VOLUME NINETY FIVE

ADVANCES IN
COMPUTERS

VOLUME NINETY FIVE

Advances in
COMPUTERS

Edited by

ATIF MEMON
University of Maryland
Williams Building
College Park, MD, USA

AMSTERDAM • BOSTON • HEIDELBERG • LONDON
NEW YORK • OXFORD • PARIS • SAN DIEGO
SAN FRANCISCO • SINGAPORE • SYDNEY • TOKYO
Academic Press is an imprint of Elsevier

Academic Press is an imprint of Elsevier
225 Wyman Street, Waltham, MA 02451, USA
525 B Street, Suite 1800, San Diego, CA 92101-4495, USA
The Boulevard, Langford Lane, Kidlington, Oxford, OX5 1GB, UK
32 Jamestown Road, London NW1 7BY, UK

First edition 2014

Notices
Knowledge and best practice in this field are constantly changing. As new research and
experience broaden our understanding, changes in research methods, professional practices,
or medical treatment may become necessary.

Practitioners and researchers must always rely on their own experience and knowledge in
evaluating and using any information, methods, compounds, or experiments described
herein. In using such information or methods they should be mindful of their own safety and
the safety of others, including parties for whom they have a professional responsibility.

To the fullest extent of the law, neither the Publisher nor the authors, contributors, or editors,
assume any liability for any injury and/or damage to persons or property as a matter of
products liability, negligence or otherwise, or from any use or operation of any methods,
products, instructions, or ideas contained in the material herein.

Library of Congress Cataloging-in-Publication Data
A catalog record for this book is available from the Library of Congress

British Library Cataloguing-in-Publication Data
A catalogue record for this book is available from the British Library

ISBN: 978-0-12-800160-8
ISSN: 0065-2458

For information on all Academic Press publications
visit our web site at store.elsevier.com

Printed and bound in USA

Working together
to grow libraries in
developing countries

www.elsevier.com • www.bookaid.org

CONTENTS

PREFACE

This volume of *Advances in Computers* is the 95th in this series. This series, which has been continuously published since 1960, presents in each volume four to seven chapters describing new developments in software, hardware, or uses of computers.

This 95th volume is eclectic in nature, the first three chapters discussing the ever important issues of software quality, the next chapter discusses issues of software design, and the last chapter discusses a fundamental question in the theoretical aspects of computing. In particular, Chapter 1, "Automated Test Oracles: A Survey," by Mauro Pezzè and Cheng Zhang, discusses test oracles, a key component of software testing. The increasing size of test suites, the growing availability of test case generators that produce enormous amount of test cases, and the repeated execution of large amounts of test cases require automated oracles. Although studied since the late 1970s, in the last decade test oracles and techniques to automatically generate test oracles have attracted a lot of attention and have witnessed an impressive growth. The chapter surveys test oracles with particular attention to their automation, overviews the main evolution of the technology, and proposes some criteria to classify the different approaches. The main techniques to automatically generate test oracles are classified according to the required information. The different forms of checkable oracles are defined as oracles expressed in a form directly checkable during the system execution.

In Chapter 2, "Automated Extraction of GUI Models for Testing," the authors, Pekka Aho, Teemu Kanstrén, Tomi Räty, and Juha Röning, posit that a significant challenge in applying model-based testing on software systems is that manually designing the test models requires considerable amount of effort and deep expertise in formal modeling. When an existing system is being modeled and tested, there are various techniques to automate the process of producing the models based on the implementation. Some approaches aim to fully automate the creation of the models, while others aim to automate the first steps to create an initial model to serve as a basis to start the manual modeling process. Especially, graphical user interface (GUI) applications, including mobile and Web applications, have been a good domain for model extraction, reverse engineering, and specification mining approaches. This chapter surveys various automated modeling techniques, with a special focus on GUI models and their usefulness in analyzing and testing of the modeled GUI applications.

Chapter 3, "Automated Test Oracles: State of the Art, Taxonomies, and Trends," by Rafael A. P. Oliveira, Upulee Kanewala, and Paulo A. Nardi also discusses test oracles, which have changed significantly over time, resulting in clear shifts in the research literature. Over the years, the testing techniques, strategies, and criteria utilized by researchers went through technical developments due to the improvement of technologies and programming languages. Software testers currently have several resources to increase their confidence in the software under test correctness. All of these software testing resources are supposed to include a mechanism to decide whether a particular execution is considered a failure or not. In software testing environments, this decision is the responsibility of the test oracle. Despite the evolution and adaptation of testing techniques over more than 30 years, test oracles remain a particular and relevant issue. This chapter uses literary evidence from a pool of about 300 studies directly related to test oracles, presenting a classification of test oracles based on a taxonomy that considers their source of information and notations.

In Chapter 4, "Anti-Pattern Detection: Methods, Challenges, and Open Issues," Fabio Palomba, Gabriele Bavota, Rocco Oliveto, and Andrea De Lucia discuss anti-patterns, which are poor solutions to recurring design problems. They occur in object-oriented systems when developers unwillingly introduce them while designing and implementing the classes of their systems. Several empirical studies have highlighted that anti-patterns have a negative impact on the comprehension and maintainability of a software systems. Consequently, their identification has received recently more attention from both researchers and practitioners who have proposed various approaches to detect them. The chapter discusses the approaches proposed in the literature. In addition, from the analysis of the state of the art, it derives a set of guidelines for building and evaluating recommendation systems supporting the detection of anti-patterns. The chapter also discusses some problems that are still open, to trace future research directions in the field. To this end, the chapter provides a support to both researchers, who are interested in comprehending the results achieved so far in the identification of anti-patterns, and practitioner, who are interested in adopting a tool to identify anti-patterns in their software systems.

Chapter 5, "Classifying Problems into Complexity Classes," by William Gasarch discusses one of the most fundamental problems in computer science. Stated informally: "Given a problem, how hard is it?" Hardness is measured by looking at the following question: Given a set A what is the fastest algorithm to determine if "$x \in A$?" The speed of an algorithm is measured by how long it takes to run on inputs of length n, as a function of n. For example, sorting a list of length n can be done in roughly $n \log n$ steps. Obtaining a fast algorithm is only half of the problem. Can one prove that there is no better algorithm? This is notoriously difficult; however, problems may be classified into complexity classes where those in the same class are roughly equally hard. This chapter defines many complexity classes and describes natural problems that are in them. The classes go all the way from regular languages to various shades of undecidable. The chapter then summarizes all that is known about these classes.

I hope that you find these chapters of interest. If you have any suggestions of topics for future chapters, or if you wish to be considered as an author for a chapter, I can be reached at atif@cs.umd.edu.

Prof. ATIF M. MEMON, Ph.D.
College Park, MD, USA

CHAPTER ONE

Automated Test Oracles: A Survey

Mauro Pezzè, Cheng Zhang

Faculty of Informatics University of Lugano, Lugano, Switzerland and Dipartimento di Informatica, Sistemi e Comunicazione, Università di Milano Bicocca, Milano, Italy

Contents

Abstract

Software testing is an essential activity of software development, and oracles are a key pillar of testing. The increasing size of test suites, the growing availability of test case generators that produce enormous amount of test cases, and the repeated execution of large amounts of test cases require automated oracles. Although studied since the late 1970s, in the last decade, test oracles and techniques to automatically generate test oracles have attracted a lot of attention and have witnessed an impressive growth.

In this chapter, we survey test oracles with particular attention to their automation. We overview the main evolution of the technology, and we propose some criteria to classify the different approaches. We present the main techniques to automatically

Advances in Computers, Volume 95
ISSN 0065-2458
http://dx.doi.org/10.1016/B978-0-12-800160-8.00001-2

generate test oracles classified according to the required information, and we discuss different forms of checkable oracles, defined as oracles expressed in a form directly checkable during the system execution.

1. INTRODUCTION

Testing is the most common activity to validate software systems and plays a key role in the software development process. Testing requires identifying test inputs by sampling the input space, executing the identified inputs on the system under test, and checking the validity of the obtained results. Each of these activities can be very expensive and has attracted the attention of researchers and practitioners who can now benefit from many techniques and tools.

In this chapter, we focus on the validation of the results of executing test cases, also known as the *oracle problem*. In particular, we focus on automated oracles for functional testing. Oracles for functional testing check the results produced with test cases that sample the functional behavior of the system, differently from the ones that deal with nonfunctional properties like performance, security, and safety. Automated oracles are executed and sometimes generated automatically. They are extremely important in reducing the costs of testing and improving the quality of software validation. The recent quick advances on automatic generation of test cases and the new tools that produce large amounts of test inputs provide new motivations for deriving efficient test oracles.

The oracle problem has been studied since the early 1970s and researchers have produced many approaches and solutions to both design automated oracles and generate them automatically. Figure 1.1 shows the main milestones in the evolution of the research on test oracles. In the 1970s, oracles evolved from simple input–output pairs that indicate the expected outputs for the given inputs to assertions inserted in the code. In the 1980s and 1990s, the main focus of research has been on deriving test oracles from formal specifications. The study of using previous versions or different programs as oracles also started in the early 1980s. Recently research on test oracles has opened new directions both in terms of application domains (like oracles for GUIs, Web applications, embedded systems, and agent systems) and new techniques, like log file analysis, test augmentation, test repair, metamorphic testing, and oracles from dynamically inferred properties and models.

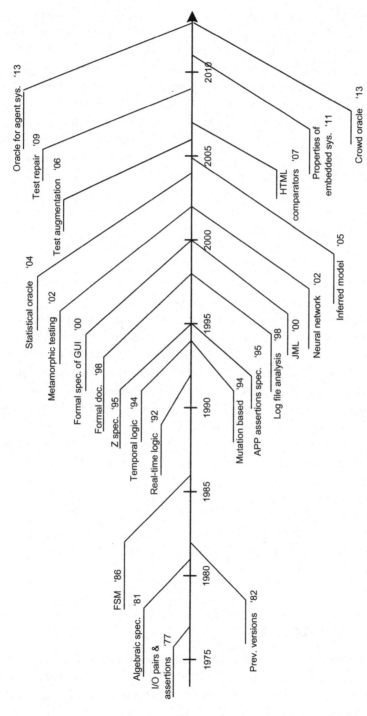

Figure 1.1 Timeline showing main milestones in the evolution of the research on test oracles.

The problem and the solutions present several trade-offs depending on the considered test inputs, the reusability across different programs, and the level of automation. Some approaches automate the execution of single test cases to validate specific properties. This is the case, for example, of common JUnit test cases whose assertions are predicated on specific inputs. Other approaches automate the execution of many test cases, such as assertions in the code that correspond to program properties. Yet other approaches deal with general program properties, like oracles that reveal the occurrence of system crashes and unexpected exceptions, and work across software systems. Some approaches make use of extra information, like the results of executing previous versions of the same system.

Program and application-specific oracles are usually more precise and can reveal many types of failures, but are also difficult and expensive to design and maintain. Oracles that refer to general properties are reusable across systems, but cannot reveal application-specific failures. Finally, oracles that compare different versions of the same system are bound to the old test suites and require strong similarities between versions.

In this chapter, we analyze different types of oracles and propose a new taxonomy based on the main component of the process that characterize automated oracles. We argue that oracles follow a general process composed of the following activities: identify the information that represents the expected behavior, choose the behaviors to be checked, translate the source information and the behaviors to be checked into an executable form, and execute the test with the generated oracle.

In this chapter, we argue that the most distinctive element of different approaches to automated oracles consists of the source information of test oracles and the way it is translated into executable form, and propose a taxonomy of automated oracles that is based on the information sources and their associate translations, and that uses the other aspects of the generation process, for instance the checkable forms, to specialize the taxonomy. We then show how the different approaches proposed in the last 50 years fit this taxonomy.

2. TEST ORACLES

The early definitions of test oracles focused on the decision process: in 1982 Weyuker defined an oracle as follows: "the tester or an external mechanism can accurately decide whether or not the output produced by a program is correct" [1], where the key element of the definition is the decision about the correctness of the output that can depend on human judgment as well as on some other mechanisms.

With the growing emphasis on automated oracles and the progress in the automated generation of test oracles, the focus has moved toward the automatic aspects of the process. In their well-cited survey, Baresi and Young defined test oracles as "some method for checking whether the system under test has behaved correctly on a particular execution" [2], where the human judgment becomes implicit. More recently in their book on software testing and analysis, Pezzè and Young defined a test oracle as "software that applies a pass/fail criterion to a program execution" [3], thus moving away completely from human judgment and assuming some automated procedure. They also relax the strict concept of correctness for a more general concept of pass/fail criterion that includes many approaches to test oracles that check only partial properties and not the complete correctness of the outputs.

We define a *test oracle* referring to the definition of Pezzè and Young as *a mechanism that determines whether or not the execution of the system under test passes or fails*. We refer to a mechanism that we assume to be automated and not relying on human judgment, and expect a pass/fail response that may not imply a decision on to the correctness of the execution.

From an abstract viewpoint, a test oracle consists of two parts: the expected behavior that is used to check the actual behavior of the system under test, and the way the behavior is checked. The expected behavior can be expressed explicitly, for example, as in a simple JUnit test case that indicates the output expected for the given input, or implicitly, for example, as a property to be satisfied or the result of another program with the same functional behavior. The behavior may be checked at the end of the execution, for example, by comparing the expected and actual outputs, or during the execution, for example, by evaluating assertions inserted in the code or by revealing unexpected execution conditions.

Test oracles differ in several aspects. Here, we distinguish between *input-specific* versus *input general*, *partial* versus *complete*, and *application-specific* versus *application general* oracles.

When the expected behavior is given for a single input or a finite set of inputs, as in the case of the simple test case of Fig. 1.2, the oracle can check only a small subset of behaviors, and we refer to these oracles as *input-specific* oracles. When the expected behavior is given for an infinite set of inputs, as in the case of the simple test case in Fig. 1.3, the oracle can be reused for different test inputs, and we refer to these oracles as *input general* oracles. The readers should notice that the test oracle in Fig. 1.2 expresses the expected output explicitly, while the oracle in Fig. 1.3 expresses it implicitly as a required property.

```
void testSum ( ) {
    int  x = 1,  y = 2;
    assertEquals (sum(x, y) = 3);
}
```

Figure 1.2 An example of input-specific test oracle. In the assertion, the expected result (3) is specific to the input values (1 and 2).

```
void testSort ( ) {
    List inputList = new ArrayList ( );
    inputList . add (3);
    inputList . add (1);
    inputLIst . add (2);
    List sortedList = sort(inputList);
    assertTrue (isSorted(sortedList));
    assertTrue (isPerm(sortedList, inputList));
}
```

Figure 1.3 An example of input general test oracle. In the assertions, the checked properties are independent from the specific input (3, 1, 2).

In the examples of Figs. 1.2 and 1.3, if a test case passes according to the oracle, the output is correct because both oracles express a sufficient condition for the output correctness. For some programs, it may be impossible or too expensive to check sufficient conditions for correctness. In these cases, oracles may check only necessary conditions, that is, if a test case fails according to the oracle, it corresponds to a failing execution, but if a test case passes according to the oracle, it may correspond to either a passing or a failing execution. We call the oracles that check necessary conditions (or incomplete properties) *partial* oracles and those that check sufficient conditions *complete* oracles.

A typical scenario of a partial oracle is in the context of testing a difficult property, for example, an input general oracle for a program that computes the shortest path on a graph. Since finding the shortest path in a directed graph is generally expensive, an oracle that checks that the output shortest path is shorter than or equal to the one found using a greedy algorithm may identify many failures, but accept incorrect outputs as well.

The oracles discussed so far in this section focus on failures that depend on the semantics of the applications, while other oracles focus on failures independent from the specific semantics of the application, like system crashes, unexpected exceptions, deadlocks, and race conditions. Csallner *et al.* proposed a series of techniques to test Java programs, JCrasher [4] that aims to reveal program crashes; Check-and-Crash [5] that combines JCrasher with ESC/Java [6]; and DSD [7] that combines Daikon [8] with ESC/Java and dynamic analysis. These techniques focus on the violations of implicit Java language rules, such as assigning an instance of a supertype to an array element, casting to an incompatible type, accessing an array outside its domain, allocating an array of negative size, dereferencing null pointers, and dividing by zero. Randoop [9] checks a group of implicit contracts in Java, .NET and in library APIs, for example, the reflexivity and transitivity of the equals() method of java.lang.Object. It also checks the absence of runtime exceptions in some APIs. In some cases, the general properties to be checked are coded as high-level rules specific to application types. For example, Ricca and Tonella [10] developed two approaches, ReWeb and TestWeb, for the analysis and testing of Web applications. These approaches detect a set of anomalies specific to Web applications, for example, unreachable pages and hyperlink inconsistencies.

Oracles based on universal implicit rules can be reused across applications that share some common general aspects. We refer to these oracles as *application general* oracles and we distinguish them from *application-specific* oracles that check the specific semantics of the program under test. By and large, application general oracles are cheaper than application-specific oracles but miss a lot of important functional failures.

3. SCOPE OF THE SURVEY AND REVIEW PROTOCOL

When surveying the status of a complex research field like the one for test oracles, the first challenge is framing the field and identifying the investigation approach. In this section, we first define the scope of the survey by clarifying the approaches and techniques that we considered and the ones we did not, and then discuss the review protocol that we followed in the survey.

We already mentioned in the former sections that we focus on oracles for functional testing and we pay special attention to automated oracles. Oracles for testing nonfunctional properties are also important, but rely on different approaches and techniques. While oracles for functional testing take into account the semantics of the programs under test, oracles for testing nonfunctional properties are usually independent from the functional semantic of the program and deserve a different treatment. Thus, we do not survey oracles for properties like performance, security, safety, and usability. A notable set of oracles that we consider only marginally in our survey are oracles that target reliability properties that may or may not be considered special cases of functional properties. In particular, we do not deal in detail with application general oracles (which are also called *implicit oracles*).

Although oracles can be completely human driven, as in the case of *inspection oracles* that are based on humans inspecting the results of program executions and deciding the pass or fail of the test cases, automation is of paramount importance in modern development processes that require many test cases to be executed repeatedly during development and maintenance. Automation can refer to both the oracle generation and execution. Automated oracles can be executed without human intervention, and automatically generated oracles are mechanically derived from some information about the program behavior. Strictly speaking, any test oracle needs some kind of human effort, since oracles rely on information about the expected system behavior expressed by software designers and users. This is obviously true for oracles based on requirement documents, behavioral models, and formal specifications. Some techniques generate test oracles using models or properties automatically inferred from either dynamic execution information or static source code semantics of previous or current program versions. In these cases, the human contribution is embedded in the programs and then extracted and used for generating oracles. In this survey, we consider the effort added to the normal software development process and we focus on approaches and techniques that generate test oracles with little or no extra human effort.

As an indispensable component of software testing, test oracles have been studied for decades and there exist a wide variety of techniques. This survey does not include all the techniques but selects the representative ones. The readers should be able to easily fit other techniques in the proposed taxonomy.

We surveyed the literature with a "snowballing" strategy. We started from a few main surveys [2,11–13], searched for relevant publications by checking their references, the references of their references, and so on. Besides the conventional backward snowballing, we also searched all the publications that cite the main surveys and papers, to discover more recent techniques. For each publication, we checked if it addressed the test oracle problem either as a main or as a minor contribution and included the publications where oracles are the main contribution.

4. THE TEST ORACLE PROCESS

Despite the great variety of test oracles, we can identify a common process that consists of few main steps that we can use to characterize and classify the different kinds of oracles: (1) identifying the source of information for deriving the oracle, (2) recognizing the program behavior to be checked, (3) translating the source of information and the program behavior into forms that can be checked against each other, and (4) executing the oracle.

Identifying the source of information amounts to identifying the expected program behavior, which can be expressed in many forms. Ultimately, oracles should check that the behavior of the program corresponds to the expectations of the end users. The source of information can be either a human being who knows about the needs addressed by the program or some artifact, typically some form of specifications. Although the ultimate source of information is always the user, referring directly to human beings to derive oracles can be expensive and difficult. Many oracles refer to other sources of information like requirement specifications, design models, API contracts, and program code. Figure 1.4 shows the main sources of information used by test oracle.

Programs present different elements that can be checked and that span from their final results to intermediate states, some properties, their traces, etc. Having identified the source of information, the oracles should *recognize the program behavior to be checked*. This choice is mainly dependent on the source of information, which determines the aspects of the program

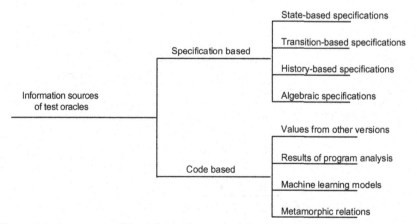

Figure 1.4 A summary of the information sources for test oracles.

behavior to be checked. A common strategy of many approaches is to maximize the behavior to be checked, that is to check all the behaviors corresponding to users' expectations that can be inferred from the source of information. However, in some cases, expectations are only partially checked, depending on factors like redundancy of program behaviors and performance overhead of the oracle execution.

There are usually discrepancies between the representations of the source of information of test oracles and the actual behavior to be checked, causing difficulties in checking them against each other directly. For example, to check the validity of a property on some program state, we often need to map the abstract names used in the specifications to the concrete names of the variables used in the program code. In general, *translating the source of information and the program behavior into a representation that we call checkable form* requires several steps. Checkable forms are executable, for example, in the form of program statements or assertions, and can have different degrees of complexity. The simplest form is the check for equality between two concrete values, like in many JUnit test cases. More complex checks may involve abstract conditions on variables. Generating complex checking procedures generally requires nontrivial translations that are extensively discussed for instance in the early work on assertion mechanisms [14,15]. A checkable form may also be only "executable" at a higher level of abstraction. A typical example is the use of finite state machines (FSMs). The oracle can check either the final state or some conditions on the transitions. Section 6 proposes a taxonomy of test oracle techniques according to their checkable form as shown in Fig. 1.5.

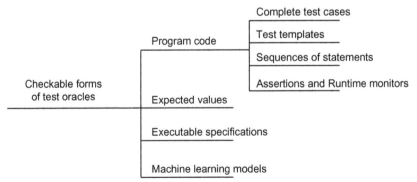

Figure 1.5 A summary of checkable forms for text oracles.

The same source of information can be translated into different checkable forms, and there can be multiple ways of translating between the same pair of sources of information and checkable forms. Nevertheless, the source of information is usually the decisive factor to determine the behavior to be checked and consequently limits the translation into checkable forms. In Section 5, we give some technical details of representative translation techniques along with their most related sources of information.

One or more steps of the common test oracle process may be skipped in a specific technique, for example, when using the JUnit test framework, testers write JUnit assertions as test oracles. These human-written assertions combine both expected and actual behaviors, which are directly checkable, and no translation is needed. In this example, the testers translate the test documents (usually in natural languages) or their domain knowledge into concrete assertions. Such mental process is beyond the scope of our discussion, which focuses on automatic translation only.

Different approaches offer various levels of automation in generating test oracles. Eclat [16] generates test oracles in the form of JUnit assertions, but because of the intrinsic incompleteness of dynamic analysis, the inferred properties may be inaccurate, and the generated oracles shall be checked by testers who shall choose the appropriate assertions. ReAssert [17] collects assertions dynamically and presents them to the testers who shall repair the broken assertions by selecting the alternative values of the variables. EvoSuite [18] and μTest [19] require the generated oracles to be analyzed by testers to determine whether they actually reveal bugs in the current version. Similar to EvoSuite and μTest, the technique proposed by Staats et al. [20] leverages mutation analysis to support test oracle generation. Specifically, it focuses on oracle data selection, (i.e., selecting the variables to be checked). As for other techniques, it requires testers' inspection to choose the proper variable and the expected values.

Recent studies have investigated the effectiveness of human testers in identifying the correctness of generated test oracles reaching contradictory results [21,22]. The results are not conclusive yet. The study of Staats et al. [22] indicates that human testers are not good at identifying correct test oracles, while the study of Pastore et al. [21] indicates that human testers can reliably identify correct test oracles and fix incorrect ones.

5. INFORMATION SOURCES AND TRANSLATIONS OF TEST ORACLES

The primary factor that impacts the level of automation of test oracles is *the information used to specify the expected behavior*, and we refer to this as the primary source of classification.

At a first glance, the source of information for test oracles can be classified either as software specifications or as a program code (see Fig. 1.4). Specifications can be further classified according to the kind of formal model into state-based specifications, transition-based specifications, history-based specifications, and algebraic specifications. Code-based information includes values from other versions, results of program analysis, machine learning models, and metamorphic relations.

As discussed in Section *4*, the source of information is tightly bounded to the translation into a checkable form. In this section, we present the main approaches to oracle generation according to the source of information, and for each of them, we discuss the main ways of translating the information into a checkable form.

5.1. State-Based Specifications

State-based specifications describe software systems in terms of states and effects of operations on states. Such specifications are supported by several specification languages, which we grouped into two sets: classic specification languages, such as Z [23], B [24], and VDM [25], and assertion languages, such as Eiffel [26], JML (Java Modeling Language) [27], and Peters and Parnas' tables [28]. While classic specification languages define states and transitions independently from the implementation, assertion languages specify states and transitions as statements or annotations of the source program.

State-based specifications are used as test oracles by verifying the compliance of the test executions with the specifications. The main problem in generating test oracles from state-based specifications comes from the different abstraction levels between the specifications and the operations monitored during the test execution; thus, the specifications of the operations will be translated in a checkable form. The specification languages are usually expressive enough to represent various data structures and state-based properties, but their expressiveness complicates the translation into executable form. Often the translation makes some simplifying assumptions, like limiting infinite sets, for instance the infinite set of natural numbers, and handling nonexecutable elements only partially and sometimes requiring some human intervention.

Here, we discuss the main approaches to translate state-based specifications into an executable form. The translation of Z, B, and VDM specifications presents the same problems related to infinite data structures, partially defined expressions and object-oriented structures. The translation of Eiffel, JML, and other assertion languages into checkable form presents similar problems but at a different abstraction level. In the following, we present the main approaches to translate state-based specifications into checkable form referring to Z; the approaches for other languages are similar. Then, we discuss the problems of compiling assertions into executable checks referring to Eiffel, JML, and Peters and Parnas' tables.

The schema predicate compiler proposed by Mikk [29] compiles Z specifications into C code. For each Z *schema*, which is the basic unit in Z, the approach generates a C function that evaluates the schema predicates using the program state passed to the function as a parameter. The generated code evaluates the predicates of the schema with a "brute force" strategy: Given a state, the code essentially replaces expressions with their values, evaluates propositional calculus formulae by using truth tables, and evaluates quantifications and set constructions by iterating through the data structures. To reduce the complexity of the generated C functions, the approach proposes an optimization step to *ensure that the generated C code always terminates*. To optimize the code, the technique defines an "executable" subset of the Z language. The subset consists of finite predicates, such as propositional calculus formulae, quantifications over finite sets, and set constructions based on finite iteration. The technique extends the set of executable predicates with a set of rules to transform special nonexecutable predicates that satisfy certain conditions into executable ones without changing their semantics. For example, the following two rules eliminate the quantifiers:

$$\frac{\forall x : M \bullet P}{M \neq \varnothing \Rightarrow P}[NotOccur(x, P)] \qquad \frac{\exists x : M \bullet P}{M \neq \varnothing \wedge P}[NotOccur(x, P)]$$

where M is a set, the variable x represents an element in M, and P is a predicate. The operator $\bullet$, also known as the "Z notation spot," means "such that" when used with the quantifier $\exists$ and "that," when used with the quantifier $\forall$. For example, $\exists x : M \bullet P$ means that there exists at least a value x in M such that predicate P is *true*. The condition $NotOccur(x, P)$ indicates that x is not a free variable in the predicate P. Although the set M can be infinite, the compiler can still compile specifications using quantifiers over M as long as the quantifiers can be eliminated by applying the above rules. For user-defined functions that may be introduced by axiomatic or generic definitions, the compiler requires the user to provide the corresponding code. Mikk proposes also a solution to the problem of partially defined specifications. He uses VDM-SL as an intermediate form and the VDM-SL compiler developed by Schmidt and Hörcher to translate Z specifications into C code [30]. When dealing with partially defined expressions, i.e., either functions or relations that may evaluate *undefined* (denoted as $\bot$) when evaluated outside their definition domain, the approach generates exception handlers.

Object-oriented extensions of Z, like Object-Z, exacerbate the problems. McDonald *et al.* translate Ojbect-Z specifications of container classes into C++ code in three stages: optimization, structural mapping, and predicate translation [31]. In the optimization stage, they rearrange the specification to simplify the subsequent translation through several steps, including replacing constant variables with their values and removing secondary variables and schema enrichments. In the structural mapping stage, they map structures in the Object-Z specification to their corresponding code elements: Specification constants and variables to variables with proper initializations, and variables types to primitive C++ types or corresponding classes in the Z toolkit library used by the technique. For example, they map the integer and boolean types to `int`, and the type of integer sets to `z_set<int>`. They map the initialization schema to a constructor, and operation schemas to member functions, create a special member function, `inv()`, to check the class invariant, and generate an exception class for each exception schema.

In the predicate translation stage, the technique focuses on how to generate code for checking program state, instead of evaluating predicates. For example, the translation prevents the `inv()` function from calling any other member function, to avoid infinite recursion. In a constructor, the class invariant is checked at its exit.

Richardson *et al.* [32] focus on time critical systems, deal with a combination of Z and temporal interval logic, and propose a translation of specifications into test oracles by means of symbolic interpretation. Symbolic interpretation assigns the symbolic names in the specifications to the stimulus inputs and the initial state variables, by referring to the data and control mappings. Then, symbolic interpretation interprets each control path in the specifications, that is, it creates an assertion expressing the condition on the specification data based on the symbolic state at each specification control point. A *specification control point* is a relevant element, such as a parameterized event, a transition, and an operation. After the symbolic interpretation of the Z specification, the oracle information is represented as a list of relevant Z schemas and their corresponding assertions, which are checked if the schema is invoked. The execution of a test case refers to a concrete test input from which concrete variables and events are bound to their counterparts in the test class (each test class is a partition of test input). The execution of the test case produces an execution profile, and the concrete events and values of variables contained in the execution profile are mapped to the oracle level to check their consistency with the oracle information.

Assertion languages merge specifications with the source code, thus simplifying but not eliminating the translation problem. Assertions are supported by different languages and methodologies. Design by contract [33] is a software design paradigm that postulates the joint design of code and assertions. Design by contract was proposed by Meyer and is fully supported by the Eiffel programming language [26]. Differently from general specification languages, like Z, the specifications in Eiffel, called *contracts*, are merged into the source code and define *obligations* and *benefits* of the software components that communicate via well-designed interfaces. In languages supporting contracts, client obligations and benefits are expressed as *pre-* and *postconditions* of the service providers. The source code is enriched with *invariants* that represent state properties that must hold during any interaction.

Contracts have been extended to many languages. *iContract* has been the first tool to support contracts in Java [34]. In iContract, contracts are written as code comments with special tags. The contracts supported by iContract are boolean expressions compliant with Java syntax, except for few syntactic extensions that include the universal quantification ($\forall$), the existential quantification ($\exists$), and the implication ($\rightarrow$). These extensions are designed to simplify their translation into Java code. For example, the syntax of $\forall$ is forall `<Class> <var> in <Enum> | <Exp_var>`, where `<Class>` is the type of the variable `<var>`, which represents an element of `<Enum>`. A reasonable translation of the $\forall$ expression is to use a Java loop to iterate over the enumeration `<Enum>` and evaluate the boolean expression `<Exp_var>` in each iteration. The existential quantification is translated similarly. An implication expression `C implies I` can be simply translated into an if statement: "if C then check I."

Besides the simple translation of boolean expressions, iContract addresses issues related to the object life cycle, the scope of variables, and inheritance, most of which are specific of object-oriented programming. The most important rules related to the object life cycle are as follows:

1. In an object construction, the preconditions must be checked at the beginning of the construction, while the invariants and the postconditions are checked only if the construction terminates normally (without exceptions).

2. For normal method invocations on objects, pre- and postconditions are checked at the entry and exit of the invoked methods, and invariants are not checked for `private` methods.

3. In object destruction, no checking is required. Thus, no checking code is inserted into the `finalize()` methods.

The predicates used in the postconditions often refer to both the return value of the method and the "old" value (or "entry-value") of some variables. iContract synthesizes a pseudo-variable, called return, to represent the `return` value, stores the variable values at the entry, and makes them accessible as the variable names with the postfix @pre. expressions, their object references are stored directly. iContract allows calls to member methods in contracts. As a result, there can be potential infinite recursions in checking invariants. To solve this problem, iContract keeps track of the recursion depth for each object within each thread and checks only invariants with depth 0. The type extension mechanisms in Java have several implications on how contracts of the types should be handled. iContract propagates contracts by following these rules:

1. Invariants are conjuncted, that is, the invariant of a subtype is the conjunction of the invariants of all its supertypes.

2. Postconditions are conjuncted, that is, the postcondition of a subtype is the conjunction of the postconditions of all its supertypes.

3. Preconditions are disjuncted, that is, the precondition of a subtype is the disjunction of the preconditions of all its supertypes.

JML is a popular behavioral specification language that supports Design by Contract in Java [27]. JML contracts are in the form of special comments in Java. JML expresses preconditions, postconditions, and invariants as boolean expressions preceded by the keywords `requires`, `ensures`, and `invariant`, respectively, and uses built-in method \ old(x) to represent the value of x before an operation. Similar to the Δ notation in Z, JML provides the keyword modifies to indicate the variables that are changed in a method body. Furthermore, JML deals with several object-oriented features, such as visibility and inheritance.

JML is the basis of many approaches to test oracle generation. Bhorkar proposed a technique to translate JML contracts into Java assertions [35]. Although supporting only preconditions, this technique addresses issues related to specification-only variables, refinement, specification inheritance, and privacy. Similar to iContract, the technique handles the inheritance of contracts by conjuncting and disjuncting the contracts according to their types. The technique also uses a hash table (per thread) to avoid recursions in runtime checking. Expressions using quantifiers are considered as nonexecutable by the technique, and no Java code is generated for such expressions.

Korat proposed a technique to generate both test cases and oracles from JML specifications [36]. Korat's technique generates test cases from preconditions and invariants and oracles from postconditions and invariants. Araujo *et al.* extended JML by adding concurrent contracts and proposed a runtime support to enable runtime checking of assertions that specify concurrent properties [37].

Peters and Parnas introduced an approach to generate test oracles from formal documentation [28,38]. The documentation is given in a tabular form that consists of relations that specify the interfaces of procedures and is translated in oracles in C and C++ code. The core element of the formal documentation consists of predicate expressions written in a variant of predicate logic with special constructs to deal with partial functions. Similar to other specification-based oracle techniques, this technique treats quantifiers by restricting them to finite sets.

To enable iterations over sets of elements with quantifiers, Peters and Parnas introduce *inductively defined predicates*. For a set S (to be used in quantifications), an inductively defined predicate P is defined with three elements I, G, and Q. The initial set I contains a finite number of elements, G is a function, called the "generator function," that generates the elements in the set, and Q is a predicate that characterizes the properties of the set. The set S is defined as the *least set* constructed in the inductive steps below:
1. $S_0 = I$
2. $S_{n+1} = S_n \cup \{ G(x) | x \in S_n \land Q(x) \}$

I, G and Q must be defined to satisfy a special condition that ensures that the constructed set S is finite [28,38].

Peters and Parnas propose an approach to translate the tabular documentations into C code [28]. Since the form of the expressions used in the documentations is well defined, the translation is done systematically.

Other state-based specifications are also used for deriving test oracles. UML models are generally informal; nevertheless, Bouquet et al. [39] defined a subset of UML 2.1, named *UML-MBT*, which is precise enough for automatically generating test cases. UML-MBT includes class diagrams, state machines, and a subset of OCL 2.0. Bouquet et al. use specifications written in VDM-SL to generate test oracles.

5.2. Transition-Based Specifications

Transition-based specifications describe software systems by specifying state transitions and constraints for their occurrence. The most popular transition-based systems are the different variants of FSMs or *finite automata*.

FSMs are executable and the translation of FSMs to checkable test oracles amounts to mapping elements of concrete program executions to those of FSM executions or the other way around. Specifically, test oracle techniques that use FSMs as sources of information need to define the mapping between program states and FSM states as well as between program operations (or events) and FSM inputs. Such test oracles determine test results based on the validity of transitions (i.e., whether a transition is allowed in the FSM specification) and/or the acceptance of the final states.

The log analyzers proposed by Andrews [40] are essentially (parallel) FSMs, specified in a special language named LFAL (log file analysis language). The FSM-based log analyzers map selected operations and events to FSM inputs. The technique analyzes runtime logs to capture relevant operations, for instance turn the heater on, and events, for instance the temperature becomes higher than a given threshold, and then executes the specified FSMs in response to each of the identified runtime operations or events by triggering the corresponding state transitions. As for mapping between states, the technique mainly specifies the correspondence between the initial FSM states and the program states.

Pradel and Gross propose an oracle defined as an API protocol checking technique [41]. They represent API protocols as deterministic FSMs in which the transitions are annotated with typed protocol parameters. In such a FSM, each node represents a state of the relevant objects, and each transition represents a method call and is labeled with an annotation in the form of $r. m(a_1, \ldots, a_n) \to o$, where m is the method name, r is the receiver object,

o is the return value, and a_i is the ith argument of the method call. The states of an FSM are distinguished between *setup* and *liable* states, and a protocol is checked only if the current state is *liable*.

To incorporate richer semantic information, the FSMs used in specific techniques have been extended in different ways. Dillon and Yu generate deterministic finite automata (DFA) from Graphical Interval Logic (GIL) specifications and use such automata for testing temporal properties [42]. The technique extracts finite sequences of system states and checks each sequence using the DFA to see whether it satisfies the GIL specification. In checking a state sequence, each state in the sequence is used to activate the possible transition in the DFA. Every node of the DFA is annotated with sets of requirements (expressed in temporal logic formulae), and at least one of the requirement sets must be satisfied by the remaining state sequence. In contrast to classic DFA, the labels on the transitions do not describe the inputs that activate the transition but propositional formulae that may be satisfied by multiple input (system) states. A transition is executable if the current state in the state sequence satisfies the formula associated with the transition.

FSMs are widely used in protocol conformance testing. The core idea is to model the protocol implementation as a FSM and check its conformance to the specification in the form of a FSM [43]. Since both the specification and the implementation are represented with FSMs, the mapping between elements of program executions and those of FSMs is not necessary.

5.3. History-Based Specifications

Time-related behaviors are specified with history-based specifications that capture the behaviors of systems evolving over time. The most popular languages for history-based specifications are temporal logics-based languages and include LTL (Linear Time Logic), CTL (Computation Tree Logic), RTIL (Real-Time Interval Logic), and GIL.

Temporal logic languages augment the set of operators of classic logic with temporal operators that challenge the translation of the specifications into a checkable form. Both temporal logic and transition-based specifications include some history information that is explicitly specified by means of temporal operators in the case of temporal logics and implicitly contained in the order of events in the case of transition-based specifications. Most translations of temporal logic specifications into a checkable form take advantage of this characteristic of transition-based specifications and target either FSMs or transition diagrams.

Dillon and Yu proposed a technique to generate test oracles from GIL specifications [42]. Their technique translates GIL formulae into FSMs that are used to check the execution traces recorded from program executions. The core of Dillon and Yu's technique is an algorithm to build DFA from temporal logic specifications. The algorithm generates DFAs from FIL (Future Interval Logic), the textual representation of GIL [44], using a decomposition procedure that factorizes a set of requirement sets into a set of *assumption–requirement* pairs. A "requirement set" is a set of formulae that must hold in the current state, and each node of the DFA is associated with a *set* of requirement sets, which represents alternative requirements on the future, i.e., remaining states in the execution trace. The decomposition procedure partitions the requirement sets with inconsistent assumptions and annotates each transition of the DFA with an assumption. The key steps in the decomposition procedure rely on both a group of operations to transform the assumption–requirement pairs and a group of rules to evaluate the acceptance of a basic formula f (as a requirement) and a propositional formula a (as an assumption). Given a FIL formula f, the oracle generation algorithm first maps it to the initial set of requirement sets (i.e., $\{\{f\}\}$), and then the decomposition procedure applies the group of transformation operations to produce the corresponding set of assumption–requirement pairs. In the end, it generates the DFA based on the assumption–requirement pairs, with some of its nodes identified as acceptance nodes according to the rules of acceptance evaluation.

Later, Dillon and Ramakrishna proposed a generic algorithm to build flow graphs (almost equivalent to DFAs) from various kinds of temporal logics [45]. The key idea is to generalize the classic tableau algorithm, making it accepting extra reduction rules for different temporal operators to produce more efficient oracles.

Other work proposes model checking for generating oracles from temporal logic specifications. Model checking verifies the validity of properties usually expressed in some form of temporal logic, like LTL or CTL, against a model of a software system usually expressed as a label transition system. In their work on using model checking to generate test sequences, Gargantini and Heitmeyer [46] translate SCR specifications into a form acceptable to model checkers. In their approach, the specifications are not checked against the implementation, but against some properties derived from event or condition tables. They express the specifications in a tabular form from which they derive a property that they check with a model checker. The translation from tables to properties acceptable to model checkers is not complex, but there are some nontrivial issues that have to be carefully addressed.

Table 1.1 shows an example of specifications expressed in tabular form: The first row states that when the water pressure goes above a threshold Low, the system moves from state TooLow to state Permitted. This table can be translated to the following code:

```
if
   □ Pressure = TooLow
       if
       □ @T(WaterPres >=Low) -> Pressure = Permitted C1
       □ (else) -> Pressure' = Pressure            C2
       fi
   ...
fi
```

from which the technique generates the following Promela specification (the input language of the model checker Spin [47]):

```
if
    :: (Pressure == TooLow) ->
       if
       :: (WaterPresP >=Low) && ! WaterPres >=Low
              -> PressureP = Permitted; CasePressure = 1;
       :: else                         CasePressure = 2;
       fi
    ...
fi
```

The code generated from the event table items is the test oracle. The *negation* of the Promela property is checked against the model of the program (generated from the SCR specifications) to identify possible violations. If the

Table 1.1 Example Table of Events Excerpted from [46]

Old Mode	Event	New Mode
Too low	@T(WaterPres $\geq$ Low)	Permitted
Permitted	@T(WaterPres $\geq$ Permit)	High
	@T(WaterPres $<$ Low)	TooLow
High	@T(WaterPres $<$ Permit)	Permitted

property is violated, the model checker generates a counterexample that shows the sequence of events that lead to the failure.

Callahan *et al.* [48] also used the result of model checking to generate test oracles as well as test drivers. The key information of oracle generation is again the counterexamples produced by the model checker. Based on a counterexample plus an action table, they generate an oracle in the form of FSM.

Memon *et al.* proposed a technique to generate oracles for GUIs [49]. They refer to a formal model of a GUI that consists of sets of objects, object properties, and a set of actions. A GUI test case is defined as an initial state and a legal sequence of actions. Given the formal model and a test case, the oracle automatically derives the expected state for every action in the test case.

5.4. Algebraic Specifications

Algebraic specifications were originally introduced to describe abstract data types (ADTs) and have found a straightforward application in object-oriented design to describe classes and interfaces. A typical algebraic specification consists of two parts that specify the syntax and the semantics of the system, respectively. The syntactical part specifies the signatures of the operations (or functions), including their names, inputs, outputs, domains, and ranges. The semantic part contains a set of *axioms* (or *equations*) that describe the equivalence relations among sequences of operations. Axioms are the key components of algebraic specifications and are the basis of all the techniques proposed so far to generate test oracles based on algebraic specifications, except for the pioneering work of DAISTS.

With DAISTS, Gannon *et al.* propose an integrated system that combines the definition and implementation of ADTs, formal algebraic specifications, and testing [50]. The algebraic specifications and the ADT specifications are written in different languages both of which are almost at the same abstraction level of implementation. Hence, the translation to generate the oracle code is simple. For example, an axiom $Top(Push(X, S)) = X$ can be translated into the following code:

```
proc Axiom(int X, Stack S)
  if Top(Push(X, S)) = X
    then /* OK, do nothing */
  else /* Failure, error message */
    write ('Axiom failed')
end
```

In the translation, the free variables of the axiom (X and S) are mapped to parameters of the procedure, and the operations (*Top* and *Push*) are mapped to invocations of the corresponding functions (implemented in the ADT). During the test execution, the test data provided by testers are passed as arguments to the procedures. To check the equality of objects, DAISTS requires a special equality function `TypeEqual`. Checking object equality is a central problem of almost all the test oracle techniques that use algebraic specifications. We will discuss this problem in detail later in this section.

An important step toward the use of algebraic specification to generate test oracles is the ASTOOT system that differs from DAISTS in several ways [51]. ASTOOT proposes the LOBAS specification language to specify object-oriented systems. In object-oriented programming, the results of the execution are not only the returned objects, but also the final (internal) states of the objects involved in the execution.

ASTOOT uses LOBAS specifications to generate test cases and check test results automatically. Similar to DAISTS, the translation from the specifications of sequences of operations to sequences of method calls in the oracle code is straightforward, that is, the generated code calls methods with the same names of the operations in the order specified by the operation sequences, using objects of the specified types. The concrete values of the free variables and the objects need to be provided by testers. ASTOOT proposes a new way of generating oracles based on the equivalence of sequences of method calls. An ASTOOT test case is a triple (S_1, S_2, tag), where S_1 and S_2 are sequences of method calls, and *tag* is a boolean value that indicates if the two sequences are equivalent, hence they should produce the same results or not. The sequences and the tag are obtained automatically from the algebraic specifications.

ASTOOT generates test cases with oracles using a compiler and a simplifier. The compiler translates an axiom in the specification into a pair of ADT trees, where paths from the root node to the leaves represent states created by executing the operations along that path. A branch in the ADT tree corresponds to an `IF_THEN_ELSE` expression on the right-hand side of the axiom. Each edge of a branch is associated with a boolean expression (called the *edge condition*) derived from the condition of the ADT `IF_THEN_ELSE` expression. The simplifier uses the ADT tree representation to generate Eiffel code as follows:

1. It finds an axiom whose left-hand side matches a partial path of the ADT tree.

2. It replaces the partial path with the right-hand side of the axiom. In this step, it matches the variables in the axiom with the arguments in the ADT tree.

3. It repeats the previous two steps until no more matching axioms can be found.

During this transformation, the simplifier can derive an expected inequality between a pair of states (represented by two paths in the pair of ADT trees) by exchanging the path condition of one path. For example, let us assume that two test cases are generated from an axiom with a IF_THEN_ELSE expression: $(S_1, S_2, equivalent)$ (with path condition $cond$) and $S'_1, S'_2, equivalent)$ (with path condition $\neg cond$). Then, other two test cases can be generated: $(S'_1, S_2, nonequivalent)$ (with path condition $\neg cond$) and $(S_1, S'_2, nonequivalent)$ (with path condition $cond$).

A common concern in using algebraic specifications as test oracles is *how to check the equality between objects*. As mentioned above, DAISTS requires the user to implement a special TypeEqual function for each ADT. Similarly, ASTOOT requires a user-defined EQN function for equality checking. In ASTOOT, two objects O_1 and O_2 of a class C are defined as *observationally equivalent* if and only if:

1. If C is a built-in class (for example, a primitive type), then the values of O_1 and O_2 are identical.

2. If C is not a built-in class, for any operation sequence S the resulting objects of $O_1.S$ and $O_2.S$ are observationally equivalent.

The definition is recursive, and in the second case, the resulting objects are not necessarily of type C. Ideally, the implementation of the EQN function checks the equality by following the above definition. The potentially huge number of combinations of operations and the depth of recursive checks make the checking of every possible operation sequence infeasible. The problem can be overcome with two strategies: (1) giving a recursive specification of the function that specifies the key logics of equality checking, or (2) providing a concrete implementation of the function that considers internal details of the underlying data structures and their operations to check the observational equivalence from another angle (instead of exploring operation sequences recursively).

The use of algebraic specifications as oracles requires side effects to be handled. The main concern of side effects is that they may result in inconsistent states for the same variable used in the specifications. Both DAISTS and ASTOOT limit side effects, thus ensuring important consistency properties and simplifying the generation of valid oracles. Specifically, DAISTS restricts side effects by requiring the implementation of a function not to modify its parameters, thus ensuring that the occurrences of a free variable in different locations represent the same value. Similar to DAISTS, ASTOOT restricts side effects by requiring parameters not to be modified by operations.

Motivated by ASTOOT [51], Chen *et al.* [52] focused on using algebraic specifications to generate test cases for object-oriented programs. Similar to ASTOOT, their technique uses the concept of fundamental pairs to select finite sets of test cases. The technique proposes a heuristic white-box technique to solve the problem of determining the observational equivalence of objects that black-box techniques do not address well. Chen *et al.* [53] extended their previous work to generate cluster-level test cases. The approach augments algebraic specifications with contract specification [54] (in the form of message-passing rules) to express cluster-level interactions.

The *CASCAT* technique [55] focuses on testing Java components. CASCAT translates algebraic specification language written in *CASOCC* to generate checkable test cases. Antoy and Hamlet [56] translated algebraic specifications into C++ code as an alternative implementation (called direct implementation).

5.5. Values from Other Versions

There are several approaches to generate test oracles from code. For large software projects, there usually exist several program versions and associated test cases. The behavior of a different version of the program can be a good source of information to generate test oracles. A "gold" (i.e., correct) version, of the program would be the perfect oracle. In their approach to testing event-driven systems, Memon and Xie [57] assume the existence of such gold versions, and extract oracles automatically from the executions of the correct versions. However, in practice, a gold version may never exist and is often substituted with historical program versions that are used as a source of test oracle information.

Sometimes a previous version is considered as a correct version, when a large portion of the output (or values to be checked) are unlikely to change in a new version. Sprenkle *et al.* [58] proposed oracle comparators for Web applications, where the HTML output generated with a previous version is used as the expected output. Using values from previous versions as test oracles is particularly suitable for regression testing that aims to check the functionalities unchanged in the new version. For example, Ostra [59] augments existing test cases with oracles for detecting regression errors.

A common and important problem of using values from other versions is *how to select the values from another version*. As there can be a huge amount of values and events in the executions of other versions, it is usually infeasible to compare every value or event. Moreover, as changes of internal implementation details are likely to be the reason for developing the new version, differences in internal states of two program versions do not necessarily indicate program faults.

To address this issue, Ostra [59] proposes three representations of object states, namely, *method-sequence representation*, *concrete-state representation*, and *observer-abstraction representation*. Each kind of representation exposes a specific level of implementation details. Ostra chooses to use one or more of these representations for capturing object states.

The oracles used by Memon and Xie [57] focus on two special kinds of events that contribute to most event-related errors. Xie and Memon studied the choices of granularity and frequency in oracle generation and execution, as weak oracles may have limited ability of fault detection and strong oracles may induce high cost [60].

5.6. Results of Program Analysis

Program analysis techniques infer information either from the source code (static analysis) or from the program executions (dynamic analysis). The information comes from the program itself, and test oracle techniques that use program analysis are usually based on some assumptions of program correctness or program faults.

A popular kind of program analysis used to generate oracles is mutation analysis. The program under test is injected with mutations (i.e., small code changes) to create faulty program versions (called "mutants"), and the mutants are tested using the test cases for the original program to see whether they can be *killed* in the test. A mutant is killed if the test cases reveal a deviation of the mutant from the original program. Mutation analysis can be viewed as a kind of dynamic analysis and is commonly used to evaluate the quality of test suites in terms of their effectiveness in killing mutants. Recently, some researchers have exploited mutation analysis to create test oracles [19,20,61]. By using mutation analysis, these techniques do not require historical versions or correct versions and can detect errors in the current version without requiring early versions as in regression testing. However, the key assumption of mutation analysis is that *the mutants are good representatives of real program faults*.

A recent approach called μTest uses mutation analysis to generate JUnit tests containing assertions [19,61]. μTest runs each test case on both the original program and all mutants and records the execution traces. The traces are analyzed to identify differences between executions of the original program and its mutants, and the technique generates an assertion for each identified difference [19].

Staats *et al.* proposed a similar technique to generate oracles using mutation analysis [20]. The technique executes the original program and its mutants and generates trace data that contain the value of every variable after every step of the execution. If the value of a variable in the execution of the original program differs from that in the execution of a mutant, the mutant is said to be killed by that variable. The variables are ranked according to the number of killed mutants. The variables that kill more mutants are more likely to be useful for creating assertions. In both [19] and [20], some assertions (or variables) have equal capability of killing mutants, and both techniques use an approximate algorithm to resolve the *set covering problem*, in order to reduce the final sets of assertions (or variables).

Daniel *et al.* focused on repairing test cases and assertions using both static and dynamic analysis [17]. To repair a broken test case, ReAssert instruments the test classes and re-executes the test case, recording the arguments of the failing assertions and the stack traces of the assertion failures. By traversing the recorded stack traces, it finds the code to repair and repairs the code by analyzing the code structure and using the recorded argument values.

5.7. Machine Learning Models

Some recent work has exploited machine learning techniques to generate test oracles. Machine learning aims to automatically learn from experience by building models to represent knowledge generalized from a set of data describing the tasks to be fulfilled [62]. The data used for building models are called *training data*.

In machine learning, a data instance is represented as a vector of *features* or *attributes*, denoted as $\langle a_1, a_2, \ldots, a_n \rangle$. Each feature describes an aspect of the data instance. The main aim of machine learning is to predict a particular feature, for example, the *output*, based on other features, for example, the *input*. In *supervised learning*, both the input and the output are known for training data, and for a new data instances, its input is known and the output needs to be predicted.

We discuss the use of models in Section **6**; in this section, we introduce common models used for generating test oracles, and the learning algorithms used to derive them, because the process of learning (i.e., model building) essentially transforms the original data into some checkable (applicable) representations.

A kind of machine learning model frequently used for software testing is the artificial neural networks (ANNs) model. An ANN is composed of a set of nodes (called *neurons*) that are interconnected as a network. There can be several layers of neurons in an ANN. The neurons at the ith layer receive the outputs of the neurons at the $(i-1)$th layer as input. In particular, there is an input layer that receives the initial input to the network and an output layer that produces the final output of the network. For each neuron, the relation between its input and output is typically characterized by a function, such as the *sigmoid function* shown below:

$$f(x) = \frac{1}{1 + e^{-x}}$$

where x is a weighted sum of the feature vector: $x = w_0 + w_1 a_1 + w_2 a_2 + \cdots + w_n a_n$. When building an ANN, a common strategy is to compute the weights to minimize the overall *error* of the output, that is, the distance between the output computed with the model and the actual output values of the training data. ANNs can express complex relations and several recent test oracle techniques use ANN or multiple ANNs as the machine learning models to compute the expected outputs, thus implementing oracles [63–65].

Another frequently used machine learning technique is *association rules learning*, in which knowledge is represented in the form of *association rules*. Each association rule has a *premise* and a *consequent* and indicates that the premise implies the consequent. Zheng *et al.* used association rules as pseudo-oracles to test search engines [66]. Their technique mines association rules from a number of search results returned by search engines in response to selected search strings. Then, they use the rules to test the search engines for other queries by checking whether the implied consequents are satisfied by the new search results.

Decision trees organize rules in tree structures and support decision making by checking against sequences of rules. A leaf node in a decision tree represents a specific decision on its corresponding data instances. A nonleaf node represents a rule or a condition. In decision making, a data instance starts from the root node, checks against each encountered nonleaf node, and decides which branch to take based on the checking result until reaching a leaf node which indicates the decision. Frounchi *et al.* [67] proposed to use decision trees as automated oracles to determine the correctness of image segmentation algorithms. They use two different algorithms, J48 and PART, for building the decision trees.

As discussed in Section **6**, common concerns in using machine learning techniques in testing are the selection and preparation of the input data (either for training or for testing) and the postprocessing (interpretation) of the model output. Specifically, for building machine learning models, the choice of the input data can largely impact on the effectiveness of the resulting models.

As in most applications of machine learning techniques, the key to success is to find a proper set of features (or attributes) based on the input and output (and probably other measurable factors) of the program under test. For example, to train classifiers to distinguish between consistent and inconsistent image segmentations, the technique by Frounchi *et al.* uses nine different attribute sets, which consist of a number of measures related to volume difference, overlap, and geometrical measures [67]. The technique also uses the correlation–based feature selection to select the attributes. In their case study, Vanmali *et al.* and Shahamiri *et al.* use 11 attributes related to credit card approval and 12 attributes related to care insurance to represent input and output factors, respectively [65,68].

Daikon is a well-known invariant inference tool. Although Daikon uses dynamic data collection during program execution and is widely acknowledged as a dynamic analysis technique, the core process of its invariant inference is essentially machine learning. Daikon generalizes from the observed data to produce a set of likely invariants to represent the knowledge of the program behavior.

The invariants inferred by Daikon do not necessarily characterize the expected behaviors of the program, but checking these properties can usually tell whether common rules are violated. The tool called Eclat [16] embodies such idea: It uses Daikon to infer operational models from a group of correct executions and derives test oracles based on properties of the operational models.

5.8. Metamorphic Relations and Intrinsic Redundancy

Recently software redundancy has been exploited to generate oracles. The most well-known approaches are metamorphic testing and cross–checking oracles.

Metamorphic testing was proposed by Chen *et al.* to alleviate the test oracle problem [69] and exploits redundancy at the input level, i.e., the presence of inputs that should produce the same results. It uses an initial set of test cases and a set of *metamorphic relations* to generate additional test cases and oracles. A metamorphic relation MR_p for a program p is a property that must hold if the program p is implemented correctly, and can be expressed as a relation over the inputs $(I_1, I_2, \ldots, I_n)$ and outputs $(O_1, O_2, \ldots, O_n)$ of p:

$$MR_p = \left\{ (I_1, I_2, \ldots, I_n, O_1, O_2, \ldots, O_n) | ir_p(I_1, I_2, \ldots, I_n) \to or_p(O_1, O_2, \ldots, O_n) \right\}$$

where ir_p and or_p are relations over the inputs and outputs and depend on the program p. We can, for example, derive a metamorphic relation MR_{sin} for an implementation of the trigonometric function sine, denoted as *sin*, from the periodic property of sine, $sin(x + 2\pi) = sin(x)$:

$$MR_{sin} = \left\{ (x, y, sin(x), sin(y)) | (y = x + 2\pi) \to (sin(y) = sin(x)) \right\}$$

where x, y are real numbers and the relations ir_{sin} and or_{sin} are defined as $ir_{sin} = \{ (x, y) | y = x + 2\pi \}$ and $or_{sin} = \{ (x, y) | x = y \}$.

Metamorphic testing does not require the expected outputs and thus can be effective in testing nontestable programs. In the above example, even if the correct value of $sin(1.23)$ is unknown, a test case can still check whether or not $sin(1.23)$ is equal to $sin(1.23 + 2\pi)$. Besides programs with rigorous (and well-known) mathematical properties, metamorphic testing is useful also in testing other kinds of programs. For example, Zhou *et al.* [70] used metamorphic testing to automatically test the consistency of Web search engines. The technique finds logical consistency properties, codes them as metamorphic relations, and checks them against multiple sets of search results.

The definition of metamorphic testing is quite general, and several testing techniques proposed before the introduction of the term itself can be deemed as instances of metamorphic testing. For example, Schroeder *et al.* proposed a technique that generates a large set of expected outputs from a small set of outputs which are known to be correct [71]. The technique is based on the simple observation that the value of a given output variable is determined by a subset of all the input variables, and this can be generalized with the following metamorphic relation $ir_p = \{ (input_1, input_2) | input_1$ and $input_2$ include the same set of variables that affect the computation of the output and these variables are given the same values in the two $inputs \}$ and $or_p = \{ (output_1, output_2) | output_1 = output_2 \}$. In a nutshell, the relation says

Table 1.2 Extensions of JML Proposed by Murphy *et al.* to Generate Metamorphic Relations

Name	Description of Operation
Additive	Increase (or decrease) numerical values by a constant
Multiplicative	Multiply numerical values by a constant
Permutative	Permute the order of elements in a set
Invertive	Reverse the order of elements in a set
Inclusive	Add a new element to a set
Exclusive	Remove an element from a set

that two inputs are equivalent if they differ only in the values of variables that do not affect the output. To facilitate metamorphic testing, Murphy *et al.* [72] extended JML to specify six kinds of metamorphic operators that generate metamorphic relations. The operators are summarized in Table 1.2.

Implementing test oracles using metamorphic information includes (1) implementing the relation *ri*, which can be used as a function to generate test inputs based on existing inputs, and (2) implementing the relation *ro*, which can be used as a property on the pair of actual and expected outputs. Conceptually, the metamorphic relations are implemented as a mechanism to derive more test cases (inputs and oracles) from the initial set of test cases.

Cross-checking oracles have been recently proposed by Carzaniga *et al.* [73]. *Cross-checking* oracles exploit the intrinsic redundancy of software systems. They focus on redundancy at the method level, which is derived from the presence of different methods or method sequences that produce equivalent results, i.e., indistinguishable outputs and states. They fork the execution of a method call, execute both the original and the equivalent call, and check for equivalence. In their study, Carzaniga *et al.* argue that redundancy is wide spread in modern software systems and present impressive results about the redundancy that they found in several well-known libraries.

6. CHECKABLE FORMS OF TEST ORACLES

In the former section, we presented the main approaches to generating test oracles classified according to the source of the information used to generate the oracle, and we discussed the techniques for translating oracles into executable form. In this section, we discuss in detail the various checkable forms of oracles. We say that an oracle is in a *checkable* form if it can be used in the execution of test cases without further transformations. The checkable forms of oracles can take different forms that span *program code* to *expected values, executable specifications,* and *machine learning models.* The checkable form is another way to classify oracles. In this section, we present the main types of checkable forms of oracles, and we discuss additional details about how to use the checkable forms produced by the various techniques discussed in the former section.

6.1. Program Code

Program code is the most common checkable form of test oracles. Depending on the specific techniques, different kinds of program code can be generated. Some techniques generate complete test cases which can be compiled and executed directly, other techniques generate test templates, yet others generate code fragments, such as statement sequences and assertions, where the variables used in the assertions are also called *oracle data* [20].

6.1.1 Complete Test Cases

Complete test cases can be easily generated from highly expressive specifications. The approach of Mikk [29] that we described in Section 5.1 translates Z specifications into C code, generating a C function for each Z schema. Similarly, the technique proposed by McDonald *et al.* [31] translates Object-Z code into C++ code. The technique generates C++ skeleton classes with function declarations based on the structure of specifications and derives the implementation of the functions from the predicates in the corresponding schemas.

Peters and Parnas translate their predicate-based tabular formal documents that we introduced in Section 5.1 into C or C++ code by generating oracle composed of four programs, namely, `initOracle`, `inCompSet`, `inDomain`, and `inRelation` [28,38]. These four programs are all executable C or C++ functions, which are called when executing the oracle to initialize and evaluate the predicates in the formal documents.

Hughes and Stotts use the algebraic specifications together with the code of ADT implementations to generate executable test drivers in Eiffel or C++ [74].

Complete test cases can be obtained also without comprehensive formal specification by adapting existing test cases or with some human effort. For example in DiffGen, Taneja and Xie generate JUnit parameterized unit test cases [75].

Both Daniel *et al.* and Mirzaaghaei *et al.* propose techniques to repair test cases that are not readily executable on the new version of program under test [17,76].

6.1.2 Test Templates

Information-rich specifications do not necessarily lead to complete test code. As mentioned in Section 5.4, Antoy and Hamlet proposed a technique to automatically generate oracle implementation templates from algebraic specifications [56]. The technique requires the programmer to write a representation function r that maps concrete to abstract states. When the manually written implementation executes an operation that changes the concrete program state s to s', a corresponding abstract operation changes the abstract state a to a', where $r(s) = a$ and the oracle checks if $r(s') = a'$. Inspired from a similar idea of mapping concrete into abstract states, Aichernig [77] proposed different approaches to check postconditions written in VDM-SL. The approach translates VDM-SL expressions into C++ code so that the oracle code can access states in the program implementation. The states are abstracted by manually implemented retrieve functions.

6.1.3 Sequences of Statements

Test cases for object-oriented software systems invoke sequences of method calls to properly exercise single classes or sets of classes, and oracles check the correctness of both the final and the intermediate outputs as well as the program states. As discussed in Section 5.4, algebraic specifications are the most common way of specifying ADTs that are at the basis of object-oriented classes, and are one of the primary sources of information for generating test cases and oracles for object-oriented systems. In algebraic specifications, axioms specify the equivalence relations between objects created by sequences of operations and are often used to generate sequences of method calls as checkable forms.

In DAIST [50], the algebraic specifications are an integral part of the program and include the code implementation and test points that indicate where to check the validity of the states. When running test cases, the axioms are translated into calls to the corresponding function implementations, and the test points are compiled into test drivers that provide test data. As described in Section 5.4, ASTOOT [51] transforms the algebraic specifications into test cases in the form of triples (S_1, S_2, tag), where S_1 and S_2 are two sequences of message invocations and *tag* is a boolean value that indicates whether the two resulting objects should be equivalent or not. The test cases, along with the

EQN function that checks the observational equivalence of objects, are the inputs of a test driver and are executed to produce test results.

Similar to ASTOOT, the algebraic specification-based technique proposed by Chen *et al.* [52] generates pairs of operation sequences as test cases and checks the observational equivalence of the two objects generated by executing the sequences. With TACCLE, Chen *et al.* further extend this technique by adding the testing of interactions among classes, called *cluster-level* testing [53]. TACCLE generates message-passing sequences based on message-passing rules specified with the Contract language. To test each individual rule, the TIM approach of TACCLE first creates the sender and receiver objects, O_{sender} and $O_{receiver}$ and randomly selects parameters that satisfy the condition of message passing. Then, TIM runs the specified operation on O_{sender} that should activate an operation on $O_{receiver}$, changing its state to $O'_{receiver}$. At the same time, TIM analyzes the rule to identify the corresponding operation that is specified to be activated on the receiver and runs this operation on $Pre\_O_{receiver}$, a copy of the receiver object right after its creation, to produce $O''_{receiver}$. By checking the equivalence of $O'_{receiver}$ and $O''_{receiver}$, TIM tests whether the rule is obeyed. TACCLE further tests composite message-passing sequences by generating sequences from the specification and the implementation, respectively, and checking whether the specification-based sequences match the implementation-based ones. As with other techniques based on algebraic specifications, the CASCAT tool generates operation sequences as test cases [55]. CASCAT includes a *Test Driver* and a *Test Result Evaluator* to execute Java components on test cases, record test results, and check their correctness.

Sequences of operations are generated also from other sources of information. Bouquet refers to a subset of UML to generate test targets that express the contexts and effects of the operations [39] and transforms test targets into paths, (i.e., sequences of method calls), by means of automated theorem proving. The results of executing the sequences can be checked to see if they produce the expected results. Gargantini *et al.* use SCR specifications to generate test sequences as consecutive input–output pairs from counterexamples reported by model checking the requirements [46].

6.1.4 Assertions and Runtime Monitors

As discussed in Section 5.1, assertion languages are a kind of state-based specifications used as a source of information for generating oracles. When expressed as runtime checks located directly in the program code, assertions are a form of checkable specifications that can be either given directly, as in the case of Eiffel, or produced from other sources of information as in the approach of Richardson *et al.* [32].

Some kinds of assertions are located in the code and can be either directly supported in the programming language with special keywords, for example, with the `assert` statement in Java, or implemented as special functions, for example, with the `assertEquals()` method in JUnit. These assertions use concrete variables or values in the program code and can be executed directly. Other kinds of assertions, so-called *abstract* assertions, predicate abstract events or variables [32]. Checking abstract assertions requires a mapping between the concrete variables used in the code and the abstract ones used in the assertions.

In contrast to assertions, runtime monitors often take into account the control flow and the order of occurrences of events, as well as program state. Runtime monitors record either the execution traces or particular events. Monitors can be either inserted in the program code or implemented as low-level agents or hooks with the support from the execution environments. While assertions are executed at runtime to check some conditions *online*, traces are usually monitored during the program execution and analyzed *offline* [32]. Offline checking usually provides more complex mechanism than online checking, since it does not suffer from typical online performance limitations.

Araujo *et al.* proposed a technique that supports runtime assertion checking of specified concurrent contracts [37]. The technique introduces extra thread-local objects, synthesizes extra methods, and instruments the original program code. Durrieu combines assertions that check general properties with expected outputs that are checked for equality [78]. The test oracle checks the traces collected during the execution of the system under test, parses human-written test schemas, and uses them to derive the expected outputs.

6.1.5 General Test Code Generation

Implicit rules can be checked at different levels. Rules can be supported directly either by the execution environment or platform or by the test oracles that generate code to explicitly collect relevant values and events and check them against the rules. For example, property-based oracles are essentially general rules of embedded programs about semaphores, message queues, and critical sections [79]. The technique generates oracles from these rules by instrumenting the program code, the operating system, and the libraries to generate runtime traces that are analyzed offline. In the technique for testing agent-based systems, the fault model consists of features (or characteristics) expected to be observed [80]. The technique instruments the code to collect the observations that will be checked by the test oracle.

Implicit rules that are supported by the execution environment or platform are likely to be enforced by the runtime environments themselves, such as the operating systems and virtual machines. For example, in JVM, an access out of the bound of an array raises a runtime exception automatically, and JVM checks the inbound property at runtime. Not all exceptions are equally interesting, as some of them are caused by test input that do not satisfy preconditions of some operations or are even intentionally thrown to transfer the control. JCrasher proposes a set of heuristics to classify each observed crash represented as an instance of Throwable at runtime [4]. Check "n" Crash (CnC) improves JCrasher by using ESC/Java to generate fault-revealing inputs more efficiently [5]. CnC focuses on the types of errors checked by ESC/Java.

Metamorphic testing focuses on relations between inputs and outputs and is applicable to various checkable forms, as long as the expected relations over the outputs of multiple test executions can be properly checked [81]. In particular, to support metamorphic testing in SOA, Chan *et al.* encapsulate the services under test into access wrappers called *metamorphic services* [82]. Based on metamorphic relations expressed as extended JML specifications, Corduroy creates a corresponding test method for each method under test and inserts a postcondition using the test method [72]. The postcondition can be translated by JML tools into test code that calls the test method to check the metamorphic relations. Although not extensively discussed, the technique by Zhou *et al.* to evaluate the quality of search engines seems to include a mechanism to automatically generate query strings and analyze the search results, for example, counting the number of URLs retrieved or to compute characteristics of ranking, using readily available APIs exposed by the search engines, for example, the Google search API [70]. Based on such a mechanism, logical consistency properties (as metamorphic relations) of multiple sets of search results can be checked automatically.

6.2. Expected Values

In general, when the expected values are known, it is straightforward to check the equality or inequality between the actual and the expected values, as, for example, discussed in [71,83–85]. This is normally done by simply using assertions or other condition checking code. However, for programs with special formats (or structures) of states, the checking procedure may need sophisticated design.

In their PATHS system, Memon *et al.* model the state of a GUI as a composition of the GUI objects with their property values [49]. Given an individual state, checking its properties can be as simple as checking normal variables. However, as GUIs mostly work in an event-driven style and a GUI test case normally includes a series of actions on the GUI, each intermediate state after an action may exhibit erroneous behavior. Moreover, there can be a large number of object properties relevant to a GUI state, and testers have to choose the granularity of the checking to balance the effectiveness and the costs. Memon *et al.* propose three strategies for selecting properties [49]. A lightweight strategy checks only the changed properties after each action. A complete strategy checks all the properties supported by the underlying language or toolkit for the GUI development. A midway strategy checks properties relevant to the GUI specification based on the GUI model proposed by the authors. Note that the state after every action is supposed to be checked. In their follow-up work, Memon and Xie studied the timing of checking GUI states [57]. They first studied two extreme strategies, namely, O_{all} and O_{last}, that check the GUI state *after each event* and *after the last event*, respectively. Based on observations on the special events relevant to transient errors (those may disappear during execution), they proposed a new strategy, called O_{new}, that checks states at selected points to balance effectiveness and efficiency. In both techniques, the actual GUI states are extracted at some points of the program executions, using an execution monitor.

HTML and XML are widely used in Web applications for representing Web pages, data exchanging, etc. Due to their specific format, these kinds of data are mostly checked in a hierarchical way. To test Web applications, Sprenkle *et al.* [58] proposed a suite of 22 oracle comparators that compare the expected and the actual HMTL outputs. The technique uses the output from a previous program version as the expected output. At a high level, the oracle comparators can be classified as document-, content- and structure-based. Each of these three categories can be further decomposed according to the treatments on lower-level entities, such as white spaces, tags, tag name, links, attributes, and forms. Sprenkle *et al.* structure the entire suite of comparators into a partial order that gives a clear overview of the relations between comparators and can be used to guide effective combinations of the comparators for specific testing tasks [58]. Kim-Park *et al.* proposed an automated oracle for XML processors that mix several kinds of information, including a relaxed golden implementation, user-defined expected nodes, and node ordering [86]. The checking process amounts to executing the XQuery code translated from the six oracle constraints.

Some programs may produce random outputs, either because they take random inputs or because of some randomness in their code implementations. For such programs, the exact expected outputs are difficult if not impossible to obtain. Mayer and Guderlei proposed a technique for testing such programs using statistical methods, based on formulae for computing statistical measures of the actual outputs available, for instance mean and variance [87]. The expected output required by the technique is computed as the expected values of the statistical measures. The technique automatically extracts the relevant outputs from the test case executions and computes the actual values of the statistical measures using the given formulae.

6.3. Executable Specifications

Executable specifications provide a way to synthesize expected executions. They differ from program implementations in that they are executed at a higher abstraction level. Test oracles can be easily derived from executable specifications by mapping the abstract states of the specifications to the concrete states of the program execution. Many techniques support executable specifications, including logic programming [88], abstract state machines [89], and FSMs. In our survey, we found that FSMs are the executable specifications most frequently used as test oracles.

Most techniques that use FSM as the sources of test oracle information do not translate the FSM specifications into other checkable forms, but use directly the FSMs as a checkable form and check the actual program executions against the FSM execution.

Pradel and Gross propose a technique for checking API protocols that checks only the execution traces derived from failing test executions [41]. They first split each execution trace into subtraces and then check each subtrace against all API protocols with protocol parameters with the same types of the subtrace. They map each receiver object used in the subtrace to a type-matching protocol parameter in each API protocol being checked.

In testing temporal properties expressed in GIL, Dillon and Yu [42] proposed an algorithm to translate GIL specifications into DFA (as described in Section 5.3). They extract finite sequences of system states from test executions and check each sequence using the DFA to see whether it satisfies the GIL specification. They use the states in the sequence to activate the possible transition in the DFA. A transition is executed if the current state in the state sequence satisfies the formulae associated with the transition. Since the automata is deterministic, for every node of the DFA, one and only one of the labels holds for any state. For testing a GIL specification p the DFA D used as the oracle represents $f = \neg p$. In this way, when D accepts a state sequence s, it detects a violation of p and computes a sequence of formulae that correspond to the violation by finding a path through the requirement sets that annotate the relevant DFA nodes. In a later work on a generic algorithm to produce oracles from temporal logic specifications, Dillon and Ramakrishna used flow graphs as the checkable form of test oracles [45]. In their work, a flow graph represents a finite state automation, and its definition is quite similar to that of the DFA used in [42]. A location L of a flow graph corresponds to a node of a DFA and is annotated with a set of temporal logic formulae that must be satisfied by the remaining state sequence. A flow graph is a bipartite graph where each arc connects a pair of location transition (T, L) or (L, T). A pair of arcs (T, L) and (T, L') corresponds to a transition (N, N') in the corresponding DFA, in which nodes N and N' correspond to locations L and L', respectively, and T is equivalent to the label of the arc. Similar to the work presented in [42], state sequences are generated from test executions and oracles execute the flow graphs and reject the sequences that do not lead to final states.

Every log file analyzer in the log analysis by Andrews [40] includes a set of parallel state machines with possibly infinite states. Each state machine is used to analyze a thread of execution; hence, a log file analyzer can analyze the log file containing log lines reported by multiple threads. Nodes of the FSMs represent specific states and transitions correspond to log file lines that represent the occurrence of specific events. In log-based testing, the programs under test are instrumented and executed to generate log files. Then, each log file analyzer processes its log file by using each line of log as input to run the underlying state machine. The analysis reports an error either if there exists no transition in the log file that exists from the current state or if the events in the log file do not lead to a final state of the state machine.

Model checking is another form of checkable specifications. The technique proposed by Callahan *et al.* starts from model checking to produce an oracle FSM, OFSM, for each partition of the test input space and use the oracles both as test drivers and as oracles [48]. As a test driver, the OFSM annotates the FSM states identifying the paths that correspond to counter-examples, generates events for all the marked paths that are sent to the units under test, and checks the conditions corresponding to the reactions of the unit under test. The OFSM enables such concrete executions referring to an action table that associates each transition event in the model to its corresponding action (to drive a test) and checks.

FSMs are widely used also in protocol conformance testing [43]. FSMs are used to model both the specification and the implementation, and the correctness of the implementation is checked by comparing the two models. When dealing with protocol specifications, classic FSMs are usually augmented with outputs associated with states and transitions.

The testing process focuses on the coverage of states, transitions, and outputs. As discussed in [2], the oracle execution in protocol conformance testing is closely coupled with the test selection. For example, the *Wp method* proposed by Fujiwara *et al.* [43] refers to both the specification and the implementation FSMs (denoted as S and I, respectively): given an input sequence $(a_1, a_2, \ldots, a_n)$, each element a_i is fed to both S and I and the two outputs are checked to detect faults.

Wang *et al.* proposed a technique for testing distributed real-time system [90]. They translate real-time temporal logic specifications into timed automata that are used as the checkable form of test oracles.

6.4. Machine Learning Models

With machine learning models built from previous executions of the same program or executions of previous versions of the program, no further translations are necessary in most cases to generate checkable oracles, since they can generate either expected outputs or the testing results directly. In this sense, machine learning models can be viewed as a kind of checkable form of test oracle. In this section, we overview how the three most frequently used machine models, association rules, decision trees, and ANNs, are used as checkable forms in test oracle techniques.

When association rules are learnt from data, the expected outputs or verdicts are determined by applying the rules on the actual outputs. In a typical application of an association rule, *premise → consequence*, the actual outputs that satisfy the *premise* must also satisfy the *consequence*. Zheng *et al.* mine association rules from existing (training) search results and compute their premises and consequences as properties of search queries and results [66].

Decision trees that are used, for example, by Frounchi *et al.* to test the consistency of image segmentations work similarly to sequences of rules [67]. Typically, a decision tree is used as a classifier to classify each data instance and the classification is interpreted as the test result of the data instance.

ANNs are also a popular machine learning model used to generate test oracles. Both Jin *et al.* and Vanmali *et al.* use a single ANN as the test oracle [63,65]. An ANN is used as an oracle by feeding it with the test inputs and using the output of the ANN as the estimated output. Since ANNs usually require inputs in the form of feature vectors and produce outputs values between 0 and 1, some preprocessing and postprocessing may be necessary to transform the original test inputs into a form acceptable to the ANN and to interpret the ANN output.

When a single ANN is not sufficient, multiple ANNs are trained and connected to form larger networks, whose final output is the combination of the outputs of the constituent ANNs. For example, Shahamiri *et al.* handle programs with complex functionalities by training one ANN for each different output [64].

Test oracles based on machine learning models may have several common limitations. Since they require sufficient data to train the models, they often use an early program version to generate training data, and then the models are used to test other program versions. Therefore, machine learning models are often used for regression testing. Since machine learning models are approximations of the expected (correct) program implementation, when used test oracles, they may generate both false positives and false negatives.

7. SUMMARY AND FUTURE DIRECTIONS

In this paper, we presented a classification of test oracles based on the source of information required to generate the oracles and we surveyed the main approaches, with particular attention to the many results produced in the last decade.

While in the 1980s and 1990s the research on automatic generation of testing oracles focused mostly on the use of different types of specifications, recent research has opened new research frontiers that span from the use of machine learning techniques to search-based techniques and techniques that exploit the intrinsic redundancy of software systems. The early results are extremely encouraging and such approaches are widely studied.

The growing availability of automated generated oracles opens new interesting research questions related to the precision of the generated oracles and the role of humans. The precision of automatically generated oracles depends on the information used for the generation. Complete and consistent formal specifications may lead to complete and precise oracles, while little information may lead to oracles able to reveal only few classes of failures, like the case of implicit oracles that can reveal system crashes and unexpected exceptions, but not functional failures. Recent research trends try to increase the completeness and precisions of oracles while keeping a small amount of required information. The increasing availability of techniques to generate automatic or semi-automatic oracles may change the role of humans who may be required to provide different forms of information to increase the effectiveness of automatic generation techniques and the precision of automated oracles.

Yet other interesting research trends are clearly indicated by some recent results concerning domain-specific applications. Recently, research has focused successfully on GUIs, Web application, and interactive applications, just to cite few interesting application domains. We will probably see a growing set of relevant application domains that may enable new approaches to generate automated oracles.

REFERENCES

[1] E.J. Weyuker, On testing non-testable programs, Comput. J. 25 (4) (1982) 465–470.
[2] Luciano Baresi, Michal Young, Test oracles, Technical report CIS-TR-01-02, University of Oregon, Department of Computer and Information Science, Eugene, OR, USA, August 2001. http://ix.cs.uoregon.edu/~michal/pubs/oracles.html.
[3] M. Pezzè, M. Young, Software Testing and Analysis: Process, Principles, and Techniques, John Wiley & Sons Inc., New York, 2008.
[4] C. Csallner, Y. Smaragdakis, JCrasher: an automatic robustness tester for Java, Softw. Pract. Exp. 34 (11) (2004) 1025–1050.
[5] C. Csallner, Y. Smaragdakis, Check 'n' crash: combining static checking and testing, in: Proceedings of the 27th International Conference on Software Engineering, ICSE '05, ACM, New York, NY, 2005, pp. 422–431.
[6] C. Flanagan, K. Rustan, M. Leino, M. Lillibridge, G. Nelson, J.B. Saxe, Extended static checking for Java, in: Proceedings of the ACM SIGPLAN 2002 Conference on Programming Language Design and Implementation, PLDI '02, ACM, New York, NY, 2002, pp. 234–245.
[7] C. Csallner, Y. Smaragdakis, T. Xie, Dsd-crasher: a hybrid analysis tool for bug finding, ACM Trans. Softw. Eng. Methodol. 17 (2) (2008) 8:1–8:37.
[8] M.D. Ernst, Dynamically discovering likely program invariants, Ph.D, University of Washington, Department of Computer Science and Engineering, Seattle, Washington, 2000.

[9] C. Pacheco, S.K. Lahiri, M.D. Ernst, T. Ball, Feedback-directed random test generation, in: Proceedings of the 29th International Conference on Software Engineering, ICSE '07, 2007, pp. 75–84.

[10] F. Ricca, P. Tonella, Detecting anomaly and failure in web applications, IEEE Multi-Media 13 (2) (2006) 44–51.

[11] S. Anand, E. Burke, T.Y. Chen, J. Clark, M.B. Cohen, W. Grieskamp, M. Harman, M.J. Harrold, P. McMinn, A. Bertolino, et al., An orchestrated survey on automated software test case generation, J. Syst. Software 86 (8) (2013) 1978–2001.

[12] A. Bertolino, Software testing research: achievements, challenges, dreams, in: 2007 Future of Software Engineering, FOSE '07, IEEE Computer Society, Washington, DC, 1978–2007, pp. 85–103.

[13] M. Harman, P. McMinn, M. Shahbaz, and S. Yoo, A comprehensive survey of trends in oracles for software testing, Technical report, Technical Report Research Memoranda CS-13-01, Department of Computer Science, University of Sheffield, 2013.

[14] D.C. Luckham, F.W. Von Henke, An overview of Anna, a specification language for Ada, IEEE Softw. 2 (2) (1985) 9–22.

[15] S. Sankar, R. Hayes, ADL—an interface definition language for specifying and testing software, in: Proceedings of the Workshop on Interface Definition Languages, IDL '94, ACM, New York, NY, 1994, pp. 13–21.

[16] C. Pacheco, M.D. Ernst, Eclat: automatic generation and classification of test inputs, in: Proceedings of the 19th European Conference on Object-Oriented Programming, ECOOP '05, 2005, pp. 504–527.

[17] B. Daniel, V. Jagannath, D. Dig, D. Marinov, ReAssert: suggesting repairs for broken unit tests, in: Proceedings of the 2009 IEEE/ACM International Conference on Automated Software Engineering, ASE '09, IEEE Computer Society, Washington, DC, 2009, pp. 433–444.

[18] G. Fraser, A. Arcuri, EvoSuite: automatic test suite generation for object-oriented software, in: Proceedings of the 19th ACM SIGSOFT Symposium and the 13th European Conference on Foundations of Software Engineering, ESEC/FSE '11, 2011, pp. 416–419.

[19] G. Fraser, A. Zeller, Mutation-driven generation of unit tests and oracles, IEEE Trans. Softw. Eng. 38 (2) (2012) 278–292.

[20] M. Staats, G. Gay, M.P.E. Heimdahl, Automated oracle creation support, or: how I learned to stop worrying about fault propagation and love mutation testing, in: Proceedings of the 2012 International Conference on Software Engineering, ICSE 2012, 2012, pp. 870–880.

[21] F. Pastore, L. Mariani, G. Fraser, Crowdoracles: can the crowd solve the oracle problem? in: Proceedings of the 2013 International Conference on Software Testing, Verification and Validation, ICST 2013, 2013, pp. 342–351.

[22] M. Staats, S. Hong, M. Kim, G. Rothermel, Understanding user understanding: determining correctness of generated program invariants, in: Proceedings of the 2012 International Symposium on Software Testing and Analysis, ISSTA 2012, 2012, pp. 188–198.

[23] J.M. Spivey, The Z Notation: A Reference Manual, Prentice Hall International (UK) Ltd., Hertfordshire, UK, 1992.

[24] J.-R. Abrial, M.K.O. Lee, D. Neilson, P.N. Scharbach, I. Sørensen, The B-method, in: Proceedings of the 4th International Symposium of VDM Europe on Formal Software Development—Volume 2: Tutorials, VDM '91, Springer-Verlag, London, UK, 1991, pp. 398–405.

[25] C.B. Jones, Systematic Software Development Using VDM, Prentice Hall International (UK) Ltd., Hertfordshire, UK, 1986.

[26] B. Meyer, Object-Oriented Software Construction, first ed., Prentice-Hall, Inc., Upper Saddle River, NJ, 1988.

[27] L. Burdy, Y. Cheon, D.R. Cok, M.D. Ernst, J.R. Kiniry, G.T. Leavens, K. Rustan, M. Leino, E. Poll, An overview of JML tools and applications, Int. J. Softw. Tools Technol. Transfer 7 (3) (2005) 212–232.

[28] D.K. Peters, D.L. Parnas, Using test oracles generated from program documentation, IEEE Trans. Softw. Eng. 24 (3) (1998) 161–173.

[29] E. Mikk, Compilation of Z specifications into C for automatic test result evaluation, in: Proceedings of the 9th International Conference of Z Users on the Z Formal Specification Notation, ZUM '95, Springer-Verlag, London, UK, 1995, pp. 167–180.

[30] U. Schmidt, H.-M. Hörcher, Programming with VDM domains, in: VDM'90 VDM and ZFormal Methods in Software Development, Springer, Berlin, Heidelberg, 1990, pp. 122–134.

[31] J. McDonald, L. Murray, P. Strooper, Translating object-z specifications to object-oriented test oracles, in: Proceedings of the Fourth Asia-Pacific Software Engineering and International Computer Science Conference, APSEC '97, IEEE Computer Society, Washington, DC, 1997, p. 414.

[32] D.J. Richardson, S.L. Aha, T.O. O'Malley, Specification-based test oracles for reactive systems, in: Proceedings of the 14th International Conference on Software Engineering, ICSE '92, 1992, pp. 105–118.

[33] B. Meyer, Applying "design by contract", Computer 25 (10) (1992) 40–51.

[34] R. Kramer, iContract—the Java(tm) design by contract(tm) tool, in: Proceedings of the Technology of Object-Oriented Languages and Systems, TOOLS '98, IEEE Computer Society, Washington, DC, 1998, p. 295.

[35] A. Bhorkar, A run-time assertion checker for Java using JML, Technical report 00-08, Department of Computer Science, Iowa State University, 2000.

[36] C. Boyapati, S. Khurshid, D. Marinov, Korat: automated testing based on Java predicates, in: Proceedings of the 2002 ACM SIGSOFT International Symposium on Software Testing and Analysis, ISSTA '02, ACM, New York, NY, 2002, pp. 123–133.

[37] W. Araujo, L.C. Briand, Y. Labiche, Enabling the runtime assertion checking of concurrent contracts for the java modeling language, in: Proceedings of the 33rd International Conference on Software Engineering, ICSE '11, ACM, New York, NY, 2011, pp. 786–795.

[38] D. Peters, D.L. Parnas, Generating a test oracle from program documentation: work in progress, in: Proceedings of the 1994 ACM SIGSOFT International Symposium on Software Testing and Analysis, ISSTA '94, ACM, New York, NY, 1994, pp. 58–65.

[39] F. Bouquet, C. Grandpierre, B. Legeard, F. Peureux, N. Vacelet, M. Utting, A subset of precise UML for model-based testing, in: Proceedings of the 3rd International Workshop on Advances in Model-Based Testing, A-MOST '07, ACM, New York, NY, 2007, pp. 95–104.

[40] J.H. Andrews, Testing using log file analysis: tools, methods, and issues, in: Proceedings of the 13th IEEE International Conference on Automated Software Engineering, ASE '98, IEEE Computer Society, Washington, DC, 1998, p. 157.

[41] M. Pradel, T.R. Gross, Leveraging test generation and specification mining for automated bug detection without false positives, in: Proceedings of the 2012 International Conference on Software Engineering, ICSE 2012, IEEE Press, Piscataway, NJ, 2012, pp. 288–298.

[42] L.K. Dillon, Q. Yu, Oracles for checking temporal properties of concurrent systems, in: Proceedings of the 2nd ACM SIGSOFT Symposium on Foundations of Software Engineering, SIGSOFT '94, ACM, New York, NY, 1994, pp. 140–153.

[43] S. Fujiwara, G. von Bochmann, F. Khendek, M. Amalou, A. Ghedamsi, Test selection based on finite state models, IEEE Trans. Softw. Eng. 17 (6) (1991) 591–603.

[44] L.K. Dillon, G. Kutty, L.E. Moser, P.M. Melliar-Smith, Y.S. Ramakrishna, Graphical specifications for concurrent software systems, in: Proceedings of the 14th International

Conference on Software Engineering, ICSE '92, ACM, New York, NY, 1992, pp. 214–224.

[45] L.K. Dillon, Y.S. Ramakrishna, Generating oracles from your favorite temporal logic specifications, in: Proceedings of the 4th ACM SIGSOFT Symposium on Foundations of Software Engineering, SIGSOFT '96, ACM, New York, NY, 1996, pp. 106–117.

[46] A. Gargantini, C. Heitmeyer, Using model checking to generate tests from requirements specifications, in: Proceedings of the 7th European Software Engineering Conference Held Jointly with the 7th ACM SIGSOFT International Symposium on Foundations of Software Engineering, ESEC/FSE-7, Springer-Verlag, London, UK, 1999, pp. 146–162.

[47] G.J. Holzmann, The model checker spin, IEEE Trans. Softw. Eng. 23 (5) (1997) 279–295.

[48] J.R. Callahan, S.M. Easterbrook, T.L. Montgomery, Generating test oracles via model checking, NASA/WVU Software Research Lab, Fairmont, WV, Technical report# NASA-IVV-98-015, 1998.

[49] A.M. Memon, M.E. Pollack, M. Lou Soffa, Automated test oracles for GUIs, in: Proceedings of the 8th ACM SIGSOFT International Symposium on Foundations of Software Engineering: Twenty-First Century Applications, SIGSOFT '00/FSE-8, ACM, New York, NY, 2000, pp. 30–39.

[50] J. Gannon, P. McMullin, R. Hamlet, Data abstraction, implementation, specification, and testing, ACM Trans. Program. Lang. Syst. 3 (3) (1981) 211–223.

[51] R.-K. Doong, P.G. Frankl, The Astoot approach to testing object-oriented programs, ACM Trans. Softw. Eng. Methodol. 3 (2) (1994) 101–130.

[52] H.Y. Chen, T.H. Tse, F.T. Chan, T.Y. Chen, In black and white: an integrated approach to class-level testing of object-oriented programs, ACM Trans. Softw. Eng. Methodol. 7 (3) (1998) 250–295.

[53] H.Y. Chen, T.H. Tse, T.Y. Chen, TACCLE: a methodology for object-oriented software testing at the class and cluster levels, ACM Trans. Softw. Eng. Methodol. 10 (1) (2001) 56–109.

[54] R. Helm, I.M. Holland, D. Gangopadhyay, Contracts: specifying behavioral compositions in object-oriented systems, in: Proceedings of the European Conference on Object-Oriented Programming on Object-Oriented Programming Systems, Languages, and Applications, OOPSLA/ECOOP '90, ACM, New York, NY, 1990, pp. 169–180.

[55] B. Yu, L. Kong, Y. Zhang, H. Zhu, Testing java components based on algebraic specifications, in: Proceedings of the 2008 International Conference on Software Testing, Verification, and Validation, ICST '08, IEEE Computer Society, Washington, DC, 2008, pp. 190–199.

[56] S. Antoy, D. Hamlet, Automatically checking an implementation against its formal specification, IEEE Trans. Softw. Eng. 26 (1) (2000) 55–69.

[57] A. Memon, Q. Xie, Using transient/persistent errors to develop automated test oracles for event-driven software, in: Proceedings of the 19th IEEE International Conference on Automated Software Engineering, ASE '04, IEEE Computer Society, Washington, DC, 2004, pp. 186–195.

[58] S. Sprenkle, L. Pollock, H. Esquivel, B. Hazelwood, S. Ecott, Automated oracle comparators for testing web applications, in: Proceedings of the 18th IEEE International Symposium on Software Reliability, ISSRE '07, IEEE Computer Society, Washington, DC, 2007, pp. 117–126.

[59] T. Xie, Augmenting automatically generated unit-test suites with regression oracle checking, in: Proceedings of the 20th European Conference on Object-Oriented Programming, ECOOP '06, 2006, pp. 380–403.

[60] Q. Xie, A.M. Memon, Designing and comparing automated test oracles for GUI-based software applications, ACM Trans. Softw. Eng. Methodol. 16 (1) (2007) 41–76.

[61] G. Fraser, A. Zeller, Mutation-driven generation of unit tests and oracles, in: Proceedings of the 19th International Symposium on Software Testing and Analysis, ISSTA '10, ACM, New York, NY, 2010, pp. 147–158.

[62] T.M. Mitchell, Machine Learning, McGraw Hill, New York, 1997.

[63] H. Jin, Y. Wang, N.-W. Chen, Z.-J. Gou, S. Wang, Artificial neural network for automatic test oracles generation, in: Proceedings of the 2008 International Conference on Computer Science and Software Engineering—Volume 02, CSSE '08, IEEE Computer Society, Washington, DC, 2008, pp. 727–730.

[64] S.R. Shahamiri, W.M.N. Wan Kadir, S. Ibrahim, S.Z. Mohd Hashim, An automated framework for software test oracle, Inform. Softw. Technol. 53 (7) (2011) 774–788.

[65] M. Vanmali, M. Last, A. Kandel, Using a neural network in the software testing process, Int. J. Intell. Syst. 17 (1) (2002) 45–62.

[66] W. Zheng, H. Ma, M.R. Lyu, T. Xie, I. King, Mining test oracles of web search engines, in: Proceedings of the 2011 26th IEEE/ACM International Conference on Automated Software Engineering, ASE '11, IEEE Computer Society, Washington, DC, 2011, pp. 408–411.

[67] K. Frounchi, L.C. Briand, L. Grady, Y. Labiche, R. Subramanyan, Automating image segmentation verification and validation by learning test oracles, Inform. Softw. Technol. 53 (12) (2011) 1337–1348.

[68] S.R. Shahamiri, W.M. Wan-Kadir, S. Ibrahim, S.Z. Hashim, Artificial neural networks as multi-networks automated test oracle, Autom. Softw. Eng. 19 (3) (2012) 303–334.

[69] T.Y. Chen, S.C. Cheung, S.M. Yiu, Metamorphic testing: a new approach for generating next test cases, Department of Computer Science, Hong Kong University of Science and Technology, Technical report HKUST-CS98-01, 1998.

[70] Z.Q. Zhou, S.J. Zhang, M. Hagenbuchner, T.H. Tse, F.-C. Kuo, T.Y. Chen, Automated functional testing of online search services, Softw. Test. Verif. Reliab. 22 (4) (2012) 221–243.

[71] P.J. Schroeder, P. Faherty, B. Korel, Generating expected results for automated black-box testing, in: Proceedings of the 17th IEEE International Conference on Automated Software Engineering, ASE '02, IEEE Computer Society, Washington, DC, 2002, p. 139.

[72] C. Murphy, K. Shen, G. Kaiser, Using JML runtime assertion checking to automate metamorphic testing in applications without test oracles, in: Proceedings of the 2009 International Conference on Software Testing Verification and Validation, ICST '09, IEEE Computer Society, Washington, DC, 2009, pp. 436–445.

[73] A. Carzaniga, A. Goffi, A. Gorla, A. Mattavelli, M. Pezzè, Cross-checking oracles from intrinsic software redundancy, in: Proceedings of the 36th International Conference on Software Engineering, ICSE '14, ACM, New York, NY, USA, 2014, pp. 931–942.

[74] M. Hughes, D. Stotts, Daistish: systematic algebraic testing for OO programs in the presence of side-effects, in: Proceedings of the 1996 ACM SIGSOFT International Symposium on Software Testing and Analysis, ISSTA '96, ACM, New York, NY, 1996, pp. 53–61.

[75] K. Taneja, T. Xie, Diffgen: automated regression unit-test generation, in: Proceedings of the 2008 23rd IEEE/ACM International Conference on Automated Software Engineering, ASE '08, 2008, pp. 407–410.

[76] M. Mirzaaghaei, F. Pastore, M. Pezzè, Supporting test suite evolution through test case adaptation, in: Proceedings of the 2012 IEEE Fifth International Conference on Software Testing, Verification and Validation, ICST '12, IEEE Computer Society, Washington, DC, 2012, pp. 231–240.

[77] B.K. Aichernig, Automated black-box testing with abstract VDM oracles, in: Proceedings of the 18th International Conference on Computer Safety, Reliability and Security, SAFECOMP '99, Springer-Verlag, London, UK, 1999, pp. 250–259.

[78] G. Durrieu, H. Waeselynck, V. Wiels, Leto—a lustre-based test oracle for airbus critical systems, in: D. Cofer, A. Fantechi (Eds.), Formal Methods for Industrial Critical Systems, Springer-Verlag, Berlin, Heidelberg, 2009, pp. 7–22.

[79] T. Yu, A. Sung, W. Srisa-an, G. Rothermel, Using property-based oracles when testing embedded system applications, in: Proceedings of the 2011 Fourth IEEE International Conference on Software Testing, Verification and Validation, ICST '11, IEEE Computer Society, Washington, DC, 2011, pp. 100–109.

[80] L. Padgham, J. Thangarajah, Z. Zhang, T. Miller, Model-based test oracle generation for automated unit testing of agent systems, IEEE Trans. Softw. Eng. 39 (9) (2013) 1230–1244.

[81] Z.Q. Zhou, D.H. Huang, T.H. Tse, Z. Yang, H. Huang, T.Y. Chen, Metamorphic testing and its applications, in: Proceedings of the 8th International Symposium on Future Software Technology (ISFST 2004), Software Engineers Association, Xian, China, 2004.

[82] W.K. Chan, S.C. Cheung, K.R.P.H. Leung, Towards a metamorphic testing methodology for service-oriented software applications, in: Proceedings of the Fifth International Conference on Quality Software, QSIC '05, IEEE Computer Society, Washington, DC, 2005, pp. 470–476.

[83] R.G. Hamlet, Testing programs with the aid of a compiler, IEEE Trans. Softw. Eng. 3 (4) (1977) 279–290.

[84] D.J. Panzl, Automatic software test drivers, Computer 11 (4) (1978) 44–50.

[85] X. Bai, K. Hou, H. Lu, Y. Zhang, L. Hu, H. Ye, Semantic-based test oracles, in: Proceedings of the 2011 IEEE 35th Annual Computer Software and Applications Conference, COMPSAC '11, IEEE Computer Society, Washington, DC, 2011, pp. 640–649.

[86] D.S. Kim-Park, C. de la Riva, J. Tuya, An automated test oracle for xml processing programs, in: Proceedings of the First International Workshop on Software Test Output Validation, STOV '10, ACM, New York, NY, 2010, pp. 5–12.

[87] J. Mayer, R. Guderlei, Test oracles using statistical methods, in: Proceedings of the First International Workshop on Software Quality, Springer, Berlin, Heidelberg, 2004, pp. 179–189.

[88] N.E. Fuchs, Specifications are (preferably) executable, Softw. Eng. J. 7 (5) (1992) 323–334.

[89] U. Glässer, Y. Gurevich, M. Veanes, High-level executable specification of the universal plug and play architecture, in: Proceedings of the 35th Annual Hawaii International Conference on System Sciences (HICSS '02)—Volume 9, HICSS '02, IEEE Computer Society, Washington, DC, 2002, p. 283.

[90] X. Wang, J. Wang, Z.-C. Qi, Automatic generation of run-time test oracles for distributed real-time systems, in: Formal Techniques for Networked and Distributed Systems, In: Lecture Notes in Computer Science, vol. 3235, Springer, Berlin, Heidelberg, 2004, pp. 199–212.

ABOUT THE AUTHORS

Mauro Pezzè is a professor of software engineering at the University of Milano Bicocca and at the University of Lugano where he served as dean from 2007 to 2013. Dr. Pezzè received his PhD in Computer Science from Politecnico di Milano. He is associated editor of IEEE Transactions on Software Engineering (TSE) since 2013 and has been associated editor of ACM Transactions of Software Engineering and Methodologies (TOSEM) from

2006 to 2013. He has served as program co-chair of the International Conference on Software Engineering (ICSE) in 2012 and as general and program chair for the ACM Sigsoft International Symposium on Software Testing and Analysis (ISSTA) in 2013 and 2006, respectively. He has been the keynote speaker at the International Conference on Software Maintenance (ICSM 2012) and at the International Symposium for Search-based Software Engineering (SSBSE 2014). He is the coauthor of the book Software Testing and Analysis: Process, Principles, and Techniques, published by John Wiley in 2007, and of more than a hundred papers appeared in the main software engineering journals and conferences.

Cheng Zhang is currently a postdoctoral fellow at the University of Waterloo. He was a postdoctoral researcher at the University of Lugano in 2013. He received his PhD degree from Shanghai Jiao Tong University in 2012. His research interests include software testing and analysis, program debugging, software maintenance, and code optimization. He has coauthored more than 10 papers in international workshops and conferences, including the International Conference on Software Engineering (ICSE), the International Conference on Automated Software Engineering (ASE), and the European Conference on Object-Oriented Programming (ECOOP).

CHAPTER TWO

Automated Extraction of GUI Models for Testing

Pekka Aho*,†, Teemu Kanstrén*,‡, Tomi Räty*,§, Juha Röning¶
*VTT Technical Research Centre of Finland, Oulu, Finland
†Department of Computer Science, University of Maryland, College Park, Maryland, USA
‡Department of Computer Science, University of Toronto, Toronto, Canada
§Department of Electrical Engineering and Computer Science, University of California, Berkeley, California, USA
¶Department of Computer Science and Engineering, University of Oulu, Oulu, Finland

Contents

Advances in Computers, Volume 95
ISSN 0065-2458
http://dx.doi.org/10.1016/B978-0-12-800160-8.00002-4

49

Abstract

A significant challenge in applying model-based testing on software systems is that manually designing the test models requires considerable amount of effort and deep expertise in formal modeling. When an existing system is being modeled and tested, there are various techniques to automate the process of producing the models based on the implementation. Some approaches aim to fully automated creation of the models, while others aim to automate the first steps to create an initial model to serve as a basis to start the manual modeling process. Especially graphical user interface (GUI) applications, including mobile and Web applications, have been a good domain for model extraction, reverse engineering, and specification mining approaches. In this chapter, we survey various automated modeling techniques, with a special focus on GUI models and their usefulness in analyzing and testing of the modeled GUI applications.

1. INTRODUCTION

Increasing, more ubiquitous use of software systems makes our daily lives more dependent on the software functioning without errors. In the worst case, a slight error in an airline coordinating system could cause a fatal accident, and a minor leak in Internet banking system could lead to loss of customers' money and major financial problems. As software systems are simplified models of their real-world counterparts, no one can claim that they are perfect and free of defects [1]. Especially, errors or weaknesses in critical infrastructure are risks that have to be minimized, and that requires software testing. Software testing is a dynamic technique for increasing confidence in the correctness of the software, i.e., that the software behaves reliably as expected [2].

Graphical user interfaces (GUIs) constitute a large part of the software being developed today [3]. Most software today is interactive, and the code related to the user interface (UI) can be more than half of all code [4]. The UI of a computer program is the part that handles the output to the display and the input from the person using the program [5]. GUI is a graphical front-end to a software system that accepts user- and system-generated events as input and produces deterministic graphical output [6]. GUI is intended to make software easier to use by providing the user with visual controls [7]. GUI software is often large and complex and requires developers to deal with elaborate graphics, multiple ways of giving commands, multiple asynchronous input devices, and rapid semantic feedback [5]. Complexity is further increased when the goal is to create simple but flexible GUIs, e.g., providing default settings for quick and simple usage but allowing more skillful users to modify the settings. The correctness of GUI's behavior is essential to the correct execution of the overall software [7].

For the most part, the challenges in automating GUI testing have remained the same for a decade [8]. It is still challenging to define and implement coverage criteria for not measuring only code coverage of the test suite, but also coverage of all the possible interactions between the GUI and the underlying application. As the amount of possible interactions tends to be impractically large for nontrivial GUI applications, the challenge is to select a test suite having a good coverage with a smaller amount of test cases. While automatically crafting the models for model-based GUI testing (MBGT) has solved some issues, it still remains challenging to verify whether the GUI executes correctly as specified or expected. A GUI test case requires interleaving the oracle invocation with the test case execution, because an incorrect GUI state can lead to an unexpected screen making further test case execution useless [8]. Also, pinpointing an error's actual cause may otherwise be difficult, especially when the final output is correct but the intermediate outputs are incorrect [8]. Automated creation of test oracles is easier for regression testing, because the behavior of an existing, presumably correct version of the GUI software can be used for extracting the expected behavior, that is then stored as oracle information [9].

Most GUI applications are built using UI software tools [10] and iterative process of redesigning the UI after user testing [5]. Most designers think that the behavior is more difficult to prototype than the appearance and communicating the behavior to the developers is more difficult than the appearance [11]. Due to the iterative "rapid prototyping" development processes, the requirements, design, and implementation of GUI software change often, making GUI testing a challenging field for test automation. The maintenance effort required for updating the test suites because of the constant changes in the GUI decreases the benefits gained from test automation. Another challenge in GUI test automation is that automated testing through a GUI is more difficult than testing the application through its API (Application Programming Interface) because it requires additional programming effort to simulate user actions, to observe the outputs produced and to check its correctness, even when using auxiliary libraries [12], such as Microsoft UI Automation [13] or Jemmy [14]. Furthermore, it is even more difficult to automate the evaluation of the user experience, as it depends also on the needs of the targeted users, and usually, end users evaluate concepts and prototypes already during development [4].

Manual testing and the use of capture/replay (CR) tools have been the most popular GUI testing approaches in industry [15]. While CR tools are an easy and straightforward first step toward more effective use of the testing resources, a large number of test cases have to be manually updated after changes in the GUI [16]. The next step, also used by the latest CR tools, is to use GUI automation at a higher level of abstraction, describing test cases with action or key words and using auxiliary libraries to translate and execute the user actions and observe the produced outputs. Usually, this protects the test cases from breaking due to the smallest changes in the GUI, and sometimes the same test cases can be used for testing the software on different platforms and test environments just by changing the auxiliary library.

A number of research results have shown that model-based testing (MBT) reduces the maintenance costs compared to the CR tools [17]. Traditionally in MBT, an abstract test model is created manually based on the requirements of the system under test (SUT), and then an MBT tool is used to generate tests based on the model and execute the tests to verify if the SUT implements the requirements correctly [18]. A significant challenge in applying MBT on software systems is that manually designing the test models requires considerable amount of effort and deep expertise in formal modeling, even more so during iterative development processes or when the documentation of the system is not accurate or updated [12]. Modeling has been one of the most significant obstacles to why MBT has not been taken into use by industry on a large scale [19]. It also requires consolidating the differences between the specification that is modeled and the implementation that is tested and providing mapping between the model and the implementation to be able to execute the derived test cases on a concrete system [12]. The manual effort in designing and maintaining the models negates a significant part of the increased efficiency gained from automated testing [16].

When an existing system is being modeled, there are various model extraction techniques to automate the process of producing the models based on the implementation. The process of automatically creating models or other specifications based on existing design and implementation artifacts is also referred to as model extraction, reverse engineering, specification mining, or specification inference. In this chapter, these terms are used interchangeably unless otherwise specified. Especially GUI applications, including mobile and Web applications, have been a good domain for reverse engineering and specification mining approaches. Usually, the goal of reverse engineering is to analyze the software and represent it in another level of abstraction, and using the abstract form for software maintenance, migrating, testing, reengineering, reuse, documenting purposes, or just to understand how the software works [20]. Our focus is on reverse engineering models of GUI applications and using the models for analysis and testing purposes.

Specification mining can be roughly divided into static, dynamic, and hybrid approaches that use a combination of both static and dynamic analysis. In the static approach, the source code or other static representation of the system is analyzed without executing the system. In the dynamic approach, the system is executed and its external behavior is analyzed [12]. Static source code analysis is well suited for extracting information about the internal structure of the system and dependencies among structural elements [12] and already available in many software engineering tools [21]. Unfortunately the dynamic behavior of the GUI is difficult to extract with static reverse engineering, because the dynamic nature of object-oriented programs, such as object creation, object deletion, garbage collection, and dynamic binding, make it very difficult to understand the behavior by just analyzing the source code [20]. Most of the modern GUI software is developed using event-handler architecture allowing developers to build complex systems using loosely coupled pieces of code and the end users to perform tasks by inputting GUI events in various ways and execution order [22], and the GUI components of modern applications are often reachable only from a particular state or with some environment constraints [23], which makes it difficult to deduce the behavior from the source code without executing it.

As the dynamic behavior of a GUI is difficult to extract with static source code analysis, dynamic reverse engineering techniques are more popular for automatically extracting GUI models, but more difficult to automate [12]. In dynamic approaches, the system is automatically executed and user actions are simulated with automated interactions, and the run-time behavior of the system is analyzed. Various algorithms are then applied to extract behavioral models of the GUI based on the collected observations. Dynamic reverse engineering does not require the source code of the system but it requires a way to programmatically observe, analyze, and interact with the GUI shown to the user. The reverse engineering tool has to be able to control and interact with the GUI application to monitor and model the behavior of dynamically changing GUIs, e.g., when the visibility of a GUI component depends on the state of another component [16].

Some reverse engineering approaches aim to fully automated creation of the models, while others aim to automate the first steps to create an initial model to serve as a basis to start the manual modeling process. There are also semiautomated modeling techniques, performed mostly automatically but are either assisted manually during the reverse engineering process, or reviewed, corrected, and extended manually after automatically generating the initial model [19]. Most techniques require human intervention and the efficiency of the technique depends on the degree of required manual effort [19]. Usually, some input from the user, e.g., a test engineer, is required during the dynamic reverse engineering process to generate models covering all the states of the GUI application, because fully automated generation of meaningful input for all elements of the SUT is extremely challenging [16]. For example, it is very improbable to find matching username and password for a login screen with random generation algorithms if the user has not provided any predefined set of test data [16]. In dynamic reverse engineering, the input generator tool would view the GUI application as a black box without knowledge of the constraints of inputs and their links. Therefore, to reach every state of the GUI, valid value combinations into the input fields of the GUI have to be provided by the user, and an easy and practical way for the user to provide the values is required [24]. Another solution for the challenge of generating meaningful input could be combining static source code analysis with dynamic reverse engineering, i.e., using a hybrid reverse engineering approach.

As the extracted models are based on the observed behavior of the implemented system, instead of the requirement specifications or expected behavior, it is challenging to use them for conformance testing or automatically generating meaningful test oracles. Conformance testing requires a link to the requirements before using the extracted models for test case or test oracle generation. In most of the dynamic GUI reverse engineering approaches for testing, the test oracle is based on the observed behavior of an earlier version of the GUI application. Using this kind of test oracles, changes, and inconsistent behavior of the GUI can be detected and the models can be used for automated regression testing, but conformance testing, i.e., validation and verification against the specifications is problematic [19]. Nevertheless, the extracted models can be utilized for automatically testing the application with a good coverage [19].

In this chapter, we survey various automated modeling and testing techniques, and present the current state-of-the-art on reverse engineering models of GUI applications and using the extracted models for automated testing and analysis. We conclude by presenting the trends we observed during this study and discussing the future directions of the research.

2. BACKGROUND

In this section, we provide background information on testing and modeling of GUIs, and software test automation in general. Automated GUI testing is introduced in Section 3.

2.1. Testing and Modeling of GUIs

2.1.1 Graphical User Interface

The UI of a computer program is the part that handles the output to the display and the input from the person using the program. The rest of the program is called the application or the application semantics [5]. A GUI is a hierarchical, graphical front-end to a software system that accepts as input user- and system-generated events from a fixed set of events and produces deterministic graphical output. A GUI contains graphical objects; each object has a fixed set of properties. At any time during the execution of the GUI, these properties have discrete values, the set of which constitutes the state of the GUI [25]. A GUI takes events (mouse clicks, selections, typing in text fields) as input from users and then changes the state of its widgets accordingly [26].

A GUI is the most widely used method for information systems to interact with end users [5]. From the user's point of view, the GUI is intended to make software easier to use by providing the user with visual controls to represent the information and actions available to the user [7]. In a typical GUI, instead of laboriously typing textual commands to control a computer program, the end user can simply choose commands by activating or manipulating the graphical objects [1]. By allowing the end users to perform multiple tasks simultaneously, GUIs can also lead to higher productivity [1].

GUIs constitute a large part of the software being developed today [3]. From the engineering's point of view, GUI software is often large, possibly more than half of all code of the program [4], and complex, requiring developers to deal with elaborate graphics, multiple ways of giving commands, multiple asynchronous input devices, and rapid semantic feedback [5]. Complexity is further increased when the goal is to create simple but flexible GUIs, e.g., providing default settings for quick and simple usage but allowing more skillful users to modify the settings. Most of the GUI applications are built by iterative process of redesigning the UI after user testing [5]. Most designers think that the behavior is more difficult to prototype than the appearance and communicating the behavior to the developers is more difficult than the appearance [11].

Most modern GUI software is developed using event-handler architecture allowing developers to build complex systems using loosely coupled pieces of code and the end users to perform tasks by inputting GUI events in various ways and execution order [27]. The end user interacts with the objects by performing actions that manipulate the GUI widgets, thus generating events at the software level. Events cause deterministic changes to the state of the software [7]. The execution outcome of an event handler may depend on its internal state, the state of other entities (objects, event handlers), and the external environment. Its execution may lead to a change in its own state or that of other entities. Moreover, the outcome of an event's execution may vary based on the sequence of preceding events or interactions seen thus far [27].

Interaction with computers has evolved from the command line interfaces (CLI) to the direct manipulation or WIMP (Windows, Icon, Mouse, and Pointer) interfaces and is currently evolving to post-WIMP interfaces [28] containing at least one interaction technique not dependent on classical 2D widgets, such as menus and icons [29]. In spite of the innovative development of interaction technology, the most usual type of UI is still extremely similar to the WIMP (Windows, Icon, Mouse, and Pointer) interface, the pointer often being one finger on a touch screen instead of a mouse or other pointing device. The most common difference between post-WIMP and WIMP interfaces is probably the replacement of zoom-in/out functionality of the mouse wheel with a two fingers swipe on multitouch screen mobile devices.

2.1.2 GUI Testing

By the definition of the IEEE Software Engineering Body of Knowledge [30], testing is an activity performed for evaluating product quality, and for improving it, by identifying defects and problems. The purpose of software testing is to reveal software faults in order to correct errors made during the implementation of the application under test (AUT) and to ensure the quality of the AUT [31]. An error is a mistake made by a programmer during the implementation of a software system [31]. A fault is a collection of program source code statements that cause a failure. A failure of an application is an external, incorrect behavior of a program [31]. A program's execution is correct when its behavior matches the functional and nonfunctional requirements in its specifications [32].

GUI testing means that an application with a GUI is tested solely by performing sequences of events or interactions on its GUI widgets and the correctness of its behavior is determined by examining only the state of the GUI widgets [33]. A typical GUI gives many degrees of freedom to an end user, leading to an enormous input event interaction space that needs to be tested [34]. Large number of permutations of events and complex event interactions of GUIs present a challenge for quality assurance and testing [34].

The GUI is one of the components in software projects that is usually subjected to less systematic testing. Its event-driven behavior and its visual essence deem unsuitable the traditional methods and tools commonly used for testing other kind of components [35]. Yet, GUI testing is crucial, as the correctness of GUI's code is essential to the correct execution of the overall software [7]. Many times all the functionality of the application can be invoked through the GUI and therefore GUI tests can cover the entire application [15]. A large proportion of faults detected with GUI testing are in the underlying business logic of the application, rather than in the GUI code itself [36].

Testing of interactive systems is a difficult task. It requires that we test the system's functionality, the interactive behavior of the system and the UI to ensure it is usable and esthetically acceptable for users [37]. As UIs become more complex and software applications become ubiquitous, often relying on new, and sometimes novel, modes of interaction, this difficulty increases [37]. A GUI's response to an event may vary depending on the current state (context) of the software, established by preceding events and their execution order. Therefore, it is not sufficient to test each event in isolation or in one state. Instead, an event has to be executed together with other events [34]. GUI testing is also extremely expensive. For example, 10,000 unit test cases can often be automatically tested within a minute, whereas 10,000 simple GUI test cases may need more than 10 h to complete [1].

2.1.3 GUI Modeling

Modeling is an activity trying to present a system in a different, usually at higher level of abstraction, capturing the relevant parts of system's structure and behavior. GUI modeling aims to present GUIs and the relevant parts of GUI's behavior and structure at a higher level of abstraction. GUI models are used for various purposes, such as communicating the designed structure and behavior to the developers of the GUI software, understanding the program, generating GUI code based on the models, reengineering, maintenance, testing, etc.

Various types of models have been used to describe GUI applications, depending on the intended use or just the preferences of the person creating the models. UI models can describe the domain over which the UI acts, the tasks that the UI supports, and others aspects of the graphical view presented to the user [38]. The use of interface models gives an abstract description of the UI, potentially allowing to:

- Express the UIs at different levels of abstraction, thus enabling choice of the most appropriate abstraction level.
- Perform incremental refinement of the models, thus increasing the guarantee of quality of the final product.
- Reuse UI specifications between projects, thus decreasing the cost of development.
- Reason about the properties of the models, thus allowing validation of the UI within its design, implementation, and maintenance processes.

In order to build any kind of model of a system, the boundaries of such system must be identified [38]. Therefore, the following kinds of models may be considered of interest for UI modeling:

- Domain models are useful for defining the domain of discourse of a given interactive system. Domain models are able to describe object relationships in a specific domain but do not express the semantic functions associated with the domain's objects.
- User models, in their simplest form, can represent the different characteristics of end users and the roles they are playing. In their more ambitious form, user models attempt to mimic user cognitive capabilities to predict how the interaction between the user and the device will progress.
- Task models express the tasks that a user performs in order to achieve goals. Task models describe the activities users should complete to accomplish their objectives. The goal of a task model is not to express how the UI behaves, but rather how a user will use it.
- Dialog models describe the behavior of the UI. Dialog model focus on the device, defining which actions are made available to users via the UI, and how it responds to them. These models capture all possible dialogs between users and the UI.
- Presentation models (PMs) define the visual appearance of the application. They describe the graphical objects in the UI and the materialization of widgets in the various dialog states.

- Navigation models define how the objects can be navigated through the UI from a user's perspective.
- Platform models define the physical devices that are intended to host the application and how they interact with each other.

2.2. Software Test Automation

The software industry is facing the challenge of developing complex software products for a great variety of execution platforms and devices, and at the same time having the pressure to increase the quality while decreasing time and costs of development [39]. In order to evaluate and improve the quality of a product, testing activities are performed to identify defects and problems. Software testing consists of the dynamic verification of the behavior of a program by executing a finite set of suitably selected test cases and comparing the observed behavior against the expected behavior [30].

The manual design and execution of the tests is time consuming and does not ensure systematic coverage of the SUT. With iterative software development process, the manual execution of the tests is even more time consuming and also very boring [17]. To reduce the amount of work required to properly test the products, the software industry is increasing the use of test automation.

Usually, the first step toward automated test process is a CR testing process, which basically means recording the manual execution of the tests once and replaying the recorded tests for every release of the SUT. Unfortunately, the requirements of a software system and therefore also the test requirements change during the development, and at least the changed test cases have to be recorded again.

The second step would be a script-based testing process, using test scripts to automate the execution of tests. Test scripts can be written in some programming language, scripting language, or a special testing language as TTCN-3 [17]. A script-based testing process reduces the amount of manual execution of tests but increases the amount of maintenance work when some requirements change.

A keyword-driven automated testing process uses a higher level of abstraction to reduce the maintenance costs of test scripts. Using abstract keywords and data values, which are then translated into executable test, it is easier to adapt to the changes in the requirements. Even though all of the previously mentioned approaches reduce manual testing, the test data and test oracles still have to be designed manually.

MBT aims to automate also the design of the test cases and expected results [17].

2.2.1 Model-Based Testing

MBT is a technique of generating test cases from behavioral models of the SUT [17]. The idea is to provide more cost-effective means for extensive testing of complex systems by decreasing the development cost and improving the test quality [39]. Instead of manually writing a large set of test cases, the SUT is represented by a smaller set of models describing its expected behavior and how it should be tested at a higher abstraction level, and a test generator tool and a set of chosen algorithms are used to automatically generate tests from these models [18]. There are several benefits, including easier test maintenance due to fewer artifacts to update, higher test coverage from the generated test cases, avoiding manual error prone activities [39], and documenting the SUT behavior in higher level models which helps in sharing the information and understanding the SUT.

MBT process can be divided into five main steps: (1) modeling the SUT and/or its environment; (2) generating abstract test cases from the models; (3) concretizing the abstract tests into executable tests; (4) executing the tests on the SUT; and (5) assigning verdicts, and analyzing the test results [17]. Traditionally, the process starts with using a modeling tool to manually describe the expected behavior of the SUT or the test environment, based on the requirements or other expectations how the system should work, and using a modeling formalism supported by the selected MBT tools. Then the model is used as input for the MBT tools to generate abstract test cases. Many of the MBT tools allow test engineer to select a test criteria to control the focus and number of the test cases. Transforming the abstract tests into executable test scripts requires mapping between the model and the actual system that is being executed, and often requires some input from the test engineer [17]. The execution of the test cases or test scripts, and generation of test reports is usually automated. If the model describes the correct behavior of the SUT, it can be used for generating test oracles and determining where incorrect behavior occurs by looking for situations which violate the model [37].

Efficient MBT should also generate tests for nonfunctional requirements, automate test evaluation, support bug reporting and tracking, support incorporation of new tests and help maintenance of existing tests when the model changes (due to changes in the requirements) [39]. To allow further improvement of the MBT process, it is important to ensure the interoperability among methods, tools, and languages [39].

While MBT itself has been an active research topic already for a long time [17], it has only recently started to be more actively adopted in the industry. The early research was rather theoretical and highly focused on formalisms and model analysis, but now there is a wide variety of tool support and available processing power. Despite the obvious benefits of MBT, modeling itself has been one of the most significant obstacles to why MBT has not been taken into use by industry on a large scale [19]. One generic barrier is its complexity, requiring analytical skills and deep expertise in formal methods [40]. The construction of a dependable and verifiable model of the software demands specialized expertise and considerable amounts of time [41].

3. AUTOMATED GUI TESTING

GUI testing is a challenging field for test automation, because GUI software is typically created using rapid prototyping [3], which means that GUI is constantly changing during the development [15], making maintenance of test cases and other test artifacts very expensive [42]. Another challenge in GUI test automation is that automated testing through a GUI is more difficult than testing the application through its API because it requires additional programming effort to simulate user actions, to observe the outputs produced and to check its correctness, even when using auxiliary libraries [12], such as Microsoft UI Automation [13] or Jemmy [14]. Usually a GUI test case includes a series of events which can only be performed one after another with time spans for the GUI to react, which makes execution of GUI test cases time consuming [1].

Furthermore, it is even more difficult to automate the evaluation of the user experience, as it depends also on the needs of the targeted users, and usually, concepts and prototypes are evaluated by the end users already during the development [4].

3.1. Unit Testing Tools—Automating The Execution of Concrete GUI Test Cases

As the first step toward GUI test automation, testers often employ unit testing tools, such as jfcUnit [43] and Jemmy [14], to manually create unit test cases for GUIs [22]. A unit test case consists of method calls to an instance of the class under test and assertions to determine whether the classes/methods executed correctly. The test cases are automatically executed on the GUI under test and assertion violations are reported as failures. The parts of the GUI state space explored depend largely on the nature of the test cases [22], relying heavily on the expertise of the test engineer to ensure sufficient test coverage [37].

Because manual coding of test cases can be tedious, it is more common use CR [44] tools to record (capture) sequences of events or interactions that testers perform manually on the GUI. These recorded test cases can be replayed (executed) automatically on the GUI.

3.2. CR Tools—Automating the Creation of Concrete GUI Test Cases

The use of CR tools has been the most popular approach to automate GUI testing in industry [15]. With CR tools, one of the developers or testers interacts with the software to exploit particular functionality while using the CR tool record the sequence of interactions. The recorded sequence can subsequently be played back automatically to repeat the test [37].

The earliest CR tools used to provide a basic automation solution by recording mouse coordinates and user actions as scripts [44]. A major problem of using mouse coordinates was that the scripts were broken with even minor changes to the GUI layout [1]. The more recent CR tools, such as Abbot [45], Squish [46], and marathonITE [47], try to overcome this problem by using GUI automation at a higher level of abstraction, capturing GUI widgets by using unique names rather than mouse coordinates. When interacting with the application, the unique name will be used to obtain a reference to the real object in the GUI and the recorded events will be performed on the designated object [1]. Usually, this protects the test cases from breaking from the smallest changes in the GUI. Another proposed solution is to capture screenshot images of the widgets and use image recognition to identify and control GUI components [48], like in Sikuli [49]. Then the test cases break if the graphical appearance of the GUI is changed. There are CR tools also for automating testing of Web applications, such as SeleniumHQ [50], and mobile applications, such as Appium [51].

While CR tools are an easy and straightforward first step toward more effective use of the testing recourses [16], a significant effort is still required to record the test cases, it is challenging to detect the failures [3], and a large number of test cases may have to be rerecorded when the layout of GUI changes [37]. CR tools also require most of the UI to be complete, being useful in postimplementation testing only [37]. As the tests are generated in a run-time environment and then stored as scripts, usually the scripts are not easy to read, interpret, or modify [37].

3.3. Keywords and Action Words—Abstracting the Concrete GUI Test Cases

Instead of capturing the test cases on the implementation level of the concrete GUI that is tested, the tests can be described using keyword or actions words on a higher level of abstraction, and using auxiliary libraries to translate and execute the user actions and observe the produced outputs. The maintenance effort after GUI changes is reduced, as usually the test cases are unaffected and only the translator has to be updated. Sometimes the same test cases can be used for testing the software on different platforms and test environments just by changing the auxiliary library.

To minimize the maintenance effort from changes and maximize the cross-platform reusability, Kervinen *et al.* [52] propose a three-tier testing architecture, illustrated in Fig. 2.1, that separates the levels of abstraction into keywords, action words, and test control. Keyword tier is the lowest level tier in the architecture, defining how to navigate in the GUI and interact with the widgets, i.e., how the concrete actions are executed and tested on the GUI. Keywords are used to describe concrete test cases. Action tier is the intermediate layer consisting of action words describing the behavior that can be tested. The action words correspond to high-level concepts that describe the problem domain rather than the solution domain. Action words are used for describing abstract test cases. Test Control tier is the highest-level tier, describing which type of tests (e.g., smoke or a long period test) are to be run, which test models are used in the runs, which test guidance heuristics should be used, and what are the coverage objectives for each run.

3.4. Model-Based GUI Testing—Automating the Creation of Abstract GUI Test Cases

In MBGT, the GUI is modeled at a different level of abstraction, using a modeling language that is supported by a test case generator tool, so that the models can used to generate test cases for the modeled GUI. Traditionally, the models for MBGT are crafted manually using a graphical modeling tool, e.g., Enterprise Architect [53], Conformiq Designer [54], and Microsoft Spec Explorer [55].

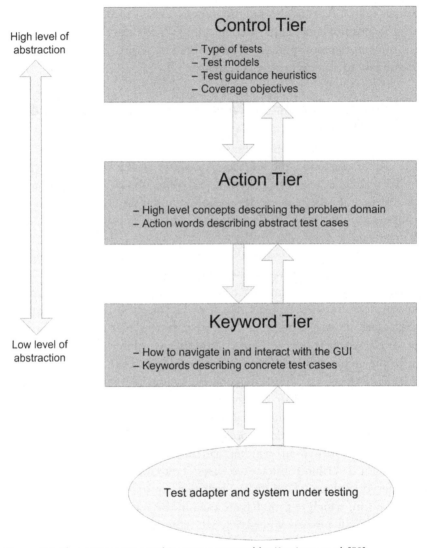

Figure 2.1 Three-tier testing architecture proposed by Kervinen *et al.* [52].

3.4.1 Models for MBGT

State-based models, such as finite-state machine (FSM), are commonly used for MBGT [34,35]. With FSM models, GUI's behavior is modeled as a state machine. Nodes of the model are states of the GUI and input events may trigger abstract state transitions in the machine. A path in the state machine, i.e., a sequence of events or interactions that trigger state transitions, represents a test case. Graph traversal algorithms can be used generate tests from the state models [56] and the abstract states of the model can be used to verify the GUI's concrete state during test case execution [25]. The challenge with FSM-based GUI models is the state space explosion, but the number of states can be reduced using only the relevant properties for distinguishing the states. However, by using too few properties and states, there is a risk of having ambiguous state transitions and losing the context information of the events or interactions.

Another type of models used for MBGT is event-based models, such as event sequence graph (ESG) [57] and event-flow graph (EFG) [58]. In event-based models, the nodes of the model are events, and all events that can be triggered following a specific event are connected to it with directed edges. The challenge with event-based models is to capture context into the model. A GUI's response to an event may vary depending on the current state (context) of the software, established by preceding events and their execution order, and models without context information may include infeasible paths [1].

3.4.2 Challenges in MBGT
For the most part, the challenges in automating the GUI testing have remained the same for a decade [8]. The first challenge in adopting MBGT is that crafting the models requires a significant amount of effort and expertise. While there are approaches for automatically crafting the models for MBGT, using these approaches introduce other kinds of challenges, explained in more detail in Section 5.1.

It is still challenging to define and implement coverage criteria for not measuring only code coverage of the test suite, but also coverage of all the possible interactions between the GUI and the underlying application. For nontrivial GUI applications, especially with long event or interaction sequences, the number of possible permutations is infinite or extremely large, making it impossible or impractical to perform exhaustive testing of the GUI [1]. Therefore, certain coverage criteria are needed to determine how to select test cases and to what extent the test will be done [1], and the challenge is to select a smaller set of test cases to fulfill the criteria efficiently.

It still remains challenging to verify whether the GUI executes correctly as specified or expected [8]. In GUI testing, the outputs are manifested by the values of properties of widgets in the GUI, and the expected values have to be prepared before testing [1]. The challenge is how to define the expected values, i.e., meaningful test oracles. Manually setting all the values of all the properties of all the widgets of each GUI state is not feasible, but setting too few values may lead to ambiguous test verdicts. Usually a GUI test case contains a sequence of events or interactions, and the oracle invocation has to be interleaved with the test case execution, because an incorrect GUI state may lead to an unexpected screen, making further test case execution useless [8]. Also, pinpointing the actual cause of an error may otherwise be difficult, especially when the final output is correct but the intermediate outputs are incorrect [8].

State space explosion is a major challenge in modeling GUI for testing. A GUI state comprises of a set of objects and their property values. Any difference in number of objects or property values may mean a different state. Some property values may have huge or even infinite number of possible values, which in turn makes the number of GUI states huge or infinite. Without a proper method to limit the explosion of GUI states, it is infeasible to perform MBGT [1].

3.4.3 Approaches for MBGT
This section gives some examples of traditional MBGT approaches, meaning that the models are manually crafted based on the requirements or other specifications of the GUI software being tested.

Belli [57] used deterministic finite-state automata (FSA) for GUI modeling, but merged GUI input and GUI state together, assigning them to the nodes of the state-transition diagram of the FSA, like in event-based models. The FSA model is used to capture both desired (correct) and undesired (faulty) events and behavior, and divided into sub graphs to allow describing the behavior of the GUI in more detail. Belli proposed to use identification of complete interaction sequences (CISs) to present meaningful expected system outputs, i.e., test oracles. Later, Belli *et al.* [59] named the model an ESG.

Vieira *et al.* [60] presented an approach to use UML models for MBGT. They used UML Use Case diagrams to describe the relationship among the use cases specified for the application and the actors who interact with the application, and UML Activity Diagrams to model the logic of a single use case. The overall behavior of the application is specified in a set of activity diagrams, used for testing the different functionalities and business rules described in the use cases specification.

Kervinen *et al.* [61] introduced a methodology for MBGT using labeled transition systems (LTSs) in conjunction with action word and keyword techniques for test modeling and MBT. The approach and the test models enable testing of concurrent systems, meaning that many applications can be tested simultaneously, allowing also interactions between the applications to be tested. Katara *et al.* [62] propose to use a CR approach to ease the test modeling by capturing GUI events directly, and use the captured information to generate the keyword tier of the testing architecture. Then the keywords are further developed into higher level action words corresponding to the three-tier testing architecture [52]. The approach was further developed [56] into TEMA tools [63], an open-source tool set for MBGT with a focus on mobile applications on Android platform.

Bowen *et al.* [37] presented a MBGT technique using PMs and presentation and interaction models (PIMs), designed to describe UI designs or implementations in a manner which enables them to be linked to a formal specification of the functionality. The models were used to derive abstract test cases that can be made concrete in various ways.

Mauser *et al.* [64] combined state charts with object-oriented programming code for MBT of embedded UIs in automotive industry. The state charts used in the approach provide a clear structure of screens and their relationships and therefore ease retracing the generated test cases. Object-oriented programming code was easy to reuse and provided efficient means to specify behavior.

3.5. Coverage and Effectiveness of GUI Testing

One of the challenges in testing is to objectively justify the decision when to stop testing. To objectively estimate the quality of the SUT, quantitative arguments, usually in the form of well-defined coverage criteria, are required [57]. Coverage criteria are sets of rules to help determine whether a test suite has adequately tested a program and to guide the testing process [65].

The most common coverage criteria are based on structural issues of the SUT (implementation orientation/white-box testing) usually measured from the source code of the system, such as statement coverage, branch coverage, and path coverage [65]. The other option is using behavioral or functional description (specification orientation/black-box testing), or a combination of both, if both implementation and specifications are available (hybrid/gray-box testing) [57].

Belli [57] proposed edge coverage to be used with event-based models for finding a minimal set of CIS and faulty/illegal CIS to cover all prototypes of legal and illegal user–system interactions, revealing all appearances of system behavior, i.e., triggering all desired and undesired events.

Memon *et al.* [65] proposed event-based coverage criteria to determine the adequacy of tested event sequences in terms of GUI events and their interactions. As the total number of permutations of event sequences in any nontrivial GUI is extremely large, the GUI's hierarchical structure is exploited to identify the important event sequences to be tested. The GUI is decomposed into GUI components, each tested in isolation. Yuan *et al.* [33] defined coverage criteria for GUI test sequences based on combinatorial interaction testing. The key motivation of using combinatorial techniques is that they enable us to incorporate "context" into the criteria in terms of event combinations, sequence length, and by including all possible positions for each event.

Usually, a good test suite is the one that is able to detect the most faults. A "good test suite" can refer also to other qualities, e.g., requires short time or otherwise few resources to create or execute, or easy to maintain [66]. Among software testing researchers, a popular way to evaluate the effectiveness of a testing technique is to try out how many faults the technique detects out of a carefully chosen "representative" sample [67]. The outcome of these evaluations depends on the type of systems and type of defects they have, as certain defects are harder or easier to detect with a specific testing technique [68], and some faults are generally harder to detect than others [69]. Because different studies usually use different samples, two-independent studies of the same techniques might report contradicting or even opposite results [70].

To objectively evaluate the effectiveness of testing, a set of suitable coverage criteria can be used, possibly together with the ability to detect faults. In general, test suites with more test cases tend to be more effective in detecting faults, but not necessarily more efficient, if you consider the time and other resources required for executing the test cases. The granularity, the amount of input given by each test case, which usually means length of the test sequence in GUI testing, affects the type of defects that are found [71]. Long test sequences are able to detect faults missed by short ones, even when the short sequences are systematically generated, and events that interact directly with the underlying program business logic, as opposed to opening/closing menus/windows, are more likely to trigger faults [33]. Usually, longer test cases are required to detect faults in more complex event handlers [71].

The diversity of states in which an event or interaction is executed and the event coverage significantly affect the fault detection effectiveness of a test suite [71], and statement coverage and GUI event coverage affect the likelihood of detecting certain kinds of faults [66]. Test designers should improve the diversity of states in which each event executes by developing a large number of short test cases to detect the majority of shallow faults, which are artifacts of modern GUI design. Additional resources should be used to develop a smaller number of long test cases to detect the deep faults [71]. Focusing on GUI testing, Strecker and Memon [66] have proposed a set of characteristics of faults and test suites that may affect fault detection.

3.6. Test Suite Reduction and Prioritization for GUI Testing

The increasing use and effectiveness of test automation tools has introduced new challenges for software testing. It is fairly easy to generate so many test cases that it takes impractically long time to execute them, even with fully automated test environment. The modern agile development processes have often short iterations, increasing the pressure for short test cycles. Therefore, it is not enough to create an effective automated test suite anymore. It has to be also efficient, not taking too much time or other resources for test execution. The main approaches for making the test suites more efficient are test suite reduction (test suite minimization) and test suite prioritization.

The goal of test suite reduction is to reduce the time and other resources required for test execution and maintenance, usually by reducing the size or number of test cases, while trying to maintain the effectiveness of the test suite [72]. Most approaches are based on eliminating test cases that are redundant relative to some coverage criterion [73]. The general approach is to instrument a set of program entities to record information about their coverage, execute a test suite and reduce it based on the collected coverage information. As different techniques monitor different program entities or behaviors, usually selecting different reduced subsets of the test suite, they have different costs, application environments, and tradeoffs between reduced suite size and fault detection effectiveness [72].

In GUI testing, test case reduction does not mean only reducing the number of test cases, but also the length of individual test cases [34]. Xie and Memon [34] defined minimal-effective event-context (MEEC) of an event that has detected a fault in a test case as the shortest sequence of preceding events or interactions required to detect the fault.

McMaster and Memon [74,75] proposed call stack coverage criterion to be used for GUI test suite reduction, and average expected probability of finding a fault [73] to be used as a metric for fault detection probability analysis during coverage-based test suite reduction. A call stack is a sequence of active calls associated with each thread in a stack-based architecture [75]. Brooks and Memon [76] presented a parameterized metric for test suite similarity, CONTeSSi(n) (CONtext Test Suite Similarity), using the context of n preceding events in test cases. The metric can be used for supporting GUI test suite reduction.

Test case prioritization means that the test cases that are expected to be most effective are executed first, and the goal is trying to detect the faults as early as possible during the test execution. Bryce and Memon [77] proposed an approach for GUI test suite prioritization of existing test suites by t-way interaction coverage. Later they generalize the approach [78] to provide a model and prioritization criteria that support testing of both GUI and Web applications. Elsaka *et al.* [79] used network centrality measures in analysis of EFG models to identify the most important GUI events and event sequences as candidates for test prioritization. Sampath *et al.* [80] formalized the notion of combining multiple criteria into one hybrid criteria for test case prioritization, test suite reduction/minimization, and regression test selection.

4. REVERSE ENGINEERING AND SPECIFICATION MINING

When an existing system is being modeled, there are various model extraction techniques to automate the process of producing the models based on the implementation. In the literature, the process of automatically creating models or other specifications based on existing design and implementation artifacts is commonly referred to as reverse engineering, specification mining, or specification inference. In this chapter, these terms are used interchangeable unless otherwise specified.

Chickofsky [81] defines reverse engineering as the process of analyzing a subject system to identify the systems' components, their relationships, and to create representations of the system in another form or at a higher level of abstraction. The specification mining can be roughly divided into static, dynamic, and hybrid approaches that use a combination of both static and dynamic analysis. In the static approach, the source code or other static representation of the system is analyzed without executing the system. In the dynamic approach, the system is executed and its external behavior is analyzed [12]. With static analysis it is difficult to have good coverage of highly dynamic applications, while dynamic analysis faces problems with guaranteeing that generated models fully capture the behavior of the system [82].

Some reverse engineering approaches aim to fully automated creation of the models, while others aim to automate the first steps to create an initial model to serve as a basis to start the manual modeling process. Usually, the goal of reverse engineering is to analyze the software and represent it in another level of abstraction, and using the abstract form for software maintenance, migrating, testing, reengineering, reuse, documenting purposes, or just to understand how the software works [20].

4.1. Static Reverse Engineering

Static source code analysis is well suited for extracting information about the internal structure of the system and dependencies among structural elements [12] and already available in many software engineering tools [21]. Usually, static analysis does not require executing the program to analyze it, saving the effort for building, deploying, and setting up an appropriate environment to execute the program being analyzed, but it requires access to the source code of the system. Sometimes static analysis requires setting up execution environment for the analyzer to have access to fully parseable source code and linked design artifacts. With static analysis it is possible to address all possible flows of the program whereas dynamic analysis covers only the observed and triggered paths [83].

Unfortunately the dynamic nature of object-oriented programs, such as object creation, object deletion, garbage collection, and dynamic binding, make it very difficult to understand the behavior by just analyzing the source code [20]. Also, it is challenging is to build a fully working static analysis environment for modern software systems with new programming language features, several abstractions, and programming languages layered and connected [83].

There are various static approaches for reverse engineering or mining interface specifications [83–85], states and relationships between objects [86], correctness rules [87], function precedence protocols [88], or function call sequences [89]. Some of the approaches are restricted to a certain programming languages, such as Java [84], or execution environments, but otherwise claim to be general purpose, working for any type of software.

A fairly recent approach by Mariani *et al.* [90], static extraction of interaction models (SEIM), uses static analysis to derive an initial FSA model capturing the interactions between a client application and its integrated Web Services, and then refining the initial FSA into two FSAs, according to the feasibility of the interactions. The approach uses a model refinement technique to identify and reduce infeasible behavior from the inferred models, and generates two FSA models, distinguishing the likely feasible interactions into one model, and the interactions with an unknown level of feasibility into another model, thus allowing engineers to distinguish the relevance of the produced information.

4.2. Dynamic Reverse Engineering

The dynamic nature of object-oriented programs is easier to reverse engineer with dynamic approaches, i.e., by executing the system [20]. In dynamic reverse engineering approaches, the system is executed and the run-time behavior of the system is analyzed [91]. Various algorithms are then applied to extract behavioral models based on the collected observations. Dynamic reverse engineering does not necessarily require the source code of the system, but usually some kind of instrumentation is required to programmatically observe and analyze the system, and the instrumentation is often made on the source code level. Besides decompilation techniques, dynamic approaches are the only option when the source code is not available [12].

Compared to static analysis, dynamic monitoring has less noise and better decidability: an executed path is possible by definition and all values can be determined at runtime [87]. Every detected failure can be shown to be caused by a real sequence of input events [92]. However, the dynamic monitoring can only see executed paths, requiring that the code it monitors is adequately exercised, e.g., by set of test cases with a good coverage. Also, dynamic approaches can only observe how the software works in the environment that was monitored, and an error can be found only when its path is executed [87].

Usually, dynamic specification mining techniques employ data mining or machine learning techniques on execution traces, captured during the execution of the system, to generate models that are useful in program verification [93]. In cases, where the system behavior executes in parallel, special considerations are needed. In cases, where the parallel execution is further distributed, yet additional considerations are required [94]. In order to apply dynamic techniques on distributed systems, the execution of each component has to be analyzed in isolation from the rest of the system [93].

Conventional mining methods have focused on either intraprocess specifications where the control flow inside each process is mined as an automaton [95,96] or extended FSMs [97], or rule-based specifications where the system behavior is summarized as temporal properties [98,99], various patterns [100], Use Case Maps [101], or Live Sequence Charts [93]. As the specification mining aims to describe the behavior of software systems, the specifications are commonly based on temporal sequences of events, e.g., Message Sequence Charts [93]. Temporal sequences describe how the system behaves over time, what events compose its behavioral functionality, and how they are composed [93].

4.3. Combining Static and Dynamic Reverse Engineering

Hybrid reverse engineering approaches try to make use of both static and dynamic analysis. Dynamic analysis alone might miss relevant aspects of the behavior and be ambiguous regarding what conditions trigger which alternative behaviors [82]. Then static analysis can be used to complement dynamic analysis [83], e.g., system interfaces can be extracted via static analysis as a form of input for dynamic analysis [96,102], to restrict the dynamic search [103], or more directly to support it [104].

For example, Systä [105] gathered both dynamic views (using a customized Java Development Kit debugger) and static views (parsing Java byte code), and afterwards improves them by merging aspects from both types of views. Whaley *et al.* [103] combined static analysis for deducing illegal call sequences, and dynamic techniques to extract models from execution runs. Then they used a dynamic model checker to ensure that the code conforms to the model.

4.4. Reverse Engineering Models for Testing

Traditionally the models for automated testing have to be crafted manually from the specifications of the SUT [62]. Providing useful models in the defined formalisms is still an issue that slows down the industrial adoption of MBT [106]. There are several approaches aiming to reduce the time needed for designing the test models by automating some parts of the modeling process, such as creating the initial models through reverse engineering. Some approaches, such as GUI ripping [107], aim to fully automated creation of the test models, while others, such as observation-based modeling [18], aim to automatically create an initial model to reduce the effort of manual modeling process.

4.4.1 Static Approaches for Testing

Most of the approaches aiming to use reverse engineered models in testing use dynamic analysis to construct the models, but there are a few that are using static analysis. To extract verification models mechanically from the source code, the extractor needs to reliably identify control states, event types, and the code fragments that constitute event responses [41].

Engler *et al.* [87] use various static analyzing techniques on the source code of the system to identify common program behaviors, extract correctness rules the system must obey, and the rules are used to locate possible errors in the system code. Their approach automatically establishes certain invariants as likely beliefs and the tool searches for bugs by finding code sequences that violate these invariants. The tool searches for invariants based on a set of standard templates and filters potential specifications with a statistical measure. Their approach has been highly effective in finding bugs in system code.

Holzmann and Smith [41] present a static model extraction approach for mechanically constructing verification models from the source code of an application. The models are obtained in a test harness that usually has to be defined only once for a given type of application. The model extraction software can create a sensible default for the test harness that the user may adopt either unmodified or accommodate as the checking process advances. With the test harness in place, the verification process can be mechanized from the beginning to the end, even when the source code of the application changes. The technique targets state-oriented and event-driven systems, such as device drivers, distributed schedulers, concurrency control algorithms, and telecommunications applications.

4.4.2 Dynamic Approaches for Testing

Observation-based modeling [18] is a dynamic reverse engineering approach that supports observation and testing of the system, analysis of different types of executions used as a basis for observations, and finally combines the different viewpoints to provide automated tool support to generate an initial test model that is suitable for MBT purposes. The generated model is then refined and verified against the specifications [18].

Mariani *et al.* [108] described a technique called "behavior capture and test" for automatically generating behavioral models that are used to derive both compatibility test suites and prioritized regression suites for commercial off-the-shelf (COTS) components. Based on execution traces of the component, interactions modeled as FSMs and data values exchanged between components as IO models are generated to describe the component behavior. The approach automatically derives small compatibility test suites for evaluating alternative candidate components that can replace a COTS component within a software system, and prioritizes test cases to improve the efficiency of regression testing of compatible COTS components. The regression testing approach is based on the execution of previous versions of the components.

Xie and Notkin [109] presented a black-box approach for unit test generation and selection without requiring a priori specifications. The approach uses Daikon [110], a dynamic invariant detection tool, to dynamically infer operational abstractions (invariants) from executions of the existing unit test suite, and then a commercial Java unit testing tool to generate the test cases. The invariants are used to guide the generation of tests to cover behavior that is not exercised by the existing suite, and then the tests that violate the operational abstractions are selected for inspection. In contrast to a formal specification that expresses desired behavior, operational abstractions express observed behavior.

Fraser and Walkinshaw [111] introduced the BESTEST (BEhavioural Software TESTing) approach, combining statistical learning theory with search-based white-box test generation strategies. The approach uses Weka toolkit [112] for model inference and Probably Approximately Correct (PAC), an evaluation framework for model inference techniques, to quantify the accuracy of the inferred models. PAC is used for assessing the adequacy of test sets and generating adequate test sets, based on behavioral adequacy.

Pradel and Gross [113] presented a fully automatic approach to reveal API protocol violations by combining test generation, protocol mining, and protocol checking. The first step is to generate tests for the classes of a program, then analyze executions of passing tests with a protocol miner, giving likely specifications of how to use API classes. The third step is to verify executions of failing tests against the mined protocols and report a warning if a test fails because of a protocol violation.

4.4.3 Hybrid Approaches for Testing
Pradel *et al.* [114] presented a fully automatic protocol conformance checker that combines dynamic analysis that infers multiobject protocols and a static

checker of API usage constraints. The combined system statically detects illegal uses of an API without human-written specifications. The dynamic specification miner runs training programs to infer specifications from program traces. These API usage protocols are translated into relationship-based specifications suitable for the static checker. The static checker checks the code of a target program against the specifications and classifies API method calls as potentially legal or illegal. Some of the potentially illegal calls may be due to incomplete protocols, so a pruner uses heuristics to remove results that are likely false positives. The final set of warnings is then presented to the user for manual inspection.

Zheng *et al.* [115] use mined models as a set of regression tests for search engines. By comparing results mined for specific queries for different search engines over time, they search for deviations from top results for specific engines. Deviations are presented to users for further analysis. The approach is a hybrid in the sense that it uses static analysis to the search results that require executing the search engines.

4.4.4 Challenges in Using Reverse Engineered Models for Testing

Test designers widely believe that the overall effectiveness and cost of software testing depends largely on the type and number of test cases executed on the software. Test oracle, a mechanism that determines whether a system is executed correctly for a test case, also significantly impacts the fault detection effectiveness and the cost of executing a test case [116].

When extracting models automatically by observing an existing system, the generated models are based on the observed implementation. As such, the generated models include also the undesirable behavior of the system, instead of capturing the requirements or expectations of the system. Without the knowledge of correct or incorrect behavior, the implementation-based models without elaboration are not well suited for generating test cases and test oracles, as in traditional MBT.

Test oracles can be defined both as generic checks for all systems or as application specific checks. Generic checks, such as unhandled exceptions [117,118] or crashes of the SUT [119], can be used in several different systems, including tests generated from extracted models. Generic test oracles can also be defined for classes of applications, such as checking for HTTP error codes in all visited pages for a Web application [120]. Application-specific test oracles have to be created or generated specifically for each case or system. In specification mining-based test generation, invariants captured from a set of execution scenarios can be used for modeling the SUT [117].

The invariants can be defined manually in order to permit more specific checks to be made on the SUT [120]. The invariants are then used as a test oracle to check that they also hold for the future executions of the SUT.

Some approaches use the "as is" models for automating various testing activities, but usually the generated models have to be manually validated and elaborated, adding the expectations and requirements into the created models. Kanstrén [18] proposes a process for elaborating the generated models and using the models for testing. The human analyst should be supported in understanding and verifying the modeled behavior by providing the models of the analyzed system in a suitably high level of abstraction for human understanding [18], and practical means to elaborate the models should be provided in tool support. Elaborating the initial reverse engineered models can provide support and a reasonable starting point for adopting MBT.

Another challenge, especially related to state-based models, is state space explosion. Any nontrivial program has a large number of possible states, depending on the definition of the state and how to distinguish them. Over the years, optimizations to the original learning algorithms have yielded significant improvements in terms of the speed of model inference and the size of extracted models, making it possible to infer state space sizes of 100,000 states or more, which is sufficient to test many kinds of industrial applications [121]. The challenge is to find the balance between increasing expressiveness to extract more accurate models and keeping the computational complexity on feasible level for model inference and model checking [121]. Abstracting away too much information from the SUT increases the risk of losing opportunities to discover faults [121].

4.5. Reverse Engineering GUI Models

GUI software is a good example of a technical application domain with existing domain-specific reverse engineering approaches that are reusable for various applications. In this survey, we have categorized not only desktop applications, but also Web and mobile applications to be GUI software.

4.5.1 Static Approaches for Reverse Engineering of GUI Models

The dynamic nature of GUI software makes it very difficult to understand the behavior by just examining the source code [20], but there are some approaches for static analysis of GUI software. Many of the static approaches target a specific language, e.g., Bouillon *et al.* [122] reverse engineer simple HTML pages; Staiger [123] is targeted at C/C++ applications that use UI libraries like Qt or TK; Guha *et al.* [124] use static control flow analysis on JavaScript applications; Ko *et al.* [125] use static analysis on JavaScript applications to search for missing feedback in applications; Bellucci *et al.* [126] perform static analysis of HTML and CSS to support adaptation of Web Applications across platforms while keeping the same JavaScript between the adaptations.

Staiger [123] presented an approach for static source code analysis for extracting GUI-related parts of a program and provide models on a higher level of abstraction. Their analysis tool is integrated into Bauhaus tool suite [127] which contains tools and techniques for recovering and visualizing program's architecture. The aim is to support maintenance tasks for legacy code, like migrating from a hand-written GUI to a GUI builder, redocumentation of the GUI, or recovering the program's architecture. The tool is restricted to C or C++ applications that use GTK or Qt.

Ko and Chang [125] presented FeedLack, a tool that statically analyzes JavaScript and HTML files of web applications' behaviors for missing feedback by enumerating control flow paths originating from user input and identifying paths that lack output-affecting code.

Ramon *et al.* [128] introduced UsiResourcer tool that uses GUI reverse engineering for modernizing GUIs of interactive applications by reengineering their resource files. The output of the tool is a platform-independent UsiXML concrete user interface (CUI) model. The approach is static, using resource decompilation to executable binary files of the GUI to unlink and decompile binary files into textual resource files.

4.5.2 Dynamic Approaches for Reverse Engineering of GUI Models

Most of the modern GUI software is developed using event-handler architecture allowing developers to build complex systems using loosely coupled pieces of code and the end users to perform tasks by inputting GUI events in various ways and execution order [22], and the GUI components of modern applications are often reachable only from a particular state or with some environment constraints [23], which makes it difficult to deduce the behavior from the source code without executing it. In many situations, the relation between UI controls and the corresponding event handlers is only defined at runtime and even the structure of the UI might be defined dynamically at runtime, with only a basic skeleton defined statically in the source code [82].

As the dynamic behavior of a GUI is difficult to extract with static source code analysis, dynamic reverse engineering techniques are more popular for automatically extracting GUI models [12]. In dynamic approaches, the system is automatically executed and user actions are simulated with automated interactions, and the run-time behavior of the system is analyzed. Various algorithms are then applied to extract behavioral models of the GUI based on the collected observations.

Dynamic reverse engineering does not require the source code of the system but more difficult to automate, as it requires a way to programmatically observe, analyze, control, and interact with the GUI shown to the user, i.e., GUI automation [12]. GUI automation is commonly used in automated GUI testing with predefined set of commands and means to verify if the expected GUI state was reached [16]. In dynamic reverse engineering, the interactions are selected from the set of available GUI components that are reverse engineered from the GUI, instead of predefined set of commands, and the behavior of the GUI is observed to generate a model or another representation of GUI [16]. GUI automation allows modeling the behavior of dynamically changing GUIs, e.g., when the visibility of a GUI component depends on the state of another component [16].

Mesbah *et al.* [129,130] presented a technique and open-source tool called Crawljax for crawling Asynchronous JavaScript and XML (AJAX) based applications to dynamically infer a state-based model, state-flow graph, modeling the various navigation paths and states within the application. The reconstructed models can be used to generate linked static pages for exposing AJAX sites to general search engines, accessibility improvements, or in automatically exercising all UI elements and conducting state-based testing of AJAX applications.

Samir *et al.* [131] proposed a semiautomated dynamic approach called GUI reverse engineering aspect (GUIRE) to reverse engineer the GUI of Java-swing applications to construct the GUI Sea models, used for migrating legacy Java GUI applications to web applications. AspectJ compiler is used for monitoring and recording GUI during manual execution of the application to generate models. The GUI is modeled as a set of all windows that ever appear in the application. Each window is modeled as a structure called a window island. Each window island contains structural and behavioral information about a certain window.

Stroulia *et al.* [132] presented CelLEST, a semiautomated method for dynamically reverse engineering state-transition models of legacy UIs and using the models for migrating to Web UIs. The models have to be manually reviewed and revised before using platform-specific translators for migration.

4.5.3 Hybrid Approaches for Reverse Engineering of GUI Models

Li and Wohlstadter [133] described a hybrid approach for view-based maintenance of GUIs. Dynamic analysis reconstructs object relationships, providing a concrete context in which maintenance can be performed. Static checking provides constraints based on static checking to limit what can be edited.

Gimblett and Thimbleby [134] presented an approach to discover a model of an interactive system by simulating user actions. Models created are directed graphs where nodes represent system states and edges correspond to user actions. The approach is dynamic but it also considers access to application source code.

Muhairat *et al.* [135] combined static and dynamic analyses in order to reverse engineer a UML Class Diagram from a Java GUI in three steps: capturing the static and the dynamic aspects of the GUI into a Petri net with transitions expressing potential navigation schemes, normalizing the transitions, and translating it into a Class Diagram.

Yang *et al.* [136] proposed a hybrid reverse engineering approach and a tool called Orbit to extract GUI models of Android mobile applications. Static analysis of the application's source code is used to extract the set of user actions supported by each widget in the GUI, and the extracted actions are used to dynamically crawl through the GUI and dynamically reverse engineer an FSM model of the application. WALA libraries [137] are used for static analysis of the source code and their crawler is built on top of the Robotium framework [138].

Azim and Neamtiu [139] present Automatic Android App Explorer (A3E), an approach and open-source tool for systematically exploring Android mobile applications running on actual phones. The approach uses static dataflow analysis on the application's bytecode to construct a high-level control flow graph that captures legal transitions among activities, and then use this graph to develop an exploration strategy that permits fast, direct exploration of activities. The extracted models, Static Activity Transition Graph (SATG) and Dynamic Activity Transition Graph (DATG) are event-based models capturing the activities of the application as nodes and represents possible activity transitions as edges.

5. USING EXTRACTED MODELS TO AUTOMATE GUI TESTING

In this section, we present some of the most active researchers and research groups in the area of reverse engineering GUI models for testing, and describe the research, tools, and approaches for reverse engineering and testing of GUI applications.

5.1. Challenges in Using Extracted Models to Automate GUI Testing

The challenges in MBGT in general have been presented in Section 3.4.2 and challenges in using reverse engineered models for testing in Section 4.4.4. However, using reverse engineered GUI models in testing brings a few additional challenges, the most important being automated creation of test oracles.

Also, using the extracted GUI models for testing increases the challenge with state space explosion, because ignoring too many properties to reduce the amount of states may lead to ambiguous results, i.e., a state of some action or event is not well defined or unique. However, if we differentiate too many different property values as different states, the number of states is too large to be computationally feasible in test case generation [1].

5.1.1 Automated Test Oracles for GUI Testing

In MBGT, the oracle information used to determine whether a test case passes or fails, consists of a set of observed properties of all the windows and widgets of the GUI [70]. Test oracles can be divided into two parts: oracle information that represents expected output, and an oracle procedure that compares the oracle information with the actual output [140]. By varying the level of detail of oracle information and changing the oracle procedure, a test designer can create different types of test oracles, depending on the goals of the specific testing process used [141]. The different types of test oracles have a significant effect on test effectiveness and cost of testing [141]. Xie and Memon [116] have presented a comparison between different types of automated test oracles for GUI testing.

The oracle procedure compares the actual output from the SUT to a presumably correct expected output [116]. Oracle procedure's frequency of comparison significantly effects on test effectiveness and cost of testing [141]. In GUI testing, the oracle procedure should compare the observed properties to their expected values after each step (event or interaction) of the test sequence during the execution of GUI test cases [70]. Otherwise it may become difficult to identify the actual cause of the error [142]. An incorrect GUI state may lead to an unexpected screen, making further execution of the test case useless as the next steps (events) of the test sequence may not be available on the unexpected GUI screen [142]. Therefore, the execution of a test case should be terminated as soon as an error is detected [142].

The oracle information may be selected or created either automatically or manually [143] based on requirements or other formal specifications of the GUI or observed behavior of an earlier, presumably correct version of the software [141]. Creating test oracles manually could in practice mean, for example, crafting or editing the test models manually, using CR tools, or using "assert" statements with unit testing tools to check if the output equals to the test oracle.

Automatically generating the oracle information for GUI applications is challenging. The oracle information can come from the design or requirements, e.g., using a formal specification language to capture the requirements, or from a base version of the application under test [115]. The formal methods are rarely used in practice, especially with increasing use of agile development processes, as the manual effort of creating the specifications is similar to manually creating the test oracles [115].

Some automated modeling tools, such as GUI Driver [118] and GUI-TAR [107], capture the observed behavior during the automated modeling process and use it as test oracle, but the weakness of capturing the implemented behavior instead of expected behavior remains, making the test oracles suitable for regression testing but not for the earlier phases of the development. In literature, this is often called reference testing. Zheng et al. [115] describe an approach for mining test oracles for Web search engines from existing search results, which is related to using results from previously executed test cases as test oracles for future test cases.

5.2. Approaches for Using Extracted Models to Automate GUI Testing

In this chapter, we introduce the work of the most active research groups on using extracted models for automated GUI testing.

5.2.1 *Memon et al.: GUI Ripping and Using Event-Based Graph Models for Automated GUI Testing*

Atif M. Memon and his team in University of Maryland (College Park, MD, USA) have extensively published their research results, the first publications on automated GUI testing being from 1999 with Pollack and Soffa from University of Pittsburgh [142]. Their GUI testing research started from using AI planning and goal-directed search for GUI test case generation [142], implemented in PATHS (Planning Assisted Tester for grapHical user interface Systems) specifications-based GUI testing approach [144–146], and then extended with an automated test oracle technique to determine if a GUI behaves as expected for a given test case [147]. Memon's PhD dissertation [58] further extended PATHS with a coverage evaluator and regression tester, presented EFG and integration tree for modeling event-based software, and used the approach not only for testing desktop applications but also for Web UI testing.

By further automation and focusing more into smoke testing and regression testing, their GUI testing approach evolved into a framework called DART (Daily Automated Regression Tester) [9,148,149]. DART automates everything from structural GUI analysis, test case generation, test oracle creation, to code instrumentation, test execution, coverage evaluation, regeneration of test cases, and their reexecution. With DART, Memon *et al.* introduced also GUI ripping, a dynamic process for automatically analyzing the structure of GUI [148] and using the captured GUI structure to create EFGs and an integration tree. GUI ripping is described in more detail in [107], with the design and implementation of GUI ripper tool, mentioning it to be part of DART and GUITAR GUI testing framework [150], and introducing GUI forest to model window structures of GUI.

During the development of GUI applications, the changes between the versions tend to break test cases of regression test suites. Therefore Memon *et al.* [3,151] presented a repairing technique using graph matching algorithms to repair previously unusable GUI test cases for regression testing. The approach helps to retain a test suite's event coverage by reusing existing test cases from the original GUI's suite that have become unusable for the modified GUI by automatically repairing them so that they can execute on the modified GUI. The repairing method was integrated into PATHS by replanning affected GUI test cases [152]. Later they continued the research by using heuristics to repair GUI test cases [153], and extend the repair framework with AutoInSpec [154], a technique for GUI model specification inference and invariant detection.

GUI windows are categorized into modal and modeless windows. Modal windows force the user to execute an event from within the modal window, regardless of what other windows are open, whereas modeless windows expand the set of executable events of the other windows of the GUI, providing more widgets for the user to choose from [155]. In EFG, each node represents an event, and all events that can be executed immediately after this event are connected with directed edges from it [58]. The EFG has evolved to a more compact GUI model called event interaction graph (EIG) [119] that can be automatically transformed from an EFG. EIG includes only system-interaction events and with the smaller set of events it better suits rapid testing, such as smoke regression testing. EIG was integrated also into DART to obtain smoke test cases for GUIs to be used for stabilizing daily software builds [156]. An example of the differences between event-based EFG and state-based FSM models can be seen in Fig. 2.2.

Xie and Memon [119] introduces also rapid crash testing and defines a tighter GUI testing cycle that is fully automatic. The key idea is to test the GUI each time it is modified, e.g., at each code commit.

For the past 10 years, GUITAR [150,157,158], a model-based system for automated GUI testing, has been the main platform for their research on automated GUI testing, and GUI ripping has been enabler for further GUI-related research also for other research groups around the world [155]. The goal has been to develop fully automated modeling and testing approaches. The GUI Ripper was initially implemented for Java SWT-based GUIs, but it has been extended to support Web-based GUIs, iOS,

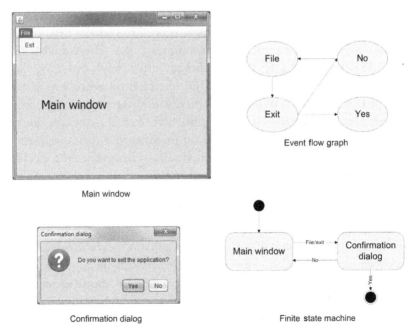

Figure 2.2 An example of a simple GUI and its EFG and FSM.

Android, Java JFC, Eclipse, and UNO (Open Office) frameworks [155]. The testing process with GUITAR consists of four main steps [150]:

1. GUI ripping: Using a crawler-like tool called GUI Ripper to automatically launch and execute the application under testing (AUT). The GUI Ripper tries to expand hidden GUI elements and all the possible GUI windows, and capture the structure of the GUI into an XML-based model called GUI Tree (or GUI Forest). Each node of the GUI Tree represents a window and encapsulates all the widgets, properties, and values in that window [107].

2. Model construction: Using gui2efg or another model converter to construct an EFG or another event-based graph model from the GUI Tree. In EFG, each node represents an event, and all events that can be executed immediately after this event are connected with directed edges from it [107].

3. Test case generation: Using graph traversal algorithms to generate test cases or event sequences by walking on the event-based graph model with a given coverage criteria, such as covering all events or all edges.

4. Replaying: Using Replayer tool to execute test cases and verify the results.

During the 10 years, various tools have been integrated into the GUITAR framework, such as a profiler tool to dynamically capture actual event-level software usage information while the GUI is being used in the field and employ the information to support refactoring [159] or to test GUI components [160,161]. GUITAR has been extended also to support automated GUI testing in open-source software projects [162] and agile development processes [163], and iteratively improve GUI test cases by run-time feedback from executed test cases [164–167] or a genetic algorithm to evolve new test cases that increase test suite's coverage while avoiding infeasible sequences [168]. GUITAR and GUI ripping has been used also for evaluating and improving usability of GUI applications [6].

After EFG and EIG models, Memon and his team have introduced Event-Flow Model [25,169], event-space exploration strategies (ESES) [25], Event Semantic Interaction (ESI) relation modeled as a graph called the ESI Graph (ESIG) [27,170], and event dependency graph (EDG) [171,172] to capture more information to the created models or make the modeling or test case generation based on the models more efficient. In the recent research, they have combined static analysis to improve the dynamic GUI ripping and testing process [172].

Memon's team has extensively published their research results also in the areas of coverage and effectiveness of GUI testing [33,34,65–67,70,71,173], and test suite reduction and prioritization for automated GUI testing [72–80], as well as characteristics of industrial GUI systems [36] and the research in the area of automated GUI testing in general [22,26].

5.2.2 Campos et al.: Static Reverse Engineering of GUI Models for Usability Analysis and Testing

José Creissac Campos and his team in University of Minho (Braga, Portugal) have numerous publications on static reverse engineering of GUI models, GUIsurfer tool, and using the generated models for usability analysis and GUI testing. Campos started his UI-related research with formal verification [174,175], formal modeling and model checking using interactor-based models to reason about the usability of interactive systems [176] in Human–Computer Interaction Group of the University of York, UK. Campos continued the research of specification based early usability analysis in University of Minho by extending the interactor-based models with tasks so that specific behavior can be analyzed more easily [177], and time and environmental factors for reasoning about the usability of a representation of real-world dynamic information on interactive devices [178,179]. Then they extended the same approach to support verifying UI behavior with model checking, still using interactors to model state, Modal Action Logic for describing behavior, and Computational Tree Logic for properties that are to be checked in SMV model checker [180], and added a separate model of context to support analysis of interactive systems [181].

Then Campos started the research on reverse engineering of GUI applications using static Java/Swing source code analysis together with Silva and Saraiva [182,183], using their earlier research on formal modeling and usability analysis as a starting point. Their GUI reverse engineering approach is based on strategic programming and slicing techniques for isolating GUI-related code the rest of the program and uses Strafunski Haskell library [184] for generic programming and language processing. The Abstract Syntax Tree (AST) representation created in this semiautomated reverse engineering process can be transformed into interactor-based models and EFGs, and used for usability analysis and model checking.

The approach was developed further and the implemented tool, named GUIsurfer [7], was capable of reverse engineering source code of GUI applications written in Java/Swing or Haskell/WxHaskell, and creating FSM models representing the behavior of the GUI. The generated models were used for MBGT, but specification of the program had to manually provided, expressed in Haskell, and QuickCheck Haskell library was used for randomly generating a large number of test cases as sequences of GUI events. The GUIsurfer tool has been extended to support also Java GWT-based rich internet applications (RIA) [185–188] and creating graph-based models using GraphViz tool [189], and using Graph-Tool [190] for manipulation and statistical analysis of the created graphs [191]. Campos *et al.* [38] have used the extracted models also for GUI reasoning, i.e., the process of validating and verifying if the modeled application behaves as expected.

Together with Couto and Ribeiro, they implement MapIt tool that uses static reverse engineering on Java source code to create platform-specific UML models that are then transformed into higher level platform-independent UML models with a pattern inference and transformation process [192,193]. With Silva, they have studied the feasibility of using GUI implementation languages for GUI modeling [194].

In the recent research [82], they combined dynamic analysis with static source code analysis for reverse engineering Web applications. First, a state-based model of the Web UI is obtained using dynamic reverse engineering, and then the relevant conditions over the input values in the UI are determined by static analysis of the event handlers attached to each UI control. An Abstract Syntax Tree (AST) is created for each event listener.

5.2.3 Paiva et al.: ReGUI Tool, Dynamic Reverse Engineering of GUI Models for Testing

Ana Paiva and her team in University of Porto (Porto, Portugal) have extensively researched GUI modeling and testing. Paiva started her GUI-related research with formal modeling and specification-based testing of UIs [195]. They used specification language based on ISO/VDM-SL standard to model the UI. Then they started writing the formal models in Spec# and using Microsoft Spec Explorer tool to convert the models into FSMs [196]. Then the FSMs are converted to hierarchical finite-state machines (HFSMs) to reduce the number of states in models. They extended Spec Explorer to support automated GUI testing [197] by adding capability to gather information about the physical GUI objects and automatically generate .NET code for simulating user actions and interacting with the GUI application. Paiva wrote also her PhD thesis [198] about formal GUI modeling and using Spec Explorer to generate test cases from the FSMs and test the conformity between the specification and the implementation.

The next research step was reverse engineering the formal GUI models using semiautomated dynamic technique, mixing manual, and automatic exploration to access parts of the GUI that are protected by a key or are in some other way difficult to access automatically [199]. The goal of the approach and presented REGUI2FM tool is to reduce the modeling effort and provide mapping information for executing abstract test cases on a concrete GUI during MBGT process. The extracted partial "as is" Spec# model is validated and completed manually into "should-be" model, including also expected outputs to be used as test oracles. During the exploration process, the intermediate code of the AUT is instrumented with Aspect-Oriented Programming (AOP) techniques in order to be able to recognize and capture a wider range of GUI controls and events, beyond native ones. Spec Explorer tool is used for transforming Spec# model into FSM, and generating and executing test cases. Paiva *et al.* [200,201] have also provided UML-based modeling tool VAN4GUIM for abstracting the complexity and visualizing the textual Spec# models.

With Silva and Campos [2], they combined dynamic GUI reverse engineering with manual GUI modeling to improve the test oracles of the created models. In this approach, they used ConcurTaskTrees (CTT) task models to describe UI interactions and TERESA tool [202] to generate FSM models from the CTT. They developed TOM (Task to Oracle Mapping) tool to generate Spec# models with test oracles from these FSM models, reverse engineered the mappings between model and concrete GUI objects into another Spec# model, combined the two Spec# models, and then used Spec Explorer to generate a new FSM model that is used for MBGT.

The reverse engineering approach was further developed with Grilo [203] by implementing the dynamic reverse engineering algorithm on top of Microsoft UI Automation library [13] and saving the GUI model in XML-based format before generating the Spec# specification for testing purposes, and the tool was renamed to REGUI [12]. The approach combines automated and manual exploration to access all parts of the GUI, but the user has to guide the tool during the creation of the model, and the generated model has to be validated and completed manually.

The ReGUI tool was developed further into version 2.0 with Morgado [204] using a different, fully automatic reverse engineering approach. The generated models include a structural model of the GUI, saved into XML-based ReGUITree model, and behavioral models saved into four GraphML models and one Spec# specification. The approach is extended by generating a Symbolic Model Verification (SMV) model for model checking purposes [205], and generating UML 2.0 FSM model and using Inductive Logic Programming (ILP) machine learning technique to solve ambiguous situations, e.g., when the same event may lead to multiple different target states. Together with Ferreira they have researched also test coverage analysis [206,207].

5.2.4 Amalfitano et al.: Dynamic Reverse Engineering of RIA and Mobile Applications

Amalfitano *et al.* in University of Naples Federico II (Naples, Italy) have been recently extremely active in publishing their research on dynamic reverse engineering of rich internet applications (RIAs) and mobile applications. Their approach for reverse engineering client-side behavior of RIAs [208] is based on dynamic analysis of the RIA execution traces and employing clustering techniques for solving the problem of state explosion of the generated FSM models. The developed RE-RIA tool creates an instantiation of a Mozilla Firefox Browser inside its Java GUI and the approach is used to model AJAX-based Web applications [209].

The approach is extended to use the generated models for testing RIAs [210] and use test reduction techniques test suites to ensure scalability. Execution traces used for the test case generation can be obtained either from user sessions, automated crawling of the application or by combining both approaches. Combining both manually and automatically obtained execution traces increased the effectiveness of testing. [210] introduces tools developed for the process: an AJAX crawling tool CrawlRIA, a dynamic RIA analysis tool CreRIA, Test Case Generator and Test Case Reducer tool TestRIA, and DynaRIA [211–213], a tool for dynamic analysis and testing of RIAs. The approach can be used also in agile processes [214], and CReRIA tool has been extended to support semiautomatic generation of user documentation for Web 2.0 applications [215].

Amalfitano *et al.* [216] have presented a Web page classification technique and WPC-CA (Web Page Classifier) tool based on the deduction of classification rules that allow the reliable classification of the pages of a Web application. A reliable classification of Web pages can be useful for supporting various engineering activities, such as reengineering, analysis, and testing. They have proposed a classification framework that characterizes existing RIA testing techniques [217].

In more recent research [218], they presented a technique and A2T2 (Android Automatic Testing Tool) for dynamic reverse engineering and automated testing of Android applications. The tool has been developed in Java and is composed of three main components: a Java code instrumentation component, the GUI Crawler, and the Test Case Generator. It supports rapid crash testing and regression testing of Android applications. Amalfitano wrote also his PhD thesis [219] on reverse engineering and testing of RIA and Android applications.

Together with Memon, Amalfitano *et al.* [220] presented AndroidRipper approach for dynamic reverse engineering of GUI models of Android mobile applications. The approach uses a high-level automation library called Robotium [138] and GUI ripper whose behavior can be configured according to application-specific testing aims. While dynamically exploring the GUI, the tool detects run-time crashes of the application. The goal of the approach is not to develop a model of the application, but automatically and systematically traverse the GUI, generating and executing test cases as new events are encountered. Test case generation is based on the automatic dynamic analysis of the GUI that is executed in order to find and fire events in the GUI. The approach is further automated [221] to reduce the manual intervention during the testing process.

Their approach for testing Android mobile applications is further extended [222] to support a broader set of events. As the earlier focus had been only on user events produced through the GUI, now they considered also context events, e.g., events coming from the external environment, events generated by the device hardware platform, events typical of mobile phones, and events from other Internet connected applications. The proposed testing techniques involve the manual definition of reusable event patterns including context events. Event patterns may be used to manually generate test cases, to mutate existing test cases, and to support the systematic exploration of the behavior of an application using the GUI Ripping technique.

5.2.5 Miao and Yang: Dynamic Reverse Engineering of GUI Test Automation Models

Miao and Yang from Victoria University (Melbourne, Australia) have proposed to address the limitations of event-based GUI models with an FSM-based GUI Test Automation Model (GuiTam) and a dynamic reverse engineering approach to automatically construct the models and use them for GUI testing [223]. Run-time GUI information is programmatically readable, which provides an opportunity to automatically generate a GuiTam for an application by traversing its GUI states [1].

In GuiTam [223], a state of the GUI is modeled as a set of opened windows, GUI objects (widgets) of each window, properties of each object, and values of the properties. Events or interaction performed on the GUI may lead to state transitions, and a transition in GuiTam captures the starting state, the event or interaction performed, and the resulting state.

To address the state space explosion problem and reduce the total number of states and state transitions, only selected object property values are considered for distinguishing different states, and only the events that lead to the state transition will be captured into GuiTam [224]. The state selection in the proposed GuiTam is at a similar level to the event flog graph (EFG) [58] model, which is also practical in terms of storage and computational complexity [223]. The algorithms and tools used for reading the widgets (objects), performing events or interactions, checking and comparing the GUI states, and generating GuiTam based on the behavior of the GUI are shortly described [223].

Test cases can be automatically generated by traversing the states of the GuiTam [223]. The test oracle information will be captured by performing the same test cases on an earlier version of the GUI application. After the oracle information is captured, the test cases can be executed on the modified version of the AUT. By comparing the observed state behavior with the corresponding oracle information, differences can be detected and possible defects can be discovered [223]. Test cases can be generated by randomly selecting a given number of paths from the GuiTam, or by traversing the states and transitions of GuiTam according to given criteria, e.g., an algorithm can select the paths from the GUITAM until all states are covered to meet the state coverage criterion [1]. The paths can be as long as possible so that the minimum number of test cases can be generated which satisfy the criterion [1].

Yang et al. [224] proposed parameterized GUI state model (PGUISM) which is basically a manually parameterized version of GuiTam, using the parameters to describe the context of the states. PGUISM is implemented in C# and uses UI Automation library [13] in Visual Studio.net 2008 to read widgets information from an application [224]. The approach is used also for model-driven GUI automation to automate the data exchange through GUI between two medical GUI applications [224].

Yang also wrote his PhD thesis [1] on GuiTam, extending the approach with an envelope model to encapsulate all possible branches of states and events related to a task or use case. To efficiently test tasks or use cases, long test cases are inevitably needed. By using a use case captured in the envelope model, task-oriented test cases can be generated automatically for effective and efficient testing within a practical time frame [1].

Yang [1] proposed also a GUI defect classification, dividing GUI defects into three groups: directly detectable defects, undetectable defects, and comparably detectable defects. Directly detectable defects can be detected without access to any specifications or information observed from an earlier version of the system, e.g., crashes that cause the AUT to stop responding to inputs, and recognizable error messages usually in the form of system error dialogs or customized message dialogs shown during the execution. Undetectable defects do not reflect any results in the GUI, and therefore cannot be detected with GUI test automation. Comparably detectable defects can be detected by comparing the actual state affected by the defects with the expected state. When a test case is executed, the actual states will be compared with the expected results and the differences will be reported. The defect classifications can be used for directing test case generation [1].

5.2.6 Aho et al.: Dynamic Reverse Engineering of State-Based GUI Models for Testing

Aho *et al.* from VTT Technical Research Centre of Finland (Oulu, Finland) have presented an approach and GUI Driver tool for dynamically reverse engineering models of Java-based GUI applications for MBT purposes [118].

Aho *et al.* [118] use a state-based GUI model to capture the behavior of the GUI application into state machine, and hierarchical tree models to capture the structure and context of the GUI in each state. The structural models, as well as screenshots of the GUI, are automatically mapped to the corresponding states in the behavioral GUI state model. Events or GUI actions are modeled as transitions between the states, and part of the context information is captured into transitions of the behavioral GUI state model.

To avoid the state space explosion, Aho *et al.* [118] disregard data values, such as texts in text fields or selected values of lists or drop-down boxes, when distinguishing new GUI states from the already visited states. Instead, the data values of the GUI are captured into properties of GUI actions or events. Therefore, the generated GUI state models may have usually an infinite number of transitions, but a reasonable number of GUI states. During the automated model extraction, the GUI is dynamically traversed or crawled through by interacting with all the detected widgets of the GUI [118]. As the number of possible event or interaction sequences is enormous,

GUI Driver attempts to drive the software into as many different states as possible, aiming for state coverage, instead of transition coverage [118].

Testing of the application begins already during the modeling, as crashes, unhandled exceptions and some usability issues are detected and reported [118]. Third party MBT tools are used for generating tests from the models. GUI Driver uses model transformation to save the GUI state model into GraphML, to allow the use of external graph traversal algorithms for generating test sequences with given coverage criteria [118]. The generated test sequences can be executed with GUI Driver and test oracles are based on an earlier, presumably correct version of the GUI application, allowing the regression testing [118].

The fully automated reverse engineering approach [118] was extended into semiautomated iterative process [24] of automated reverse engineering and manually providing valid input, such as username and password, when the reverse engineering algorithm does not find any more new states from the GUI application. The user provides the input combinations into the GUI that is being modeled and then allows the GUI Driver tool to continue automated reverse engineering [24].

Aho *et al.* [16] have highlighted the importance of diverse GUI automation and interacting with all enabled widgets of the GUI during the dynamic reverse engineering in order to produce more comprehensive models of the dynamic behavior of GUI applications. Therefore, they proposed a widget classification to support GUI automation strategies for effective model extraction [16] and presented some easy-to-implement strategies to demonstrate the feasibility of the classification. The goal of the GUI automation strategies is to reach as many states as possible with as few events or interactions as possible [16], in similar way as in test suite prioritization.

Together with Suarez from F-Secure Ltd (Helsinki, Finland) they presented Murphy, a dynamic GUI reverse engineering and testing toolset developed as internal tool at F-Secure [225]. The idea of Murphy tool is similar to GUI Driver: traversing or crawling through all the possible states of the GUI application and automatically constructing a state-based GUI model of the behavior observed during the execution. Most of the model extraction approaches have limitations and restrictions on the GUI applications that can be modeled, but Murphy is more platform independent, supporting most GUI platforms regardless of the implementation language [225]. Murphy provides also a variety of tools to use the extracted GUI models for automated testing and supporting manual testing activities, supports virtualized test execution environment, and integrates to other tools in automated test environment, e.g., Jenkins [226] open-source continuous integration tool.

Murphy tool [225] uses state-based directed graph for capturing the behavior of the GUI application and models events or interactions as transitions between the states. During the UI crawling, screenshots of the GUI are automatically captured after each interaction and used for visualization of the resulting graph models [225]. In addition to using the traditional means of dynamically observing the GUI, such as UI Automation library [13], Murphy provides its own window scrapping libraries. One of the libraries innovatively uses image recognition and comparison to provide platform-independent way to detect widgets for interaction and changes in the GUI for observing the state changes and possible defects [225].

As the extracted models are based on the observed implementation, instead of requirements of the system, visual inspection, and manual approval of the models is required to make sure that the modeled application behaves as expected [227]. Using screenshots of the modeled GUI application to visualize each state of the model helps in reading the models and understanding the behavior of the modeled application [227]. In addition to detecting crashes and unhandled exceptions during model extraction and testing, test oracles are based on approved behavior of an earlier version of the GUI application [225]. The extracted models of a new version are compared with the models of the previous version using model comparison functionality, and Murphy reports deviations, showing screenshots of both versions and highlighting the changes in the images. Then the user has to decide which changes were desired features and which are deviations from the expected behavior [227].

One of the main contributions of Aho and Suarez [225,227] was presenting experiences from using the Murphy tool to automatically extract models from commercial GUI software products and using the models to automate and support GUI testing activities in highly automated industrial development and testing environment.

5.2.7 Other Approaches Using Extracted Models for Automating GUI Testing

Chen and Subramaniam [228] presented an approach and VESP, a Visual Editor for testing Specifications, tool for automated specification-based testing of GUI-based Java applications. The approach uses a visual environment to pre-run a GUI application and to obtain test specifications in the form of FSMs, and enriches existing architecture for automated specification-based testing. The testers can graphically manipulate the test specifications within the true GUI environment of the AUT and the recorded input and output contain the same references as those in the AUT, so that the test cases generated from the edited specification can be used directly by test oracles during the automated testing procedure.

Mesbah and van Deursen [120,229] presented an approach for invariant-based automatic testing of AJAX UIs and Atusa tool, offering generic invariant checking components, a plugin-mechanism to add application-specific state validators, and generation of a test suite covering the paths obtained during crawling. They use Crawljax tool [129] to dynamically reverse engineer FSM-based state-flow graphs of the AJAX applications. Crawljax traverses a website in a depth-first order until no more new GUI elements are found. Duda *et al.* [230] proposed a similar approach, but uses a breadth-first strategy to support parallel crawling and speed up the reverse engineering process. Joorabchi and Mesbah [231] implement a tool called iCrawler to automatically reverse engineer the structure of the GUI of an iPhone operating system (iOS) application. The authors use a low-level Objective-C run-time reference library to hook into the executing iOS application. iCrawler automatically sends events to the UI to cover the interaction state space, dynamically reverse engineering a state model of the GUI application.

Iglesias and Castro [35] introduced GUITester tool and a semiautomated approach using property-based testing strategies for GUI testing by assisting the developer in modeling a GUI using FSM models, and using the models for GUI testing. The GUI is manually executed while instrumented with Javassist library [232] to obtain a trace file with information about correct and incorrect interactions. FSM model is extracted from the trace file using model inference tools, and the final FSM model is used as a basis for random generation for producing the test cases and the test data. Once an error is found, a shrinking feature is used to minimize the failing test case, providing support for debugging, and fixing purposes. When the GUI grows in size and complexity, the number of execution traces needed to infer the FSM model makes the assisted trace generation process infeasible.

Mariani *et al.* [233] present AutoBlackTest, a tool using dynamic analysis for model extraction and test suite generation for GUI applications. AutoBlackTest interacts with the application through its GUI, identifies system crashes and other domain-independent problems, and uses Q-learning techniques to understand the interaction modalities and to generate relevant testing scenarios. IBM Rational Functional Tester (RFT) [234] is used for extracting the list of widgets present in a given GUI, to access the state of the widgets and to interact with the widgets. TeachingBox [235] is used to implement the Q learning algorithm that can be adapted to the specific needs by implementing the state abstraction functions, the actions, and the reward function. AutoBlackTest also provides the capability to generate a test suite that can be automatically reexecuted with RFT from the model obtained as a result of the learning phase. As the Q-values represent the relevance of each action, prioritized test suites of desired size can be generated by covering transitions with Q-values above a threshold defined by the tester.

Gross *et al.* [92] presented EXSYST, a hybrid model extraction and test generation tool that uses dynamic analysis for exploring Java GUI applications while guided by static analysis aiming to maximize the code coverage of the generated test suite. It applies a search-based approach for systematically generating GUI events or interactions while observing which events correspond to which behavior in the code. EXSYST uses a genetic algorithm from EvoSuite test generation tool [236] to evolve a population of GUI test suites with the goal of achieving maximum possible coverage. To guide the exploration and the search operators, a nondeterministic state machine model of the GUI is created and evolved alongside the test cases. Model is used to guide the exploration process by giving preference to unexplored parts of the GUI and to repair invalid sequences when mutating interaction sequences. The approach detects exceptions, but does not automatically create test oracles.

6. CONCLUSION AND DISCUSSION

During the past 5 years, automated extraction of GUI models for testing has become a popular research topic. Software industry is obviously interested in effective ways to automate GUI testing, but another important reason for increasing popularity are the GUI frameworks that provide an easy access to observe and interact with the GUI, e.g., Jemmy [14], Micsosoft UI Automation [13] and Robotium [138]. These GUI frameworks have solved many technical issues in model extraction, but many challenges remain and new ones emerge as the research goes on. Also, there are practical issues hindering the large scale industrial adoption of the tools and approaches, such as usability and scalability of the tools.

6.1. Trends

Based on this state-of-the-art study on automated extraction of GUI models for testing, we observed the following trends: (1) the use of hybrid methods for model extraction is increasing, (2) the first long term industrial experiences have been published with promising results, (3) new ways of using extracted GUI models for testing, and (4) the use of virtual machines for model extraction will increase.

In their latest work, many researchers of this research area combine static and dynamic analysis to extract better and more detailed models [136] or to generate better tests from the extracted models [92]. Dynamic analysis has been the prominent method for GUI model extraction, but static methods have been revisited and combined to dynamic methods as the extraction techniques have evolved and more detailed analysis is required.

Although the industrial adoption of using extracted models for automated GUI testing is still lacking, the first long term industrial evaluations with large commercial GUI applications have been published and the results were promising [227]. As the approaches and tools evolve and the usability and scalability improves, the large scale industrial adoption will follow. Many of the tools mentioned in this study have been published as open-source software, and hopefully the increasing use will speed up the development.

Most approaches use the extracted GUI models for generating test cases with test oracles based on the behavior of an earlier version of the GUI application. This way it is possible to detect changes in the behavior. A recent study [227] uses model comparison instead of test case generation for regression testing. The basic idea is to extract a new model of each new version and automatically compare the models to detect changes. Another new way of utilizing the extracted GUI models is providing automated tool support to speed up manual GUI testing activities [227].

Virtual machines can be used to minimize the nondeterministic behavior during model extraction and GUI testing, e.g., external changes and events in the test environment, such as operating system notifying the user about new software updates available [237]. Restoring a clean snapshot of a virtual machine every time the GUI is restarted during model extraction, as in [227], removes also unintentional context information, such as event history or long event sequences that affect the state of the GUI but the cause is not captured into the model. We expect that the use of virtual machines for model extraction and GUI testing will increase.

6.2. Future

As the computers get faster and better, keeping the model extraction fast and extracted models small will be less problematic. Until then, we have to keep finding the balance between not covering all possible interactions of the GUI to keep the extraction fast but still extracting models with good enough coverage of the GUI, and abstracting the unnecessary details away to keep the size of the extracted models small enough to be computationally feasible but still capture enough details to unambiguously determine the state of the GUI and maintain the usefulness of the extracted models.

Although some approaches aim for a fully automated GUI testing process, in practice some manual effort is always required. The question is if the optimal place for the manual effort is in providing meaningful input, validating the correctness of the extracted models, guiding the test generation to get better tests or less false positives, linking the extracted models to the requirements of the modeled system, or somewhere else. Most of these steps can be automated but require manual effort either before or after the automated step.

REFERENCES

[1] X. Yang, Graphic user interface modelling and testing automation, PhD thesis, School of Engineering and Science, Victoria University, Melbourne, Australia, 2011.

[2] J.L. Silva, J.C. Campos, A.C.R. Paiva, Model-based user interface testing with spec explorer and ConcurTaskTrees, in: Proc. 2nd Int. Workshop on Formal Methods for Interactive Systems (FMIS 2007), 4 Sep 2007, Lancaster, UK, 2007, pp. 77–93.

[3] A.M. Memon, Automatically repairing event sequence-based GUI test suites for regression testing, ACM Trans. Softw. Eng. Methodol. 18 (2) (2008), article no. 4. ACM, New York, NY, pp. 1–36.

[4] J. Canny, The future of human–computer interaction, ACM Queue 4 (6) (2006) 24–32, ACM, New York, NY.

[5] B.A. Myers, UIMSs, toolkits, interface builders, ACM Trans. Comput. Hum. Interact. 2 (1) (1995) 64–103, Human Computer Interaction Institute, Carnegie Mellon University, May 24, 1996. A revised version from "User Interface Software Tools".

[6] A.M. Memon, Using reverse engineering for automated usability evaluation of GUI-based applications, in: A. Seffah, J. Vanderdonckt, M.C. Desmarais (Eds.), Human-Centered Software Engineering: Software Engineering Models, Patterns and Architectures for HCI, Springer, London, 2009, pp. 335–355.

[7] J.C. Silva, J.A. Saraiva, J.C. Campos, A generic library for GUI reasoning and testing, in: Proc. 2009 ACM Symposium on Applied Computing (SAC'09), 8–12 Mar 2009, Honolulu, HI, USA, 2009, pp. 121–128.

[8] A.M. Memon, GUI testing: pitfalls and process, Computer 35 (8) (2002) 87–88, IEEE Computer Society.

[9] A.M. Memon, A. Nagarajan, Q. Xie, Automating regression testing for evolving GUI software, J. Softw. Maint. Evol. Res. Pract. 17 (1) (2005) 27–64, John Wiley & Sons Inc.

[10] B.A. Myers, S.E. Hudson, R. Pausch, Past, present, and future of user interface software tools, ACM Trans. Comput. Hum. Interact. 7 (1) (2000) 3–28.

[11] B.A. Myers, S.Y. Park, Y. Nakano, G. Mueller, A. Ko, How designers design and program interactive behaviors, in: Proc. 2008 IEEE Symposium on Visual Languages and Human-Centric Computing (VL/HCC), 15–19 Sep 2008, Herrsching, Germany, 2008, pp. 177–184.

[12] A.M.P. Grilo, A.C.R. Paiva, J.P. Faria, Reverse engineering of GUI models for testing, in: Proc. 2010 5th Iberian Conf. Information Systems and Technologies (CISTI), 16–19 Jun 2010, Santiago de Compostela, Spain, 2010, pp. 1–6.

[13] Microsoft UI Automation. http://msdn.microsoft.com/en-us/library/ms747327 (v=vs.110).aspx.

[14] Jemmy, an open source Java library for GUI automation. http://jemmy.java.net.

[15] K. Li, M. Wu, Effective GUI Test Automation: Developing an Automated GUI Testing Tool, SYBEX Inc., Alameda, CA, 2004.

[16] P. Aho, N. Menz, T. Räty, Dynamic reverse engineering of GUI models for testing, in: Proc. 2013 Int. Conf. Control, Decision and Information Technologies (CoDIT'13), 6–8 May 2013, Hammamet, Tunisia, 2013, pp. 441–447.

[17] M. Utting, B. Legeard, Practical Model-Based Testing: A Tools Approach, Morgan Kaufmann Publishers Inc, San Francisco, CA, 2006.

[18] T. Kanstrén, A Framework for Observation-Based Modelling in Model-Based Testing, VTT Publications 727, Espoo, Finland, 2010.

[19] A. Kull, Automatic GUI model generation: state of the art, in: Proc. 2012 IEEE 23rd Int. Symposium on Software Reliability Engineering Workshops (ISSREW), 27–30 Nov 2012, Dallas, TX, USA, 2012, pp. 207–212.

[20] T. Systä, Static and Dynamic Reverse Engineering Techniques for Java Software Systems, Acta Electronica Universitatis Tamperensis 30, Tampere, Finland, 2000.

[21] R. Kollmann, P. Selonen, E. Stroulia, T. Systä, A. Zündorf, A study on the current state of the art in tool-supported UML-based static reverse engineering, in: Proc. 9th Working Conf. on Reverse Engineering (WCRE'02), 29 Oct 2002, Richmond, VA, USA, 2002, pp. 22–32.

[22] A.M. Memon, B.N. Nguyen, Advances in automated model-based system testing of software applications with a GUI front-end, Adv. Comput. 80 (2010) 121–162, Elsevier Inc.

[23] B. Nguyen, Testing GUI-Based Software with Undetermined Input Spaces, PhD dissertation, Department of Computer Science, University of Maryland, College Park, 2013.

[24] P. Aho, N. Menz, T. Räty, Enhancing generated Java GUI models with valid test data, in: Proc. 2011 IEEE Conf. on Open Systems (ICOS 2011), 25–28 Sep 2011, Langawi, Malaysia, 2011, pp. 310–315.

[25] A.M. Memon, An event-flow model of GUI-based applications for testing, Softw. Test. Verif. Reliab. 17 (3) (2007) 137–157, John Wiley and Sons Ltd., Chichester, UK.

[26] I. Banerjee, B. Nguyen, V. Garousi, A.M. Memon, Graphical user interface (GUI) testing: systematic mapping and repository, Inform. Softw. Technol. 55 (10) (2013) 1679–1694, Elsevier.

[27] X. Yuan, A.M. Memon, Generating event sequence-based test cases using GUI runtime state feedback, IEEE Trans. Softw. Eng. 36 (1) (2010) 81–95, IEEE Computer Society.

[28] R.J.K. Jacob, A. Girouard, L.M. Hirshfield, M.S. Horn, O. Shaer, E.T. Solovey, J. Zigelbaum, Reality-based interaction: a framework for post-WIMP interfaces, in: Proc. SIGCHI Conf. on Human Factors in Computing Systems (CHI '08), 5–10 Apr 2008, Florence, Italy, 2008, pp. 201–210.

[29] A. Dam, Post-WIMP user interfaces, ACM Commun. 40 (2) (1997) 63–67, ACM, New York, NY.

[30] IEEE Computer Society Professional Practices Committee, Guide to the Software Engineering Body of Knowledge: 2004 Version, IEEE Computer Society, 2004.

[31] IEEE, IEEE Standard Glossary of Software Engineering Terminology, ANSI/IEEE Std 610.12-1990, IEEE Standards Association, New York, NY, Reaffirmed 2002.

[32] F. Belli, M. Linschulte, Event-driven modeling and testing of web services, in: Proc. 32nd Annual IEEE Int. Computer Software and Applications Conf. (COMPSAC'08), 28 Jul 2008, Turku, Finland, 2008, pp. 1168–1173.

[33] X. Yuan, M. Cohen, A.M. Memon, GUI interaction testing: incorporating event context, IEEE Trans. Softw. Eng. 37 (4) (2011) 559–574, IEEE Computer Society.

[34] Q. Xie, A.M. Memon, Using a pilot study to derive a GUI model for automated testing, ACM Trans. Softw. Eng. Methodol. 18 (2) (2008), article no. 7. ACM, New York, NY.

[35] D. Iglesias, L.M. Castro, Property-based testing for graphical user interfaces, J. Comput. Inform. Technol. 1 (3) (2011) 60–71, Academy Publish.

[36] P. Brooks, B. Robinson, A.M. Memon, An initial characterization of industrial graphical user interface systems, in: Proc. 2nd IEEE Int. Conf. on Software Testing, Verification and Validation (ICST 2009), 1–4 Apr 2009, Denver, CO, USA, 2009, pp. 11–20.

[37] J. Bowen, S. Reeves, UI-design driven model-based testing, Innov. Syst. Softw. Eng. 9 (3) (2013) 201–215, Springer, London.

[38] J.C. Campos, J. Saraiva, C. Silva, J.C. Silva, GUIsurfer: a reverse engineering framework for user interface software, in: Reverse Engineering—Recent Advances and Applications, March 2012, InTech, 2012, pp. 31–54.

[39] P. Santos-Neto, R. Resende, C. Pâdua, Requirements for information systems model-based testing, in: Proc. 2007 ACM Symposium on Applied Computing (SAC), 11–15 Mar 2007, Seoul, Korea, 2007, pp. 1409–1415.

[40] A. Bertolino, A. Polini, P. Inverardi, H. Muccini, Towards anti-model-based testing, in: Proc. Int. Conf. on Dependable Systems and Networks (DSN2004), 28 Jun 2004, Florence, Italy, 2004, pp. 124–125.

[41] G.Z. Holzmann, M.H. Smith, An automated verification method for distributed systems software based on model extraction, IEEE Trans. Softw. Eng. 28 (4) (2002) 364–377, IEEE Computer Society.

[42] M. Grechanik, Q. Xie, C. Fu, Maintaining and evolving GUI-directed test scripts, in: Proc. 2009 IEEE 31st Int. Conf. on Software Engineering (ICSE 2009), 16–24 May 2009, Vancouver, Canada, 2009, pp. 408–418.

[43] jfcUnit, an extension to JUnit framework for testing Java Swing based applications. http://jfcunit.sourceforge.net.

[44] J. Andersson, G. Bache, The video store revisited yet again: adventures in GUI acceptance testing, in: Proc. 5th Int. Conf. on eXtreme Programming and Agile Processes in Software Engineering (XP'2004), 6–10 Jun 2004, Garmisch-Partenkirchen, Germany, 2004, pp. 1–10.

[45] Abbot, a framework for automated testing of Java GUI components and programs. http://abbot.sourceforge.net.

[46] Squish, a GUI test automation tool for functional GUI regression tests. http://www.froglogic.com/squish/gui-testing.

[47] marathonITE, a Java GUI Test automation framework. http://marathontesting.com.

[48] T. Yeh, T. Chang, R.C. Miller, Sikuli: using GUI screenshots for search and automation, in: Proc. 22nd Annual ACM Symposium on User Interface Software and Technology, 4–7 Oct 2009, Victoria, Canada, 2009, pp. 183–192.

[49] Sikuli, a tool using screenshot images for automating and testing GUIs. http://www.sikuli.org.

[50] SeleniumHQ, a tool for automating testing of web applications. http://docs.seleniumhq.org.

[51] Appium, an open source test automation framework for native and hybrid mobile apps. http://appium.io.

[52] A. Kervinen, M. Maunumaa, M. Katara, Controlling testing using three-tier model architecture, in: Proc. 2nd Workshop on Model Based Testing (MBT 2006), 25–26 Mar 2006, Vienna, Austria, 2006, pp. 53–66.

[53] Enterprise Architect, a commercial UML modeling tool. http://www.sparxsystems.com/products/ea/.

[54] Conformiq Designer, a commercial test modeling and MBT tool. http://www.conformiq.com/products/conformiq-designer/.

[55] Microsoft Spec Explorer, a tool that extends Microsoft Visual Studio for creating models of software behavior. http://msdn.microsoft.com/en-us/library/ee620411.aspx.

[56] T. Takala, M. Katara, J. Harty, Experiences of system-level model-based GUI testing of an android application, in: Proc. 2011 IEEE 4th Int. Conf. on Software Testing, Verification and Validation (ICST), 21–25 Mar 2011, Berlin, Germany, 2011, pp. 377–386.

[57] F. Belli, Finite-state testing and analysis of graphical user interfaces, in: Proc. 12th Int. Symposium on Software Reliability Engineering (ISSRE'01), 27–30 Nov 2001, Hong Kong, China, 2001, pp. 34–43.

[58] A.M. Memon, A Comprehensive Framework for Testing Graphical User Interfaces, PhD dissertation, Department of Computer Science, University of Pittsburgh, 2001.

[59] F. Belli, N. Nissanke, C.J. Budnik, A. Mathur, Test generation using event sequence graphs: Technical Report 2005/6, Institute for Electrical Engineering and Information Technology, University of Paderborn, Germany, 2005.

[60] M. Vieira, J. Leduc, B. Hasling, R. Subramanyan, J. Kazmeier, Automation of GUI testing using a model-driven approach, in: Proc. 2006 Int. Workshop on Automation of Software Test (AST), 20–28 May 2006, Shanghai, China, 2006, pp. 9–14.

[61] A. Kervinen, M. Maunumaa, T. Pääkkönen, M. Katara, Model-based testing through a GUI, in: Proc. 5th Int. Conf. on Formal Approaches to Software Testing (FATES'05), 11 Jul 2005, Edinburgh, UK, 2005, pp. 16–31.

[62] M. Katara, A. Kervinen, M. Maunumaa, T. Pääkkönen, M. Satama, Towards deploying model-based testing with a domain-specific modeling approach, in: Proc. Testing: Academic and Industrial Conf.—Practice and Research Techniques (TAIC PART 2006), 29–31 Aug 2006, Windsor, UK, 2006, pp. 81–89.

[63] TEMA tools, an open source tool set for MBGT. http://tema.cs.tut.fi.

[64] D. Mauser, A. Klaus, K. Holl, Towards a GUI test model using state charts and programming code, in: Proc. 25th IFIP Int. Conf. on Testing Software and Systems (ICTSS'13), 13–15 Nov 2013, Istanbul, Turkey, 2013, pp. 271–276.

[65] A.M. Memon, M.L. Soffa, M.E. Pollack, Coverage criteria for GUI testing, in: Proc. 8th European Software Engineering Conf. (ESEC)/9th ACM SIGSOFT Int. Symposium on Foundations of Software Engineering (FSE-9), 10–14 Sep 2001, Vienna, Austria, 2001, pp. 256–267.

[66] J. Strecker, A.M. Memon, Relationships between test suites, faults, and fault detection in GUI testing, in: Proc. 1st Int. Conf. on Software Testing, Verification, and Validation (ICST), 9–11 Apr 2008, Lillehammer, Norway, 2008, pp. 12–21.

[67] J. Strecker, A.M. Memon, Faults' context matters, in: Proc. 4th Int. Workshop on Software Quality Assurance (SOQUA'07), 3–7 Sep 2007, Dubrovnik, Croatia, 2007, pp. 112–115.

[68] V.R. Basili, R.W. Selby, Comparing the effectiveness of software testing strategies, IEEE Trans. Softw. Eng. 13 (12) (1987) 1278–1296, IEEE Computer Society.

[69] A.J. Offutt, J.H. Hayes, A semantic model of program faults, in: Proc. 1996 ACM SIGSOFT Int. Symposium on Software Testing and Analysis (ISSTA), 8–10 Jan 1996, San Diego, CA, USA, 1996, pp. 195–200.

[70] J. Strecker, A.M. Memon, Accounting for defect characteristics in evaluations of testing techniques, ACM Trans. Softw. Eng. Methodol. 21 (3) (2012), article no. 17. ACM, New York, NY.

[71] Q. Xie, A.M. Memon, Studying the characteristics of a "Good" GUI test suite, in: Proc. 17th IEEE Int. Symposium on Software Reliability Engineering (ISSRE 2006), 7–10 Nov 2006, Raleigh, NC, USA, 2006, pp. 159–168.

[72] S. McMaster, A.M. Memon, Call stack coverage for test suite reduction, in: Proc. 21st IEEE Int. Conf. on Software Maintenance (ICSM'05), 25–30 Sep 2005, Budapest, Hungary, 2005, pp. 539–548.

[73] S. McMaster, A.M. Memon, Fault detection probability analysis for coverage-based test suite reduction, in: Proc. 21st IEEE Int. Conf. on Software Maintenance (ICSM), 2–5 Oct 2007, Paris, France, 2007, pp. 335–344.

[74] S. McMaster, A.M. Memon, Call stack coverage for GUI test-suite reduction, in: Proc. 17th IEEE Int. Symposium on Software Reliability Engineering (ISSRE), 7–10 Nov 2006, Raleigh, NC, USA, 2006, pp. 33–44.

[75] S. McMaster, A.M. Memon, Call-stack coverage for GUI test suite reduction, IEEE Trans. Softw. Eng. 34 (1) (2008) 99–115, IEEE Computer Society.

[76] P. Brooks, A.M. Memon, Introducing a test suite similarity metric for event sequence-based test cases, in: Proc. 23rd IEEE Int. Conf. on Software Maintenance (ICSM'09), 20–26 Sep 2009, Edmonton, Canada, 2009, pp. 243–252.

[77] R.C. Bryce, A.M. Memon, Test suite prioritization by interaction coverage, in: Proc. Workshop on Domain-Specific Approaches to Software Test Automation (DoSTA 2007), 3–7 Sep 2007, Dubrovnik, Croatia, 2007, pp. 1–7.

[78] R.C. Bryce, S. Sampath, A.M. Memon, Developing a single model and test prioritization strategies for event-driven software, IEEE Trans. Softw. Eng. 37 (1) (2011) 48–64, IEEE Computer Society.

[79] E. Elsaka, W.E. Moustafa, B. Nguyen, A.M. Memon, Using methods & measures from network analysis for GUI testing, in: Proc. Int. Workshop on TESTing Techniques & Experimentation Benchmarks for Event-Driven Software (TESTBEDS 2010), 6–10 Apr 2010, Paris, France, 2010, pp. 240–246.

[80] S. Sampath, R. Bryce, A.M. Memon, A uniform representation of hybrid criteria for regression testing, IEEE Trans. Softw. Eng. 39 (1) (2013) 1326–1344, IEEE Computer Society.

[81] E.J. Chikofsky, J.H. Cross II, Reverse engineering and design recovery: a taxonomy, IEEE Softw. 7 (1) (1990) 13–17, IEEE Computer Society.

[82] C.E. Silva, J.C. Campos, Combining static and dynamic analysis for the reverse engineering of web applications, in: Proc. 5th ACM SIGCHI Symposium on Engineering Interactive Computing Systems (EICS '13), 24–27 Jun 2013, London, UK, 2013, pp. 107–112.

[83] S. Shoham, E. Yahav, S.J. Fink, M. Pistoia, Static specification mining using automata-based abstractions, IEEE Trans. Softw. Eng. 34 (5) (2008) 651–666, IEEE Computer Society.

[84] R. Alur, P. Cerny, P. Madhusudan, W. Nam, Synthesis of interface specifications for Java classes, in: Proc. 32nd ACM SIGPLAN-SIGACT Symp. on Principles of Programming Languages (POPL '05), 12–14 Jan 2005, Long Beach, CA, USA, 2005, pp. 98–109.

[85] M. Acharya, T. Xie, J. Xu, Mining interface specifications for generating checkable robustness properties, in: 17th Int. Symp. on Software Reliability Engineering (ISSRE '06), 7–10 Nov 2006, Raleigh, NC, USA, 2006, pp. 311–320.

[86] M.G. Nanda, C. Grothoff, S. Chandra, Deriving object type states in the presence of inter-object references, in: Proc. 20th Annual ACM SIGPLAN Conf. on Object Oriented Programming, Systems, Languages, and Applications (OOPSLA '05), 16–20 Oct 2005, San Diego, CA, USA, 2005, pp. 77–96.

[87] D. Engler, D.Y. Chen, S. Hallem, A. Chou, B. Chelf, Bugs as deviant behavior: a general approach to inferring errors in systems code, in: Proc. 18th ACM Symposium on Operating Systems Principles (SOSP '01), 21–24 Oct 2001, Chateau Lake Louise, Banff, Canada, 2001, pp. 57–72.

[88] M.K. Ramanathan, A. Grama, S. Jagannathan, Path-sensitive inference of function precedence protocols, in: Proc. 29th Int. Conf. on Software Engineering (ICSE '07), 19–27 May 2007, Minneapolis, MN, USA, 2007, pp. 240–250.

[89] A. Wasylkowski, A. Zeller, C. Lindig, Detecting object usage anomalies, in: Proc. 6th Joint Meeting of the European Software Engineering Conf. and the ACM SIGSOFT Symp. Foundations of Software Eng. (ESEC/SFE 2007), 3–7 Sep 2007, Dubrovnik, Croatia, 2007, pp. 35–44.

[90] L. Mariani, M. Pezzè, O. Riganelli, M. Santoro, SEIM: static extraction of interaction models, in: Proc. 2nd Int. Workshop on Principles of Engineering Service-Oriented Systems (PESOS '10), 1–2 May 2010, Cape Town, South Africa, 2010, pp. 22–28.

[91] L.C. Briand, Y. Labiche, J. Leduc, Towards the reverse engineering of UML sequence diagrams for distributed, multithreaded Java software: Technical Report, Carleton University (SCE-04-04), 2004.

[92] F. Gross, G. Fraser, A. Zeller, EXSYST: search-based GUI testing, in: 2012 34th Int. Conf. on Software Engineering (ICSE 2012), 2–9 Jun 2012, Zurich, Switzerland, 2012, pp. 1423–1426.

[93] S. Kumar, S.-C. Khoo, A. Roychoudhury, D. Lo, Mining message sequence graphs, in: Proc. 33rd Int. Conf. on Software Engineering (ICSE '11), 21–28 May 2011, Waikiki, Honolulu, HI, USA, 2011, pp. 91–100.

[94] L. Briand, Y. Labiche, J. Leduc, Toward the reverse engineering of UML sequence diagrams for distributed Java software, IEEE Trans. Softw. Eng. 32 (9) (2006) 642–663, IEEE Computer Society.

[95] G. Ammons, R. Bodik, J.R. Larus, Mining specifications, in: Proc. 29th ACM SIGPLAN-SIGACT Symp. Principles of Programming Languages (POPL'02), 16–18 Jan 2002, Portland, OR, USA, 2002, pp. 4–16.

[96] D. Lo, S. Maoz, Mining scenario-based triggers and effects, in: Proc. 23rd Int. Conf. on Automated Software Engineering (ASE 2008), 15–19 Sep 2008, L'Aquila, Italy, 2008, pp. 109–118.

[97] D. Lorenzoli, L. Mariani, M. Pezze, Automatic generation of software behavioral models, in: ACM/IEEE 30th Int. Conf. on Software Engineering (ICSE '08), 10–18 May 2008, Leipzig, Germany, 2008, pp. 501–510.

[98] V. Dallmeier, C. Lindig, A. Wasylkowski, A. Zeller, Mining object behavior with ADABU, in: Proc. Int. Workshop on Dynamic Systems Analysis, 20–28 May 2006, Shanghai, China, 2006, pp. 17–24.

[99] J. Yang, D. Evans, D. Bhardwaj, T. Bhat, M. Das, Perracotta: mining temporal API rules from imperfect traces, in: Proc. 28th Int. Conf. Software Engineering (ICSE'06), 20–28 May 2006, Shanghai, China, 2006, pp. 282–291.

[100] M. Gabel, Z. Su, Javert: fully automatic mining of general temporal properties from dynamic traces, in: Proc. 16th ACM SIGSOFT Int. Symp. on the Foundations of Software Engineering (FSE 2008), 9–14 Nov 2008, Atlanta, GA, USA, 2008, pp. 339–349.

[101] A. Hamou-Lhadj, E. Braun, D. Amyot, T. Lethbridge, Recovering behavioral design models from execution traces, in: Proc. 9th European Conf. on Software Maintenance and Reengineering (CSMR 2005), 21–23 Mar 2005, Manchester, UK, 2005, pp. 112–121.

[102] P.J. Guo, J.H. Perkins, S. McCamant, M.D. Ernst, Dynamic inference of abstract types, in: Int. Symposium on Software Testing and Analysis (ISSTA 2006), 17–20 Jul 2006, Portland, ME, USA, 2006, pp. 255–265.

[103] J. Whaley, M.C. Martin, M.S. Lam, Automatic extraction of object-oriented component interfaces, in: Proc. 2002 ACM SIGSOFT Int. Symposium on Software Testing and Analysis (ISSTA '02), 22–24 Jul 2002, Rome, Italy, 2002, pp. 218–228.

[104] L. Burdy, Y. Cheon, D. Cok, M. Ernst, J. Kiniry, G.T. Leavens, K.R.M. Leino, E. Poll, An overview of JML tools and applications, Int. J. Softw. Tool Technol. Trans. 7 (3) (2005) 212–232, Springer-Verlag, Berlin, Heidelberg.

[105] T. Systä, On the relationships between static and dynamic models in reverse engineering Java software, in: Proc. 6th Working Conference on Reverse Engineering (WCRE 1999), 6–8 Oct 1999, Atlanta, GA, USA, 1999, pp. 304–313.

[106] M. Schur, Experimental specification mining for enterprise applications, in: Proc. 19th European Software Engineering Conf. (ESEC)/ACM Symposium on Fundamentals of Software Engineering (FSE), 5–9 Sep 2011, Szeged, Hungary, 2011, pp. 388–391.

[107] A.M. Memon, I. Banerjee, A. Nagarajan, GUI ripping: reverse engineering of graphical user interfaces for testing, in: Proc. 10th Working Conf. on Reverse Engineering (WCRE'03), 13–16 Nov 2003, Victoria, Canada, 2003, pp. 260–269.

[108] L. Mariani, S. Papagiannakis, M. Pezzé, Compatibility and regression testing of COTS-component-based software, in: Proc. 29th Int. Conf. on Software Engineering (ICSE'07), 19–27 May 2007, Minneapolis, MN, USA, 2007, pp. 85–95.

[109] T. Xie, D. Notkin, Tool-assisted unit test generation and selection based on operational abstractions, Autom. Softw. Eng. 13 (3) (2006) 345–371, Springer, Kluwer Academic Publishers.

[110] M.D. Ernst, J. Cockrell, W.G. Griswold, D. Notkin, Dynamically discovering likely program invariants to support program evolution, IEEE Trans. Softw. Eng. 27 (2) (2001) 1–25, IEEE Computer Society.

[111] G. Fraser, N. Walkinshaw, Behaviourally adequate software testing, in: 2012 IEEE 5th Int. Conf. on Software Testing, Verification and Validation (ICST), 17–21 Apr 2012, Montreal, Canada, 2012, pp. 300–309.

[112] Weka, a collection of machine learning algorithms for data mining tasks. http://www.cs.waikato.ac.nz/ml/weka.

[113] M. Pradel, T.R. Gross, Leveraging test generation and specification mining for automated bug detection without false positives, in: Proc. 34th Int. Conf. on Software Engineering (ICSE), 2–9 Jun 2012, Zurich, Switzerland, 2012, pp. 288–298.

[114] M. Pradel, C. Jaspan, J. Aldrich, T.R. Gross, Statically checking API protocol conformance with mined multi-object specifications, in: Proc. 34th Int. Conf. on Software Engineering (ICSE), 2–9 Jun 2012, Zurich, Switzerland, 2012, pp. 925–935.

[115] W. Zheng, H. Ma, M.R. Lyu, T. Xie, I. King, Mining test oracles of web search engines, in: Proc. 26th IEEE/ACM Int. Conf. on Automated Software Engineering (ASE '11), 6–12 Nov 2011, Lawrence, KS, USA, 2011, pp. 408–411.

[116] Q. Xie, A.M. Memon, Designing and comparing automated test oracles for GUI-based software applications, ACM Trans. Softw. Eng. Methodol. 16 (1) (2007), article no. 4. ACM, New York, NY.

[117] M. d'Amorim, C. Pacheco, D. Marinov, T. Xie, M.D. Ernst, An empirical comparison of automated generation and classification techniques for object-oriented unit testing, in: Proc. 21st Int. Conf. on Automated Software Engineering (ASE'06), 18–22 Sep 2006, Tokyo, Japan, 2006, pp. 59–68.

[118] P. Aho, N. Menz, T. Räty, I. Schieferdecker, Automated Java GUI modeling for model-based testing purposes, in: Proc. 8th Int. Conf. on Information Technology: New Generations (ITNG2011), 11–13 Apr 2011, Las Vegas, NV, USA, 2011, pp. 268–273.

[119] Q. Xie, A.M. Memon, Rapid crash testing for continuously evolving GUI-based software applications, in: Proc. 21st IEEE Int. Conf. on Software Maintenance (ICSM'05), 25–30 Sep 2005, Budapest, Hungary, 2005, pp. 473–482.

[120] A. Mesbah, A.V. Deursen, Invariant-based automatic testing of AJAX user interfaces, in: Proc. 31st Int. Conf. on Software Engineering (ICSE'09), 16–24 May 2009, Vancouver, Canada, 2009, pp. 210–220.

[121] K. Meinke, N. Walkinshaw, Model-based testing and model inference, in: Proc. 5th Int. Symposium on Leveraging Applications of Formal Methods (ISOLA 2012), 15–18 Oct 2012, Heraklion, Crete, Greece, 2012, pp. 440–443.

[122] L. Bouillon, Q. Limbourg, J. Vanderdonckt, B. Michotte, Reverse engineering of web pages based on derivations and transformations, in: Proc. 3rd Latin American Web Congress (LA-WEB 2005), 31 Oct 2005, Buenos Aires, Argentina, 2005, pp. 3–13.

[123] S. Staiger, Reverse engineering of graphical user interfaces using static analyses, in: Proc. 14th Working Conf. on Reverse Engineering (WCRE2007), 28–31 Oct 2007, Vancouver, Canada, 2007, pp. 189–198.

[124] A. Guha, S. Krishnamurthi, T. Jim, Using static analysis for Ajax intrusion detection, in: Proc. 18th Int. World Wide Web Conf. (WWW '09), 20–24 Apr 2009, Madrid, Spain, 2009, pp. 561–570.

[125] A.J. Ko, X. Zhang, FeedLack detects missing feedback in web applications, in: Proc. SIGCHI Conference on Human Factors in Computing Systems (CHI '11), 7–12 May 2011, Vancouver, Canada, 2011, pp. 2177–2186.

[126] F. Bellucci, G. Ghiani, F. Paternò, C. Porta, Automatic reverse engineering of inter-active dynamic web applications to support adaptation across platforms, in: Proc. 2012 ACM Int. Conf. on Intelligent User Interfaces (IUI'12), 14–17 Feb 2012, Lisbon, Portugal, 2012, pp. 217–226.

[127] Bauhaus project, tools for program analysis. http://www.iste.uni-stuttgart.de/en/ps/project-bauhaus.html.

[128] O.S. Ramón, J. Vanderdonckt, J.G. Molina, Re-engineering graphical user interfaces from their resource files with UsiResourcer, in: Proc. 2013 IEEE Seventh Int. Conf. on Research Challenges in Information Science (RCIS), 29–31 May 2013, Paris, France, 2013, pp. 1–12.

[129] A. Mesbah, E. Bozdag, A. van Deursen, Crawling AJAX by inferring user interface state changes, in: Proc. 8th Int. Conf. on Web Engineering (ICWE '08), 14–18 Jul 2008, Yorktown Heights, NJ, USA, 2008, pp. 122–134.

[130] A. Mesbah, A. van Deursen, S. Lenselink, Crawling Ajax-based web applications through dynamic analysis of user interface state changes, ACM Trans. Web 6 (1) (2012), article no. 3. ACM, New York, NY.

[131] H. Samir, A. Kamel, Automated reverse engineering of Java graphical user interfaces for web migration, in: Proc. ITI 5th Int. Conf. on Information and Communications Technology (ICICT), 16–18 Dec 2007, Cairo, Egypt, 2007, pp. 157–162.

[132] E. Stroulia, M. El-Ramly, P. Iglinski, P. Sorenson, User interface reverse engineering in support of interface migration to the web, Autom. Softw. Eng. 10 (3) (2003) 271–301, Kluwer Academic Publishers, Hingham, MA.

[133] P. Li, E. Wohlstadter, View-based maintenance of graphical user interfaces, in: Proc. 7th Int. Conf. on Aspect-Oriented Software Development (AOSD '08), 31 Mar 2008, Brussels, Belgium, 2008, pp. 156–167.

[134] A. Gimblett, H. Thimbleby, User interface model discovery: towards a generic approach, in: Proc. ACM SIGCHI Symposium on Engineering Interactive Comput-ing Systems (EICS '10), 19–23 Jun 2010, Berlin, Germany, 2010, pp. 145–154.

[135] M.I. Muhairat, R.E. Al-Qutaish, B.M. Athamena, From graphical user interface to domain class diagram: a reverse engineering approach, J. Theor. Appl. Inf. Technol. 24 (1) (2011) 28–40, Little Lion Scientific, Islamabad, Pakistan.

[136] W. Yang, M.R. Prasad, T. Xie, A grey-box approach for automated GUI-model gen-eration of mobile applications, in: Proc. 16th Int. Conf. on Fundamental Approaches

to Software Engineering (FASE'13), 16–24 Mar 2013, Rome, Italy, 2013, pp. 250–265.

[137] T. J. Watson Libraries for Analysis (WALA). http://wala.sourceforge.net/wiki/index.php/Main_Page.

[138] Robotium, an Android test automation framework. https://code.google.com/p/robotium.

[139] T. Azim, I. Neamtiu, Targeted and depth-first exploration for systematic testing of Android Apps, in: Proc. 2013 ACM SIGPLAN Int. Conf. on Object-Oriented Programming, Systems, Languages & Applications (OOPSLA), 26–31 Oct 2013, Indianapolis, IN, USA, 2013, pp. 641–660.

[140] D.J. Richardson, S.L. Aha, T.O. O'Malley, Specification-based test oracles for reactive systems, in: Proc. 14th Int. Conf. on Software Engineering (ICSE '92), 11–15 May 1992, Melbourne, Australia, 1992, pp. 105–118.

[141] A.M. Memon, I. Banerjee, A. Nagarajan, What test oracle should i use for effective GUI testing? in: Proc. 18th IEEE Int. Conf. on Automated Software Engineering (ASE), 6–10 Oct 2003, Montreal, Canada, 2003, pp. 164–173.

[142] A.M. Memon, M.E. Pollack, M.L. Soffa, Using a goal-driven approach to generate test cases for GUIs, in: Proc. 21st Int. Conf. Software Engineering (ICSE), 16–22 May 1999, Los Angeles, CA, USA, 1999, pp. 257–266.

[143] A.M. Memon, Q. Xie, Using transient/persistent errors to develop automated test oracles for event-driven software, in: Proc. 19th IEEE Int. Conf. on Automated Software Engineering (ASE), 20–24 Sep 2004, Linz, Austria, 2004, pp. 186–195.

[144] A.M. Memon, M.E. Pollack, M.L. Soffa, A planning-based approach to GUI testing, in: Proc. 13th Int. Software/Internet Quality Week (QW2000), 30 May–2 Jun 2000, San Francisco, CA, USA, 2000.

[145] A.M. Memon, M.E. Pollack, M.L. Soffa, Plan generation for GUI testing, in: Proc. 5th Int. Conf. on Artificial Intelligence Planning and Scheduling (AIPS), 14–17 Apr 2000, Breckenridge, CO, USA, 2000, pp. 226–235.

[146] A.M. Memon, M.E. Pollack, M.L. Soffa, Hierarchical GUI test case generation using automated planning, IEEE Trans. Softw. Eng. 27 (2) (2001) 144–155, IEEE Computer Society.

[147] A.M. Memon, M. Pollack, M. Soffa, Automated test oracles for GUIs, in: Proc. 8th ACM SIGSOFT Int. Symposium on Foundations of Software Engineering (FSE-8): 21st Century Applications, 6–10 Nov 2000, San Diego, CA, USA, 2000, pp. 30–39.

[148] A.M. Memon, I. Banerjee, A. Nagarajan, DART: a framework for regression testing nightly/daily builds of GUI applications, in: Proc. Int. Conf. on Software Maintenance (ICSM), 22–26 Sep 2003, Amsterdam, The Netherlands, 2003, pp. 410–420.

[149] A.M. Memon, Q. Xie, Empirical evaluation of the fault-detection effectiveness of smoke regression test cases for GUI-based software, in: Proc. 20th IEEE Int. Conf. on Software Maintenance (ICSM), 11–14 Sep 2004, Chicago, IL, USA, 2004, pp. 8–17.

[150] GUITAR, a GUI testing framework. http://guitar.sourceforge.net.

[151] A.M. Memon, M.L. Soffa, Regression testing of GUIs, in: Proc. 9th European Software Engineering Conf. (ESEC)/11th ACM SIGSOFT Int. symposium on Foundations of Software Engineering (FSE-11), 1–5 Sep 2003, Helsinki, Finland, 2003, pp. 118–127.

[152] A.M. Memon, Using tasks to automate regression testing of GUIs, in: Proc. IASTED Int. Conf. on Artificial Intelligence and Applications (AIA 2004), 16–18 Feb 2004, Innsbruck, Austria, 2004.

[153] S. McMaster, A.M. Memon, An extensible heuristic-based framework for GUI test case maintenance, in: Proc. 1st Int. Workshop on TESTing Techniques &

Experimentation Benchmarks for Event-Driven Software (TESTBEDS), 1-4 Apr 2009, Denver, CO, USA, 2009, pp. 251–254.

[154] M. Cohen, S. Huang, A.M. Memon, AutoInSpec: using missing test coverage to improve specifications in GUIs, in: Proc. 23rd IEEE Int. Symposium on Software Reliability Engineering (ISSRE'12), 27–30 Nov 2012, Dallas, TX, USA, 2012, pp. 251–260.

[155] A.M. Memon, I. Banerjee, B. Nguyen, B. Robbins, The first decade of GUI ripping: extensions, applications, and broader impacts, in: Proc. 20th Working Conf. on Reverse Engineering (WCRE), 14–17 Oct 2013, Koblenz, Germany, 2013, pp. 11–20.

[156] A.M. Memon, Q. Xie, Studying the fault-detection effectiveness of GUI test cases for rapidly evolving software, IEEE Trans. Softw. Eng. 31 (10) (2005) 884–896, IEEE Press, Piscataway, NJ.

[157] B. Nguyen, B. Robbins, I. Banerjee, A.M. Memon, GUITAR: an innovative tool for automated testing of GUI-driven software, Autom. Softw. Eng. 21 (1) (2013) 65–105, Springer, US.

[158] D. Hackner, A.M. Memon, Test case generator for GUITAR, in: Proc. Companion of the 30th Int. Conf. on Software Engineering (ICSE Companion '08), 10–18 May 2008, Leipzig, Germany, 2008, pp. 959–960.

[159] A. Nagarajan, A.M. Memon, Refactoring using event-based profiling, in: Proc. First Int. Workshop on REFactoring: Achievements, Challenges, and Effects (REFACE), 13–16 Nov 2003, Victoria, Canada, 2003.

[160] A.M. Memon, Employing user profiles to test a new version of a GUI component in its context of use, Softw. Qual. J. 14 (4) (2006) 359–377, Kluwer Academic Publishers, Hingham, MA.

[161] P. Brooks, A.M. Memon, Automated GUI testing guided by usage profiles, in: Proc. 22nd IEEE/ACM Int. Conf. on Automated Software Engineering (ASE'07), 05–09 Nov 2007, Atlanta, GA, USA, 2007, pp. 333–342.

[162] Q. Xie, A.M. Memon, Model-based testing of community-driven open-source GUI applications, in: Proc. 22nd IEEE Int. Conf. on Software Maintenance (ICSM'06), 24–27 Sep 2006, Philadelphia, PA, USA, 2006, pp. 145–154.

[163] A.M. Memon, Q. Xie, Agile quality assurance techniques for GUI-based applications, in: I.G. Stamelos, P. Sfetsos (Eds.), Agile Software Development Quality Assurance, Idea Group Inc., Hershey, PA, 2007, pp. 114–135

[164] X. Yuan, A.M. Memon, Using GUI run-time state as feedback to generate test cases, in: Proc. 29th Int. Conf. on Software Engineering (ICSE '07), 20–26 May 2007, Minneapolis, MN, USA, 2007, pp. 396–405.

[165] X. Yuan, A.M. Memon, Alternating GUI test generation and execution, in: Proc. IEEE Testing: Academic and Industrial Conf. (TAIC PART '08), 29–31 Aug 2008, Windsor, UK, 2008, pp. 23–32.

[166] X. Yuan, M. Cohen, A.M. Memon, Towards dynamic adaptive automated test generation for graphical user interfaces, in: Proc. 1st Int. Workshop on TESTing Techniques & Experimentation Benchmarks for Event-Driven Software (TESTBEDS'09), 1–4 Apr 2009, Denver, CO, USA, 2009, pp. 263–266.

[167] X. Yuan, A.M. Memon, Iterative execution-feedback model-directed GUI testing, Inform. Softw. Technol. 52 (5) (2010) 559–575, Butterworth-Heinemann, Newton, MA.

[168] S. Huang, M. Cohen, A.M. Memon, Repairing GUI test suites using a genetic algorithm, in: Proc. 3rd IEEE Int. Conf. on Software Testing, Verification and Validation (ICST 2010), 7–9 Apr 2010, Paris, France, 2010, pp. 245–254.

[169] A.M. Memon, Developing testing techniques for event-driven pervasive computing applications, in: Proc. OOPSLA 2004 Workshop on Building Software for Pervasive Computing (BSPC), 25 Oct 2004, Vancouver, Canada, 2004.

[170] X. Yuan, M. Cohen, A.M. Memon, Covering array sampling of input event sequences for automated GUI testing, in: Proc. 22nd IEEE Int. Conf. on Automated Software Engineering (ASE'07), 5–9 Nov 2007, Atlanta, GA, USA, 2007, pp. 405–408.

[171] S. Arlt, I. Banerjee, C. Bertolini, A.M. Memon, M. Schäf, Grey-box GUI testing: efficient generation of event sequences, Comput. Res. Repos. (2012), arXiv:1205.4928.

[172] S. Arlt, A. Podelski, C. Bertolini, M. Schäf, I. Banerjee, A.M. Memon, Lightweight static analysis for GUI testing, in: Proc. 2012 IEEE 23rd Int. Symposium on Software Reliability Engineering (ISSRE), 27–30 Nov 2012, Dallas, TX, USA, 2012, pp. 301–310.

[173] Q. Xie, Developing cost-effective model-based techniques for GUI testing, in: Proc. 28th Int. Conf. on Software Engineering (ICSE'06), 20–28 May 2006, Shanghai, China, 2006, pp. 997–1000.

[174] J.C. Campos, M.D. Harrison, Formally verifying interactive systems: a review, in: Proc. Eurographics Workshop on Design, Specification and Verification of Interactive Systems (DSV-IS '97), 4–6 Jun 1997, Granada, Spain, 1997, pp. 109–124.

[175] J.C. Campos, M.D. Harrison, The role of verification in interactive systems design, in: Proc. Eurographics Workshop on Design, Specification and Verification of Interactive Systems (DSV-IS '98), 3–5 Jun 1998, Abingdon, UK, 1998, pp. 155–170.

[176] J.C. Campos, M.D. Harrison, Model checking interactor specifications, Autom. Softw. Eng. 8 (3–4) (2001) 275–310, Kluwer Academic Publishers, Hingham, MA.

[177] J.C. Campos, Using task knowledge to guide interactor specifications analysis, in: Proc. 10th Int. Workshop on Design, Specification and Verification of Interactive Systems (DSV-IS 2003), 2003, 11–13 Jun 2003, Funchal, Madeira, Portugal, 2003, pp. 171–186.

[178] J.C. Campos, G.J. Doherty, Reasoning about dynamic information displays, in: Proc. 10th Int. Workshop on Design, Specification and Verification of Interactive Systems (DSV-IS 2003), 2003, 11–13 Jun 2003, Funchal, Madeira, Portugal, 2003, pp. 288–302.

[179] J.C. Campos, M.D. Harrison, From HCI to software engineering and back, in: Proc. ICSE Workshop on Bridging the Gaps Between Software Engineering and Human-Computer Interaction (SE-HCI 2003), 3–10 May 2003, Portland, OR, USA, 2003, pp. 49–56.

[180] J.C. Campos, M.D. Harrison, K. Loer, Verifying user interface behaviour with model checking, in: Proc. of the 2nd Int. Workshop on Verification and Validation of Enterprise Information Systems (VVEIS 2004), 14–17 Apr 2004, Porto, Portugal, 2004, pp. 87–96.

[181] J.C. Campos, M.D. Harrison, Considering context and users in interactive systems analysis, in: Proc. EIS 2007 Joint Working Conferences (EHCI 2007, DSV-IS 2007, and HCSE 2007), 22–24 Mar 2007, Salamanca, Spain, 2007, pp. 193–209.

[182] J.C. Silva, J.A. Saraiva, J.C. Campos, Combining formal methods and functional strategies regarding the reverse engineering of interactive applications, in: Proc. 13th Int. Workshop on Design, Specification, and Verification of Interactive Systems (DSVIS 2006), 26–28 Jul 2006, Dublin, Ireland, 2006, pp. 137–150.

[183] J.C. Silva, J.C. Campos, J. Saraiva, Models for the reverse engineering of Java/Swing applications, in: Proc. 3rd Int. Workshop on Metamodels, Schemas, Grammars, and Ontologies for Reverse Engineering (ATEM 2006), 1 Oct 2006, Genoa, Italy, 2006.

[184] Strafunski Haskell library. http://www.haskell.org/haskellwiki/Applications_and_libraries/Generic_programming/Strafunski.

[185] C.E. Silva, Reverse Engineering of Rich Internet Applications, Master's thesis, University of Minho, Portugal, 2010.

[186] J.C. Silva, C.C. Silva, R.D. Gonçalo, J.A. Saraiva, J.C. Campos, The GUISurfer tool: towards a language independent approach to reverse engineering GUI code, in: Proc.

2nd ACM SIGCHI Symposium on Engineering Interactive Computing Systems (EICS'10), 19–23 Jun 2010, Berlin, Germany, 2010, pp. 181–186.

[187] J.C. Silva, C.E. Silva, J.C. Campos, J.A. Saraiva, GUI behavior from source code analysis, in: Proc. Conf. Nacional em Interacção Humano-Computador (Interacção 2010), 14–15 Oct 2010, Aveiro, Portugal, 2010, pp. 81–88.

[188] C.E. Silva, Reverse engineering of GWT applications, in: Proc. 4th ACM SIGCHI Symposium on Engineering Interactive Computing Systems (EICS'12), 25–28 Jun 2012, Copenhagen, Denmark, 2012, pp. 325–328.

[189] Graphviz, an open source graph visualization software. http://www.graphviz.org.

[190] Graph-tool, a Python module. http://graph-tool.skewed.de.

[191] J.C. Silva, J.C. Campos, J.A. Saraiva, GUI Inspection from source code analysis, in: Proc. 4th Int. Workshop on Foundations and Techniques for Open Source Software Certification (OpenCert 2010), 17–18 Sep 2010, Pisa, Italy, 2010, article no. 11.

[192] R. Couto, A.N. Ribeiro, J.C. Campos, A patterns based reverse engineering approach for Java source code, in: Proc. 2012 35th Annual IEEE Software Engineering Workshop (SEW), 12–13 Oct 2012, Heraclion, Crete, Greece, 2012, pp. 140–147.

[193] R. Couto, A.N. Ribeiro, J.C. Campos, MapIt: a model based pattern recovery tool, in: Proc. 8th Int. Workshop on Model-Based Methodologies for Pervasive and Embedded Software (MOMPES 2012), 3–7 Sep 2012, Essen, Germany, 2012, pp. 19–37.

[194] C.E. Silva, J.C. Campos, Can GUI implementation markup languages be used for modelling? in: Proc. 4th Int. Conf. on Human-Centered Software Engineering (HCSE'12), 29–31 Oct 2012, Toulouse, France, 2012, pp. 112–129.

[195] A. Paiva, J. Faria, R. Vidal, Specification-based testing of user interfaces, in: Proc. 10th Int. Workshop on Design, Specification and Verification of Interactive Systems (DSV-IS), 11–13 Jun 2003, Funchal, Madeira, Portugal, 2003, pp. 139–153.

[196] A.C.R. Paiva, N. Tillmann, J.C.P. Faria, R.F.A.M. Vidal, Modeling and testing hierarchical GUIs, in: Proc. 12th Int. Workshop on Abstract State Machines (ASM), 8–11 Mar 2005, Paris, France, 2005, pp. 329–344.

[197] A. Paiva, J. Faria, N. Tillmann, R. Vidal, A model-to-implementation mapping tool for automated model-based GUI testing, in: Proc. 7th Int. Conf. on Formal Engineering Methods (ICFEM), 1–4 Nov 2005, Manchester, UK, 2005, pp. 450–464.

[198] A.C.R. Paiva, Automated Specification-Based Testing of Graphical User Interfaces, PhD thesis, Department of Electrical and Computer Engineering, University of Porto, Portugal, 2007.

[199] A.C.R. Paiva, J.C.P. Faria, P. Mendes, Reverse engineered formal models for GUI testing, in: Proc. 12th Int. Workshop on Formal Methods for Industrial Critical Systems (FMICS), 1–2 Jul 2007, Berlin, Germany, 2007, pp. 218–233.

[200] A.C.R. Paiva, J.C.P. Faria, R.F.A.M. Vidal, Towards the integration of visual and formal models for GUI testing, in: Proc. 3rd Workshop on Model-Based Testing (MBT), 31 Mar–1 Apr 2007, Braga, Portugal, 2007, pp. 99–111.

[201] R.M.L.M. Moreira, A.C.R. Paiva, Visual abstract notation for gui modelling and testing—VAN4GUIM, in: Proc. 3rd Int. Conf. on Software and Data Technologies (ICSOFT 2008), 5–8 Jul 2008, Porto, Portugal, 2008, pp. 104–111.

[202] Multimodal TERESA, a tool for design and development of multi-platform applications. http://giove.isti.cnr.it/teresa.html.

[203] A.M.P. Grilo, A.C.R. Paiva, J.P. Faria, Reverse engineering of GUI models, in: INForum '09, 10–11 Sep 2009, Lisbon, Portugal, 2009, pp. 527–538.

[204] I. Morgado, A. Paiva, J. Faria, Reverse engineering of graphical user interfaces, in: Proc. 6th Int. Conf. on Software Engineering Advances (ICSEA '11), 23–29 Oct 2011, Barcelona, Spain, 2011, pp. 293–298.

[205] I. Morgado, A. Paiva, J. Faria, Dynamic reverse engineering of graphical user interfaces, Int. J. Adv. Softw. 5 (3 –4) (2012) 224–246, IARIA.

[206] R.D.F. Ferreira, J.C.P. Faria, A.C.R. Paiva, Test coverage analysis of UML activity diagrams for interactive systems, in: Proc. 2010 7th Int. Conf. on the Quality of Information and Communications Technology (QUATIC 2010), 29 Sep 2010, Porto, Portugal, 2010, pp. 268–273.

[207] R.D.F. Ferreira, J.C.P. Faria, A.C.R. Paiva, Test coverage analysis of UML state machines. Software testing, in: Proc. 2010 3rd Int. Conf. on Verification, and Validation Workshops (ICSTW), 6–10 Apr 2010, Paris, France, 2010, pp. 284–289.

[208] D. Amalfitano, A.R. Fasolino, P. Tramontana, Reverse engineering finite state machines from rich internet applications, in: Proc. 15th Working Conf. on Reverse Engineering (WCRE'08), 15–18 Oct 2008, Antwerp, Belgium, 2008, pp. 69–73.

[209] D. Amalfitano, A.R. Fasolino, P. Tramontana, Experimenting a reverse engineering technique for modelling the behaviour of rich internet applications, in: Proc. IEEE Int. Conf. on Software Maintenance (ICSM 2009), 20–26 Sep 2009, Edmonton, Canada, 2009, pp. 571–574.

[210] D. Amalfitano, A.R. Fasolino, P. Tramontana, Rich internet application testing using execution trace data, in: Proc. 2010 3rd Int. Conf. on Software Testing, Verification, and Validation Workshops (ICSTW), 6–10 Apr 2010, Paris, France, 2010, pp. 274–283.

[211] D. Amalfitano, A.R. Fasolino, A. Polcaro, P. Tramontana, DynaRIA: a tool for Ajax web application comprehension, in: Proc. 2010 IEEE 18th Int. Conf. on Program Comprehension (ICPC), 30 Jun 2010, Braga, Portugal, 2010, pp. 46–47.

[212] D. Amalfitano, A.R. Fasolino, A. Polcaro, P. Tramontana, Comprehending Ajax web applications by the DynaRIA tool, in: Proc. 2010 Seventh Int. Conf. on the Quality of Information and Communications Technology (QUATIC), 29 Sep 2010, Porto, Portugal, 2010, pp. 122–131.

[213] D. Amalfitano, A.R. Fasolino, A. Polcaro, P. Tramontana, The DynaRIA tool for the comprehension of Ajax web applications by dynamic analysis, Innov. Syst. Softw. Eng. 10 (2014), pp. 41–57, Springer-Verlag.

[214] D. Amalfitano, A.R. Fasolino, P. Tramontana, An Iterative approach for the reverse engineering of rich internet application user interfaces, in: Proc. 2010 Fifth Int. Conf. on Internet and Web Applications and Services (ICIW), 9–15 May 2010, Barcelona, Spain, 2010, pp. 401–410.

[215] D. Amalfitano, A.R. Fasolino, P. Tramontana, Using dynamic analysis for generating end user documentation for Web 2.0 applications, in: Proc. 2011 13th IEEE Int. Symposium on Web Systems Evolution (WSE), 30–30 Sep 2011, Williamsburg, VA, USA, 2011, pp. 11–20.

[216] D. Amalfitano, A.R. Fasolino, P. Tramontana, A tool-supported process for reliable classification of web pages, in: Proc. Int. Conf. on Advanced Software Engineering and Its Applications (ASEA), 10–12 Dec 2009, Jeju Island, Korea, 2009, pp. 338–345.

[217] D. Amalfitano, A.R. Fasolino, P. Tramontana, Techniques and tools for rich internet applications testing, in: Proc. 2010 12th IEEE Int. Symposium on Web Systems Evolution (WSE), 17–18 Sep 2010, Timisoara, Romania, 2010, pp. 63–72.

[218] D. Amalfitano, A.R. Fasolino, P. Tramontana, A GUI crawling-based technique for android mobile application testing, in: Proc. 3rd Int. Workshop on Testing Techniques & Experimentation Benchmarks for Event-Driven Software (TESTBEDS 2011), 21 Mar 2011, Berlin, Germany, 2011, pp. 252–261.

[219] D. Amalfitano, Reverse Engineering and Testing of Rich Internet Applications, PhD thesis, Facoltà di Ingegneria, Dipartimento di Informatica e Sistemistica, Università degli Studi di Napoli Federico II, 2011.

[220] D. Amalfitano, A.R. Fasolino, S. Carmine, A.M. Memon, P. Tramontana, Using GUI ripping for automated testing of android applications, in: Proc. 27th IEEE Int. Conf. on

Automated Software Engineering (ASE'12), 3–7 Sep 2012, Essen, Germany, 2012, pp. 258–261.

[221] D. Amalfitano, A.R. Fasolino, P. Tramontana, S. Carmine, G. Imparato, A toolset for GUI testing of android applications, in: Proc. 2012 28th IEEE Int. Conf. on Software Maintenance (ICSM), 23–28 Sep 2012, Trento, Italy, 2012, pp. 650–653.

[222] D. Amalfitano, A.R. Fasolino, P. Tramontana, N. Amatucci, Considering context events in event-based testing of mobile applications, in: Proc. 2013 IEEE Sixth Int. Conf. on Software Testing, Verification and Validation Workshops (ICSTW), 18–22 Mar 2013, Luxembourg, 2013, pp. 126–133.

[223] Y. Miao, X. Yang, An FSM based GUI test automation model, in: Proc. 2010 11th Int. Conf. on Control, Automation, Robotics & Vision (ICARCV), 7–10 Dec 2010, Singapore, 2010, pp. 120–126.

[224] X. Yang, Y. Miao, Y. Zhang, Model-driven GUI automation for efficient information exchange between heterogeneous electronic medical record systems, in: J. Pokorny, V. Repa, K. Richta, W. Wojtkowski, H. Linger, C. Barry, M. Lang (Eds.), Information Systems Development, Business Systems and Services: Modeling and Development, Springer, New York, NY, 2011, pp. 799–810.

[225] P. Aho, M. Suarez, T. Kanstren, A.M. Memon, Industrial adoption of automatically extracted GUI models for testing, in: Proc. Int. Workshop on Experiences and Empirical Studies in Software Modelling (EESSMod 2013), 1 Oct 2013, Miami, FL, USA, 2013, pp. 49–54.

[226] Jenkins, an open source continuous integration server. http://jenkins-ci.org.

[227] P. Aho, M. Suarez, T. Kanstren, A.M. Memon, Murphy tools: utilizing extracted GUI models for industrial software testing, in: Testing: Academic & Industrial Conference—Practice and Research Techniques (TAIC PART), 4 Apr 2014, Cleveland, OH, USA, 2014.

[228] J. Chen, S. Subramaniam, Specification-based testing for GUI-based applications, Softw. Qual. J. 10 (3) (2002) 205–224, Kluwer Academic Publishers.

[229] A. Mesbah, A. van Deursen, D. Roest, Invariant-based automatic testing of modern web applications, IEEE Trans. Softw. Eng. 38 (1) (2012) 35–53, IEEE Computer Society.

[230] C. Duda, G. Frey, D. Kossmann, R. Matter, C. Zhou, AJAX Crawl: making AJAX applications searchable, in: Proc. 2009 IEEE 25th Int. Conf. on Data Engineering (ICDE '09), 29 Mar 2009, Shanghai, China, 2009, pp. 78–89.

[231] M. Joorabchi, A. Mesbah, Reverse engineering iOS mobile applications, in: Proc. 2012 19th Working Conf. on Reverse Engineering (WCRE), 15–18 Oct 2012, Kingston, ON, Canada, 2012, pp. 177–186.

[232] Javassist, an open source library for Java bytecode manipulation. http://www.jboss.org/javassist.

[233] L. Mariani, M. Pezzè, O. Riganelli, M. Santoro, AutoBlackTest: a tool for automatic black-box testing, in: 2011 33rd Int. Conf. on Software Engineering (ICSE), 21–28 May 2011, Honolulu, HI, USA, 2011, pp. 1013–1015.

[234] IBM Rational Functional Tester, a commercial tool for automated functional testing and regression testing. http://www.ibm.com/software/products/en/functional.

[235] TeachingBox, an open source tool providing advanced machine learning techniques. http://sourceforge.net/projects/teachingbox.

[236] G. Fraser, A. Arcuri, EvoSuite: automatic test suite generation for object-oriented software, in: Proc. Joint Meeting of the European Software Engineering Conf. and the ACM SIGSOFT Symp. on the Foundations of Software Engineering (ESEC/FSE'11), 5–9 Sep 2011, Szeged, Hungary, 2011, pp. 416–419.

[237] S. Arlt, C. Bertolini, S. Pahl, M. Schäf, Trends in model-based GUI testing, Adv. Comput. 86 (2012) 183–222, Academic Press.

ABOUT THE AUTHORS

Pekka Aho works as a Research Scientist at the VTT Technical Research Centre of Finland, Oulu. He received his master's degree in computer engineering from University of Oulu, Finland in 2009 and is currently finishing his Ph.D. degree under the supervision of Dr. Juha Röning. His research interests include software test automation and model-based testing with current focus on automatically extracting models of graphical user interfaces for testing. Before his academic career, he has worked as Software Designer and Project Manager in the industry.

Teemu Kanstrén is a Senior Researcher at the VTT Technical Research Centre of Finland, Oulu, and at the time of writing this chapter, he was a Visiting Post-Doctoral Fellow at University of Toronto. His work involves research and development in software engineering with the aim to improve the state of the art, to produce practically useful solutions, and help industry partners adopt them. His specific topics of interest include advanced test automation solutions such as model-based testing, and he is the main author of the open source model-based testing tool OSMO Tester. He got his Ph.D. degree on test automation and model-based testing at the University of Oulu, Finland in 2010.

Dr. Tomi Räty received his Ph.D. degree in information processing science from the University of Oulu, Finland. He is currently a Principal Research Scientist at the VTT Technical Research Centre of Finland, Oulu. His current research interests include data analysis, machine-learning technologies, model-based testing, and software platforms. He is the author or co-author of more than 30 papers published in various conferences and journals, and he has served as a Reviewer for multiple journals and at numerous conferences.

Dr. Juha Röning is Professor of Embedded Systems in the Department of Computer Science and Engineering at the University of Oulu, Finland. He is a principal investigator of the Biometics and Intelligent Systems Group (BISG). In 1985, he received Asla/Fullbright scholarship. From 1985 to 1986, he was a visiting research scientist in the Center for Robotic Research at the University of Cincinnati. From 1986 to 1989, he held a Young Researcher Position in the Finnish Academy. In 2000, he was nominated as Fellow of SPIE. He has two patents and has published more than 300 papers in the areas of computer vision, robotics, intelligent signal analysis, and software security.

CHAPTER THREE

Automated Test Oracles: State of the Art, Taxonomies, and Trends

Rafael A.P. Oliveira*, Upulee Kanewala[†], Paulo A. Nardi*
*Department of Computer Systems, University of São Paulo (ICMC/USP), São Carlos, SP, Brazil
[†]Computer Science Department, Colorado State University (CSU), Fort Collins, Colorado, USA

Contents

Abstract

Test oracle methods have changed significantly over time, which has resulted in clear shifts in the research literature. Over the years, the testing techniques, strategies, and criteria utilized by researchers went through technical developments due to the improvement of technologies and programming languages. Software testing designers, known as testers, currently have several resources to increase their confidence in the software under test correctness. All of these software testing resources are supposed to include a mechanism to decide whether a particular execution is considered a failure or not. In software testing environments, this decision is the responsibility of the test oracle. Despite the evolution and adaptation of testing techniques over more than 30 years, test oracles remain a particular and relevant issue. In this chapter, using literary evidence from a pool of about 300 studies directly related to test oracles, we present a classification of test oracles based on a taxonomy that considers their source of information and notations. Based on this classification, we perform a quantitative analysis to highlight the shifts in (evolution of) research on test oracles. Exploring geographical and quantitative information, we analyzed the maturity of this field using coauthorship networks among studies published between 1978 and 2013. Further, we determine the most prolific authors and their countries, main conferences and journals, supporting tools, and academic efforts and use a comparative analysis between academia and industry. Finally, from these analyses, we draw an analytic reflection about contemporary test oracle approaches and a criticism about oracle trends.

1. INTRODUCTION

A fundamental element in the automated testing processes is the *test oracle*, which represents a method (program, function, set of data, or table of values) to verify whether the SUT (Software Under Test) behaves correctly on a particular execution [1–3]. This element plays a decisive role in software testing processes establishing a decision about the correctness of an SUT result [4–6]. According to Ivory and Hearst [7], test oracles must support testers' decision about the SUT behavior against an input, establishing which results/behaviors are acceptable. In this sense, test oracles are reliable sources of information that testers can trust to decide the correct test results [8–10]. In technical terms, a test oracle can be carried out in different ways: functions, assertions, processes, data, parallel programs, and others [11]. On the other hand, even a human being can play the role of test oracle deciding about the correctness of test results. Regardless of the different ways of implementation, oracles bear a fundamental responsibility for the whole testing process: they judge and report to testers whether the result of an execution is correct [1,12,13].

Developing an adequate test oracle for particular test domains offers a number of challenges. First, oracles are generally separated from the SUT and, then, one needs complex pre-/postconditions to automate them in testing environments [14]. Second, developing test oracles involves controllability and observability issues [15]. This means that often it is necessary to determine external mechanisms to control and observe the functionality of the SUT, controlling and observing different inputs' effects on SUT's outputs. In addition, there are cases in which the tester must expend a precious amount of project time verifying test outputs in order to define whether they are acceptable. Finally, depending on the complexity of the output, in some occasions, it is not possible to establish a test oracle. In these cases, the tester could explore heuristics (statistical functions or models) to provide expected results, establishing an oracle assumption.

Although much of the Software Engineering (SE) literature provides evidence about the importance of automated testing activities, in practice test oracle automation is well known as being a difficult task. During the development of an automated test environment (including a test oracle) in practical software projects, the tester deals with at least four different delicate issues. First is defining what should be tested. Second is defining what are acceptable outputs and under which conditions. Third is establishing acceptable outputs. Fourth is identifying reliable sources of information and models which one can trust as a reference for test oracles.

Identifying the correct aspects related to each issue presented previously is essential for testers. Once testers have an adequate and automated test scenario, including a mechanism to support their final decisions (oracle), the software product can be evaluated in a productive and effective way. Then, testers can load and run test cases automatically, without the necessity of human intervention after setting test cases, allowing automatic setting of system conditions and persistence of these conditions. This automated test scenario must include resources for comparisons between current and expected results. In other words, methods to analyze each individual test case result (pass/fail).

The current scenario in the sense of software quality reveals that there is no more space for poorly tested software systems. Despite significant improvements of software development resources, testing activities have become increasingly important and crucial to the daily life of common people. Software systems developed within the last 5 years reach more people in a shorter time than decades ago, so delivering nontested software might decree the unacceptability of a product [15]. Demanding customers, ranking in software centers, customer's reviews, etc., drive the current software systems to be literally viewed as a product and not a solution to be chosen by consumers. These aspects increase the software industry competitiveness. Therefore, developers regard the test as one of the most important activities during the software development process.

The central theme of this chapter has to do with the test oracles, which represent indispensable mechanisms in automated test environments. A test oracle is a relevant topic in SE, and researchers and practitioners have studied them for more than 30 years. Among the main goals of this chapter, we present the following:

- A broad taxonomy about test oracles, with practical examples and detailed descriptions;
- A temporal evolution of research on test oracle;
- Demographic and quantitative information based on a pool of studies directly related to test oracles; and
- A critical view about trends and relevant issues to be faced by the researchers in the next years.

Following Section 1, the rest of this chapter is organized as follows:

- Section 2 introduces basic concepts of software testing and presents comparative information about manual testing and automated testing. In addition, this section describes oracle definitions using a high level of information and giving practical examples;
- Section 3 describes various test oracle approaches to establish an oracle taxonomy. This information was collected and classified from scientific studies related to test oracles. Practical examples and code excerpts are presented to illustrate the oracle rule in real software testing scenarios;
- Section 4 reports the test oracle's state of the art. This section uses a pool of about 300 test oracle scientific studies to compose a survey. We explore quantitative and geographical analysis to describe the general scenario of oracle research over more than 30 years. In addition, we present similar surveys available, supporting tools, and academic dissertations available;
- Section 5 drives forward a set of oracle relevant issues that must be faced by researchers and practitioners on software testing. Using Section 4 as background, these thoughts are based on our own point of view about present and future research on test oracles; and
- Section 6 observes the final and concluding remarks addressed to test oracles in this chapter. Furthermore, this section reproduces relevance and importance of test oracles for automated software testing environments.

2. BACKGROUND

Despite the advanced resources of software development available, programmers can make *mistakes* during the process of writing code. Such mistakes set *faults* for performing a process, method, or activity. Manifestations of faults can lead software systems to inconsistent states and then several *errors* might be revealed [16]. In essence, the execution of a defective source code leads the program to an unexpected state and that is visible by means of the system output, revealing failures [17,18]. The central point of this chapter refers to the means for defining whether the current results agree with the expected outcomes in software testing scenarios—test oracle. This section presents a wide view of software testing concepts and, after that, it introduces the concept of test oracles in this scenario.

2.1. Software Testing Concepts

Myers *et al.* [16] emphasized that software testing activities can be the process, or series of processes, whose goal is running a system in order to find errors. According to Bertolino [19,20], software testing is the execution process of a software product aiming to check whether it reaches its specifications considering the environment in which it was designed. Hunter and Strooper [21] agree that software testing is the main resource to check specifications against current behaviors. The standard way of thinking about software testing is that there are different useful definitions to describe it. In this study, we define software testing as a way to verify whether the SUT behaves in accordance with its specification through a controlled execution. Furthermore, Bertolino [19] considers the following software testing definition as a reference framework, allowing different associations with testing concepts: ". . . Software testing consists of the dynamic verification of the behavior of a program on a finite set of test cases, suitably selected from the usually infinite execution domain, against the specified expected behavior . . ."

In this introductory scenario, one can realize that over more than 30 years of research and practice, software testing environments have suffered significant changes and advances [15]. New software testing activities incorporate innovations in order to follow trends such as object-oriented (OO) [22], aspect-oriented [23–25], Web applications [26–28], and embedded systems [29,30]. This would allow one to affirm that test activities are highly dependent on the SUT. As a consequence of this dependence and particularity of the SUTs, many software companies allocate a specific team of practitioners to develop their own testing tools [1].

Despite particularities testing activities have generic points, as well. These general points are techniques and criteria that aim to mitigate efforts to discover errors and to decrease testing costs [18]. Testing techniques and criteria support the achievement of testing activities in a systematic and judicious way. Each technique has the support of various test criteria to perform the exercise of different features of the SUT [16,19]. Therefore, testing techniques can be considered strategies to minimize effort and maximize efficiency for detecting defects [18]. Regarding only testing techniques, one can highlight mainly *functional testing*, *structural testing*, and *error-based testing* [15].

Conventional wisdom has it that functional testing, also known as blackbox testing, consists of a testing strategy based only on the program's specifications [16]. This testing strategy disregards SUT's internal structures, and it can be carried out using a set of test cases. On the other hand, structural testing, also called white-box testing, employs SUT's internal structures as a source of information for different tests and coverage analysis. Finally, error-based testing uses information about frequent errors that are common during the process of writing code in software development projects [15].

In addition, during software development processes, there are testing phases to be considered. Among these phases the most popular are unit testing, which is the phase where the main test focus is to assess the correctness of the smaller units of the SUT (e.g., functions and modules); integration testing, whose goal is to verify the adequacy of different software modules working together as whole solution; and system testing, which aims at detecting faults in systems [16,18,19].

Applying appropriate software testing techniques and criteria during all phases of the development process implies a general increase of project costs for developers and, consequently, customers [18]. However, according to Seo and Choi [31], complexity and costs of software testing increase as do the size of the SUT. Consequently, at every stage of the development life cycle, it is necessary to apply testing techniques and strategies. Thus, many times, testing activities take more than 50% of the time of development [16]. For instance, it is possible to mention that a proper test for an SUT as a whole would take enough time to delay official commitments and deadlines. Therefore, different software companies have a policy of releasing unfinished systems under development and waiting for complaints from users to improve the system's quality and reliability [32,33]. It is often said that software developers and testers, generally, do not have enough time for testing their projects.

The most appropriate solution to alleviate the problems of cost and time associated with software testing is using automated tests during different stages of the development process and in different modules of the SUT [20]. An adequate automated testing has to provide productive and reliable approaches [7]. Test automation is a matter of emphasis on the SE area because they promote more systematic testing approaches [7,20]. Automated testing activities can bring significant cost savings to software development projects and are a key factor to help reducing analysis costs [15]. Section 2.2 presents common practical aspects associated with the automated test.

2.2. Automated Software Testing

Due to the plurality of software systems available in the last years, it is possible to determine different meanings for the term automated testing. According to Dustin *et al.* [34], an automated test may mean a wide variety of aspects associated with the testing processes such as using capture/record/playback tools, test-driven development, unit testing, and custom scripts. In spite of these variations, the authors highlight four fundamental characteristics that differ between manual and automated testing approaches: (1) automated tests are software development; (2) test automation enhances manual efforts once its focus is on automating hard manual tests; (3) automated testing activities do not replace manual tests and human intervention with testing strategies and techniques; and (4) automated tests cannot be separated from manual tests because these approaches are complementary.

To figure out an adequate definition of automated software testing, we prefer to list some basic conditions that should be achieved in a testing scenario. Some of these conditions were suggested by Hoffman [13]. According to this author, all conditions need not necessarily be satisfied to set an automated testing environment. These conditions are as follows:
- Loading and running test cases automatically;
- Lacking human intervention after setting test cases;
- Allowing automatic system conditions setting and persistence of these conditions;
- Including resources for getting relevant results;
- Including resources for comparisons between current and expected results; and
- Including methods to analyze each individual test case result (pass/fail).

On the other hand, for the manual test, a human (the tester) provides inputs to the SUT and manually verifies its outputs. Manual testing involves six steps that do not necessarily need to be performed completely [16,35]: (1) coding; (2) code update in some excerpts; (3) build/compilation; (4) running code and, sometimes, filling out test forms; (5) checking log files, databases, external services, screen outputs, variable's values, etc.; and (6) tester/developer results checking. In this scenario, manual approaches have become a common practice among software developers before they deliver a version for a testing team. In case the code does not work as it is expected to, some previous steps should be reconsidered [20,36].

Table 3.1 presents basic comparative characteristics regarding automated and manual testing environments. These characteristics should be fairly presented pondering important aspects of a development and test environment such as cost and productivity [36]. The advantages of adopting automated testing are worthy: simple replay, regression support, time to market, and high productivity are some of them [11,20]. On the other hand, manual testing is simple to adopt and has a low cost in the short term [36].

There are many deep and fair comparisons between manual and automated testing regarding variations in project and team size. Using this thinking as a premise, Table 3.2 draws a comparison where advantages and disadvantages are numbered. In this comparison, we consider several aspects such as complexity, efficiency, efficacy, productivity, and cost. For the most of these aspects, automated approaches work better than manual ones. Although it is true, that human monitoring is necessary and imperative for a wide variety of test scenarios. The most notable advantage of manual approaches is the fact that a person running tests manually can identify unexpected behaviors that automated testing might not be able to identify. A human being is able to notice screen oscillations, delays, or any unexpected behavior that an automated testing system would have difficulty identifying [13,36].

Over the last three decades, automated testing approaches have suffered from advancements. As a representative illustration of these advancements, one can include the improvement of test oracles approaches. Year after year,

Table 3.1 Implications for Manual and Automated Testing

	Manual	Automated
Test conduction	Human based	Machine based
Reexecution	Time consuming	Quick
Regression support	No	Yes
Coding	Simple	Complex
Project time	Time consuming	Short
Productivity	Low	High

Table 3.2 Comparison Between Manual and Automated Testing

Advantages	Disadvantages
Manual testing	
• A human being monitoring might notice unexpected behaviors • Notification of inconsistencies regarding different executions of data, states, settings, and environments	• Efficiency in detecting errors must consider human fatigue • Determined test data, iterations, and combinations may require automation • Certain aspects may not have manual solutions (i.e., performance analysis) • When testers are waiting for certain errors, after a few repetitions, this may impairs the detection of defects
Automated testing	
• More complex, efficient, and well-elaborated test cases • Tools are able to match amount, productivity, and efficiency • Possibility of technology transfer between industry and academia • Efficiency for error detections in specific domains	• Some complex domains of test provide extreme difficulty for automations • Only check the conditions for which the automation was designed to investigate • Difficulties on defining which conditions should be checked to consider a test as successful • Implementations to generate efficient test cases are complex • Difficulty in predicting the way an SUT should behave and what consequences are expected after an execution

new studies provide more efficient and productive ways for SUTs have their outputs checked, aiming to reduce human efforts. Section 2.3 presents the main conceptual aspects associated with test oracles in automated testing environments.

2.3. Test Oracles

A plurality of definitions and concepts can be associated with test oracles. According to Machado [9] and Hamlet [37], the definition of test oracles concerns decision procedures and strategies for interpreting and judging the test results. When a set of test cases TC are available, the tester might implement test oracles as an object comparator between test case outputs and SUT's current output. In this case, regarding an SUT **P**, one can consider an input domain $\mathbf{D}$, an output domain $\mathbf{X}$ and, then, $\mathbf{TC}$ should be a function for matching the inputs $\mathbf{D'} \subseteq \mathbf{D}$ and the outputs $\mathbf{X'} \in \mathbf{X}$. In this scenario, $\mathbf{D'}$ corresponds to a valid input in the domain $\mathbf{D}$ and $\mathbf{dom(TC)=D'}$ denotes the domain of $\mathbf{TC}$. In this sense, $\mathbf{TC(t)}$ should be considered a valid output for each $\mathbf{t} \in \mathbf{dom(TC)}$. Then, $\mathbf{P(t)}$ represents the result of $\mathbf{P}$ executing with input $\mathbf{t}$. Then, one can define that the program $\mathbf{P}$ meets $\mathbf{TC}$ if and only if it meets it on all inputs in $\mathbf{dom(TC)}$. Therefore, considering that $\mathbf{TC}$ might have infinite correspondences, a finite set of test cases should be selected. Considering this scenario, a function $\mathbf{O}$ called oracle for $\mathbf{P}$ on $\mathbf{TC}$ if for all $\mathbf{t} \in \mathbf{D}$:

$$O(t) = \begin{cases} \text{true (pass)} & P(t) = TC(t) \\ \text{false (fail)} & P(t) \neq TC(t) \\ \text{true (pass)} & t \notin \text{dom(TC)} \end{cases}$$

Technically, test oracles represent a mechanism to check test outputs. One can consider this short definition as satisfactory, however real software testing scenarios and different test output domains provide ample evidence that this premise must be interpreted in different ways to be considered true [38–40]. To put it succinctly, before presenting more deep definitions, it is necessary to consider test oracles as a piece inside the software testing context. This piece can be represented, for example, by a tester checking outputs and writing test reports. In this case, in particular, the oracle is called a *human oracle*. On the other hand, this piece can be totally automated by several processes able to judge the correctness of test outputs.

Regarding the automated testing scenario presented in Section 2.2, one can observe that it is possible to set a test environment in which an automated oracle is not included. In this scenario, generally, testers apply several techniques for achieving structural coverage and in generating test data. However, the SUT's outputs or behaviors should be checked or evaluated by a human tester (human oracle). The efforts and project time expended by the tester on evaluating test outputs are known as the *human oracle cost* [41]. Human oracles are common in several situations such as evaluating the effectiveness of new test techniques, using the tester know-how about the SUT behavior, and detecting unexpected errors.

In order to achieve productive software testing in large scales, testers should automate their test oracles to mitigate manual efforts. Disregarding manual approaches, oracles play a vital role in automated testing and their neglect can result in an unproductive test. To illustrate this, Fig. 3.1 presents a wide concept map of software testing context and it illustrates test oracles as a supportive technology [42]. The concept map represents a general view of software testing matching sources of information, test phases, test techniques, testing criteria, processes, and test oracles. According to this figure, a test oracle is a software testing technology that can be associated with different processes and test techniques.

Figure 3.1 provides a concept from which it is possible to infer that test oracles are independent from any other software testing aspects. Regarding a more specific software test environment, test oracles play a fundamental rule as the conclusion of a series of processes that might include test case generation, test data selection, test sequencing, and test execution. In order to illustrate a scenario like this, Machado [9] suggested a generic model of a black-box testing process including test case generation, test data selection, automated execution, and test oracle. Figure 3.2 provides a practical example of a generic association among all of these phases in a practical scenario.

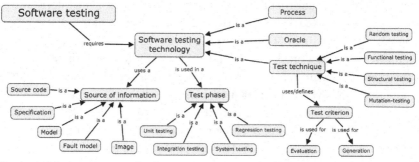

Figure 3.1 A concept map of software testing. *Extracted from Durelli et al. [42] with kind permission from the authors.*

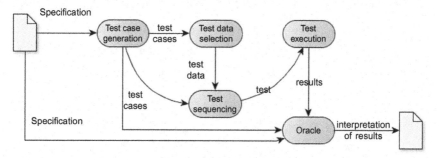

Figure 3.2 A generic model of a black-box testing process.

In Fig. 3.2, depending on the output domain, a tester can implement a productive test oracle in the form of a program, a set of assertions, a function, a heuristic, or a data structure with expected outputs. Addressing these varieties, according to Chan and Tse [43], under practical and theoretical points of view, test oracles can frame fundamental differences. Concerning the theory, Chan and Tse [43] argue that by means of the program's specifications one is able to determine appropriate test oracles. However, it is important to highlight that, in practice, oracle mechanisms could be costly, hard to implement, or may not exist [6,11,44]. So, the implementation of an automated mechanism to the same end as a human being judging test outputs is a challenging task to be faced by test designers [45].

Despite the variety, in practice, aspects related to test oracles deal with a primary issue in software testing activities—deciding about the correctness of an SUT P, against predetermined test data. Figure 3.3 presents a traditional and generic test oracle structure using flowchart elements. In this case, the test oracle accesses the set of data needed to evaluate the correctness of the test output. This set of data comes from the specification of the SUT and contains sufficient information for supporting the oracle's final decision.

Figure 3.4 introduces several structures which represent test oracle functions. In the figure, it is possible to notice that, in order to adequately play their rules, some test oracles may require test cases. However, there are cases where test oracles are able to provide a test result based on test data (inputs). There are cases where a set of information and data about the expected results are needed to decide about the correctness of SUTs (Fig. 3.4A) [46–51]. On the other hand, test designers can create test oracles from formal methods or specifications (Fig. 3.4B) [52–56]. Regarding most sophisticated cases, test oracles can place into service test data inputs to derive expected outputs of the SUT (Fig. 3.4C) [57–61]. Finally, as we already mentioned, one can consider the human oracles, where testers can use their own knowledge about the SUT to check if outputs are in accordance with specifications

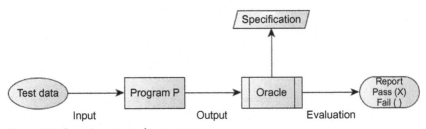

Figure 3.3 Generic test oracle structure.

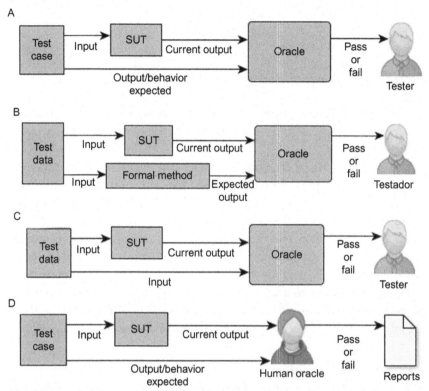

Figure 3.4 Test oracles using different sources of information. (A) Using expected output/behaviors. (B) Using formal models/specifications. (C) Using test data. (D) Human oracles.

(Fig. 3.4D) [41,62–64]. Other possibilities could be contemplated, for example, a test oracle can be designed considering a reliable model of output from which basic features can be extracted to be compared with current outputs from the SUT [39,40].

Regarding complexity and costs, one can consider test oracles based on expected output/behaviors as unsophisticated and quick to implement. Regarding Fig. 3.4A, a tester can deal with these oracles using one of the various frameworks that have come to be known collectively as an *xUnit* family. xUnit frameworks allow the unit testing in SUTs implemented in different programming languages [65]. For example, in *JUnit* [66], which is an *xUnit* framework for Java, testers can get different test oracles in their code using assertions, which mean a true/false statement placed in a program to check unit and partial results. Figure 3.5 presents an example of a test

```
1     public void testDVDInStore ( ) {
2     Store store = new Store ( ) ;
3     boolean result = store.checkByTitle ("The Godfather III") ;
4     assertEquals (true , result) ;
5     }
```

Figure 3.5 Test oracle using an *xUnit* framework.

oracle using the *JUnit* framework. In this example, line of code 4 represents a test oracle to check the correctness of the method *boolean Store. checkByTitle(String)*.

According to Fig. 3.4B, when testers have at their disposal a mathematical model that faithfully represents the SUT such as a Finite-State Machine (FSM) or a Petri net, it is possible to automate a test oracle from this model. Along the same lines of the example presented, regarding to Fig. 3.4C, it is possible to set a test oracle using test data. For instance, through outputs given from parallel executions or using another versions of the SUT, a tester can build a test oracle to compare those outputs and current outputs. In these cases, it is important to assume that the version used, called the reference program, meets all the specifications of the SUT. This sort of test oracle frequently uses the cases of a regression test and a mutation test.

2.3.1 The Oracle Problem

The decision about the correctness of an execution and, consequently, revelations of failures is the most essential aspect related to any testing activity, even the manual ones [3,45]. In a software testing environment, test oracles play this essential aspect, which is a hard task because it is not trivial to find out a set of expected outputs for SUTs [43]. For instance, we can wonder about a situation in which the SUT **P** must figure out the value of π on a determined precision of decimal numbers. Unless it has another program **Q**, which is working properly to solve the same problem, it is impossible to determine if **P**'s outputs are right or not [6]. Another similar case is when **P** represents a nondeterministic program and **P(vk)** matches different possible outputs, all of them correct [43,45]. That means that the process of deciding about correctness of SUT's is often much harder than it seems and involves finding solutions for different kind of problems [4,6,67]. Problems like these have been frequent in the software industry during the last three decades. Due to this, testers consider the task to determine reliable sources to judge all SUT's outputs a complex and nontrivial.

The *oracle problem* is set in cases when, using practical means, it is impossible or too difficult to decide about the correctness of test cases and test outputs [6]. Along the same lines, we would define the oracle problem as the absence of oracle or cases when it is too expensive to apply the oracle. There are not enough test oracles to always support the right decisions. Due to this fact, the oracle problem is a fundamental challenge presented in the literature often [2,4,9,68]. This is one reason why testers classify the design of test oracle as a complex and cognitive activity rather than being a routine activity [37,43]. Even having a test oracle to support evaluations of test results, practitioners frequently identify unpredictable points about the use of oracles [68]. Depending on the oracle, the following problems may occur:

- False positives: the test result passes; however, some inconsistent state might not be checked. Regarding a test scenario, a false positive is when a test result incorrectly rejects a true null hypothesis; and
- False negatives: cases in which the test result fails while the SUT is working well. In a test scenario, a false negative is the failure to reject a false null hypothesis.

Some research aims to alleviate the oracle problem using specific techniques. In these cases, testing tools are able to support testers' decisions about the correctness of an SUT execution [39,40,69]. However, testers must also consider the possibility that oracles can often support them making wrong decisions. Depending on the SUT, it is extremely difficult to predict expected behaviors to be compared against current behaviors [39,70]. Failures can come out under different situations which make checking the result complex or impossible to be performed [71]. The oracle problem can be challenging when SUT outputs are given in complex formats such as images, sounds, and virtual environments [39].

2.3.2 Trade-off on Test Oracles

Dealing with test oracles brings some trade-offs. For testers, these situations involve losing project time and increasing costs in return for gaining quality aspects. Scientific studies explore the trade-off between efficiency in identifying failures in SUTs and complexity in developing oracles [72–74]. The more effective the oracle, the more complex the information that it uses to determine if the program execution is in line with the expected results. Consequently, defining an oracle as complex as the original program is usually not acceptable.

Other trade-offs must be explored as well. For instance, if it is possible to define a fully automated oracle to identify all possible failures present in the SUT's outputs, there would be no need for the program itself because the oracle could be used instead. Then, we could consider that, regardless of the goal in studying a new oracle approach, it is important to know: What already exists? Where does the new approach fit? And how do we compare them? This allows, for example, one to identify what position in the trade-off a new study fits. For practitioners, it becomes easier to identify what kind of approach is best suited for a particular problem, that is, which oracle approach should best be used to support the test of a software product.

Considering broader scenarios of test automation including test oracles, testers should anticipate dealing with more complex trade-off situations. In these cases, the trade-offs increase because an important aspect is that both the reliable test set problem [75] and the oracle problem [6] are open issues. A set of test data $\mathbf{T}$ for a software system $\mathbf{P}$ is reliable if it reveals that $\mathbf{P}$ contains an error whenever $\mathbf{P}$ is incorrect. According to Howden [75], an effective testing strategy which is reliable for all software systems cannot be implemented. In this context, there is often no way to define in practice a criterion test that, once applied, can identify all errors in every program; likewise, there is no way to define in practice a test oracle that identifies all wrong outputs in every program [4]. In particular cases, this means that one must consider existing resources, the number of possible inputs (input domain), complexity in defining the respective outputs for all inputs, time, and cost. Thus, the tester must always weigh the resources available with time and test effectiveness.

A lot of research on software testing focuses on approaches that seek to change the balance of the trade-off in favor of some variable related to it. In the case of reliable test set problems, for example, many studies aim to find an approach or data selection criteria to identify more errors with a fixed and finite amount of resources for an application domain [51,76]. Other areas of research involve the generalization of results, i.e., whether an approach for a specific domain can be used in other domains, and how effective it is [77,78]. Comparative studies are often published to answer such questions [3,79]. Section 3 brings explanations about the most studied and reported test oracle taxonomies in accordance with researchers and practitioners.

3. ORACLES TAXONOMIES

Different authors [1,11–13,36,45,80] have dedicated their efforts in writing theories and classifications and taxonomies of test oracles. Due to the diversity of software domains, currently there is no standardized test oracle taxonomy and the existing classifications could depend on the source of information, the SUT's output, or the automation method considered by the oracle. In this section, we present some of the most common oracle taxonomies and classifications. We present oracle taxonomies found in different kinds of SE studies conducted by academia members and practitioners. In this section, we separated these classifications into three groups: (1) generic taxonomies; (2) specific taxonomies; and (3) taxonomy using oracle information characteristics. In addition, we present some example to support theoretical descriptions.

3.1. Generic Classifications

In this section, we introduce general classifications in which test oracles can or cannot fit. Although these classifications are well known by many researchers and practitioners, they are not often mentioned in studies of the test oracle. These classifications are associated with the general purpose of the test oracles and they are not associated with technical aspects applied in order to implement the oracle function such as source of information or automation level. Below we present some characteristics that oracles can or cannot meet.

3.1.1 Pseudo-Oracles and Partial Oracles [81,82]

Davis and Weyuker [4] were two of the first authors to formalize and discuss the oracle problem. They sought solutions that alleviate the fact that it is impossible in practice to define a complete and totally reliable oracle for all SUTs. Given the impossibility of defining an ideal oracle, the authors discuss two possible options: *pseudo-oracles* and *partial oracles*.

According to Davis and Weyuker [4], pseudo-oracles are programs written by a second team, in parallel to the SUT, and following the same specifications. Both oracle and SUT run with the same input data and outputs are compared. This concept can be considered in two aspects. First, one could consider any code or executable model as a pseudo-oracle. Second, the margin of accuracy between the pseudo-oracle and SUT could be applied to allow acceptable discrepancies between results.

There is no guarantee that an oracle is free of faults hence *pseudo*. Accordingly, when the SUT's output is not equivalent to the oracle output, one must go through the debug process to check which one actually has the fault. As we mentioned before, if the oracle is incorrect, i.e., the oracle indicates a failure when there is no failure, this is a false negative. On the other hand, if both programs present the same wrong result, the verdict will be that the SUT passed the test when it actually did not—false positive.

Along the same lines, partial oracles aim to identify where test results are incorrect, even without knowledge of the correct output [6]. In other words, a partial oracle should support the tester's decision about the correctness of a test execution without expected outputs. Testers might resort to partial oracles when it is impossible or too difficult to define the expected result. That is, they must account for what is certainly wrong and analyze whether the SUT's output is plausible. For instance, one can affirm that a result of a sin function cannot be outside the "−1" and "1" boundary. If it is outside such a range, the result is clearly wrong. Examples of partial oracles are found in many different ways [21,83,84]. Pre- and postconditions often define contracts which must be respected in the code. Although it is true that if an SUT passes a test and no error is found, it may still be incorrect because the partial oracle only indicates that the program produces data within a plausible result, but it does not mean the result is confidently correct.

Partial oracles may seem impractical or inefficient in the present day, as it was presented in 1981 and it is natural to think that nowadays larger and more complex programs make it impractical to implement parallel and costly versions of the SUT. However, a literature review shows that pseudo-oracles can still be viable and studies are still in use [85]. For instance, 24 years after Davis and Weyuker's [4] proposal, Hummel and Atkinson [86] exploit technologies to find components for reuse as a means of discovering pseudo-oracles on the Internet. In this case, the components found have the same function of an SUT and can be used as pseudo-oracles to support statistical testing of a self-built component implementation. This idea is explored further in the present day by other research, as with the use of Web services.

3.1.2 Passive and Active Oracles

Along the same lines of the classification presented before, the literature presents a generic classification among test oracles: passive and active oracles. It is often said that active oracles directly drive their own testing activities reproducing the SUT behavior and generating expected outputs [87–90]. Contrary to this premise, passive oracles act as simple comparators between current and expected test results. According to Pasala et al. [91], an active oracle mimics the behavior of the SUT and a passive oracle verifies the SUT behavior, but it does not reproduce it.

Active test oracles are common in the literature. A traditional example is test oracles using formal models to reproduce expected outputs. On the other hand, as an example of a passive test oracle, one can mention the approach present by McDonald and Strooper [72], in which passive test oracles are implemented from translations of Object-Z specifications. Another example is provided in the study conducted by Shukla *et al.* [92]. In this approach, the authors present a passive oracle built as a wrapper with checking functions based on the API (Application Program Interface) of a software component. According to the authors, this technique can be applied in a wide variety of software components in most programming languages.

The active–passive oracle concept is transverse to the pseudo- and partial oracles (Section 3.1.1). A program written in parallel, i.e., a pseudo-oracle, reproduces the behavior of the SUT; therefore, it is also an active oracle. The partial oracle that does not reproduce the result but compares it with a set of constraints is a passive oracle.

3.2. Specific Taxonomies

The general purpose of this section describes specific test oracle taxonomies on software testing presented in the literature. Research on test oracles defined the majority of these classifications regarding different aspects such as source of information, automation process, and information characteristics. In this section, we present these classifications highlighting their particularities. Each subsection represents a particular classification and the context in which this classification was suggested. We use a broad variety of practical examples to support our explanations.

3.2.1 Source of Oracles [80]

Beizer [80], interested in characteristics used as sources of information in different test oracles, identified five different types of oracles. According to him, oracles are defined following different aspects such as source of information, data input, and generation of expected outputs. Beizer [80] then defined five types of oracles according to their sources of information:

- Input/outcome oracle: more complex and the most common, this test oracle specifies the expected outcome for a specified input;
- Kiddie testing: the principle of these oracles is common; it runs the test using test data and reporting whether the application crashes. In more complex cases, this type of oracle should verify some characteristics searching for incoherency, and after this, it gives a verdict;
- Regression test: expected outputs are given from the previous version of the SUT.
- Besides having a new version of the SUT, the tester should consider test data with the same outcome as the last version;

- Pattern test set: decisions are based on a pattern previously created and validated. This type of oracle is common for validating compilers, Web browsers, and word processors; and
- Existing programs: the test is performed based on the results of entries executed on an existing and similar system.

3.2.2 Classification by Automation Process [12,13,36]

According to Hoffman [13], besides serving as a reference for comparison of current outputs with expected results, the expression test oracle could be used to describe the generation of expected results (data). Then, disregarding manual approaches, behind every test oracle exists an automation process. In three different studies [12,13,36], the researcher Douglas Hoffman described several characteristics useful to the process of oracle automation. In the same studies, Hoffman presents a different oracle taxonomy. In this context, we compiled these characteristics defining a taxonomy based on the automation processes described by Hoffman. This taxonomy is presented in Table 3.3. The table shows the oracle classification, expressive features, advantages, and disadvantages classified into different classes.

3.2.3 Oracle Categories According to Harman et al. [11]

In a recent scientific study, Harman *et al.* [11] provide a broad analysis of trends in research on test oracles regarding current approaches. In their analysis, the authors considered the works on test oracles into four different categories:

- Specified oracles: in this category, Harman *et al.* [11] include all test oracle that specifications in order to judge test outputs and behaviors. Naturally, a lot of different studies could be included in this category. Among these studies, the authors highlight specification-based languages, models, assertions, contracts, and algebraic specification;
- Derived oracles: in this group of test oracles, tests included approaches using any type of artifacts or resources from which test oracles may be created. Given this definition, the authors highlight that derived oracles may become an uncompleted specified oracle. The common resources cited are MR, regression test suites, system executions (trace), textual documentation, and strategies for pseudo-oracles;
- Implicit oracles: are intended to identify situations in which the presence of a fault in the SUT is obvious such as crashes. Harman *et al.* [11] highlight that implementing these oracles requires no domain knowledge and

Table 3.3 Compilation of Testing Oracles by Their Automation Process

Oracle	Definition	Advantage	Disadvantage
No oracle	Approach without verification of results	Large amount of data can be executed	Only notable errors are detected
Human oracle	A human figure verify results	Can detect unpredictable errors	Time consuming and its efficiency are influenced by physiological factors, such as tiredness
True or complete	The oracle generates outputs from inputs	All possible errors, considering the test set, are detected	Expensive implementation. Its execution is time consuming
Consistency	It compares current results to previous results (regression testing)	Quick verification. Can verify large amount of data	Does not detect errors in the original program
Stochastic or random	Checks a random test data sample	Could automate testing in a simple manner	May not notice specific errors and it is time consuming to check
Sampling	Verifies a previously selected test data sample	Generally promotes a quick check	May not detect specific errors
Self-referenced	Promotes responses to data via messaging	Allows wide posttest analysis. The verdict is given in the message content	The system must submit test results so that messages are received
Heuristic	Verify specific characteristics	Quick, simple, and inexpensive	Generally could bring false positive/negative results
Model based	Uses a digital model data about the behavior of the SUT	Tests can be used across multiple systems using different models	Maintenance is expensive. Complex models must match the expected behavior
Manual	Results should be carefully defined by a test engineer	Useful for complex SUTs	It always performs the same procedures and is limited by a number of test cases

Continued

Table 3.3 Compilation of Testing Oracles by Their Automation Process—cont'd

Oracle	Definition	Advantage	Disadvantage
Statistics	Makes statistical correlations between inputs and outputs	Enables checking large scale and real data systems	May not detect apparent errors
Computational	Explores the behavior of the SUT to convert inputs into results	Very useful for simple mathematical functions and transformations	May not detect some errors and generate false positive/negative results

the technique can be used in all runtime problems. A function which is always waiting for handles of exceptions is an example of this test oracle;

- No oracles: in this group of study, the authors include some approaches on test oracles which try to deal with the test oracle as a whole. In these studies, despite the absence of automated oracles, the researchers' target is generally to reduce the human efforts on the judgment of test outputs. Among these targets, the authors highlight reducing human oracle cost, reducing qualitative human oracle cost, and crowdsourcing the oracle.

3.3. A Taxonomy by Oracle Information Characteristics

Oracle information is a standardized term by researchers of test oracle use in order to reference data about expected test outputs [94]. Then, oracle information represents the SUT's expected behavior [95], which might be obtained from the specification, stored results, parallel program execution, learning machines, and other sources. The oracle information can be concrete (that is, the expected result itself), or abstract, as the acceptable boundary of results, expressed by a constraint. Complementing the concept of oracle information, oracle procedure is another standardized term used by researchers and it represents the processes used to compare the oracle information with the current output. According to Durrieu *et al.* [96], systems perform this comparison at runtime (online) or after the execution (offline).

Given this introductory scenario, the source of information and the way this information is represented can influence the accuracy, complexity, expressiveness, and many other aspects of the oracle's effectiveness. Furthermore, the sources of information are critical components to determine the ease of writing and interpreting their meaning. In this section, we suggest an oracle classification regarding the oracle information explored by studies on test oracles. This taxonomy assumes that studies on test oracles fit into four basic types: (1) *specification-based* oracles, (2) *metamorphic relation (MR)-based* oracles, (3) *machine learning* (ML) oracles, and (4) *version-based* oracles. Disregarding a few differences, our taxonomy is quite similar to classification suggested by Harman *et al.* [11]. It is important to highlight that this classification is used in the mapping presented in Section 4. So, this section presents this taxonomy in more detail and with practical examples.

3.3.1 Specification-Based Oracles[1]

Baresi and Young [1] present a specific survey highlighting the main characteristics of automated test oracles that require neither precomputed input/output pairs nor a previous version of the SUT. Consequently, regardless of precomputed outputs, software specifications are the most important source of information to derive test inputs and test outputs. This category of test oracle can be named specification based. Due to the popularity of this test oracle approach, this section brings several examples of differences forms to implement test oracles using SUT's specifications.

Technically, a specification can be defined as a detailed formulation, in document form, which provides a definitive description of a system for the purpose of developing or validating the system [17]. When this formulation is used for validation, it is regarded as the oracle information. The language used to describe such a formulation is called a specification language, which is capable of being interpreted by a compiler or interpreter and allows the creation of an automated oracle procedure.

The interest in using specification languages as oracle information is also supported by a variety of studies found in the literature (Section 4). Specification-based oracles can be classified according to the paradigm, automation features, levels of abstraction, and other characteristics. Here, we present specification-based oracles regarding three general aspects: (1) their *location* in relation to the SUT, (2) their *paradigm*, and (3) their *temporal* property representation.

3.3.1.1 Specification Location

Baresi and Young [1] present groups of oracles according to certain similarities, among them: oracles of pure specification language, embedded assertion languages, and extrinsic interface contracts. These three oracle contracts differ from each other in the way they are written with respect to the code.

Oracles based on *pure specification* are those in which the tester uses a specification language to describe the desired behavior of a system or part of it for later use as a source for the oracle, i.e., as the oracle information. Such languages are usually not designed with the concern of being automatically interpreted. Therefore, defining procedures to interpret oracles which use such a source of information can be challenging.

Embedded assertion languages[1] allow one to insert expressions of intent within the code to be tested. They usually represent pre- or postconditions at some control point in the program. Such expressions are checked during the code execution and, if a violation is detected, a message is presented. In this way, they are executable code which may be an extension of the same language used to implement the SUT or from a different language. Java and other programming languages natively support embedded assertions. There are also specification notation languages, such as Anna [97–99] and JML [85,100], in which the assertions can be written in the code. In such cases, assertions are marked with reserved words recognized by an outside interpreter/compiler and executed as a separated part of the code.

For example, consider a Java code snippet which was modified to increase its performance, where the tester wants to be sure that the output is the same as its original output. In this context, one may introduce an assertion in the SUT to ensure that an error will occur if the refactoring method for coordinate calculation differs from its original. As an illustration, in Fig. 3.6, the first line contains the embedded assertion recognized by the Java compiler and, consequently, JVM (Java Virtual Machine) given the reserved word *assert*. During the program execution, if the expression is not true, a runtime error is thrown. Technically, this is the oracle strategy explored by JUnit (Fig. 3.5 and Section 2.3).

Extrinsic interface contracts keep the specification, in the form of assertions, separate from the implementation and less closely tied to the target programming language. There are several assertion languages that allow extrinsic interface contracts, known as ADL (Architecture Description Language). Developers must define the bindings between the specification and the functions in the program [101,102]. This is usually achieved by the use of wrappers. A wrapper is a checker that surrounds the component under test [103]

```
1    assert (calculate_coord() = newCalculate_Coord());
2    float new_coordinate = newCalculate_Coord(coordinate);
```

Figure 3.6 Excerpt from an assertion code.

---

[1] Assertion may be defined as a logical expression specifying a program state that must exist or a set of conditions that program variables must satisfy at a particular point during program execution [17].

without modifying its code. For instance, when testing a given class on an OO code, another class (the wrapper) is created with the same interface as the original but with other methods which are responsible to check some constraint.

Figure 3.7 presents a code example, adapted from Shukla *et al.* [90], in which the objective is testing a class which is a list of integers, using an insert method. The code represents the list class to be tested. A list of integers, in this program, should have a maximum length of 1000 elements and 3 methods: *insert()*, *size()*, and *exists()*. To test the *insert()* method, two basic assumptions are considered: (i) if a value is inserted, it must exist in the list; and (ii) if a value is inserted, the list must have one more element than before the value is inserted. Both assumptions can be tested without inserting intrusive code (embedded assertions) with a wrapper.

Figure 3.8 represents such a wrapper. It extends the original class and overrides the method to be tested. The new *insert()* method (i) retrieves the size of the list before the insertion, (ii) calls the method under test, (iii) retrieves the size of the list after the insertion, and (iv) calls the method which will evaluate the assumptions. If the value is not inserted into the list or if the list does not contain one more element after an insertion, a message

```
1    public class ListOfInteger{
2              public final int MAX_LENGTH=1000;
3              private int index=0;
4              public int[] list = new int[MAX_LENGTH];
5              public void insert(int value){
6                      //The code insertion code is here
7              }
8              public int size(){
9                      return index;
10             }
11             public boolean exists(int value){
12                     //the code to check if an element exists is here
13             }
14   }
```

Figure 3.7 A program to be tested using interface contracts.

```
1    public class Wrapper extends ListOfInteger{
2              public void insert(int value){
3                      int before = size();
4                      super.insert(value);
5                      int after = size();
6                      checkInsert(value, before, after);
7              }
8              void checkInsert(int value, int before, int after) {
9                      if ((!super.exists(value))||((before+1) != after));
10                     System.out.println("Error on insert()");
11             }
12   }
```

Figure.3.8 Code representing class to be tested.

is sent. A driver calls the method *insert()* from the wrapper and the class under test is evaluated without the need for intrusive code.

Other specification languages may be related to the SUT by some variation of the presented approaches. For example, a specification does not need to be a contract, but can be any other language paradigm which can be translated by the oracle procedure. The mapping between oracle information and SUT can also be achieved by instrumenting the SUT to dump the target outputs to a log which can then be used by the oracle procedure in the analysis.

3.3.1.2 Specification Paradigm

There are several specification languages and their respective paradigms are reflected in many different oracle approaches. Because any programming language can actually be interpreted as oracle information, there are as many oracle information paradigms as language paradigms. Here, we present some of the most common paradigms that can be found in the literature to write oracle information.

Embedded assertions, discussed in the last section, are *declarative languages* that are nonprocedural languages that permit the user to declare a set of facts and to express queries or problems that use these facts [17]. Other examples of declarative languages are OCL (Object Constraint Language) and Alloy, which are not embedded assertions. Such oracles are examples of partial oracles.

OCL, for example, is an extension of UML (Unified Modeling Language) proposed by the OMG (Object Management Group). It allows the definition of constraint limits of values to variables and pre- and post-conditions of methods [104–107]. An example of a study of automation is presented by Cheon and Avila [106], in which OCL constraints are translated to runtime checks in AspectJ[2] separated from the implementation code, and mapped into the SUT with pointcuts.

Other languages provide *procedural* or *OO* resources, such as Object Z which allows the tester to plan his oracle information with such concepts as inheritance. An external checker is needed to translate specification sentences, as previously stated. Perfect Developer [81] is a tool that incorporates an automated theorem to verify that specifications written with Object Z (or a specification language called Perfect) are sound. Such a tool is not an oracle

---

[2] AspectJ is an extension of a program paradigm known by Aspect-Oriented Programming (AOP) for the Java programming language.

in the sense that it does not compare the specification with the SUT. Rather, it analyzes whether the specification has flows that work as contradictions.

Another specification paradigm encompasses *executable models*, which can be simulated in tools such as Simulink, XCos, and Scicos. They are suitable as oracle information because it is possible to simulate the SUT behavior. An oracle procedure should retrieve the SUT results and compare them with the model results. Such an oracle is a simplistic example of pseudo-oracles because it uses another version of the SUT to test it—the executable model [70].

A practical example of the use of executable models as oracles is presented by Lasalle *et al.* [108]. The authors apply a Simulink model as oracle information. Its simulation calculates the expected results of a vehicle reaction with respect to the road characteristics when steering.

State machines and other models can also be used as oracle specifications. A parser can be applied to generate an analyzer from the machine. The SUT's output is inserted into the analyzer. After that, if the output is not expected in the machine, an error is detected. In this case, the state machine plays the role of the oracle information and the analyzer represents the oracle procedure.

Andrews and Zhang [53] give an example of state machines as oracles to test an elevator system. In their model, the output is stored into a log file. The requirements are the following: (i) the door must be closed if the elevator is moving; (ii) the elevator must be stopped when the controller program terminates; and (iii) the door must never be open for more than 30 s. A sample of SUT's output is presented in Fig. 3.9.

The testers have created two machines: one for requirements 1 and 2 (Fig. 3.10 (door safe)) and another for requirement 3 (Fig. 3.10 (no delay)).

An analyzer receives the following inputs: the state machine and the log file. If the analyzer cannot recognize a line from the log or if there is no transition in the machine, the file is rejected and an error is identified. Eventually, the analyzer may be modified to ignore valid log lines that are not represented in the state machines. In the example, *call* and *reach* are expected

1	call 3
2	go_up
3	reach 2
4	reach 3
5	stop
6	door_open 3 103325
7	door_close 3 103340
8	go_down

Figure 3.9 A sample of SUT's output regarding state machines as oracle.

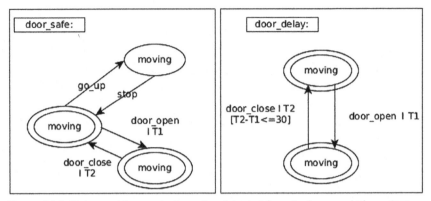

Figure 3.10 State machines as test oracles. *Adapted from Andrews and Zhang [53].*

lines in the log file, but they are not represented in the state machines. In this case, they must be ignored by the analyzer so as to not trigger an error.

3.3.1.3 Temporal Specifications

Some software systems must be in agreement with requirements that express temporal properties. This is common for embedded systems, as in Avionics and Telco. A requirement example of a Mars probe [109] is expressed as follows:

> ... When the TimerInt reaches the Control System and the reading of acceleration is not completed, the status should change to Emergency within 60 milliseconds ...

One can observe that a behavior (status changing) must be true within 60 ms, that is, not necessarily at the same instant as the other triggering behaviors. The oracle must have the ability to check such requirements in the SUT. There are many specification languages from diverse paradigms which can be used to write temporal properties. TRIO [110,111], MITL [109], EAGLE, GIL, time Petri nets [112], and timed automata [109] are other instances.

Higher expressive temporal languages should express time quantitatively, qualitatively and provide some representation of existential ($\exists$) and universal ($\forall$) quantifiers. Quantitative operators allow the representation of intervals of time in relation to other events. For example, "event X must hold until event Y happens." Qualitative operators provide ways to measure distances, as "X must hold k units of time from the current instant." For instance, Felder and Morzenti [113] provide such operators.

As with pure specification language, the execution of a temporal language is not always the main concern. There are studies which tackle the adaptation of pure languages on automated testing tools which are capable of translation. Given the high complexity of such languages and the difficulty of defining a complete solution, the adaptation is usually accomplished partially in exchange of some expressiveness.

This is the case with the research on oracles for Simulink-like models [70], where a tool is capable of analyzing results with respect to a TRIO-adapted specification (TRIO/Apolom). Although a recursive capability is not implemented, the oracle procedure is capable of analyzing quantitative and qualitative operators, such as existential and universal quantifiers.

The following requirements are used as a base to write an oracle information example in TRIO/Apolom language:

> ... If the temperature of a system is greater than x for an interval of time (interval) of more than t1 instants, then a red indicator must be on to indicate a critical situation until it lowers to a safer temperature. A safety protocol (safety) must be started within the next t2 instants and should last the same number of instants as interval. Also, a yellow indicator must be on after the safe temperature is reached and until the alarm is turned off ...

The requirement above can be translated to TRIO/Apolom as presented in Fig. 3.11.

According to Nardi [70], the left part of connector Λ in the first line identifies the first instant (the starting point) when a temperature is greater than **x**. The right side of the connector has an operator to count how many instants the temperature is above x from the starting point and verifies whether it endures longer than is allowed (**t1**). If both conditions hold, then the second line guarantees that the red indicator is on for the same interval of time as the critical temperature. It also verifies whether the safety protocol is activated for the next **t2** instants and that it endures for the same interval of time as the interval. Line three insures that the yellow indicator is turned on the next instant that the temperature is below the critical point until the alarm is switched off.

3.3.2 MR-Based Oracles
The oracle information may not be based directly on the system specification, but rather on known relationships between multiple inputs and

---

Starts(greaterthan(temp;x)) Λ interval = NowOn(greaterthan(temp;x)) > t1
Lasts(on(red),interval-1) Λ $\exists$ (Lasts(on(safety),interval-1),0,t2) Λ
UntilW(on(yellow),instant() + interval, off(alarm))

Figure 3.11 Example of a TRIO/Apolom translation.

outputs, known as MRs. MR specifies how the output of the program should change according to a specific change made to the input and represent some necessary properties of the [114]. MRs are used as test oracles in metamorphic testing to identify faults in the SUT [115]. Following are the basic steps in applying metamorphic testing:

1. Identify set of MRs that should be satisfied by the SUT;
2. Create set of test cases using a traditional test selection approach such as random testing or fault-based testing. These test cases are referred as initial test cases or source test cases;
3. Create follow-up test cases by applying the input transformations specified by the MRs identified in step 1 to the initial test cases created in step 2; and
4. Execute the initial and follow-up test case pairs to check whether the output change at runtime complies with the output change specified by the MR.

As an illustration, the sin function must always obey the following property: $\sin(x) = \sin(180 - x)$. Such necessary properties of the sin function may not be a part of its specification. However, this property specifies a relationship between a pair of input data, x and $180-x$, and their respective outputs $\sin(x)$ and $\sin(180 - x)$. In the given example, the follow-up test case can be created by subtracting 180 from the initial input. Testing of an implementation of sin can be performed by executing the following initial and follow-up test case pairs and checking whether the produced output pairs are equal:

$$(3,\ 177),\ (15,\ 165),\ (45,\ 135),\ (125,\ 55),\ (277,\ -97)$$

Although this is a trivial example, MR-based oracles are applied for testing applications in different domains, including bioinformatics [116], ML programs [117,118], embedded software [119], healthcare simulations [120], Monte Carlo modeling [121], and programs with partial differential equations [122]. In addition, Xie et al. [123] integrated MRs with program slicing and used that for fault localization in programs that face the oracle problem.

The set of MRs used in testing has a big impact on the effectiveness of metamorphic testing. Liu et al. [124] found that using more diverse MRs can improve the effectiveness of testing [124]. Usually, MRs used for testing are identified manually by the tester, based on her knowledge of the program specification. Recently, there have been developments of automated methods that use ML techniques to detect MRs [125].

These approaches use a set of features that represent the static control flow information of a program to develop ML prediction models that are used to predict MRs.

Some taxonomies on test oracles consider MR-based oracles as a sub-category of derived oracles or specification-based oracles [11]. For the context of this chapter, due to the increase of approaches on metamorphic testing over the years, we have considered metamorphic approaches as their own category. We think that studies on metamorphic testing are mature enough to be analyzed and discussed separately.

3.3.3 ML-Based Oracles

ML is a set of computational methods that use collected data and is capable of making predictions. There are a variety of ML techniques applied as oracles, such as Supervised Learning Machines (SLA): (1) artificial neural networks (ANNs) [126–129], (2) support vector machines [130,131], and (3) info-fuzzy networks (IFNs) [79,132].

These three SLAs share a characteristic: they use collected and labeled data to train a machine to predict new, unlabeled data. ANN, for example, can be trained with pairs of inputs and already known outputs (training set). The resulting machine may be seen as an approximated function of the SUT. If a new input is used in the trained ANN, it is capable of predicting an approximated output, even if this input–output pair is not part of the training set. Therefore, the ANN can be used as an oracle. If the same input is used in the ANN and the SUT, a procedure can both compare and identify if there are irregular discrepancies.

A similar application of ML as oracles is the use of them as classifiers. In the same way, pairs of elements and the class or category in which they belong are used to train an ANN. At the end of the training step, the ANN may be capable of identifying in which category new elements belong. For instance, Aggarwal *et al.* [126] and Jin *et al.* [128] present a case study with oracles for triangle classification into isosceles, scalene, equilateral, or not a triangle. The ANN receives two inputs: a triplet which represents three sides of a triangle and the category in which it fits. After the ANN is trained, it is capable of predicting in which category new triplets belong.

Such an oracle approach is appealing because of the ability to approximate functions. However, it has limitations to overcome. Input data may not be easily represented as characters and strings for use in ML. Also, deciding the structure of the network, such as the number of layers and neurons, may not be easy. The selection of training sets from test cases is another key problem that must be considered carefully: it should first be evaluated, which requires the use of other oracles.

3.3.4 Version-Based Oracles

Version-based oracles are mechanisms that explore different versions of the SUT to support decisions about the correctness of a test execution. The use of other versions of the SUT to implement test oracles was previously discussed in the introduction of pseudo-oracle concepts. This classification is very similar to the Derived Oracles, presented by Harman *et al.* [11]. Here, we briefly discuss different approaches to SUT versions as oracle information and how new versions can be used, namely:

- *N*-version: an *N*-version approach requires that *N* independently written versions of an SUT are also implemented [133]. If different outputs are produced by any version, a majority vote decides which output is likely correct. If the same team implements all versions of the SUT in the same language, it is possible that the same defect in the program will be present in other versions (correlated defects). To avoid such a drawback, Manolache and Kourie [134] suggest that different teams and language paradigms should be used. However, Knight and Leveson [135] found that even independently developed programs may contain correlated faults; and

- M-mp (m-model Program testing): an M-mp approach is a variation of the *N*-version. In this case, only different versions of SUT are implemented, instead of a complete system, with the objective of reducing the test cost.

Other similar approaches of version-based oracles may include three strategy variation of strategies. First, *regression testing* in which previously tested stable versions are used as oracle information to test programs developed by iterative processes [95]. Second, *third-party components* that can use tools such as extreme harvesting [86] to search for artifacts (as metadata) produced during normal development processes as the basis for component retrieval and matching on Web search engines. The retrieved components are then used as an oracle and information. Third, one can mention oracles based on *mutation test* that uses outputs taken from programs generated from the original code with small modified source code (mutant programs). Then, the oracle compares these outputs with outputs from the original code.

Section 4 presents a mapping with a quantitative analysis of studies on test oracles.

4. A QUANTITATIVE ANALYSIS AND A MAPPING OF STUDIES

Most test engineers agree that test oracles are a recent issue in software testing. Two decades ago, considering the huge number of conferences and journals on SE, the studies that dealt directly with test oracles were limited. They were confined to a portion of the literature addressing automated test strategies. Nowadays, this context is different and there are several researchers from academia and industry dedicating their efforts specifically to studies on test oracles. In this section, using a pool of more than 300 studies on test oracles, we map the oracle state of the art in several ways:

- Counting the number of publications directly related to test oracles from 1978 to 2013;
- Mapping authors' affiliations in order to measure the industry interest in test oracles and technology transfers from academia to industry;
- Presenting a list of academic efforts to test oracles (Ph.D. and Masters);
- Ranking countries of authors' affiliations in order to discover the most active groups of researchers and universities;
- Presenting supporting tools;
- Analyzing the SUTs explored in empirical evaluation;
- Establishing a coauthorship network to understand the most prolific groups and highlight their interests; and
- Understanding the test oracle evolutions in terms quantitatively using line graphs of SUTs and approaches.

4.1. A Literature Review on Test Oracles

In the following section, we present the methodology we have used to acquire a pool of 304 test oracle studies. We have created an online repository[3] including all of these studies and important information such as title, authors, year and medium of publication, abstract, and others. After constructing the repository, we defined a series of data points to be collected from these studies in order to provide a bird's-eye view of the issue. In this section, we explain our methods and protocols for research and present the numbers that we derived from our analyses.

---

[3] Repository available in: http://www.labes.icmc.usp.br/~rpaes/repo/repo.html.

4.1.1 Study Selection

Aiming to obtain a significant number of useful studies on test oracles, we searched for studies on indexed databases. In the context of this chapter, the term "study" means any written document published and available online such as journal articles, conference papers, and technical reports (gray literature).

We have conducted Web searches for studies in IEEE (Institute of Electrical and Electronics Engineers)[4] and ACM (Association for Computing Machinery)[5] using the following search string: "(('test' OR 'testing') AND ('oracle' OR 'oracles'))." We searched for these terms in three different fields: title, abstract, and keywords. We did not customize the searches for specific years, journals, or conferences. All of this information is important for possible replications and future updates.

After making adjustments for each database, we collected more than 400 studies, combining ACM and IEEE results. After that, we read each paper's abstract, analyzed the studies (excluding repeated entries) and selected the ones related directly to test oracles. In addition, this part of the analysis aims to identify off-topic studies such as research on Oracle® database systems. Studies on SE topics other than test oracles were excluded as well. On the other hand, any study describing, examining, or developing any kind of test oracle was included in our analysis. We avoided imposing many restrictions on study selection in order to get a broad publication overview.

Following this manual selection, we added some already known primary studies related to this topic. These papers did not appear in our original pool because they had appeared in publications not indexed by the two selected databases. Then, at end of the process described, we gathered a pool of 304 studies directly related to test oracles in an automated software testing scenario. One can access online the complete list of these studies and information about them through the repository Web page. Figure 3.12 shows the work flow we have used in our selection process.

4.1.2 Study Classification

We have classified the selected studies according to the oracle taxonomy by oracle information characteristics, detailed in Section 3.3. This means that we have read each selected study, classifying them in four different categories: (i) specification based, (ii) MR, (iii) ML, and (iv) N-version or similar.

---

[4] See: http://ieeexplore.ieee.org/.
[5] See http://dl.acm.org/.

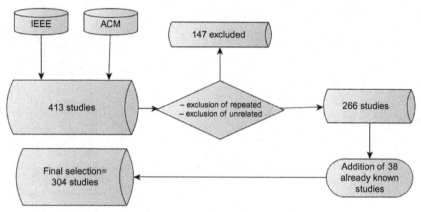

Figure 3.12 Study selection: work flow.

During this analysis, we found some secondary studies, which are studies that analyze other studies with new contributions and results (primary studies) [136]. Then, we classified these sorts of studies as (v) surveys. In our survey, we identified secondary studies with classifications or surveying test oracles aspects.

In order to classify all of the papers, we carried out a consensus process to decide on pending papers, where the authors discussed whether such papers met our criteria. In this context, a subset of studies was read by each author of this chapter. At first, based solely on title and abstract, we decided about the study inclusion or not. Afterward, studies deemed as relevant according to goals were read.

4.2. A Quantitative Analysis on Studies

Analyzing our pool of studies, one can note that, in a generic way, the interest from research of test oracles grew during the years. It is possible to note that the amount of research about this field has increased year after year since 2008. Using a line graph, Fig. 3.13 presents a visual analysis of the number of studies included in our pool from 1978 to 2013. In addition, the same figure presents a table including the number of studies identified each 3-year period from 1978 to 2013.

These quantitative aspects show a considerable evolution of research on test oracles. The upshot of all this analysis is that the oracle issue is growing year after year, receiving increasing attention from researchers. Research on test oracles has been quite constant throughout the underlying 25-year period, since 1987. Considering the selectivity of the conferences and

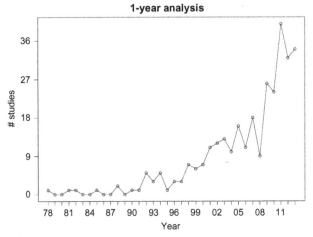

Figure 3.13 Analysis of published research on test oracles.

3-year period	#
1978–1980	1
1981–1986	2
1984–1986	1
1987–1989	2
1990–1992	7
1993–1995	9
1996–1998	13
1999–2001	24
2002–2004	35
2005–2007	45
2008–2010	59
2011–2013	106
Total	304

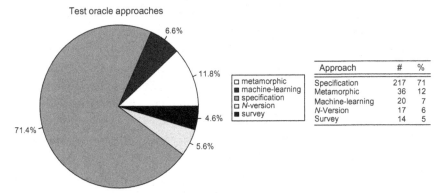

Approach	#	%
Specification	217	71
Metamorphic	36	12
Machine-learning	20	7
N-Version	17	6
Survey	14	5

Figure 3.14 Pie chart of test oracle approaches.

journals and its broad coverage, it is fair to assume that research on test oracles have been playing a substantial role in the SE context.

4.2.1 Study Analysis per Area

Our analysis and classification show that research on test oracles has been published under the five distinct categories in the following proportion: specification-based approaches are responsible for 71% (217/304) of our selected studies; MR-based account for 12% (36/304); N-version and related studies account for 6% (17/304); ML approaches represent 7% (20/304) of the approaches considered; finally, surveys compose 5% (14/304) of the studies. Figure 3.14 draws a fan plot that illustrates the differences among the approaches considered in this study. In addition, the same figure includes a table that presents these numbers sorted from the highest to the lowest.

The line plot in Fig. 3.15 illustrates the relative quantities and differences among studies selected for our study. At a glance, specification-based approaches have been in a continuous evolution since 1995. Considering approaches related to MR, it is possible to note a considerable evolution after the year 2000. The evolution has established a regular constancy, showing that this area has been widely exploited by new research. Considering ML approaches, one can notice that this area has maintained certain constancy without many significant developments. Along those the same lines, the N-version and similar approaches appear as a supporting approach that did not show many evolutions. Finally, as a consequence of the popularity of automated testing activities, surveys on test oracles are becoming common among other approaches.

Complementing the analysis on the evolution of software testing approaches, Fig. 3.16 shows graphically the number of oracle publications during each 3-year period since 1978. Regarding this visual information, one can notice that since about 2004 the four approaches were firm and they appear together on subsequent research. Using this analysis, one can infer that sketches of research on N-version-based oracles were noted first at

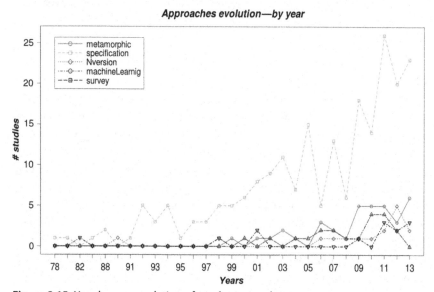

Figure 3.15 Year-by-year evolution of oracle approaches.

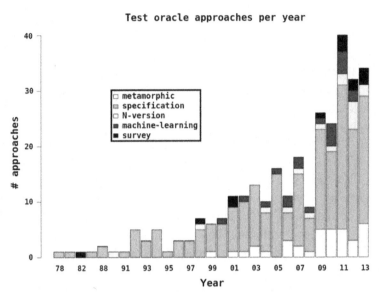

Figure 3.16 Comparative of oracle approaches year by year.

the end of the 1980s and, after almost a 10-year period with no new results, these approaches came out again, although it is true that after 2009 research has exploited more of these approaches. Finally, considering the visual information plot in this figure, it is evident to note how much bigger the number of specification-based approaches when it is compared to other approaches.

4.2.2 SUT Analysis

Our analysis identified 87% (263/304) studies that have presented at least one experiment to support their findings about test oracles. Then, we designed an analysis to compare between practical and theoretical works (Fig. 3.17A). We made a deeper analysis to ascertain methods and strategies used by researchers on test oracles to validate their approaches. In the context of this analysis, we considered all study cases, proof of concepts, examples of usage, quasi-experiments, controlled experiments, and general empirical analysis as experiments. The first experimental analysis preformed was directed to access the usage of *toy programs* and *real programs*. Toy programs, which are very common in SE experiments, are systems with limited functions that generally are set to work for a specific purpose. Despite this fact, concepts applied to toy programs may often be generalized for wide scenarios. In terms of this analysis, we considered the following as toys: single specific functions, code excerpts, and SUT versions developed by the

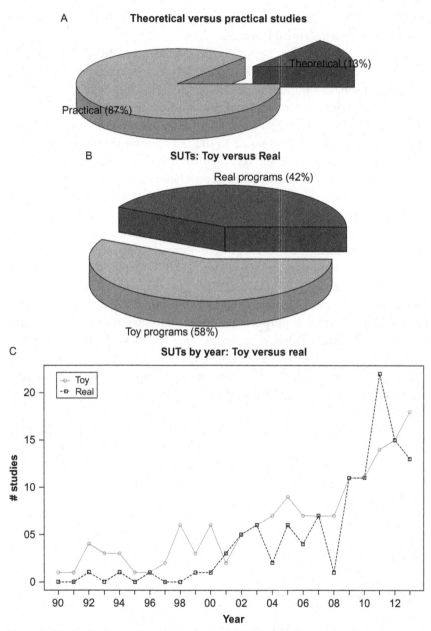

Figure 3.17 Analysis on validation strategies and SUTs. (A) Theoretical versus practical studies. (B) Toy versus real programs. (C) Toy and real programs: year-by-year after 1990.

researchers. On the other hand, real programs are commercial systems or open source systems available for final users.

Regarding the studies, 58% (152/263) used toys and 42% (111/263) exploited real software systems. Figure 3.17B presents a pie chart illustrating this comparison. In addition, Fig. 3.17C presents the number of toy and real programs experimented in approaches published since 1990. An outcome observed was that results regarding experiments using one or more real systems are much reliable. This is due to the fact that sometimes toys are generally of little practical use and less sophisticated than real programs.

Over 36 years of research, on new development systems on test oracles arose, as did APIs, programming paradigms, and languages with built-in tools. Regarding these changes, we accomplished an analysis to investigate test oracle research considering many systems implemented over these years. We have classified the SUTs in five distinct categories: (1) mobile/embedded or real-time reactive systems; (2) GUI (graphical user interface); (3) general purpose; (4) Web and Internet applications (including SOA (Service-Oriented Architecture)); and (5) distributed and concurrent applications. Among general purpose, we identified single functions and other popular SUTs and validation strategies such as clock alarms, calculators, specific-domain tools, triangle classification, credit approval applications, ATMs (Automated Teller Machine) systems, cryptographic systems, numerical problems, and sort algorithms (bubble, quick, etc.). Table 3.4 presents the number of SUTs per category identified in our analysis.

About this SUT analysis, we highlight the number of Web application (13%, 35/264) and the number of embedded/reactive systems (17%, 44/264). Further, Fig. 3.18 presents this analysis in a line graph that represents a distribution including the number of each SUT category by year from 1990 to 2013.

Table 3.4 Number of SUTs and Categories

SUT Category	#	%
(1) Mobile/embedded or real-time/reactive	44	17
(2) GUIs	15	6
(3) General purpose	164	62
(4) Web applications	35	13
(5) Distributed and concurrent	6	2

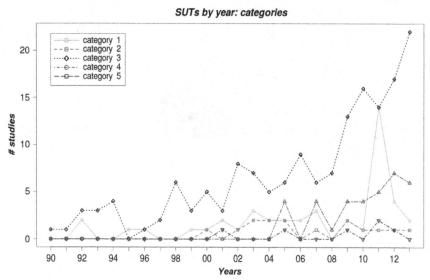

Figure 3.18 SUT categories year by year.

4.2.3 Projects Analysis

Other aspects considered in our study were related to authors' affiliation. We performed this analysis to raise two basic types of information:

- What is the participation of industry members and practitioners?
- Which countries have more universities and/or software companies researching test oracles?

Regarding this premise, we have checked all of the authors' affiliations, classifying the studies as coming from academia (universities/colleges), industry (research institutes or private companies), or collaboration in cases of one or more authors from academia and industry in the same study. In this sense, we could note only 11% (32/304) of the test oracles studies selected belong to industry; 12% of the studies were classified as collaboration; and 78% (237/304) of the selected studies were held in academic environments. Figure 3.19 presents this comparison using a fan plot.

Regarding a temporal comparative analysis of studies from industry and academia, Fig. 3.20 presents a graphical design of a year-by-year analysis between the numbers. This analysis shows a significant superiority of studies originated in academia. However, we noticed slight increase in industry and collaboration studies since 2008. This increase raises an important question: Are testing oracles becoming more applicable in industry scenarios? Possible answers to these questions are given in Section 5. To sum up this context, we

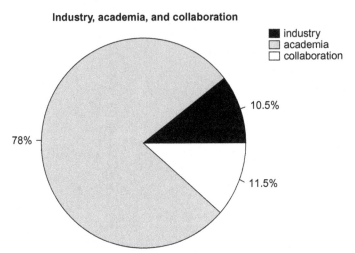

Figure 3.19 Research on test oracles: industry, academia, and collaboration.

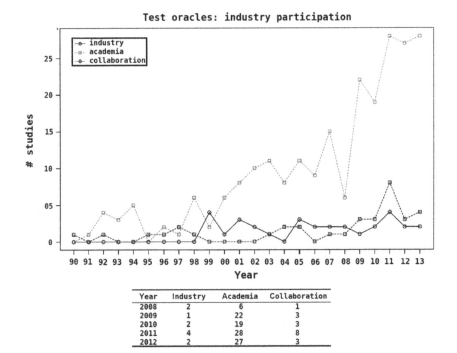

Year	Industry	Academia	Collaboration
2008	2	6	1
2009	1	22	3
2010	2	19	3
2011	4	28	8
2012	2	27	3

Figure 3.20 Test oracles: industry, academia, and collaboration.

consider that the industry participation in research on test oracles is quite weak; however, it is becoming as important as automated testing activities.

4.2.4 Demographical Analysis

In order to provide a wide demographic view about the research on test oracles, we have collected information about where each study published was conducted. We found the first author's affiliated research institutes, universities/colleges, and private companies. Then, using the country of each professional address indicated on the publication, we counted the most active countries conducting research on test oracles. Table 3.5 presents the data collected from this analysis. We observed that together the United States and China host about a half of the research on test oracles analyzed. The United States has 104 (34%) and China has 42 (13%) of the studies considered in our survey. Considering the geographical analysis provided, we highlight the research held in Australia, which represents 24 (8%) of the total studies.

Aiming to provide a wide view about each the contributions from each country, using a visualization tool [137], we designed a colorful world map demonstrated in Fig. 3.21. In this world map, the level of contribution of each country is presented using colors. Stronger colors represent countries with more contributions. Therefore, the color red represents the most prolific country and the color white represents no contribution at all. A brief visual evaluation of this map shows that India, Brazil, and Germany have contributed little so far.

4.2.5 Publication Strategies

This aim of the analysis is to verify the strategies used by researchers of test oracles and to communicate their new findings. Taking our repository of 304 studies, there were 4 technical reports and 300 studies published in conferences or journals of SE and related areas. Then, we took note of the means used of each publication in order to answer the following question: What are the most common venues and periodicals for research on test oracles?

Considering this investigation, before a more deep analysis, we can define that the number of conference studies (78%, 240/304) is four times higher than the number of journal studies (19%, 60/304). Figure 3.22 shows a fan plot that represents the number of periodical and conference publications.

Regarding the studies identified from periodicals, we can define that the most desirable target of test oracle research is the Journal IEEE Transactions

Table 3.5 Most Prolific Countries by Authors' Affiliation

Country	#	%
USA	104	34
China	42	13
Australia	24	8
Canada	19	6
France	19	6
UK	16	5
Germany	11	3
Italy	10	3
Malaysia	8	2
India	7	2
Brazil	7	2
Spain	7	2
Netherlands	4	1
Japan	3	0.9
Finland	3	0.9
South Korea	3	0.9
Austria	2	0.6
Taiwan	2	0.6
Switzerland	2	0.6
Others	11	3

on Software Engineering.[6] In this periodical, we found more than 33% (20/60) of the studies, representing 20 studies. The second periodical most used by test oracle research is *Information and Software Technology*[7] in which 10% (6/60) of the selected studies were published. Table 3.6 presents the complete relationship among studies and periodicals considered for this work.

---

[6] See http://www.computer.org/portal/web/tse.
[7] See http://www.journals.elsevier.com/information-and-software-technology/.

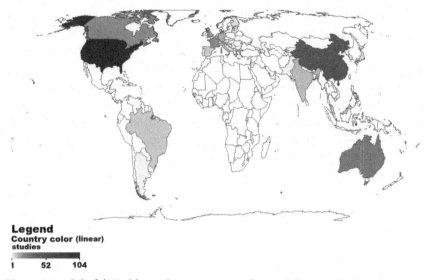

Legend
Country color (linear)
studies

1   52   104

Figure 3.21 Colorful World map by country contributions. Generated using Cs2 [137].

Analysis: conference and journal studies

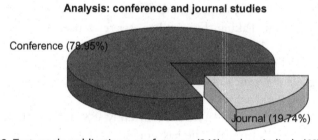

Conference (78.95%)

Journal (19.74%)

Figure 3.22 Test oracle publications: conferences (240) and periodicals (60).

Table 3.6 Test Oracle Studies Published in Periodicals

Journals	#	%
IEEE Transactions on Software Engineering	20	33.33
Information and Software Technology	6	10.00
ACM SIGSOFT Software Engineering Notes	3	5.00
Lecture Notes in Computer Science	3	5.00
IET Software	2	3.33
Software Testing, Verification and Reliability	2	3.33
IEEE Software	1	1.67
Others	23	38.33

Considering studies published in conferences, we note a large variety of targets likely due to the existence of different conferences on software testing and automated testing. We highlight five main preferred targets followed by researchers on test oracles. Four of these congresses are ICST (International Conference on Software Testing, Verification and Validation), ASE (International Conference on Automated Software Engineering), ICSE (International Conference on Software Engineering), and QSIC (International Conference on Quality Software), where were published 64 studies included in our analysis, 16 studies in each conference. Finally, the fifth most common conference found on our analysis was COMPSAC (Annual International Computers, Software & Applications Conference), where 15 studies were found. Table 3.7 draws a wide scenario about the most popular conferences among researchers on test oracles.

4.2.6 Prolific Researchers

One of the goals of this chapter is the identification of productive researchers on test oracles. Regarding the 304 studies, we identified 595 different authors. Only 149 (25%) of these authors have two or more studies considered in this survey. Taking this number as a reference, we preview more contributions for the next years, once an expressive number of authors may be concluding more research on test oracles.

Among 595 different authors, according to our analysis, we highlight the most prominent and active:

- Professor T. Y. Chen—14 studies (currently at Swinburne University of Technology—Australia), who has worked several years on metamorphic testing and some extensions in the areas of program testing, proving, and debugging;
- Professor Paul Strooper—11 studies (currently at University of Queensland—Australia), who has worked on test oracles based on formal specifications;
- Professor T. H. Tse—11 studies (currently at University of Hong Kong—China), who has worked mainly with test oracles considering MR;
- Professor Atif Memon—nine studies (currently at University of Maryland—USA), who works with test oracle for GUI testing;
- Professor ZhiQuan (George) Zhou—seven studies (currently at University of Wollongong—Australia), whose studies are aimed at alleviating the oracle problem using, mainly, MR; and

Table 3.7 Test Oracle Studies published in Conferences and Workshops

Acronym	Conference	#	%
ICST	International Conference on Software Testing, Verification and Validation	16	6.6
ASE	International Conference on Automated Software Engineering	16	6.6
ICSE	International Conference on Software Engineering	16	6.6
QSIC	International Conference on Quality Software	16	6.6
COMPSAC	Annual International Computers, Software & Applications Conference	15	6.2
ASPEC	Asia-Pacific Software Engineering Conference	12	5.0
ICSTW	International Conference on Software Testing Verification and Validation Workshops	10	4.1
AST	Workshop on Automation of Software Test	7	2.9
ISSRE	International Symposium on Software Reliability Engineering	6	2.5
ITNG	International Conference on Information Technology New Generations	4	1.6
TAIC PART	Testing: Academic and Industrial Conference—Practice and Research Techniques	4	1.6
SMC	International Conference on Systems, Man, and Cybernetics	4	1.6
SSIRI	Secure Software Integration and Reliability Improvement	3	1.2
ICSESS	International Conference on Software Engineering and Service Science	3	1.2
SEFM	International Conference on Software Engineering and Formal Methods	3	1.2
ISSTA	International Symposium on Software Testing and Analysis	2	0.8
SERE	International Conference on Software Security and Reliability	2	0.8
CiSE	International Conference on Computational Intelligence and Software Engineering	2	0.8
Other events		101	41.6

- Professor Wing-Kwong Chan—seven studies (currently at City University of Hong Kong—China), who works with methodologies of pattern classification for metamorphic testing.

Regarding the authorship in a wider scenario, an analysis shows that only 6.2% (37/595) of the authors had four or more studies included. Table 3.8 presents the citation name and the number of studies of our survey for the 36 more prolific authors identified.

4.3. Author's Collaboration

To measure the level of collaboration among the authors, we prepared a coauthorship network including all studies of our survey. This network matches all authors and coauthors who have published together at least

Table 3.8 Most Prolific Authors of the Survey

Author	#	Author	#
Bai, X.	4	Kuo, F.-C.	6
Bieman, J.M.	4	Labiche, Y.	5
Briand, L.C.	5	Liu, H.	5
Carrington, D.	5	Mcdonald, J.	4
Chan, W.K.	7	Mcminn, P.	6
Chen, T.Y.	14	Memon, A.	9
Chen, Y.	6	Murphy, C.	6
Guderlei, R.	4	Peters, D.K.	4
Harman, M.	4	Schweiggert, F.	5
Heimdahl, M.P.E.	4	Shahamiri, S.R.	5
Hoffman, D.	4	Staats, M.	4
Hoffman, D.M.	4	Strooper, P.	11
Huang, H.	4	Tonella, P.	4
Ibrahim, S.	4	Tsai, W.-T.	6
Just, R.	5	Tse, T.H.	11
Kadir, W.M.N.W.	5	Xie, Q.	5
Kaiser, G.E.	5	Xie, T.	4
Kapfhammer, G.M.	4	Zhou, Z.Q.	7

Figure 3.23 General coauthorship network among test oracle studies. Generated using Cs2 [137].

one time. This network is graphically presented in Fig. 3.23. Each node represents an author and each edge represents a collaboration between authors in at least one publication. It is important to highlight that in this network we do not consider unique authors. The network of authors and papers clearly identifies the collaboration level among authors. The distinguished members of each group are usually at the center of each clique. This visual organization shows the main research groups on the test oracle scenario, but it conceals quantitative information on the authors' contribution.

A visual analysis of this coauthorship network reveals a huge group including more than 50 researchers (center of Fig. 3.23). Visually, it is fair to assume that this is a result of the union of more than four major research groups. In addition, it is possible to note a huge group with more than 30 researchers (bottom of Fig. 3.23). Besides these two groups, it is possible to note more than 15 small groups with at least 5 researchers. In a generic way, over the years, the trend is that these groups increase in number of researchers and join with larger groups. Thus, the exchange of experiences between groups anticipates excellence and improvement in future research.

In order to match the network presented in Fig. 3.23 and the numbers presented by Table 3.8, we present a graphical association in Fig. 3.24. Analyzing the figure, one can verify where the most prolific authors are located in a wide scenario. Each node represents an author, and the sizes of the nodes are directly proportional to their number of studies. In addition, it is possible to note that a large amount of these authors are associated with the biggest groups identified. On the other hand, it is possible to note that there are 6 small groups (less than 12 authors) with an expressive number of contributions.

In addition, it is possible to note that a large amount of these authors are associated with the biggest groups identified. On the other hand, it is possible to note that there are 6 small groups (less than 12 authors) with an

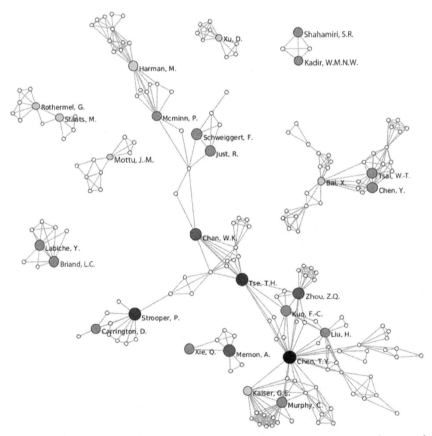

Figure 3.24 Active researchers on test oracles and their respective groups. Generated using Cs2 [137].

expressive number of contributions. In addition, Fig. 3.25 presents the coauthorship collaboration regarding each approach in our study classification (Section 4.1.2). Using this figure, we reach a visual analysis about the maturity of collaboration for each test oracle approach. The group of authors that have published contributions to the test oracles using MR (Fig. 3.25A) seems to be very connected and collaborative. Note the connections between large groups of authors. Among the studies presented in this analysis, it is possible to note mainly two focuses: (1) test of programs without test oracles [44,68,114,125,138–143] and (2) failure identification and classification [38,144,145].

The coauthorship network of studies on ML strategies (Fig. 3.25B) differs totally from the metamorphic area for two main reasons. First, there is no connection among the research groups and the biggest group has only seven authors. Second, the groups identified use different approaches from different and huge areas such as Petri nets [111], *Backpropagation* method [61], Ontologies [57], and artificial intelligence (AI), and other ANNs [126,128,129,146–151]. Then, it is possible to identify ten separate groups with at least four authors.

Only 17 studies related to *N*-version-based test oracles (Fig. 3.14). A coauthorship network could not be meaningful with this number of studies. Figure 3.25C represents the graphical collaboration among authors who played efforts to develop test oracles using *N*-version strategies. Among these strategies we highlight mainly regression test [71,152–155], mutation analysis [156,157], multiple version [158], *N*-version programming [159], and partial oracles [83,160].

Due to the variety of approaches, it was expected that there would be more collaboration among researchers who have dedicated efforts on specification-based test oracles. One can confirm this through the coauthorship network of authors presented in Fig. 3.25D. A visual analysis reveals 3 major groups of more than 10 researchers and more than 10 small groups with at least 5 authors each. Among the large number of approaches, we highlight assertion based [161–165], bytecode based and decision trees [166,167], passive test oracles [90,92], human oracle [41,50,64,78], image based [39,40], statistical analysis [168–172], log analysis [173,174], ADA [21,97], UML [104,105,175–177], event driven [178–180], natural languages [62,181], and others [182,183].

In addition to the approaches outlined above, many of the approaches presented explored formal specifications to alleviate the oracle problem. Among these formal specifications, we can identify a wide range of

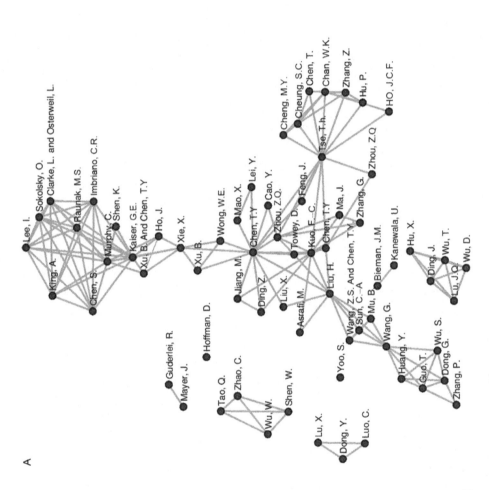

Figure 3.25—Cont'd

Figure 3.25—Cont'd

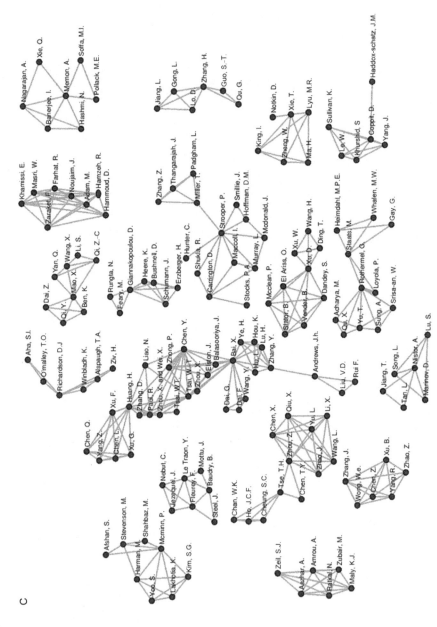

Figure 3.25—Cont'd

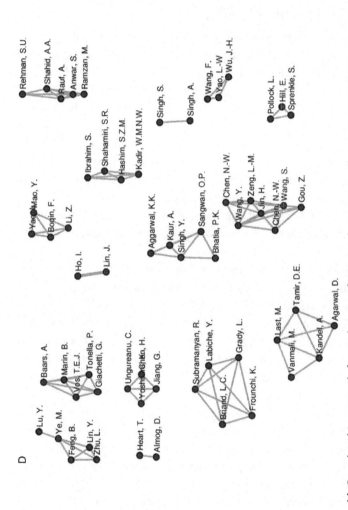

Figure 3.25—Cont'd Coauthorship network for each type of test oracle (generated using Cs2 [137]). (A) Metamorphic-relation based, (B) N-version based, (C) specification based, and (D) machine-learning based.

approaches. We highlight finite state machine [54,184–189], algebraic specifications [99,190–193], Object Z [72,88,194,195], model checking [196–199], OCL [106,107], Alloy [200], AspectJ [201], and Eiffel contracts [202].

4.4. Surveys and Position Studies

In our study, we identified some works about complete or partial surveys on test oracles. In addition, we identify some opinion studies, also known as position studies, where the authors' point of view is expressed. Therefore, in this subsection, we present the main points raised by these works.

Chronologically, one can consider the study presented by Weyuker [6] (already mentioned in Section 3), which was the first significant opinion paper about test oracles. In this study, the authors present their considerations of the practical use of test oracles regarding cases in which an oracle does not exist or the tester must expend some extraordinary amount of time to determine whether or not the current output is correct. This kind of software system is called a "nontestable" program. In that study, the authors highlight options of test strategies to be used instead of test oracles and their consequences.

In 1998, Hoffman [12] (already mentioned in Section 3) presented a study categorizing test oracles in classes regarding their various types of automated software verification and validation regarding real industrial approaches. In this analysis, the authors identified five different classes of oracles: True, Stochastic, Heuristic, Sampling, and Consistent oracles. In addition, in this classification, the authors present comparisons among the advantages and disadvantages for each class covered. Later, the study Hoffman [13] was written by the same author with a different classification in which four types of oracle strategies (and not using any oracle) are identified and outlined: True, Consistency, Self Referential, and Heuristic.

In 2001, Baresi and Young [1] surveyed the proposed approaches related to test oracles that require neither precomputed test cases nor previous versions of the SUT. Here, the authors analyze test oracle strategies and approaches dealing with Transducers, Embedded Assertion Languages, Extrinsic Interface Contracts, Pure Specification Languages, Trace Checking, and Log File Analysis. However, generally, this analysis is not comprehensive and it considers only a part of the research on test oracles.

In 2009, Shahamiri et al. [3] presented a comparative analysis among six categories of test oracles: N-Version Diverse Systems and M-Model

Program Testing; Decision Table; IFN Regression Tester; AI Planner Test Oracle; ANN-Based Test Oracle; and Input/output Analysis-Based Automatic Expected Output Generator. The authors highlight that all of the methods mentioned have advantages and disadvantages and then they present an analysis aiming to compare the approaches regarding several aspects: Automation Tool, Automated Oracle Activities, and Limitations. The study concludes mainly two fundamental aspects to be considered about the oracle problem. First, it is not possible to completely automate the entire oracle process. Second, there is no unique approach to reach all oracle activities in different circumstances. Then, the upshot of all this study is that research on test oracles should develop a complete automated test oracle which is applicable in any type of software testing, while all oracle activities are automated.

In 2011, Staats et al. [203] raised that several improvements to testing activities can be achieved regarding the problem of the oracle selection. Basically, this study proposes an analysis that includes test oracles in a revisitation of the fundamentals of testing in order to get better test results.

Chen et al. [67] revealed that oracle mismatches are one of the main causes of failed tests produced in automated testing. This study considered 197 failed tests produced in automated testing in GUI-based automated regression testing for a real industrial project in order to identify the main cause of false positives. Shende and Byagar [204] provided an opinion study in which automated test oracles are considered a fundamental challenge to be handled by testers in the software industry. In a similar approach, Itkonen et al. [205] presented a field study in which 12 testing sessions in 4 industrial organizations were recorded to measure how testers use knowledge while performing Exploratory Software Testing (ET). This study revealed that testers apply their knowledge of test oracles to determine whether a result was correct or not. The results showed that a considerable number of failures could be found outside the actual focus areas, showing the effectiveness of the exploratory testing approach.

Chan and Tse [43] summarized 15 years of their own research on test automation when a test oracle may not exist using MR. In order to do this analysis, the authors selected three relevant issues: (1) testing without a mechanism to determine the expected outcomes, (2) testing without a mechanism to gauge the actual results, and (3) testing without a mechanism to decide whether the actual results agree with the expected outcomes. Considering the first and the second issues, the authors presented their studies on metamorphic testing. About the third issue, the authors described their findings on pattern classification and formal object equivalence and nonequivalence.

In 2013, Harman *et al.* [11], trying to overcome the fragmented community of researchers and practitioners of automated test oracles, present a comprehensive investigation about the studies on a test oracle. The authors have constructed a repository of 611 publications on test oracles and their related areas. The survey covers specified, derived, and implicit oracles and techniques that cater to the absence of oracles. However, the main focus of this study is to provide an analysis of trends related to test oracles by means of a road map for future work at the interfaces between existing definitions. Among these trend analyses, the authors presented some future research direction like the potential of metamorphic testing.

4.5. Supporting Tools

During our analysis, we found *tools* to support the oracle automation. We have considered as tools any means of automation associated with oracles, including specification language translators, development environments that support oracles, and frameworks. Table 3.9 presents a list of the most common tools we identified with a brief description and their references.

4.6. Academic Efforts on Test Oracles (Ph.D. and Masters)

In order to provide a comprehensive analysis covering relevant academic efforts related to test oracles, we also searched for Masters theses and Ph.D. dissertations that have made important contributions to the development of test oracles. These are listed in Table 3.10.

In Section 5, we discuss aspects related to the research on test oracles. This discussion is based on the analyses and numbers we have presented in this section. We highlight some evidence and shifts revealed by our study. In addition, we raise some personal and particular points of view concerning the research on test oracles as a whole.

5. DISCUSSIONS

The purpose of this section is to use the numbers eminent from Section 4 to introduce a discussion about possible areas for investigation by researchers. Briefly, the target of our discussion is an attempt to achieve advances in oracle approaches that fit test oracles in contemporary concepts, reducing human efforts on activities of verification. Typically, this discussion

Table 3.9 Test Oracles: Supporting Tools

Tool/Framework	Specification	References
Prosper	Uses postconditions	[8]
TROMLAB	Formal specification for real-time systems	[206]
JUnit	Unit testing for Java programs	[100,207–210]
BIT	Framework for automated black-box testing	[103]
ISAO	Uses machine learning to construct an oracle for image segmentations	[211]
ClassBench	A tool for executing and evaluating tests	[194,195]
DART	Regression test for GUIs	[71,178,180]
Amsterdam	Automates metamorphic testing	[142]
O-FIm	Supports the test of programs with GUIs	[39,40]
JTOC	Uses Java annotations and Java inner class to construct intelligible contracts for programmers	[162]
Gourlay's framework	Is theoretical framework for testing	[45]
Test templates	Used to derive tests from model-based specifications	[212]
ASTRAR	Group testing technique for Web services	[82]
TROMLAB	Framework for rigorous development of real-time reactive systems	[206]
Circe	A grammar-based oracle for testing Web applications	[170]
GUIdiff	A regression testing tool for graphical user interfaces	[213]
ZARBI	Combines multiresolution static analysis and testing oracles	[171]
SPIN	A model checking tool	[196]
STG	Generates oracles from operational specifications	[214]
EvoSuite	Automatic test suite generation for Java	[215]
ADEPT	Executable specifications for automation behavior and user interaction	[216]
Roast	A framework for table-driven testing of Java classes	[217]

Continued

Table 3.9 Test Oracles: Supporting Tools—cont'd

Tool/Framework	Specification	References
TROT	Automates the testing of equation execution	[93,97]
Zoltar	A toolset for automatic fault localization	[48]
Fault Evaluator	Experimental investigation of testing logical expressions in software	[218]
Warlock	Generates oracles from Object-Z specification	[88]
Web Testing Explorer	Automates the test of Web application	[27]
ATUSA	Automates the invariant-based automatic testing	[219]
TOG	Oracles from specifications	[187,220]
TAOS toolkit	A set of tools to test automation	[152]
Teager	Conformance testing based on UML state machines	[177]
muJava	Mutation test for Java programs	[221]
STSC	Statistical testing of software components	[90]
SafeRefactor	Supports a technique to test Java refactoring engines	[222]
WebVizOr	Automated oracles and analyzing test results of Web applications	[223]
SpecTRM-RL	Supports the generation of test cases from specifications	[76]
Mettoc	Metamorphic testing from compilers	[224]
Orstra	Automates unit-test suites with regression oracle checking	[155]
ConfDiagnoser	An automated configuration error diagnosis tool for Java software	[210,225]
LETO	A luster-based test oracle for airbus critical systems	[96]
PLASMA	A real-time verification-based oracle for this system	[226]
Extreme Harvesting	Finds and collects components from Internet	[86]

Table 3.9 Test Oracles: Supporting Tools—cont'd

Tool/Framework	Specification	References
Corduroy	Converts metamorphic properties in testing methods that can be run using assertions checking at run-time JML	[68]
PATHS	Supports using AI and formal model on test oracles for GUIs	[227]
MD-TEST	Verifies behaviors and internal data structure of SUTs	[228]
MaC	A run-time monitoring tool	[164]
CaslTest	Testing tool with support to Casl specification-based oracles	[192]
Dresden OCL Toolkit	Interprets OCL constraints from a UML model and generates AspectJ code	[106]
NeuronDotNet	Builds different NNs	[60]

is related to our own point of view about present and future research on test oracles. Thereby, the content presented in this section expresses the opinion of the authors under their personal experiences and paradigms.

In this context, we raise three fundamental issues to be considered in contemporary oracle approaches: (1) the high level of tool and specification languages; (2) the complexity of SUT's outputs; and (3) the necessity of generalization of oracle strategies and properties. In the following subsections, we present explanations and details to justify these issues. Next, we expand our discussion through the inclusion of some possible trends.

5.1. High Level of Tools and Specification Languages

An objection in the research on the oracle problem of finding the middle ground: what lies between the unfeasible complete automation and the manual means? This is a question that is hard to answer. There are many variables that can influence such a trade-off. Therefore, we believe there are many paths to be explored. Moreover, how to define a solution of (partially) automated oracle that is welcome in the software industry?

Based on our analysis, generically, a testing team may be reluctant to adopt a solution that is too hard to learn or too intrinsically domain/technology dependent if such variables change frequently. Even for long-term

Table 3.10 A Relation of Ph.D. and Master Work on Test Oracles

Year	Author	Title	University	Type
1993	Zhang [229]	The construction of oracles for software testing	Durham University	Master
1994	Viravan [230]	Enhancing debugging technology	Purdue University	Ph.D.
1995	Peters [231]	Generating a test oracle from program documentation	McMaster University	Master
2000	Takahashi [232]	An automated oracle for verifying GUI objects	Florida Institute of Technology	Master
2000	Manolache [233]	Testing algorithmically complex software using model programs	University of Pretoria	Master
2000	Machado [9]	Testing from structured algebraic specifications: the oracle problem	University of Edinburgh	Ph.D.
2001	Memon [234]	A comprehensive framework for testing graphical user interfaces	University of Pittsburgh	Ph.D.
2001	Sandhu [235]	Relational specification as a testing oracle	West Virginia University	Master
2003	Feng [236]	On the effectiveness of metamorphic testing for numerical programs	The University of Hong Kong	Master
2003	Moe [237]	Observing the dynamic behavior of large distributed systems to improve development and testing: an empirical study in software engineering	Linköping University	Ph.D.
2004	Agarwal [238]	A comparative study of artificial neural networks and info fuzzy networks on their use in software testing	University of South Florida	Master
2005	Pacheco [239]	Eclat: automatic generation and classification of test inputs	Massachusetts Institute of Technology	Master
2006	Edvardsson [240]	Techniques for automatic generation of tests from programs and specifications	Linköping University	Ph.D.

Table 3.10 A Relation of Ph.D. and Master Work on Test Oracles—cont'd

Year	Author	Title	University	Type
2006	Xie [241]	Developing cost-effective model-based techniques for GUI testing	University of Maryland	Ph.D.
2008	Huse [242]	Is using images to test Web pages the solution to a Sisyphean task?	University of Oslo	Master
2008	Dookhoo [243]	Automated regression testing approach to expansion and refinement of speech recognition grammars	University of Central Florida	Master
2010	Park [244]	An approach for oracle data selection criterion	The University of Minnesota	Ph.D.
2010	Lozano [245]	Constraint programming for random testing of a trading system	KTH Royal Institute of Technology	Master
2010	Bessayah [246]	A complementary approach for testing system robustness based on passive testing and fault injection techniques	University of Pierre and Marie Curie (Paris 6)	Ph.D.
2010	Jagannath [247]	Reducing the costs of bounded-exhaustive testing	University of Illinois	Master
2010	Roest [248]	Automated regression testing of Ajax Web applications	Faculty EEMCS, Delft University of Technology	Master
2010	Shrestha [249]	An empirical evaluation of the effectiveness of JML assertions as test oracles	University of Denver	Master
2010	Murphy [250]	Metamorphic testing techniques to detect defects in applications without test oracles	Columbia University	Ph.D.
2011	Shahamiri [251]	An automated framework for software test oracle based on multinetworks	Universiti Teknologi Malaysia	Ph.D.
2011	Zuo [252]	Metamorphic testing research based on circling FSCS	East China Normal University	Master

Continued

Table 3.10 A Relation of Ph.D. and Master Work on Test Oracles—cont'd

Year	Author	Title	University	Type
2011	Kudari [253]	An ontology-based automated test oracle comparator for testing Web applications	Malmö University	Master
2011	Wu [254]	Self-checked metamorphic testing of Monte Carlo simulation	East Carolina University	Master
2011	Liu [255]	Metamorphic testing and its application on hardware fault tolerance	University of Wisconsin	Master
2012	Asrafi [256]	On testing effectiveness of metamorphic relations	Swinburne University of Technology	Master
2012	Just [257]	On Effective and Efficient Mutation Analysis for Unit and Integration	Testing University of Ulm	Ph.D.
2013	Nardi [70]	On test oracles for Simulink-like models	University of São Paulo	Ph.D.
2013	Afshan [258]	Search-based generation of human readable test data and its impact on human oracle costs	The University of Sheeld	Ph.D.
2013	Vieira [259]	A generic and automatic test strategy for compiler testing	Faculty EEMCS, Delft University of Technology	Master

projects and test benches, SE methods teach us that it is sometimes difficult to change mature patterns when they have been applied for a long time. Tools regarding test oracle approaches seem to be complex. A tool should be attractive to its user, that is, easy enough to be used and extensible to allow new technologies to be added in the future. Due to this, it is possible to note that the acceptance of research on the oracle problem by the industry is a challenge. This problem of technology transfer became clear from the numbers provided by the comparative analysis among studies from industry, academia, or collaborations (Fig. 3.19).

We believe that a possible solution to the problem of technology transfer is the development of effective methodologies to transfer results of test oracle research to industry. It seems that a considerable amount of researchers on test oracles does not produce products from their findings or thesis. Many times, impressive and impactful studies on the oracle problem are published but their practical exploration are not well presented and documented. Disregarding some exceptions, this lack of products is due to the fragmentation of the research groups. We feel that, despite some collaboration among research groups (Fig. 3.23), there is a lack of cooperation to create a product with several resources.

Another point to be considered in dealing with problems related to technology transfer is the supply of training materials and tutorials about practical approaches. Available frameworks, tools, and APIs seem to be difficult to handle for testers who are not involved in their original design. Tutorials and practical examples are not usually mentioned by the authors of studies. Likewise, internet repositories including code samples and templates are not common. Due to this, practitioners and researchers interested in following new strategies have to expend a lot of time to learn to adopt new concepts and paradigms.

In addition, in our analysis, we observed many studies on parts of an oracle, but they do not treat the problem as a whole. For example, there are many studies on specification languages that discourse on how expressive they are with regard to other languages, their applications in different domains or how it is possible to translate them to automata and how to turn expressions more efficiently. But there is no study on the tracing from a document to a specification language that is used as oracle information and how expressive a specification language actually should be to fit as oracle information. In addition, there is a lack of studies on how to facilitate the specification writing for complex requirements in the oracle context. A similar situation occurs for MR where describing metamorphic testing can be a manually intensive technique for complex cases [142].

All the timely challenges, namely, the difficulty in generalizing automated solutions and in learning a specification language and writing requirements, usability and support mechanisms, initial configurations, and input and output parameters, hamper the oracle automation and make their acceptance difficult in the industry. Such points must be considered in a context where an oracle procedure must analyze its information to allow the automation. For instance, on the ML research, there are many studies that demonstrate their role as oracles, but there is not much effort on presenting how to prepare the data of an SUT to feed the network.

5.2. Complexity of SUT's Outputs

Another delicate issue to be faced by researchers and practitioners on test oracles is the complex format of the SUT's outputs. Complex formats are those for which the decision on their correctness requires sensory and perceptual aspects of a human being, such as vision and human hearing. For example, systems with sophisticated GUIs, some Web applications, and virtual reality environments have typical instances of these complex outputs. Moreover, our analysis has revealed few practical studies directed to these systems (Fig. 3.18 and Table 3.4).

Systems with complex outputs are becoming common nowadays. The competitiveness makes the software industry develop ever more attractive and exquisite outputs. Then, naturally, the complexity of outputs is inherent from this generation of contemporary software. In addition, the contemporary software has a vast array of technologies including the hardware platforms, operating systems, and programming languages to support complex scenarios.

Testing technologies can be updated in the same proportion to this *new generation of systems* bringing benefits to final users. In particular, test oracles are supposed to support a productive evaluation of complex outputs. To illustrate this situation, when an SUT has a value or string as an output, the oracle rule is alleviated. Then, testers are able to define automated approaches in a *friendly* way. On the other hand, when the system output is given in a complex format, the oracle problem involves an *extra problem*—defining adequate methods for productive automation.

Following, we present several output formats that could make the oracle problem worse:

- Web applications: they should work well visually in several browsers. For final users it is common to see, *text fields*, *checkboxes*, and *comboboxes* not working properly under different browsers. Visual nondetected errors could be defining the failure to a company;
- Virtual Reality (VR) or Augmented Reality (AR) systems: these systems could carry visual errors, regarding positioning and dimensioning of virtual objects in the three-dimensional environments. Automated testing strategies for these applications are highly manual and ad hoc;
- Text-to-Speech (TTS) systems: a system whose outputs are provided by means of an audio signal (such as representing speech) are commonly evaluated by human audition and scoring. Then, the automation of test oracles for this context can be considered an abstract and hard task. Despite the complexity related to the test, TTS systems have several

applications, such as support for computer–human interaction for blind people, automatic reading of e-mails in embedded and mobile applications, reading of social network updates, and call center automation;

- GUIs: software systems whose output is promoted by means of a GUI (including mobile applications) must work properly independently of platform, screen resolutions, screen orientation, touch screens sensibilities, color systems, monitor settings, and Look and Feels (L&Fs). In addition, event-driven systems are a well-known problem when the issue is processes of quality assurance. In this way, the complexity associated with SUT's outputs is transferred for automated test strategies. For instance, generally, rippers and record/playback tools are necessities;

- Images or graphical outputs: systems whose outputs are given by a processed image, such as CAD (computer-aided diagnosis) systems are naturally hard to be tested automatically. This kind of system, generally, is designed to support decisions in diagnosis. Visual analysis is necessary for CAD system testing; and

- Videos: systems whose outputs are given in video formats require synchronization between sounds and frames of images. Quality aspects have to be verified independently of platforms. Additionally, these systems may need to be associated with subtitles for videos and delays can occur.

As a result, these complex characteristics limit the alternatives for test automation and, consequently, test oracles. Implementing automated test oracles for SUT with complex outputs requires the application of specific techniques. These techniques might be directed at evaluating specific characteristics of the SUT's outputs. Further, these characteristics should represent the main essence of the output as whole, working as information sources for testing activities. For example, regarding complex GUIs or images, these characteristics may be represented by colors, contrast, forms, textures, or components' positioning. On the other hand, considering TTS systems, these characteristics may be represented by naturalness, volume, energy, duration, pauses, etc.

In this context, an expressive contribution can be held by means of the composition and update of repositories including open source tools, frameworks, and APIs on the test oracle. Regarding our pool of more than 300 studies, few researchers provided their resources and technologies to access the Internet. Further, when the researchers provided their products for public access, generally, there were not enough support materials for other researchers using/extending these tools and frameworks. However, we believe tool repositories would help to advance the state-of-the-art faster.

Since open source tools could be improved and extended, this would help avoiding groups starting new research from scratch.

5.3. Generalization of Test Oracle Strategies and Properties

It is necessary to make a generalization of test oracle research. This necessity was introduced by Harman *et al.* [11]. We believe this generalization should be held under two fundamental aspects: (1) theoretical, by means of oracle properties and (2) practical, by means of generic oracle strategies. Below, we present aspects associated with these two generalization perspectives:

- Theoretical generalizations: future studies on test oracles may consider the standardization of theoretical definitions and properties. Section 3 presented plenty of definitions and categories of test oracles. Future research may be focused on establishing more general theoretical definitions and properties on test oracles. We see several benefits associated with this standardization:
  - More broad definitions and taxonomies for test oracles: generally, each test oracle researcher presents particular definitions closer to their own interests. This makes the research on test oracles a fragmented issue, instead of continuous;
  - Possibilities of Systematic Literature Reviews (SLRs): SLRs are a means of aggregating knowledge about an SE topic or research question. In other words, SLR is a means of identifying, evaluating, and interpreting all available research relevant to a particular research question or topic area. It is useful for researchers and practitioners to find out techniques and strategies in their particular interest area. In SE, generally, the study selection for SLRs is performed by means of a research string with a set of key words in an indexed basis of scientific articles [113]. Then, for specific domains and contexts, theoretical generalizations of test oracles may facilitate the access of the state of the art; and
  - Maturity: well-explored areas of software testing have standards and patterns for their basic properties and definitions, such as mutation testing, model testing, and regression testing. Standardized definitions of properties are propitious to research collaboration and group integrations.
- Practical generalizations: as we presented in Section 2, test oracles are particular processes useful in a specific testing scenario. Due to these processes, new research on test oracles may include strategies that offer

support to more than one field output test. We present two consequences associated with the generalization of test oracle strategies:

- Flexibility: due to the variety of domains, researchers should consider
  the development of more adaptable tools and flexible frameworks.
  A possible way to realize the tools and frameworks is the implementation of plug-in-oriented resources and technologies. In this context,
  a plug-in represents a software component that adds a specific testing
  feature to an existing tool/framework; and
- Integration of tools and frameworks: considering the large number of
  tools and frameworks presented in Table 3.9, research to generalize
  approaches to oracles would be favorable for the possibility of integration in frameworks and tools.

Using our survey as background, in the following section, we present particular thoughts about future research on test oracles.

5.4. Trends on Test Oracle

The investigation of trends presented in this section is based on the quantitative analysis obtained through the evaluation of the evolution of oracle
approaches (Fig. 3.15) and the type of SUT exploited in experiments
(Fig. 3.18). Below, we present some trends in a high-level description
regardless of technical aspects associated with each trend.

The first trend to be considered by researchers on test oracles is the con-
duction of *multidisciplinary approaches*. Current SE projects associate different
forms and concepts from distinct areas of computing. For instance, the association of ANN and software testing can result in significant evolutions, alleviating human oracle costs and automating test oracles. These evolutions are
results of a well-conducted multidisciplinary project associating concepts of
AI and SE. Regarding test oracles, one can mention future research associating concepts of Processing Image (PI) for checking results of SUTs which
include GUIs, Web application, and images in their outputs. In the same
context, techniques of Signal Processing can be included in testing strategies
of systems of voice synthesis or TTS systems.

A visible trend on test oracles is the *improvement and development of new
strategies associated to metamorphic testing*. Besides a connected group of
researchers (Fig. 3.25A), our analysis demonstrated a considerable evolution
of research on metamorphic testing over the last 5 years (Fig. 3.15). Research
efforts in metamorphic testing have branched out into two main directions:
(1) applying metamorphic testing to programs in different domains as a

solution to overcome the oracle problem and (2) improving/extending the metamorphic testing technique itself, such as automatic detection of MRs and utilizing MRs in fault localization. In this sense, through proper associations with traditional concepts of the test, metamorphic testing must fit itself as a consolidated solution to alleviate the oracle problem.

Another trend is the *integration of the test oracle in rippers and testing tools developed for ubiquitous and pervasive systems*. Ubiquitous and pervasive systems compose an expressive advance in computing that involves the development of applications to be executed everywhere and anywhere. In practical terms, to support these advances, one can consider the different embedded systems and mobile devices available nowadays. Appropriate automated test environments (including a test oracle) for ubiquitous and pervasive systems have to ensure testers that the application is able to run properly under different conditions, such as operational system versions, screen resolutions, screen orientations, and hardware configurations. Technically, this trend might consider the development of integrated environments with SUT and testing technologies. These environments might allow several dynamic changes and adaptations in both SUT and testing technologies.

Finally, using the analysis presented in Section 4, our study has revealed a trend of test oracle research towards the *exploration of secondary studies*, such as surveys and judicious literature reviews. Secondary studies are useful tools to support decisions by researchers and practitioners about the correct technologies to be applied in their projects. Over more than 30 years of research on test oracles, there are several approaches available in the literature. Then, before defining their testing strategies, professionals may use secondary studies to support their decision about which test oracle they might use. According to Fig. 3.15, this trend can already be visualized as a result of the last 3 years of research.

6. FINAL AND CONCLUDING REMARKS

Test oracles perform an elementary function on testing activities—to ascertain whether a test execution is correct or not. In automated testing scenarios, test oracles may be implemented to ensure the productivity to check the correctness of SUT's outputs. Otherwise, the process of verifying test outputs should be conducted by testers, requiring several human efforts. Once a testing designer has a well-implemented test oracle, it is possible to design huge test sequences including more test cases in a systematic approach. Hence, these increase the reliability that the SUT is close to its specifications. However, it is not always a simple task to estimate and evaluate test outputs. In some cases, due to the complexity of the SUT requirements or output, even a human oracle expends a lot of time defining whether test results are acceptable. Given the relevance of this issue, several groups are trying to develop practical approaches for incorporating test oracle mechanisms in their testing processes. Due to this, over more than 30 years of research on test oracles, one can identify clear shifts in the research literature. We have therefore surveyed more than 300 studies on test oracles to measure and report these shifts and predict some trends for future evaluation.

In this chapter, besides some trends and discussions, we have presented a quantitative analysis of a huge pool of studies on test oracles. We have categorized the approaches reported and their experiments. In addition, we present an amount of data sufficient to measure the state of the art on test oracles. To support our study, we have graphically presented approach evolution, SUT classification, identification of research groups, coauthorship of networks, collaboration maps, a broad taxonomy commonly found in the literature, a critical view about issues to be regarded by contemporary oracle approaches, and other analyses. Further, we shared out particular thoughts about trends to be faced by researchers and practitioners test oracles in the next years regarding contemporary software systems. In this sense, under a general and high-level description, our goal was to offer the knowledge gathered by the authors through the years of research on that field and point to what may be the next challenge: defining solutions which will shape the coming state-of-the-art practice.

Our final analysis, giving us an upshot of all this, states that test oracles are obtaining more and more space in industry projects. Daily, researchers have been dedicating their efforts to set a space for test oracles among standardized testing concepts. Future software testing activities will need a verdict about the output of the SUT—requiring a test oracle mechanism. This provision is clear and primary and then test oracles are welcome in contemporary test projects. Due to this, we strongly encourage everyone who is starting studies on test oracles to read this chapter. Then, we believe that quantitative analysis and taxonomy specifications are a good reference to be extended for students and practitioners. In addition, through the reading of this chapter, researchers and practitioners can notice that there is a wide field of research yet to be explored. As for the integration of already known and well-established approaches aiming at the industry acceptance, this fact enriches the monograph presented by means of this chapter.

ACKNOWLEDGMENTS

The authors are grateful to Márcio E. Delamaro and Fátima L.S. Nunes for valuable comments. A thank you to Norine Walker, Juliana Oliveira, and the UMD writing fellows for their accurate reviews and comments. Currently, R. A. P. O is a student visitor at University of Maryland and Prof. Atif Memon is his supervisor. R. A. P. O is supported by FAPESP (Fundaçãao de Amparo à Pesquisa do Estado de São Paulo)—Grant Numbers 2012/06474-1 and 2013/01775-6.

REFERENCES

[1] L. Baresi, M. Young, Test oracles, Technical report CIS-TR-01-02, Department of Computer and Information Science University of Oregon, Eugene, OR, USA. http://bit.ly/9fkDwJ, 2001 (accessed 09.02.11).

[2] W. Howden, Theoretical and empirical studies of program testing, IEEE Trans. Softw. Eng. SE-4 (4) (1978) 293–298.

[3] S. Shahamiri, W. Kadir, S. Hashim, A comparative study on automated software test oracle methods, in: Proceedings of the 4th International Conference on Software Engineering Advances (ICSEA 2009), Porto, Portugal, 2009, pp. 140–145.

[4] M.D. Davis, E.J. Weyuker, Pseudo-oracles for non-testable programs, in: Proceedings of the ACM Conference (ACM 1981), New York, NY, USA, 1981, pp. 254–257.

[5] J. Day, J. Gannon, A test oracle based on formal specifications, in: Proceedings of the 2nd Conference on Software Development Tools, Techniques, and Alternatives (SDTTA 1985), Los Alamitos, CA, USA, 1985, pp. 126–130.

[6] E. Weyuker, On testing non-testable programs, Comput. J. 25 (4) (1982) 465–470.

[7] M.Y. Ivory, M.A. Hearst, The state of the art in automating usability evaluation of user interfaces, ACM Comput. Surv. 33 (4) (2001) 470–516.

[8] J. Bieman, H. Yin, Designing for software testability using automated oracles, in: Proceedings of the International Test Conference (ITC 1992), Baltimore, MD, 1992, pp. 900–907.

[9] P.D.L. Machado, Testing from structured algebraic specifications: the oracle problem, Ph.D. Dissertation, University of Edinburgh, 2000.

[10] J. Takahashi, An automated oracle for verifying GUI objects, ACM SIGSOFT 26 (4) (2001) 83–88.

[11] M. Harman, P. McMinn, M. Shahbaz, S. Yoo, A comprehensive survey of trends in oracles for software testing, Technical report, Department of Computer Science, University College London (UCL), UK. http://bit.ly/1kFX0T3, 2013. (accessed 12.04.13).

[12] D. Hoffman, A taxonomy for test oracles, in: Proceedings of the 11th International Quality Week (QW 98), San Francisco, CA, USA, 1998, pp. 1–8.

[13] D. Hoffman, Using oracles in test automation, in: Proceedings of the 19th Pacific Northwest Software Quality Conference (PNSQC 2001), Portland, OR, USA, 2001, pp. 91–102.

[14] P. Jalote, An Integrated Approach to Software Engineering, third ed., Springer-Verlag New York, Inc., New York, USA, 2005.

[15] P. Ammann, J. Offutt, Introduction to Software Testing, first ed., Cambridge University Press, Cambridge, UK, 2008.

[16] G. Myers, C. Sandler, T. Badgett, The Art of Software Testing, third ed., John Wiley and Sons Inc., New York, USA, 2011.

[17] IEEE Systems and Software Engineering—Vocabulary. 24765:2010(E), ISO/IEC/IEEE, vol. 1, 2010, pp. 1–418. http://dx.doi.org/10.1109/IEEESTD.2010.5733835. (accessed 30.06.2014).

[18] A.P. Mathur, Foundations of Software Testing, first ed., Addison-Wesley Professional, Boston, USA, 2007.

[19] A. Bertolino, Software testing research and practice, in: E. Borger, A. Gargantini, E. Riccobene (Eds.), Abstract State Machines 2003, v. 2589 de Lecture Notes in Computer Science, Springer, Berlin, Heidelberg, 2003, pp. 1–21.

[20] A. Bertolino, Software testing research: achievements, challenges, dreams, in: Proceedings of the Future of Software Engineering (FOSE 2007), Minneapolis, MN, USA, 2007, pp. 85–103.

[21] C. Hunter, P. Strooper, Systematically deriving partial oracles for testing concurrent programs, in: Proceedings of the 24th Australasian Computer Science Conference (ACSC 2001), Gold Coast, Australia, 2001, pp. 83–91.

[22] H.Y. Chen, T. Tse, Equality to equals and unequals: a revisit of the equivalence and nonequivalence criteria in class-level testing of object-oriented software, IEEE Trans. Softw. Eng. 39 (11) (2013) 1549–1563.

[23] B. Cafeo, P. Masiero, Contextual integration testing of object-oriented and aspect-oriented programs: a structural approach for Java and AspectJ, in: Proceedings of the 25th Brazilian Symposium on Software Engineering (SBES 2011), Sao Paulo, Brazil, 2011, pp. 214–223.

[24] F. Ferrari, J. Maldonado, A. Rashid, Mutation testing for aspect-oriented programs, in: Proceedings of the 1st International Conference on Software Testing, Verification, and Validation (ICST 2008), Lillehammer, Norway, 2008, pp. 52–61.

[25] M. Kumar, A. Sharma, S. Garg, A study of aspect oriented testing techniques, in: Proceedings of the IEEE Symposium on Industrial Electronics Applications (ISIEA 2009), Kuala Lumpur, Malaysia, 2009, pp. 996–1001.

[26] M. Leotta, D. Clerissi, F. Ricca, P. Tonella, Capture-replay vs. programmable web testing: an empirical assessment during test case evolution, in: Proceedings of the 20th Working Conference on Reverse Engineering (WCRE 2013), Koblenz, Germany, 2013, pp. 272–281.

[27] S. McMaster, X. Yuan, Developing a feedback-driven automated testing tool for Web applications, in: Proceedings of the 12th International Conference on Quality Software (QSIC 2012), Xi'an, China, 2012, pp. 210–213.

[28] U. Praphamontripong, Web mutation testing, in: Proceedings of the 5th IEEE International Conference on Software Testing, Verification and Validation (ICST 2012), Berlin, Germany, 2012, pp. 495–498.

[29] A. Latoui, F. Djahli, An optical BILBO for online testing of embedded systems, IEEE Des. Test 30 (3) (2013) 34–48.

[30] Y. Yin, B. Liu, H. Ni, Real-time embedded software testing method based on extended finite state machine, J. Syst. Eng. Electron. 23 (2) (2012) 276–285.

[31] K.I. Seo, E.M. Choi, Rigorous vertical software system testing in IDE, in: Proceedings of the 5th ACIS International Conference on Software Engineering Research, Management & Applications (SERA 2007), Busan, Korea, 2007, pp. 847–854.

[32] P. Imperatore, E. Salvadori, I. Chlamtac, Path loss measurements at 3.5 GHz: a trial test WiMAX based in rural environment, in: Proceedings of the 3rd International Conference on Testbeds and Research Infrastructure for the Development of Networks and Communities (TridentCom 2007), Orland, FL, USA, 2007, pp. 1–8.

[33] J. Sun, G. Li, C. Xu, Prior distribution of missile range trial successive test data based on random weighting, in: Proceedings of the 4th International Conference on Computational and Information Sciences (ICCIS 2012), Kuala Lumpur, Malaysia, 2012, pp. 1163–1166.

[34] E. Dustin, T. Garrett, B. Gauf, Implementing Automated Software Testing: How to Save Time and Lower Costs While Raising Quality, first ed., Addison-Wesley Professional, Boston, USA, 2009.

[35] J. Humble, D. Farley, Continuous Delivery: Reliable Software Releases Through Build, Test, and Deployment Automation, first ed., Addison-Wesley Professional, Boston, USA, 2010.

[36] D. Hoffman, Using oracles in testing and test automation, Testing, (2006), Available in http://goo.gl/d3Fb6 LogiGear—Software.

[37] R.G. Hamlet, Software quality, software process, and software testing, Adv. Comput. 41 (1995) 191–229.

[38] W. Chan, J. Ho, T. Tse, Piping classification to metamorphic testing: an empirical study towards better effectiveness for the identification of failures in mesh simplification programs, in: Proceedings of the 31st Annual International Computer Software and Applications Conference (COMPSAC 2007), Beijing, China, 2007, pp. 397–404.

[39] M. Delamaro, F. Nunes, R. Oliveira, Using concepts of content-based image retrieval to implement graphical testing oracles, Softw. Test. Verif. Rel. 23 (3) (2013) 171–198.

[40] R. Oliveira, M. Delamaro, F. Nunes, Exploring the O-FIm framework to support the test of programs with GUIs, in: Proceedings of the 4th Brazilian Workshop on Systematic and Automated Software Testing (SAST 2010), Natal, Brazil, 2010, pp. 31–40.

[41] P. McMinn, M. Stevenson, M. Harman, Reducing qualitative human oracle costs associated with automatically generated test data, in: Proceedings of the 1st International Workshop on Software Test Output Validation (STOV 2010), Trento, Italy, 2010, pp. 1–4.

[42] V. Durelli, R. Araujo, M. Silva, R. Oliveira, J. Maldonado, M. Delamaro, A scoping study on the 25 years of research into software testing in Brazil and an outlook on the future of the area, J. Syst. Softw. 86 (4) (2013) 934–950.

[43] W. Chan, T. Tse, Oracles are hardly attain'd, and hardly understood: confessions of software testing researchers, in: Proceedings of the 13rd International Conference on Quality Software (QSIC 2013), Boston, MA, USA, 2013, pp. 245–252.

[44] M. Asrafi, H. Liu, F.-C. Kuo, On testing effectiveness of metamorphic relations: a case study, in: Proceedings of the 5th International Conference on Secure Software Integration and Reliability Improvement (SSIRI 2011), Jeju Island, Korea, 2011, pp. 147–156.

[45] M. Staats, M. Whalen, M. Heimdahl, Programs, tests, and oracles: the foundations of testing revisited, in: Proceedings of the 33rd International Conference on Software Engineering (ICSE 2011), Waikiki, HI, USA, 2011, pp. 391–400.

[46] R. Guderlei, R. Just, C. Schneckenburger, F. Schweiggert, Benchmarking testing strategies with tools from mutation analysis, in: Proceedings of the IEEE International Conference on Software Testing Verification and Validation Workshop (ICSTW 2008), Berlin, Germany, 2008, pp. 360–364.

[47] D. Hoffman, P. Strooper, Automated module testing in prolog, IEEE Trans. Softw. Eng. 17 (9) (1991) 934–943.

[48] T. Janssen, R. Abreu, A. van Gemund, Zoltar: a toolset for automatic fault localization, in: Proceedings of the 24th IEEE/ACM International Conference on Automated Software Engineering (ASE 2009), Auckland, New Zealand, 2009, pp. 662–664.

[49] D. Kim-Park, C. de la Riva, J. Tuya, An automated test oracle for XML processing programs, in: Proceedings of the 1st International Workshop on Software Test Output Validation (STOV 2010), Trento, Italy, 2010, pp. 5–12.

[50] P. McMinn, M. Shahbaz, M. Stevenson, Search-based test input generation for string data types using the results of Web queries, in: Proceedings of the 5th IEEE International Conference on Software Testing, Verification and Validation (ICST 2012), Montreal, Canada, 2012, pp. 141–150.

[51] M. Staats, G. Gay, M. Heimdahl, Automated oracle creation support, or: how I learned to stop worrying about fault propagation and love mutation testing, in: Proceedings of

the 34th International Conference on Software Engineering (ICSE 2012), Zurich, Switzerland, 2012, pp. 870–880.

[52] B. Aichernig, A. Griesmayer, E. Johnsen, R. Schlatte, A. Stam, Conformance testing of distributed concurrent systems with executable designs, in: Proceedings of the 7th International Symposium on Formal Methods for Components and Objects (FMCO 2009), Sophia Antipolis, France, 2009, pp. 61–81.

[53] J. Andrews, Y. Zhang, General test result checking with log file analysis, IEEE Trans. Softw. Eng. 29 (7) (2003) 634–648.

[54] J. Chen, S. Subramaniam, Specification-based testing for GUI-based applications, Softw. Q. J. 10 (3) (2002) 205–224.

[55] D. D'Souza, M. Gopinathan, Computing complete test graphs for hierarchical systems, in: Proceedings of the 4th IEEE International Conference on Software Engineering and Formal Methods (SEFM 2006), Pune, India, 2006, pp. 70–79.

[56] D. Giannakopoulou, D. Bushnell, J. Schumann, H. Erzberger, K. Heere, Formal testing for separation assurance, Ann. Math. Artif. Intell. 63 (2011) 5–30.

[57] A. Rauf, S. Anwar, M. Ramzan, S. Rehman, A. Shahid, Ontology driven semantic annotation based GUI testing, in: Proceedings of the 6th International Conference on Emerging Technologies (ICET 2010), Islamabad, Pakistan, 2010, pp. 261–264.

[58] O. Sangwan, P. Bhatia, Y. Singh, Radial basis function neural network based approach to test oracle, ACM SIGSOFT 36 (5) (2011) 1–5.

[59] S. Shahamiri, W. Kadir, S. Ibrahim, An automated oracle approach to test decision-making structures, in: Proceedings of the 3rd IEEE International Conference on Computer Science and Information Technology (ICCSIT 2010), Chengdu, China, 2010, pp. 30–34.

[60] S. Shahamiri, W. Kadir, S. Ibrahim, A single-network ANN-based oracle to verify logical software modules, in: Proceedings of the 2nd International Conference on Software Technology and Engineering (ICSTE 2010), San Juan, Puerto Rico, 2010, pp. 272–276.

[61] M. Vanmali, M. Last, A. Kandel, Using a neural network in the software testing process, Int. J. Intell. Syst. 17 (1) (2002) 45–62.

[62] S. Afshan, P. McMinn, M. Stevenson, Evolving readable string test inputs using a natural language model to reduce human oracle cost, in: Proceedings of the 6th IEEE International Conference on Software Testing, Verification and Validation (ICST 2013), Luxembourg, 2013, pp. 352–361.

[63] D. Hook, D. Kelly, Testing for trustworthiness in scientific software, in: Proceedings of the ICSE Workshop on Software Engineering for Computational Science and Engineering (SECSE 2009), Vancouver, Canada, 2009, pp. 59–64.

[64] H. Sneed, State coverage of embedded realtime programs, in: Proceedings of the 2nd Workshop on Software Testing, Verification, and Analysis (STVA 1988), Banff, Canada, 1988, pp. 245–250.

[65] A.Z. Javed, P. Strooper, G. Watson, Automated generation of test cases using model-driven architecture, in: Proceedings of the 2nd International Workshop on Automation of Software Test (AST 2007), Minneapolis, MN, USA, 2007, pp. 1–3.

[66] Team, J. Junit 4. http://junit.org/, 2013 (accessed 12.15.13).

[67] J. Chen, M. Lin, K. Yu, B. Shao, When a GUI regression test failed, what should be blamed? in: Proceedings of the 5th IEEE International Conference on Software Testing, Verification and Validation (ICST 2012), Montreal, Canada, 2012, pp. 467–470.

[68] C. Murphy, K. Shen, G. Kaiser, Using JML runtime assertion checking to automate metamorphic testing in applications without test oracles, in: Proceedings of the International Conference on Software Testing Verification and Validation (ICST 2009), Denver, CO, USA, 2009, pp. 436–445.

[69] M. Jiang, T. Chen, F.-C. Kuo, Z. Ding, Testing central processing unit scheduling algorithms using metamorphic testing, in: Proceedings of the 4th IEEE International Conference on Software Engineering and Service Science (ICSESS 2013), Beijing, China, 2013, pp. 530–536.

[70] P. Nardi, On test oracles for Simulink-like models, Ph.D. Dissertation, University São Paulo, 2013.

[71] A. Memon, Q. Xie, Empirical evaluation of the fault-detection effectiveness of smoke regression test cases for GUI-based software, in: Proceedings of the 20th IEEE International Conference on Software Maintenance (ICSM 2004), Chicago, IL, USA, 2004, pp. 8–17.

[72] J. McDonald, P. Strooper, Translating object-Z specifications to passive test oracles, in: Proceedings of the 2nd IEEE International Conference on Formal Engineering Methods (ICEFEM 1998), Brisbane, Australia, 1998, pp. 165–175.

[73] L. Rose, S. Poulding, Efficient probabilistic testing of model transformations using search, in: Proceedings of the 1st International Workshop on Combining Modelling and Search-Based Software Engineering (CMSBSE 2013), San Francisco, CA, USA, 2013, pp. 16–21.

[74] Z. Zhang, W. Chan, T. Tse, P. Hu, Experimental study to compare the use of metamorphic testing and assertion checking, J. Softw. 20 (10) (2009) 2637–2654.

[75] W. Howden, Reliability of the path analysis testing strategy, IEEE Trans. Softw. Eng. SE-2 (3) (1976) 208–215.

[76] J. Srinivasan, N. Leveson, Automated testing from specifications, in: Proceedings of the 21st Digital Avionics Systems Conference (DASC 2002), Irvine, CA, USA, 2002, pp. 1–8.

[77] A.-M. Torsel, Automated test case generation for Web applications from a domain specific model, in: Proceedings of the 35th IEEE Annual Computer Software and Applications Conference Workshops (COMPSACW 2011), Munich, Germany, 2011, pp. 137–142.

[78] D. Vazquez, J. Xu, S. Ramos, A. Lopez, D. Ponsa, Weakly supervised automatic annotation of pedestrian bounding boxes, in: Proceedings of the IEEE Conference on Computer Vision and Pattern Recognition Workshops (CVPRW 2013), Portland, OR, USA, 2013, pp. 706–711.

[79] D. Agarwal, D. Tamir, M. Last, A. Kandel, A comparative study of artificial neural networks and info-fuzzy networks as automated oracles in software testing, IEEE Trans. Syst. Man Cyber. A Syst. Hum. 42 (5) (2012) 1183–1193.

[80] B. Beizer, Software Testing Techniques, second ed., International Thomson Computer Press—Van Nostrand Reinhold Co, New York, USA, 1990, 580 pp.

[81] D. Crocker, Perfect developer: a tool for object-oriented formal specification and refinement, in: Proceedings of the International Symposium of Formal Methods Europe (FME 2003)—Tools Exhibition Notes, Pisa, Italy, 2003, pp. 1–5.

[82] W.-T. Tsai, X. Bai, Y. Chen, X. Zhou, Web service group testing with windowing mechanisms, in: Proceedings of the IEEE International Workshop Service-Oriented System Engineering (SOSE 2005), Beijing, China, 2005, pp. 213–218.

[83] R. Just, F. Schweiggert, Automating software tests with partial oracles in integrated environments, in: Proceedings of the 5th Workshop on Automation of Software Test (AST 2010), Cape Town, South Africa, 2010, pp. 91–94.

[84] L. Ran, C. Dyreson, A. Andrews, R. Bryce, C. Mallery, Building test cases and oracles to automate the testing of Web database applications, Inform. Softw. Technol. 51 (2) (2009) 460–477.

[85] C. Murphy, G. Kaiser, Metamorphic runtime checking of non-testable programs, Technical report, Columbia University. http://bit.ly/1p8rGfR, 2009 (accessed 12.09.13).

[86] O. Hummel, C. Atkinson, Automated harvesting of test oracles for reliability testing, in: Proceedings of the 29th Annual International Computer Software and Applications Conference (COMPSAC 2005), Edinburgh, UK, 2005, pp. 196–202.

[87] J. McDonald, D. Hoffman, P. Strooper, Programmatic testing of the standard template library containers, in: Proceedings of the 13th IEEE International Conference on Automated Software Engineering (ASE 1998), Honolulu, HI, USA, 1998, pp. 147–156.

[88] J. McDonald, P. Strooper, D. Hoffman, Tool support for generating passive C++ test oracles from object-z specifications, in: Proceedings of the 10th Asia-Pacific Software Engineering Conference Software Engineering Conference (APSEC 2003), Chiang Mai, Thailand, 2003, pp. 322–332.

[89] T. Miller, P. Strooper, Supporting the software testing process through specification animation, in: Proceedings of the 1st International Conference on Software Engineering and Formal Methods (SEFM 2003), Brisbane, Australia, 2003, pp. 14–23.

[90] R. Shukla, P. Strooper, D. Carrington, Tool support for statistical testing of software components, in: Proceedings of the 12th Asia-Pacific Software Engineering Conference (APSEC 2005), Taipei, Taiwan, 2005, pp. 16–24.

[91] A. Pasala, S. Rao, A. Gupta, S. Gunturu, On the validation of API execution-sequence to assess the correctness of application upon COTS upgrades deployment, in: Proceedings of the 6th International IEEE Conference on Commercial-off-the-Shelf (COTS)-Based Software Systems (ICCBSS 2007), Banff, Canada, 2007, pp. 225–232.

[92] R. Shukla, D. Carrington, P. Strooper, A passive test oracle using a component's API, in: Proceedings of the 12th Asia-Pacific Software Engineering Conference (APSEC 2005), Taipei, Taiwan, 2005, pp. 7–15.

[93] J. Hagar, J. Bieman, Adding formal specifications to a proven V&V process for system-critical flight software, in: Proceedings of the Workshop on Industrial-Strength Formal Specification Techniques (WIFT 1995), Boca Raton, FL, USA, 1995, pp. 76–85.

[94] P. Nardi, M. Delamaro, Test oracles associated with dynamical system models, Technical report CIS-TR-01-02, University of São Paulo (USP), ICMC. http://bit.ly/1ll0mCW, 2011 (accessed 12.18.13).

[95] A. Memon, I. Banerjee, A. Nagarajan, What test oracle should I use for effective GUI testing? in: Proceedings of the 18th IEEE International Conference on Automated Software Engineering (ASE 2003), Montreal, Canada, 2003, pp. 164–173.

[96] G. Durrieu, H. Waeselynck, V. Wiels, LETO—a lustre-based test oracle for airbus critical systems, in: Proceedings of the 13th International Workshop on Formal Methods for Industrial Critical Systems (FMICS 2009), Eindhoven, The Netherlands, 2009, pp. 7–22.

[97] J. Hagar, J. Bieman, Using formal specifications as test oracles for system-critical software, ACM SIGAda Ada Lett. 16 (6) (1996) 55–72.

[98] D. Luckham, F. Von Henke, An overview of Anna, a specification language for Ada, IEEE Softw. 2 (2) (1985) 9–22.

[99] S. Sankar, A. Goyal, P. Sikchi, Software testing using algebraic specification based test oracles, Technical report, Stanford University. http://1.usa.gov/Oz2Avd, 1993 (accessed 12.15.13).

[100] Y. Cheon, G. Leavens, A simple and practical approach to unit testing: the JML and JUnit way, in: Proceedings of the European Conference on Object-Oriented Programming (ECOOP 2002), Malaga, Spain, 2002, pp. 1789–1901.

[101] G. Dai, X. Bai, Y. Wang, F. Dai, Contract-based testing for Web services, in: Proceedings of the 31st Annual International Computer Software and Applications Conference (COMPSAC 2007), Beijing, China, 2007, pp. 517–526.

[102] M. Harman, S. Kim, K. Lakhotia, P. McMinn, S. Yoo, Optimizing for the number of tests generated in search based test data generation with an application to the oracle cost problem, in: Proceedings of the 3rd International Conference on Software Testing, Verification, and Validation Workshops (ICSTW 2010), Paris, France, 2010, pp. 182–191.

[103] S. Edwards, A framework for practical, automated black-box testing of component-based software, Softw. Test. Verif. Rel. 11 (2) (2001) 97–111.

[104] L. Briand, Y. Labiche, A UML-based approach to system testing, Softw. Syst. Modell. 1 (1) (2002) 10–42.

[105] L. Briand, Y. Labiche, H. Sun, Investigating the use of analysis contracts to improve the testability of object-oriented code, Softw. Pract. Exp. 33 (7) (2003) 637–672.

[106] Y. Cheon, C. Avila, Automating java program testing using OCL and AspectJ, in: Proceedings of the 7th International Conference on Information Technology: New Generations (ITNG 2010), Las Vegas, NV, USA, 2010, pp. 1020–1025.

[107] S. Packevicus, U. Andrej, E. Bareisa, Software testing using imprecise OCL constraints as oracles, in: Proceedings of the 2007 International Conference on Computer Systems and Technologies (CompSysTech 2007), Ruse, Bulgaria, 2007, pp. 1–6.

[108] J. Lasalle, F. Peureux, J. Guillet, Automatic test concretization to supply end-to-end MBT for automotive mechatronic systems, in: Proceedings of the 1st International Workshop on End-to-End Test Script Engineering (ETSE 2011), Toronto, Canada, 2011, pp. 16–23.

[109] X. Wang, Z.-C. Qi, S. Li, An optimized method for automatic test oracle generation from real-time specification, in: Proceedings of the 10th IEEE International Conference on Engineering of Complex Computer Systems (ICECCS 2005), Shanghai, China, 2005, pp. 440–449.

[110] M. Felder, A. Morzenti, Validating real-time systems by history-checking TRIO specifications, in: Proceedings of the International Conference on Software Engineering (ICSE 1992), Melbourne, Australia, 1992, pp. 199–211.

[111] J. Lin, I. Ho, A new perspective on formal testing method for real-time software, in: Proceedings of the 26th Euromicro Conference 2000 (Euromicro 2000), Maastricht, Netherlands, 2000, pp. 270–276.

[112] J. Lin, I. Ho, Generating timed test cases with oracles for real-time software, Adv. Eng. Softw. 32 (9) (2001) 705–715.

[113] T. Dyba, B. Kitchenham, M. Jorgensen, Evidence-based software engineering for practitioners, IEEE Softw. 22 (1) (2005) 58–65.

[114] T. Chen, T. Tse, Z. Zhou, Fault-based testing without the need of oracles, Inform. Softw. Technol. 45 (1) (2003) 1–9.

[115] T.Y. Chen, S.C. Cheung, S.M. Yiu, Metamorphic testing: a new approach for generating next test cases, Technical report, Department of Computer Science, Hong Kong University of Science and Technology, Hong Kong. http://bit.ly/1nTs6HM, 1998 (accessed 02.13.14).

[116] T. Chen, J. Ho, H. Liu, X. Xie, An innovative approach for testing bioinformatics programs using metamorphic testing, BMC Bioinformatics 10 (1) (2009) 1–12.

[117] C. Murphy, G.E. Kaiser, L. Hu, L. Wu, Properties of machine learning applications for use in metamorphic testing, in: Proceedings of the 20th International Conference on Software Engineering & Knowledge Engineering (SEKE 2008), San Francisco, CA, USA, 2008.

[118] X. Xie, J.W.K. Ho, C. Murphy, G. Kaiser, B. Xu, T.Y. Chen, Testing and validating machine learning classifiers by metamorphic testing, J. Syst. Softw. 84 (4) (2011) 544–558.

[119] F.-C. Kuo, T.Y. Chen, W. Tam, Testing embedded software by metamorphic testing: a wireless metering system case study, in: Proceedings of the 36th IEEE Conference on Local Computer Networks (LCN 2011), Bonn, Germany, 2011, pp. 291–294.

[120] C. Murphy, M. Raunak, A. King, S. Chen, C. Imbriano, G. Kaiser, I. Lee, O. Sokolsky, L. Clarke, L. Osterweil, On effective testing of health care simulation software, in: Proceedings of the 3rd Workshop on Software Engineering in Health Care (SEHC 2011), Waikiki, HI, USA, 2011, pp. 40–47.

[121] J. Ding, T. Wu, D. Wu, J. Lu, X. Hu, Metamorphic testing of a Monte Carlo modeling program, in: Proceedings of the 6th International Workshop on Automation of Software Test (AST 2011), Waikiki, Honolulu, HI, USA, 2011, pp. 1–7.

[122] T. Chen, J. Feng, T. Tse, Metamorphic testing of programs on partial differential equations: a case study, in: Proceedings of the 26th Annual International Computer Software and Applications Conference (COMPSAC 2002), Oxford, England, 2002, pp. 327–333.

[123] X. Xie, W.E. Wong, T.Y. Chen, B. Xu, Metamorphic slice: an application in spectrum-based fault localization, Inform. Softw. Technol. 55 (5) (2013) 866–879.

[124] H. Liu, F.-C. Kuo, D. Towey, T.Y. Chen, How effectively does metamorphic testing alleviate the oracle problem? IEEE Trans. Softw. Eng. 40 (1) (2014) 4–22.

[125] U. Kanewala, J. Bieman, Techniques for testing scientific programs without an oracle, in: Proceedings of the 5th International Workshop on Software Engineering for Computational Science and Engineering (SE-CSE 2013), San Francisco, CA, USA, 2013, pp. 48–57.

[126] K. Aggarwal, Y. Singh, A. Kaur, O. Sangwan, A neural net based approach to test oracle, ACM SIGSOFT 29 (3) (2004) 1–6.

[127] D. Almog, T. Heart, Developing the basic verification action (BVA) structure towards test oracle automation, in: Proceedings of the International Conference on Computational Intelligence and Software Engineering (CiSE 2010), Wuhan, China, 2010, pp. 1–4.

[128] H. Jin, Y. Wang, N.-W. Chen, Z. Gou, S. Wang, Artificial neural network for automatic test oracles generation, in: Proceedings of the International Conference on Computer Science and Software Engineering (CSSE 2008), Wuhan, China, 2008, pp. 727–730.

[129] Y. Mao, F. Boqin, Z. Li, L. Yao, Neural networks based automated test oracle for software testing, in: Proceedings of the 13th International Conference on Neural Information Processing (ICONIP 2006), Berlin, Heidelberg, 2006, pp. 498–507.

[130] F. Wang, J.-H. Wu, C.-H. Huang, K.-H. Chang, Evolving a test oracle in black-box testing, in: Proceedings of the 14th International Conference on Fundamental Approaches to Software Engineering: Part of the Joint European Conferences on Theory and Practice of Software (FASE 2011), Saarbrucken, Germany, 2011, pp. 310–325.

[131] F. Wang, L.-W. Yao, J.-H. Wu, Intelligent test oracle construction for reactive systems without explicit specifications, in: Proceedings of the 9th IEEE International Conference on Dependable, Autonomic and Secure Computing (DASC 2011), Sydney, Australia, 2011, pp. 89–96.

[132] F. Zaraket, W. Masri, M. Adam, D. Hammoud, R. Hamzeh, R. Farhat, E. Khamissi, J. Noujaim, GUICOP: specification-based GUI testing, in: Proceedings of the 5th IEEE International Conference on Software Testing, Verification and Validation (ICST 2012), Montreal, Canada, 2012, pp. 747–751.

[133] D.E.J. Eckhardt, L.D. Lee, A theoretical basis for the analysis of multiversion software subject to coincident errors, IEEE Trans. Softw. Eng. SE-11 (12) (1985) 1511–1517.

[134] L. Manolache, D. Kourie, Software testing using model programs, Softw. Pract. Exp. 31 (13) (2001) 1211–1236.

[135] J.C. Knight, N.G. Leveson, An experimental evaluation of the assumption of independence in multi-version programming, IEEE Trans. Softw. Eng. 12 (1986) 96–109.

[136] B. Kitchenham, R. Pretorius, D. Budgen, O.P. Brereton, M. Turner, M. Niazi, S. Linkman, Systematic literature reviews in software engineering—a tertiary study, Inform. Softw. Technol. 52 (8) (2010) 792–805.

[137] S. Team, Science of science (Sci2) tool, in: Indiana University and SciTech Strategies, 2009, http://sci2.cns.iu.edu.

[138] T. Chen, T. Tse, Z. Zhou, Fault-based testing in the absence of an oracle, in: Proceedings of the 25th Annual International Computer Software and Applications Conference (COMPSAC 2001), Chicago, IL, USA, 2001, pp. 172–178.

[139] Y. Lei, X. Mao, T. Chen, Backward-slice-based statistical fault localization without test oracles, in: Proceedings of the 13th International Conference on Quality Software (QSIC 2013), Boston, MA, USA, 2013, pp. 212–221.

[140] H. Liu, X. Liu, T. Chen, A new method for constructing metamorphic relations, in: Proceedings of the 12th International Conference on Quality Software (QSIC 2012), Xi'an, China, 2012, pp. 59–68.

[141] C. Murphy, Using runtime testing to detect defects in applications without test oracles, in: Proceedings of the 2008 Foundations of Software Engineering Doctoral Symposium (FSEDS 2008), Atlanta, GA, USA, 2008, pp. 21–24.

[142] C. Murphy, K. Shen, G. Kaiser, Automatic system testing of programs without test oracles, in: Proceedings of the 18th International Symposium on Software Testing and Analysis (ISTAA 2009), Chicago, IL, USA, 2009, pp. 189–200.

[143] X. Xie, W. Wong, T. Chen, B. Xu, Spectrum-based fault localization: testing oracles are no longer mandatory, in: Proceedings of the 11th International Conference on Quality Software (QSIC 2011), Madrid, Spain, 2011, pp. 1–10.

[144] W. Chan, M. Cheng, S. Cheung, T. Tse, Automatic goal-oriented classification of failure behaviors for testing XML-based multimedia software applications: an experimental case study, J. Syst. Softw. 79 (5) (2006) 602–612.

[145] X. Xie, J. Ho, C. Murphy, G. Kaiser, B. Xu, T. Chen, Application of metamorphic testing to supervised classifiers, in: Proceedings of the 9th International Conference on Quality Software (QSIC 2009), Jeju, Korea, 2009, pp. 135–144.

[146] G. Jiang, H. Chen, C. Ungureanu, K. Yoshihira, Multi-resolution abnormal trace detection using varied-length N-grams and automata, in: Proceedings of the 2nd International Conference on Autonomic Computing (ICAC 2005), Seattle, WA, USA, 2005, pp. 111–122.

[147] H. Jin, Y. Wang, N.-W. Chen, S. Wang, L.-M. Zeng, Predication of program behaviours for functionality testing, in: Proceedings of the 1st International Conference on Information Science and Engineering (ICISE 2009), Nanjing, China, 2009, pp. 4993–4996.

[148] Y. Lu, M. Ye, Oracle model based on RBF neural networks for automated software testing, Inform. Technol. J. 6 (3) (2007) 469–474.

[149] S. Shahamiri, W. Kadir, S. Ibrahim, S. Hashim, An automated framework for software test oracle, Inform. Softw. Technol. 53 (7) (2011) 774–788.

[150] S. Sprenkle, E. Hill, L. Pollock, Learning effective oracle comparator combinations for Web applications, in: Proceedings of the 7th International Conference on Quality Software (QSIC 2007), Portland, OR, USA, 2007, pp. 372–379.

[151] M. Ye, B. Feng, L. Zhu, Y. Lin, Automated test oracle based on neural networks, in: Proceedings of the 5th IEEE International Conference on Cognitive Informatics (ICCI 2006), Beijing, China, 2006, pp. 517–522.

[152] D. Richardson, TAOS: testing with analysis and oracle support, in: Proceedings of the 1994 ACM SIGSOFT International Symposium on Software Testing and Analysis (ISSTA 1994), Seattle, WA, USA, 1994, pp. 138–153.

[153] T. Salima, A. Askarunisha, N. Ramaraj, Enhancing the efficiency of regression testing through intelligent agents, in: International Conference on Conference on Computational Intelligence and Multimedia Applications (ICCIMA 2007), Sivakasi, India, 2007, pp. 103–108.

[154] S. Tiwari, K. Mishra, A. Kumr, A. Misra, Spectrum-based fault localization in regression testing, in: Proceedings of the 8th International Conference on Information Technology: New Generations (ITNG 2011), Las Vegas, NE, USA, 2011, pp. 191–195.

[155] T. Xie, Augmenting automatically generated unit-test suites with regression oracle checking, in: Proceedings of the 20th European Conference on Object-Oriented Programming (ECOOP 2006), Nantes, France, 2006, pp. 380–403.

[156] D. Powell, J. Arlat, H. Chu, F. Ingrand, M.-O. Killijian, Testing the input timing robustness of real-time control software for autonomous systems, in: Proceedings of the 9th European Dependable Computing Conference (EDCC 2012), Sibiu, Romania, 2012, pp. 73–83.

[157] C. Wright, G. Kapfhammer, P. McMinn, Efficient mutation analysis of relational database structure using mutant schemata and parallelisation, in: Proceedings of the 6th IEEE International Conference on Software Testing, Verification and Validation Workshops (ICSTW 2013), Luxembourg, 2013, pp. 63–72.

[158] C. Atkinson, O. Hummel, W. Janjic, Search-enhanced testing: NIER track, in: Proceedings of the 33rd International Conference on Software Engineering (ICSE 2011), Honolulu, HI, USA, 2011, pp. 880–883.

[159] T. Shimeall, N. Leveson, An empirical comparison of software fault tolerance and fault elimination, in: Proceedings of the 2nd Workshop on Software Testing, Verification, and Analysis (STVA 1988), Banff, Canada, 1988, pp. 180–187.

[160] R. Just, F. Schweiggert, Evaluating testing strategies for imaging software by means of mutation analysis, in: Proceedings of the International Conference on Software Testing, Verification and Validation Workshops (ICSTW 2009), Denver, CO, USA, 2009, pp. 205–209.

[161] Y. Cheon, Abstraction in assertion-based test oracles, in: Proceedings of the 7th International Conference on Quality Software (QSIC 2007), Portland, OR, USA, 2007, pp. 410–414.

[162] G. Qu, S.-T. Guo, H. Zhang, A practical approach to assertion testing framework based on inner class, in: Proceedings of the 2nd IEEE International Conference on Software Engineering and Service Science (ICSESS 2011), Beijing, China, 2011, pp. 133–137.

[163] A. Rajan, L. du Bousquet, Y. Ledru, G. Vega, J.-L. Richier, Assertion-based test oracles for home automation systems, in: Proceedings of the 7th International Workshop on Model-Based Methodologies for Pervasive and Embedded Software (MOMPES 2010), Silicon Valley, CA, USA, 2010, pp. 45–52.

[164] Q. Xie, A. Memon, Designing and comparing automated test oracles for GUI-based software applications, ACM Trans. Softw. Eng. Methodol. 16 (1) (2007) 1–38.

[165] J. Zhi, V. Garousi, On adequacy of assertions in automated test suites: an empirical investigation, in: Proceedings of the 6th IEEE International Conference on Software Testing, Verification and Validation Workshops (ICSTW 2013), Luxembourg, 2013, pp. 382–391.

[166] W. Xu, T. Ding, H. Wang, D. Xu, Mining test oracles for test inputs generated from Java bytecode, in: Proceedings of the 37th IEEE Annual Computer Software and Applications Conference (COMPSAC 2013), Kyoto, Japan, 2013, pp. 27–32.

[167] W. Xu, H. Wang, T. Ding, Mining auto-generated test inputs for test oracle, in: Proceedings of the 10th International Conference on Information Technology: New Generations (ITNG 2013), Las Vegas, NE, USA, 2013, pp. 89–94.

[168] A. Avancini, Security testing of web applications: a research plan, in: Proceedings of the 34th International Conference on Software Engineering (ICSE 2012), Zurich, Switzerland, 2012, pp. 1491–1494.

[169] A. Avancini, M. Ceccato, Grammar based oracle for security testing of web applications, in: Proceedings of the 7th International Workshop on Automation of Software Test (AST 2012), Zurich, Switzerland, 2012, pp. 15–21.

[170] A. Avancini, M. Ceccato, Circe: a grammar-based oracle for testing cross-site scripting in web applications, in: Proceedings of the 20th Working Conference on Reverse Engineering (WCRE 2013), Koblenz, Germany, 2013, pp. 262–271.

[171] D. Brylow, J. Palsberg, Deadline analysis of interrupt-driven software, IEEE Trans. Softw. Eng. 30 (10) (2004) 634–655.

[172] S. Zhang, ConfDiagnoser: an automated configuration error diagnosis tool for Java software, in: Proceedings of the 35th International Conference on Software Engineering (ICSE 2013), San Francisco, CA, USA, 2013, pp. 1438–1440.

[173] J. Andrews, Testing using log file analysis: tools, methods, and issues, in: Proceedings of the 13th IEEE International Conference on Automated Software Engineering (ASE 1998), Honolulu, HI, USA, 1998, pp. 157–166.

[174] D. Tu, R. Chen, Z. Du, Y. Liu, A method of log file analysis for test oracle, in: Proceedings of the 8th International Conference on Embedded Computing—Co-located with International Conference on Scalable Computing and Communications (EmbeddedCom 2009), Dalian, China, 2009, pp. 351–354.

[175] L. Briand, M. Di Penta, Y. Labiche, Assessing and improving state-based class testing: a series of experiments, IEEE Trans. Softw. Eng. 30 (11) (2004) 770–783.

[176] X. Li, X. Qiu, L. Wang, X. Chen, Z. Zhou, L. Yu, J. Zhao, UML interaction model-driven runtime verification of Java programs, IET Softw. 5 (2) (2011) 142–156.

[177] D. Seifert, Conformance testing based on UML state machines, in: Proceedings of the 10th International Conference on Formal Methods and Software Engineering (ICFEM 2008), Kitakyushu-City, Japan, 2008, pp. 45–65.

[178] A. Memon, I. Banerjee, N. Hashmi, A. Nagarajan, DART: a framework for regression testing "nightly/daily builds" of GUI applications, in: Proceedings of the International Conference on Software Maintenance (ICSM 2003), Amsterdam, The Netherlands, 2003, pp. 410–419.

[179] A. Memon, Q. Xie, Using transient/persistent errors to develop automated test oracles for event-driven software, in: Proceedings of the 19th IEEE International Conference on Automated Software Engineering (ASE 2004), Linz, Austria, 2004, pp. 186–195.

[180] A. Memon, Q. Xie, Studying the fault-detection effectiveness of GUI test cases for rapidly evolving software, IEEE Trans. Softw. Eng. 31 (10) (2005) 884–896.

[181] B. Smith, L. Williams, On the effective use of security test patterns, in: Proceedings of the 6th IEEE International Conference on Software Security and Reliability (SERE 2012), Washington, DC, USA, 2012, pp. 108–117.

[182] Z. Dai, X. Mao, Y. Qi, K. Ben, Light-weight test oracles for resource leaks based on finalizers, in: Proceedings of the 19th Asia-Pacific Software Engineering Conference (APSEC 2012), Hong Kong, China, 2012, pp. 73–79.

[183] A. Mesbah, A. van Deursen, D. Roest, Invariant-based automatic testing of modern Web applications, IEEE Trans. Softw. Eng. 38 (1) (2012) 35–53.

[184] P. Arcaini, A. Gargantini, E. Riccobene, Combining model-based testing and runtime monitoring for program testing in the presence of nondeterminism, in: Proceedings of the 6th IEEE International Conference on Software Testing, Verification and Validation (ICSTW 2013), Luxembourg, 2013, pp. 178–187.

[185] R. Hierons, Oracles for distributed testing, IEEE Trans. Softw. Eng. 38 (3) (2012) 629–641.

[186] B. Hofer, B. Peischl, F. Wotawa, GUI savvy end-to-end testing with smart monkeys, in: Proceedings of the ICSE Workshop on Automation of Software Test (AST 2009), Vancouver, Canada, 2009, pp. 130–137.

[187] D. Peters, D. Parnas, Using test oracles generated from program documentation, IEEE Trans. Softw. Eng. 24 (3) (1998) 161–173.

[188] R. Yang, Z. Chen, B. Xu, W. Wong, J. Zhang, Improve the effectiveness of test case generation on EFSM via automatic path feasibility analysis, in: Proceedings of the 13th IEEE International Symposium on High-Assurance Systems Engineering (HASE 2011), Boca Raton, FL, USA, 2011, pp. 17–24.

[189] J. Zhang, R. Yang, Z. Chen, Z. Zhao, B. Xu, Automated EFSM-based test case generation with scatter search, in: Proceedings of the 7th International Workshop on Automation of Software Test (AST 2012), Zurich, Switzerland, 2012, pp. 76–82.

[190] S. Antoy, D. Hamlet, Automatically checking an implementation against its formal specification, IEEE Trans. Softw. Eng. 26 (1) (2000) 55–69.

[191] H. Chen, The application of an algebraic design method to deal with oracle problem in object-oriented class level testing, in: Proceedings of the IEEE International Conference on Systems, Man, and Cybernetics (SMC 1999), Tokyo, Japan, 1999, pp. 928–932.

[192] P. Machado, E. Oliveira, P. Barbosa, C. Rodrigues, Testing from structured algebraic specifications: the veritas case study, Electron. Notes Theoret. Comput. Sci. 130 (2005) 235–261.

[193] H. Zhu, A note on test oracles and semantics of algebraic specifications, in: Proceedings of the 3rd International Conference on Quality Software (QSIC 2013), Nanjing, China, 2003, pp. 91–100.

[194] I. MacColl, L. Murray, P. Strooper, D. Carrington, Specification-based class testing: a case study, in: Proceedings of the 2nd International Conference on Formal Engineering Methods (ICFEM 1998), Brisbane, Australia, 1998, pp. 222–231.

[195] J. McDonald, L. Murray, P. Strooper, Translating object-Z specifications to object-oriented test oracles, in: Proceedings of the 4th Asia-Pacific Software Engineering and International Computer Science Conference (APSEC 1997), Hong Kong, China, 1997, p. 414.

[196] J. Chen, T. Aoki, Conformance testing for OSEK/VDX operating system using model checking, in: Proceedings of the 18th Asia Pacific Software Engineering Conference (APSEC 2011), Ho Chi Minh, Vietnam, 2011, pp. 274–281.

[197] D. Kuhn, V. Okun, Pseudo-exhaustive testing for software, in: Proceedings of the 30th Annual IEEE/NASA Software Engineering Workshop (SEW 2006), Columbia, MD, USA, 2006, pp. 153–158.

[198] R. Kuhn, Y. Lei, R. Kacker, Practical combinatorial testing: beyond pairwise, IT Prof. 10 (3) (2008) 19–23.

[199] N. Malik, J. Baumgartner, S. Roberts, R. Dobson, A toolset for assisted formal verification, in: Proceedings of the IEEE International Performance, Computing and Communications Conference (IPCCC 1999), Phoenix/Scottsdale, AR, USA, 1999, pp. 489–492.

[200] D. Coppit, J. Yang, S. Khurshid, W. Le, K. Sullivan, Software assurance by bounded exhaustive testing, IEEE Trans. Softw. Eng. 31 (4) (2005) 328–339.

[201] W. Xu, D. Xu, Automated evaluation of runtime object states against model-level states for state-based test execution, in: Proceedings of the International Conference on Software Testing, Verification and Validation Workshops (ICSTW 2009), Denver, CO, USA, 2009, pp. 3–9.

[202] B. Meyer, I. Ciupa, A. Leitner, L. Liu, Automatic testing of object-oriented software, in: Proceedings of the 33rd Conference on Current Trends in Theory and Practice of Computer Science (SOFSEM 2007), Harrachov, Czech Republic, 2007, pp. 114–129.

[203] M. Staats, M. Whalen, M. Heimdahl, Better testing through oracle selection: (NIER track), in: Proceedings of the 33rd International Conference on Software Engineering (ICSE 2011), Waikiki, HI, USA, 2011, pp. 892–895.

[204] P. Shende, S. Byagar, Test automation and designing test cases using designing techniques: challenges, in: International Conference on Advances in Computing and Management (ICACM 2012), Pune, India, 2012, pp. 1–10.

[205] J. Itkonen, M. Mantyla, C. Lassenius, The role of the tester's knowledge in exploratory software testing, IEEE Trans. Softw. Eng. 39 (5) (2013) 707–724.

[206] V. Alagar, M. Chen, O. Ormandjieva, M. Zheng, Automated test generation from object-oriented specifications of real-time reactive systems, in: Proceedings of the 10th Asia-Pacific Software Engineering Conference (APSEC 2003), Chiang Mai, Thailand, 2003, pp. 406–414.

[207] S. Alawneh, D. Peters, Specification-based test oracles with JUnit, in: Proceedings of the 23rd Canadian Conference on Electrical and Computer Engineering (CCECE 2010), Calgary, Alberta, Canada, 2010, pp. 1–7.

[208] J. Gibson, J. Raffy, E. Lallet, Formal object-oriented development of a voting system test oracle, Innov. Syst. Softw. Eng. 7 (4) (2011) 237–245.

[209] A. Nistor, L. Song, D. Marinov, S. Lu, Toddler: detecting performance problems via similar memory-access patterns, in: Proceedings of the 35th International Conference on Software Engineering (ICSE 2013), San Francisco, CA, USA, 2013, pp. 562–571.

[210] G. Xu, Z. Yang, H. Huang, Q. Chen, L. Chen, F. Xu, JAOUT: automated generation of aspect-oriented unit test, in: Proceedings of the 11th Asia-Pacific Software Engineering Conference (APSEC 2004), Busan, Korea, 2004, pp. 374–381.

[211] K. Frounchi, L. Briand, L. Grady, Y. Labiche, R. Subramanyan, Automating image segmentation verification and validation by learning test oracles, Inform. Softw. Technol. 53 (12) (2011) 1337–1348.

[212] P. Stocks, D. Carrington, Test templates: a specification-based testing framework, in: Proceedings of the 5th International Conference on Software Engineering (ICSE 1993), Baltimore, MD, USA, 1993, pp. 405–414.

[213] S. Bauersfeld, GUIdiff—a regression testing tool for graphical user interfaces, in: Proceedings of the 6th IEEE International Conference on Software Testing, Verification and Validation (ICST 2013), Luxembourg, 2013, pp. 499–500.

[214] D. Clarke, T. Jeron, V. Rusu, E. Zinovieva, STG: a tool for generating symbolic test programs and oracles from operational specifications, in: Proceedings of the 8th European Software Engineering Conference Held Jointly with 9th ACM SIGSOFT International Symposium on Foundations of Software Engineering (ESEC/FSE), New York, NY, USA, 2001, pp. 301–302.

[215] G. Fraser, A. Arcuri, Whole test suite generation, IEEE Trans. Softw. Eng. 39 (2) (2013) 276–291.

[216] D. Giannakopoulou, N. Rungta, M. Feary, Automated test case generation for an autopilot requirement prototype, in: Proceedings of the IEEE International Conference on Systems, Man, and Cybernetics (SMC 2011), Anchorage, AK, USA, 2011, pp. 1825–1830.

[217] A. Gotlieb, Exploiting symmetries to test programs, in: Proceedings of the 14th International Symposium on Software Reliability Engineering (ISSRE 2003), Denver, CO, USA, 2003, pp. 365–374.

[218] W. Jenkins, S. Vilkomir, W. Ballance, Fault evaluator: a tool for experimental investigation of effectiveness in software testing, in: Proceedings of the IEEE International Conference on Progress in Informatics and Computing (PIC 2010), Shanghai, China, 2010, pp. 1077–1083.

[219] A. Mesbah, A. van Deursen, Invariant-based automatic testing of Ajax user interfaces, in: Proceedings of the 31st IEEE International Conference on Software Engineering (ICSE 2009), Vancouver, Canada, 2009, pp. 210–220.

[220] D. Peters, D. Parnas, Generating a test oracle from program documentation: work in progress, in: Proceedings of the 1994 ACM SIGSOFT International Symposium on Software Testing and Analysis (ISSTA 1994), Seattle, WA, USA, 1994, pp. 58–65.

[221] K. Shrestha, M. Rutherford, An empirical evaluation of assertions as oracles, in: Proceedings of the 4th IEEE International Conference on Software Testing, Verification and Validation (ICST 2011), Berlin, Germany, 2011, pp. 110–119.

[222] G. Soares, R. Gheyi, T. Massoni, Automated behavioral testing of refactoring engines, IEEE Trans. Softw. Eng. 39 (2) (2013) 147–162.

[223] S. Sprenkle, H. Esquivel, B. Hazelwood, L. Pollock, WebVizOr: a visualization tool for applying automated oracles and analyzing test results of Web applications, in: Proceedings of the Testing: Academic & Industrial Conference—Practice and Research Techniques (TAIC PART 2008), Windsor, UK, 2008, pp. 89–93.

[224] Q. Tao, W. Wu, C. Zhao, W. Shen, An automatic testing approach for compiler based on metamorphic testing technique, in: Proceedings of the 17th Asia Pacific Software Engineering Conference (APSEC 2010), Sydney, Australia, 2010, pp. 270–279.

[225] S. Zhang, M. Ernst, Automated diagnosis of software configuration errors, in: Proceedings of the 35th International Conference on Software Engineering (ICSE 2013), San Francisco, CA, 2013, pp. 312–321.

[226] A. Goldberg, K. Havelund, C. McGann, Runtime verification for autonomous spacecraft software, in: Proceedings of the IEEE Aerospace Conference (IAC 2005), Big Sky, MT, USA, 2005, pp. 507–516.

[227] A. Memon, M. Pollack, M. Soffa, Automated test oracles for GUIs, ACM SIGSOFT 25 (6) (2000) 30–39.

[228] S. Baharom, Z. Shukur, An experimental assessment of module documentation-based testing, Inform. Softw. Technol. 53 (7) (2011) 747–760.

[229] X. Zhang, The construction of oracles for software testing, Master's Thesis, Durham University, 1993.

[230] C. Viravan, Enhancing debugging technology, Ph.D. Dissertation, Purdue University, 1994.

[231] D. Peters, Generating a test oracle from program documentation, Master's Thesis, McMaster University, 1995.

[232] J. Takahashi, An automated oracle for verifying GUI objects, Master's Thesis, Florida Institute of Technology, 2000.

[233] L.-I. Manolache, Testing algorithmically complex software using model programs, Master's Thesis, University of Pretoria, 2000.

[234] A.M. Memon, A comprehensive framework for testing graphical user interfaces, Ph.D. Dissertation, University of Pittsburgh, 2001.

[235] H. Sandhu, Relational specification as a testing oracle, Master's Thesis, Virginia University, West, 2001.

[236] J. Feng, On the effectiveness of metamorphic testing for numerical programs, Master's Thesis, The University of Hong Kong, 2003.

[237] J. Moe, Observing the dynamic behaviour of large distributed systems to improve development and testing: an empirical study in software engineering, Ph.D. Dissertation, Linköping universitet, 2003.

[238] D. Agarwal, A comparative study of artificial neural networks and info fuzzy networks on their use in software testing, Master's Thesis, University of South Florida, 2004.

[239] C. Pacheco, Eclat: automatic generation and classification of test inputs, Master's Thesis, Massachusetts Institute of Technology, 2005.

[240] J. Edvardsson, Techniques for automatic generation of tests from programs and specifications, Ph.D. Dissertation, Linköping universitet, 2006.

[241] Q. Xie, Developing cost-effective model-based techniques for GUI testing, Ph.D. Dissertation, University of Maryland (College Park), 2006.

[242] T. Huse, Is using images to test web pages the solution to a sisyphean task? Master's Thesis, University of Oslo, 2008.

[243] R.A. Dookhoo, Automated regression testing approach to expansion and refinement of speech recognition grammars, Master's Thesis, University of Central Florida, 2008.

[244] M.-H. Park, An approach for oracle data selection criterion, Ph.D. Dissertation, The University of Minnesota, 2010.

[245] R.C. Lozano, Constraint programming for random testing of a trading system, Master's Thesis, School of Information and Communication Technology—KTH Royal Institute of Technology, 2010.

[246] F. Bessayah, A complementary approach for testing system robustness based on passive testing and fault injection techniques, Ph.D. Dissertation, Telecom & Management SudPari—University of Pierre and Marie Curie (Paris 6)—UPMC, 2010.

[247] V.S.B. Jagannath, Reducing the costs of bounded-exhaustive testing, Master's Thesis, University of Illinois, Urbana-Champaign, 2010.

[248] D. Roest, Automated regression testing of Ajax Web applications, Master's Thesis, Faculty EEMCS, Delft University of Technology, 2010.

[249] K. Shrestha, An empirical evaluation of the effectiveness of JML assertions as test oracles, Master's Thesis, University of Denver, 2010.

[250] C. Murphy, Metamorphic testing techniques to detect defects in applications without test oracles, Ph.D. Dissertation, Columbia University, 2010.

[251] S.R. Shahamiri, An automated framework for software test oracle based on multi-networks, Ph.D. Dissertation, Universiti Teknologi Malaysia, 2011.

[252] G.J. Zuo, Metamorphic testing research based on circling FSCS, Master's Thesis, East China Normal University, 2011.

[253] S. Kudari, An ontology-based automated test oracle comparator for testing Web applications, Master's Thesis, Malmö University, 2011.

[254] T. Wu, Self-checked metamorphic testing of Monte Carlo simulation, Master's Thesis, East Carolina University (ECU), 2011.

[255] J. Liu, Metamorphic testing and its application on hardware fault-tolerance, Master's Thesis, University of Wisconsin, 2011.

[256] M. Asrafi, On testing effectiveness of metamorphic relations, Master's Thesis, Swinburne University of Technology, 2012.

[257] R. Just, On effective and efficient mutation analysis for unit and integration testing, Master's Thesis, Universität Ulm, 2012.

[258] S. Afshan, Search-based generation of human readable test data and its impact on human oracle costs, Ph.D. Dissertation, The University of Sheeld, 2013.

[259] A.M. Vieira, A generic and automatic test strategy for compiler testing, Master's Thesis, Faculty EEMCS, Delft University of Technology, 2013.

ABOUT THE AUTHORS

Rafael A. P. Oliveira is a Ph.D. candidate at University of São Paulo (USP/ICMC). He has received his M.Sc. in 2012 from the University of São Paulo. He is a visiting scholar at the University of Maryland (UMD, College Park, MD, USA), where much of this book chapter was conducted. His research focuses on alleviating human testing efforts, automated and systematic testing strategies, automated test oracles, and GUI and TTS testing. In addition, his main interests are software testing, quality, and reliability. His main publications can be found in his personal site (http://www.labes.icmc.usp.br/~rpaes/) and on Lattes Platform (http://lattes.cnpq.br/0793753941171478).

Upulee Kanewala is a Ph.D. candidate in the Computer Science Department at the Colorado State University. Her research interests include developing automated test oracles, effects of test oracles in testing, and automatic detection of metamorphic relations that can be used as test oracles.

Paulo Augusto Nardi is a Ph.D. candidate in Computer Science and Computational Mathematics at the University of São Paulo, Brazil. As part of his doctoral studies, from 2011 to 2012, he was a visiting scholar at the Politecnico di Milano, Milan, Italy. He received his M.S. in Computer Science from UNIVEM in 2006. His current research interests include software testing, test oracles, empirical software engineering, and embedded systems. His main publications can be found on Lattes Platform (http://lattes.cnpq.br/5154586471030104).

CHAPTER FOUR

Anti-Pattern Detection: Methods, Challenges, and Open Issues

Fabio Palomba*, Andrea De Lucia*, Gabriele Bavota†, Rocco Oliveto‡
*Department of Management and Information Technology, University of Salerno, Fisciano, Italy
†Department of Engineering, University of Sannio, Benevento, Italy
‡Department of Bioscience and Territory, University of Molise, Pesche, Italy

Contents

Advances in Computers, Volume 95
ISSN 0065-2458
http://dx.doi.org/10.1016/B978-0-12-800160-8.00004-8

Abstract

Anti-patterns are poor solutions to recurring design problems. They occur in object-oriented systems when developers unwillingly introduce them while designing and implementing the classes of their systems. Several empirical studies have highlighted that anti-patterns have a negative impact on the comprehension and maintainability of a software systems. Consequently, their identification has received recently more attention from both researchers and practitioners who have proposed various approaches to detect them. This chapter discusses on the approaches proposed in the literature. In addition, from the analysis of the state-of-the-art, we will (i) derive a set of guidelines for building and evaluating recommendation systems supporting the detection of anti-patterns; and (ii) discuss some problems that are still open, to trace future research directions in the field. For this reason, the chapter provides a support to both researchers, who are interested in comprehending the results achieved so far in the identification of anti-patterns, and practitioner, who are interested in adopting a tool to identify anti-patterns in their software systems.

1. ANTI-PATTERN: DEFINITIONS AND MOTIVATIONS

During lifecycle, a software system undergoes continuous changes aiming at maintaining high its business level [1]. Unfortunately, these changes are often made by developers in a rush due to market/customers constraints. As a consequence, source code quality is often neglected with the risk of introducing *code bad smell* (or simply *code smells* or *smells*) [2], i.e., symptoms of possible design problems in source code. For example, developers might add several responsibilities to a class feeling that it is not required to include them in separate classes. As a result, the class grows rapidly and when the added responsibilities grow and breed, the class becomes too complex and its quality deteriorates. Such classes are know as *Large Class* [2] and could be the cause of a design problem in source code, i.e., *anti-pattern*.[1] Fowler [2] and Brown *et al.* [3] defined a catalogue of more than 30 anti-patterns. For each anti-pattern, they reported the definition of the anti-pattern as well as specific refactoring operations aimed at removing it in order to improve the quality of source code.

Even if there is anecdotal evidence that design problems (such as anti-patterns) negatively impacts software comprehension and maintenance, in

---

[1] Very often code bad smells and anti-pattern are used as synonym. However, the scenario we report allows to understand the difference between code smells and anti-patterns. Specifically, code smell represents something "probably wrong" in the code, while an anti-pattern is certainly a design problem in source code. In other words, a code smell might indicate an anti-pattern.

the last decade, anti-patterns have been the subject of empirical studies aiming at empirically analyzing their impact on software maintainability. We now have empirical evidence that code-containing code smells or participating in anti-patterns is significantly more change prone than "clean" code [4]. Also, code participating in anti-patterns has a higher fault-proneness than the rest of the system code [4,5].

Other studies aimed at understanding the impact of anti-patterns on program comprehension [6] showed that the presence of an anti-pattern in the source code does not decrease the developers' performance, while a combination of anti-patterns results in a significant decrease of their performance [6,7]. While the results of this study indicate that single anti-patterns are not harmful, they also reveal that anti-patterns are quite diffuse in software systems and very often code components are affected by more than one anti-pattern. In addition, we have empirical evidence that the number of anti-patterns in software systems increases over time and only in few cases they are removed through refactoring operations [8,9].

All these findings suggest that code smells and anti-pattern need to be carefully detected and monitored and, whenever necessary, refactoring operations should be planned and performed to deal with them. Unfortunately, the identification and the correction of design flaws in large and nontrivial software systems can be very challenging. These observations call for recommendation systems supporting the software engineer in (i) identifying anti-patterns and (ii) designing and applying a refactoring solution to remove them.

In this chapter, we will focus on the analysis of different techniques aimed at detecting anti-patterns in source code.[2] By analyzing these approaches, we will derive a set of guidelines for building and evaluating recommendation systems supporting the detection of anti-patterns. In addition, we will also discuss some problems that are still open, to trace future research directions in the field.

2. METHODS FOR THE DETECTION OF ANTI-PATTERNS

Among the 30+ anti-patterns defined in the literature [2,3], only for a subset of them we have approaches and tools for their automatic identification. Table 4.1 reports the list of such anti-patterns, while in the next

---

[2] The interested reader can find a survey on recommendation systems supporting refactoring operations in the Chapter 15 of the book "Recommendation Systems in Software Engineering" [10].

Table 4.1 List of Anti-Patterns for Which a Detection Strategy Has Been Proposed in the Literature

Anti-Pattern	Description	References
Blob (God Class)	A class having huge size and implementing different responsibilities	[11–15]
Feature Envy	A method making too many calls to methods of another class to obtain data and/or functionality	[15–18]
Duplicate Code	Classes that show the same code structure in more than one place	[19–23]
Refused Bequest	A class inheriting functionalities that it never uses	[24]
Divergent Change	A class commonly changed in different ways for different reasons	[15,25,26]
Shotgun Surgery	A class where a change implies cascading changes in several related classes	[15,25]
Parallel Inheritance	Pair of classes where the addition of a subclass in a hierarchy implies the addition of a subclass in another hierarchy	[15]
Functional Decomposition	A class implemented following a procedural-style	[13]
Spaghetti Code	A class without structure that declare long methods without parameters	[13]
Swiss Army Knife	A class that exhibits high complexity and offers a large number of different services	[13]
Type Checking	A class that shows complicated conditional statements	[27]

sections, we discuss in details each of them. Specifically, for each anti-pattern, we present (i) its definition; (ii) the approaches proposed for its identification; and (iii) the results of the empirical evaluation conducted to assess the detection accuracy of the approaches proposed in the literature.

2.1. Blob

2.1.1 Definition

The *Blob*, also named *God Class*, is a class implementing different responsibilities, generally characterized by the presence of a high number of attributes and methods, which implement different functionalities, and by many dependencies with data classes (i.e., classes implementing only getter and setter methods) [2].

2.1.2 Detection Strategies

The problem to identify classes affected by the Blob anti-pattern has been analyzed under three perspectives. First, researchers focused their attention on the definition of heuristic-based approaches that exploit several software quality metrics (e.g., cohesion and coupling [28]). For instance, DECOR (DEtection and CORrection of Design Flaws) [13], use a set of rules, called "rule card,"[3] describing the intrinsic characteristics of a class affected by Blob (see Fig. 4.1). As described in the rule card, DECOR detects a Blob when the class has an LCOM5 (Lack of Cohesion Of Methods) [28] higher than 20, a number of methods and attributes higher than 20, a name that contains a suffix in the set {Process, Control, Command, Manage, Drive, System}, and it has an one-to-many association with data classes.

Beside DECOR, other approaches rely on metrics to identify Blobs in source code. For example, Marinescu [12] presented a detection strategy able to identify Blobs looking at deviations from good design principles (see Fig. 4.2). Specifically, for each class a combination of cohesion and coupling metrics is computed and Blobs are identified as classes that exhibit an overall quality lower than other classes (absolute and relative thresholds are used in order to discriminate between Blobs and "clean" classes).

Although Blob can be detected solely using structural properties, historical analysis can aid the identification of complementary, additional useful information. In fact, as the Blob is a class that centralizes most of the system's behavior, is possible to think that despite the kind of change a developer has

```
RULE_CARD: Blob {
   RULE: Blob {ASSOC: associated FROM: mainClass ONE
                TO: DataClass MANY}
   RULE: mainClass {UNION LargeClassLowCohesion ControllerClass}
   RULE: LargeClassLowCohesion {UNION LargeClass LowCohesion}
   RULE: LargeClass {(METRIC: NMD + NAD, VERY_HIGH, 20)}
   RULE: LowCohesion {(METRIC: LCOM5, VERY_HIGH, 20)}
   RULE: ControllerClass {UNION (SEMANTIC: METHODNAME,
          {Process, Control, Command, Manage, Drive, System}),
          (SEMANTIC: CLASSNAME, {Process, Control, Command,
          Manage, Drive, System}}
   RULE: DataClass {(STRUCT: METHOD_ACCESSOR, 90)}
};
```

Figure 4.1 Rule card for the Blob identification in DECOR [13].

[3] http://www.ptidej.net/research/designsmells/.

$$GodClass(S) = S' | \frac{S' \subseteq S, \forall C \in S'}{(WMC(C), TopValues(25\%)) \wedge (ATFD(C), HigherThan(1)) \wedge (TCC, BottomValues(25\%))}$$

$$GodClass(S) = S' | \frac{S' \subseteq S, \forall C \in S'}{(ATFD(C), HigherThan(1)) \wedge ((WMC(C), TopValues(25\%)) \vee (TCC, BottomValues(25\%)))}$$

Figure 4.2 Detection strategy to identify Blobs proposed by Marinescu [12].

to perform in a software system, if a Blob class is present, it is very likely that something will need to be changed in it [15]. This conjecture is on the basis of HIST (*H*istorical *I*nformation for *S*mell de*T*ection) [15]. In HIST, Blobs are detected as classes modified in more than α% of commits involving at least one another class. The parameter α has been empirically evaluated, and a value that provides good detection accuracy is $\alpha = 8$.

The approaches reported above classify classes strictly as being or not anti-patterns, while an accurate analysis for the borderline classes is missing [11]. To mitigate such a problem, it is possible to build an identification model able to assign a probability that a class is affected by a Blob. Specifically, the DECOR identification rule card can be translated into a Bayesian Network using a discretization of the metric values. Then, a probability that a class is affected by a Blob is computed [11]. On the same line, Oliveto *et al.* [14] proposed the identification of Blobs by building the signature of Blobs. Given a set of Blobs is possible to derive their signature (represented by a curve) that synthetize the quality of the class. Specifically, each point of the curve is the value of a specific quality metrics (e.g., the CK metric suite). Then, the identification of Blob is simply obtained by comparing the curve (signature) of a class given in input with the (curves) signatures of the previous identified Blobs. The higher the similarity, the higher the likelihood that the new class is a Blob as well.

Blob classes could be also detected indirectly. There are approaches used to recommend Extract Class Refactoring (ECR) operations, which are operations specialized for removing Blob from a software system [14]. For instance, Fokaefs *et al.* [29] proposed an approach that takes in input a software system and suggests a set of ECR operations. In other words, the tool suggests to split a set of classes in several classes in order to have a better distribution of the responsibility. Clearly, the original classes are candidate Blob. The approach proposed by Fokaefs *et al.* [29] formulated the detection of ECR operations (and thus, indirectly, of Blobs) as a cluster analysis problem, where it is necessary to identify the optimal partitioning of methods in different classes. In particular, for each class, they analyze the structural dependencies between the entities of a class, i.e., attributes and methods, in order to build, for each entity, the entity set, i.e., the set of methods using it. The Jaccard distance between all couples of entity sets of the class is computed in order to cluster together cohesive groups of entities that can be extracted as separate classes. The Jaccard distance is computed as follows:

$$Jaccard\left(E_i, E_j\right) = 1 - \frac{\left|E_i \cap E_j\right|}{\left|E_i \cup E_j\right|}$$

where E_i and E_j are two entity sets, the numerator is the number of common entities between the two sets and the denominator is the total number of unique entities in the two sets. If splitting the class in separate classes the overall quality (in terms of cohesion and coupling) of the system improves, the approach proposed the splitting as a candidate ECR operation. In other words, a Blob has been identified. The approach proposed by Fokaefs et al. [29] has been implemented as an Eclipse plugin called JDeodorant.[4]

2.1.3 Analysis of the Detection Accuracy

All the approaches described above have been empirically evaluated in order to understand the accuracy of the suggestions provided to the software engineer. DECOR has been empirically validated first on an open source system, called Xerces,[5] and then on other eight systems [13]. Overall, the precision of the approach is 88.6%, while the recall reaches 100% [13]. Regarding the detection strategy proposed by Marinescu, the empirical study revealed 60% of accuracy [12]. As for HIST, the accuracy has been evaluated in terms of precision and recall on 8 open source systems. The study showed that the overall precision of HIST is 76%, while the recall is 61% [15]. More importantly, HIST has been compared with DECOR showing that the historical analysis can support the software engineer better than the structural ones. Oliveto et al. [14] provided a comparison of their approach based on the signature of Blobs with DECOR [13] and the approach based on Bayesian Belief Network proposed by Khomh et al. [11]. The study revealed that the accuracy of their approach generally outperform the other ones. Finally, the benefits of JDeodorant have also been empirically analyzed. The empirical evaluation indicated that the refactoring operations provided by

[4] http://www.jdeodorant.com.
[5] http://xerces.apache.org.

JDeodorant are meaningful and they approximate the refactoring operations previously performed by three developers with 67% precision and 82% recall [29]. Clearly, the accuracy of the refactoring operations identified represents a good proxy for the accuracy of the identification of Blobs.

2.2. Feature Envy

2.2.1 Definition

A method suffers of the *Feature Envy* anti-pattern if it is more interested in another class (also named envied class with respect the one it actually is in). It is often characterized by a large number of dependencies with the envied class [2]. Usually, this negatively influences the cohesion and the coupling of the class in which the method is implemented. In fact, the method suffering of Feature Envy reduces the cohesion of the class because it likely implements different responsibilities with respect to those implemented by the other methods of the class and increases the coupling, due to the many dependencies with methods of the envied class.

2.2.2 Detection Strategies

A first simple way to detect Feature Envy in source code is to traverse the Abstract Syntax Tree (AST) of a software system in order to identify, for each field, the set of the referencing classes [16]. So, using a threshold it is possible to discriminate the fields having too many references with other classes.

Although the Feature Envy is one of the most studied anti-patterns in literature, the only automatic approach defined to detect it is the one proposed by Palomba *et al.* [15], namely HIST. The conjecture is that a method affected by Feature Envy changes more often with the envied class than with the class it is actually in. Given this conjecture, HIST identifies methods affected by these anti-patterns as those involved in commits with methods of another class of the system β% more than in commits with methods of their class. The parameter β underwent an empirical calibration that showed how better performance can be obtained with $\beta = 70$.

Despite the lacking of automatic techniques to detect this kind of anti-pattern, there are several approaches able to identify *Move Method Refactoring* (MMR), i.e., operations aimed at removing the Feature Envy anti-pattern [17,18]. In some way, these approaches can aid the software engineer also in the identification of the Feature Envy: if the suggestion proposed by the refactoring tool is correct, then an instance of the Feature Envy anti-pattern is present in the source code.

```
extractMoveMethodRefactoringSuggestions(Method m)
    T = {}
    S = entity set of m
    for i = 1 to size of S
        entity = S[i]
        T = T ∪ {entity.ownerClass}
    sort(T)
    suggestions = {}
    for i = 1 to size of T
        if(T[i] ≠ m.ownerClass ∧ modifiesDataStructureInTargetClass(m, T[i]) ∧
        preconditionsSatisfied(m, T[i]))
            suggestions = suggestions ∪
            {moveMethodSuggestions(m → T[i])}
        if(suggestions ≠ φ)
            return suggestions
        else
            for i = 1 to size of T
                if(T[i] = m.ownerClass
                    return {}
                else if preconditionsSatisfied(m, T[i])
                    return moveMethodSuggestions(m → T[i])
        return {}
```

Figure 4.3 Algorithm used by JDeodorant for the identification of Move Method Refactoring operations [18].

Besides ECR operations, JDeodorant also support MMR operations. The underlined approach uses a clustering analysis algorithm (see Fig. 4.3). Given a method m, the approach forms a set of candidate target classes where m should be moved (set T in Fig. 4.3). This set is obtained by examining the entities (i.e., attributes and methods) that m accesses from the other classes (entity set S in Fig. 4.3). In particular, each class in the system containing at least one of the entities accessed by m is added to T. Then, the candidate target classes in T are sorted in descending order according to the number of entities that m accesses from each of them ($sort(T)$ in Fig. 4.3). In the following steps, each target class T_i is analyzed to verify its suitability to be the recommended class. In particular, T_i must satisfy three conditions to be considered in the set of candidate suggestions: (i) T_i is not the class m currently belongs to, (ii) m modifies at least one data structure in T_i, and (iii) moving m in T_i satisfies a set of behavior preserving preconditions [18]. The set of classes in T satisfying all the conditions above are put in the *suggestions* set (see Fig. 4.3). If *suggestions* is not empty, the approach suggests to move m in the first candidate target class following the order of the sorted set T. On the other side, if *suggestions* is empty, the classes in the sorted set T are again analyzed by applying milder constraints than before. In particular, if a class T_i is the m owner class, then no refactoring suggestion is performed and the algorithm stops. Otherwise, the approach checks if moving the method m into T_i satisfies the behavior preserving preconditions. If so, the approach suggests to move m into T_i. Thus, an instance of the Feature Envy anti-pattern is identified.

This technique uses structural information to suggest MMR operations. However, there are cases where the Feature Envy and the envied class are related by a conceptual linkage rather than a structural one. Here, the lexical properties of source code can aid in the identification of the right refactoring to perform. This is the reason why Bavota *et al.* presented Methodbook [17], in which methods and classes play the same role of the people and groups, respectively, in Facebook.[6] In particular, methods represent people, and so they have their own information as, for example, method calls or conceptual relationships with the other methods in the same class as well as the methods in the other classes. To identify the envied class, Methodbook use Relational Topic Model (RTM). Following the Facebook metaphor, the use of RTM is able to identify "friends" of the method under analysis. If the class having the highest number of "friends" of the considered method is not the current owner class, a refactoring operation is suggested (i.e., a Feature Envy is detected).

2.2.3 Analysis of the Detection Accuracy
The evaluation on the detection algorithm provided by HIST has been conducted on 8 open source systems in terms of precision and recall [15]. The results show that HIST is able to suggest candidate Feature Envy anti-patterns with a precision of 71% and a recall of 81%. HIST has also been compared with the tool JDeodorant and the results have shown that the precision of the two approaches are comparable (71% against 68%), while the recall of HIST is quite higher than the one achieved by JDeodorant (81% against 60%) [15]. Also Methodbook has been compared with JDeodorant on 6 open source systems. The comparison performed with JDeodorant highlighted that Methodbook is generally more precise than JDeodorant, providing less suggestions to the developers of an average higher quality. However, the results also clearly highlighted that JDeodorant is able to identify good refactoring operations (and thus correct instances of Feature Envy) that are missed by Methodbook [17].

2.3. Duplicate Code
2.3.1 Definition
Classes that show the same code structure in more than one place in the system are affected by *Duplicate Code* anti-pattern. Code duplication is a

---

[6] https://www.facebook.com.

potentially serious problem that affects the maintainability of a software system, but also its comprehensibility. The problem of the identification of code duplication is very challenging simply because, during the evolution, different copies of a feature suffer different changes and this affects the possibility of the identification of the common functionality provided by different copied features. Moreover, having duplicate components in source code implies the increase of the effort in the maintenance of a system because when a change request involving such duplicate components is received, developer needs to modify several times the same feature because several copies are disseminated in different places. For all these reasons, the problem of finding duplicate code, has been recognized as a potentially serious problem affecting the stability of an application, but also its fault-proneness [30].

2.3.2 Detection Strategies

In the literature, several approaches for clone detection have been proposed. It is worth noting that a semantic detection of clones could be very hard to perform and, in general, this is an undecidable problem. This is the reason why most of the proposed techniques focus their attention on the detection of syntactic or structural similarity of source code. For example, the AST of the given program is built in order to find matches of sub-trees in Refs. [19,20,23]. Alternatively, Kamiya *et al.* [22] introduced the tool *CCFinder*, where a program is divided in lexemes and the token sequences are compared in order to find matches between two subsequences.

However, such approaches appear to be ineffective in cases where duplicated code suffers several modifications during its evolution. To mitigate such a problem, Jiang *et al.* [21] introduced DECKARD, a technique able to identify clones using a mix of tree-based and syntactic-based approaches. The process, they follow can be summarized as follows:

1. Given a program, a parser translates source code into parse tree;
2. Syntactic trees are processed in order to produce a set of vectors capturing the syntactic information of parse tree;
3. The Euclidean distances are performed. Thus, the vectors are clustered;
4. Heuristics are applied to detect clones.

2.3.3 Analysis of the Detection Accuracy

The detection methods based on AST [19,20] have been applied on one process-control system written in C, having 400 KLOC. The authors found that most of detected clones were of small size and they were functions performing the same operations in different places. The main problem of this approach is that it is able to determine only exact tree match. The empirical evaluation conducted on DECKARD involved large systems as JDK and the Linux kernel and showed that the tool performs significantly better than the other state-of-art technique to detect clones [21].

2.4. Refused Bequest

2.4.1 Definition

In Object-Oriented development, one of the key features aiming at reducing the effort and the cost in software maintenance is inheritance [2]. For example, if there is something wrong in the definition of an attribute inherited by some children classes, such attribute needs to be changed only in the parent of such classes. However, it is not uncommon that developers make improper use of the concept of inheritance, especially in the cases where other kind of relationships would be more correct. The *Refused Bequest* anti-pattern arises when a subclass does not support the interface of the superclass [2]. On one hand, this happens when a subclass overrides a lot of methods inherited by its parent, on the other hand, the relationship of inheritance can be wrong also if the subclass does not override the methods inherited from the parent, but never uses them or such methods are never called by the clients of the subclass. In some cases, this anti-pattern simply means that the relationship of inheritance is wrong, namely the subclass is not a specialization of the parent.

2.4.2 Detection Strategies

A simple naive method to estimate the presence of Refused Bequest anti-pattern in a software system is by looking for classes having the following characteristics: (i) the class is in a hierarchy and (ii) the class overrides more than γ% of the methods defined by the parent. However, such a method does not take into account the semantics established by an "is-a" relationship between two classes of the system. For this reason, Ligu *et al.* [24] introduced the identification of Refused Bequest using a combination of static source code analysis and dynamic unit test execution. In particular, the approach identifies classes affected by this anti-pattern by looking at the classes that really *"wants to support the interface of the superclass"* [2]. If a class does not support the behavior of its parent, a Refused Bequest is detected. In order to understand if a method of a superclass is actually called on subclass instances by other classes of the system, Ligu *et al.* [24] intentionally override these methods introducing an error in the new implementation (e.g., division by zero). If there are classes in the system invoking the method, then a failure will occurs. Otherwise, if the execution of all the test cases does not lead to a failure, the inherited superclass methods are never used by the other classes of the system and, thus, an instance of Refused Bequest is found. The approach proposed by Ligu *et al.* [24] has been implemented as an extension of the JDeodorant Eclipse plugin [18].

2.4.3 Analysis of the Detection Accuracy
Unfortunately, the approach proposed by Ligu *et al.* [24] for the identification of Refused Bequest has not been empirically evaluated yet. The authors only applied the approach on one medium-size open source system in order to have a preliminary idea of its accuracy.

2.5. Divergent Change
2.5.1 Definition
Fowler describes a *Divergent Change* as a class that is *"commonly changed in different ways for different reasons"* [2]. Classes affected by this anti-pattern generally have low cohesion.

2.5.2 Detection Strategies
The definition of Divergent Change provided by Fowler suggests that structural techniques are not completely suitable to detect instances of such an anti-pattern. The reason is that in order to identify Divergent Change anti-patterns it is necessary to analyze how the system evolves over time. Only one approach provides an attempt to exploit structural information (i.e., coupling) to identify this anti-pattern [25]. In particular, using coupling information it is possible to build a Design Change Propagation Probability (DCPP) matrix. The DCPP is an $n \times n$ matrix where the generic entry A_{ij} is the probability that a design change on the artifact i requires a change also to the artifact j. Such probability is given by the *cdegree* [26], i.e., an indicator of the number of dependencies between two artifacts. Once the matrix is built, a Divergent Change instance is detected if a column in the matrix contains high values for a particular artifact. In other words, high values on the columns of the matrix correspond to have a high number of artifacts related to the one under analysis and so the probability to have a Divergent Change increase.

However, by looking at the definition, it is reasonable to think to detect this kind of anti-pattern using the historical information that a system can have (i.e., change log). The conjecture is that classes affected by this anti-pattern present different sets of methods each one containing methods changing together but independently from methods in the other sets. Such a conjecture has been implemented in HIST that uses association rules discovery to detect a subsets of methods in the same class that often change together [15]. Once HIST detects these change rules between methods of the same class, the approach identifies Divergent Change as those containing at least two or more sets of methods with the following characteristics:

1. The cardinality of the set is at least γ;
2. All methods in the set change together, as detected by the association rules;
3. Each method in the set does not change with methods in other sets as detected by the association rules.

2.5.3 Analysis of the Detection Accuracy

Unfortunately, there is not a real empirical evaluation of the approach based on structural information to detect Divergent Change anti-pattern. The authors of this approach only proposed two example scenarios in which the defined approach is able to detect instances of Divergent Change [25,26]. They planned to make an empirical study in order to validate their technique in a real context. Regarding HIST, the evaluation was not only focused on the accuracy of the detection algorithm but also on its behavior when compared with a static approach using solely structural information (i.e., methods' calls). The results indicated that HIST has higher precision (73% vs. 20%) and recall (79% vs. 7%) than the technique that exploits only structural information [15].

2.6. Shotgun Surgery

2.6.1 Definition

This anti-pattern appears when "*every time you make a kind of change, you have to make a lot of little changes to a lot of different classes*" [2]. As for Divergent Change, also in this case finding a purely structural technique able to provide an accurate detection of this anti-pattern is rather challenging.

2.6.2 Detection Strategies

There are only two approaches able to identify this anti-pattern in the source code: the first is proposed by Rao and Reddy [25] and it is based on the DCPP matrix, the second is included in HIST and relies on historical information [15]. As for the former, after the construction of the DCPP matrix (as for the identification of Divergent Change), the approach detects instances of Shotgun Surgery in a way complementary to that for the Divergent

Change detection. In fact, if a row of the matrix contains high values for an artifact, it means that there is high probability that a change involving the artifact impact on more than one artifact. Regarding the latter, HIST implements the following conjecture: *"a class affected by Shotgun Surgery contains at least one method changing together with several other methods contained in other classes"* [15]. As for the Divergent Change, association rule discovery allows to identify a set of methods belonging to different classes often changing together. Thus, a class is affected by Shotgun Surgery if it contains at least one method that changes with methods contained in more than δ different classes. The parameter δ has been empirically calibrated and the empirical analysis revealed that the best performance are achieved with $\delta = 3$.

2.6.3 Analysis of the Detection Accuracy

The empirical evaluation of the approach based on the DCPP matrix was only planned and not available yet [25]. Instead, the detection algorithm of HIST has been validated on 8 open source systems in terms of accuracy. The results showed that on one hand, the first point highlighted is that this anti-pattern is not quite common (only four instances on the eight systems), on the other hand, HIST was able to detect all the instances found, reaching a precision and a recall of 100% [15].

2.7. Parallel Inheritance Hierarchies

2.7.1 Definition

Fowler defined the *Parallel Inheritance* as a special case of Shotgun Surgery, where *"every time you make a subclass of one class, you also have to make a subclass of another"* [2].

2.7.2 Detection Strategies

Since this anti-pattern is considered a special case of Shotgun Surgery, it is reasonable to think that, also in this case, detecting it using structural properties of source code might be very challenging. The only technique able to identify instances of Parallel Inheritance Hierarchies is the one included in HIST [15] that relies on historical information. Following the definition provided by Fowler, HIST detects the Parallel Inheritance Hierarchies as pairs of classes for which the addition of a subclass for one class implies the addition of a subclass for the other class. Also in this case, association rule discovery is used to mine pairs of classes that respect this rule [15].

2.7.3 Analysis of the Detection Accuracy

HIST has been evaluated in terms of precision and recall and compared with a static technique constructed by the authors of HIST for providing some insights about the usefulness of historical analysis when detecting this anti-pattern. Such a technique exploits lexical properties of source code and it is based on the heuristic provided by Fowler for the identification of this anti-pattern: *"You can recognize this smell because the prefixes of the class names in one hierarchy are the same as the prefixes in another hierarchy"* [2]. The results showed that HIST reaches 61% of precision and recall, while the lexical-based technique identifies instances of Parallel Inheritance Hierarchies with a recall of 45%. Also, only 17% of the correct instances are detected by both the approaches, while 43% of instances are identified only by HIST, the remaining 40% only by the lexical-based technique. This result highlights that the combination of structural/lexical and historical analysis could be worthwhile for detecting this kind of anti-pattern.

2.8. Functional Decomposition

2.8.1 Definition

A class in which inheritance and polymorphism are poorly used, declaring many private fields and implementing few methods [3]. It can be symptom of procedural-style programming. The concepts of Object-Oriented development are not always clear to developers working for the first time using such a paradigm. Indeed, a developer with high experience in functional paradigm tends to apply procedural rules in the development of Object-Oriented software, producing errors in the design of the application. The anti-pattern coined as *Functional Decomposition* is the most common anti-pattern appearing in these cases. Brown *et al.* [3] define Functional Decomposition as *"a main routine that calls many subroutines."*

2.8.2 Detection Strategies

In order to detect this anti-pattern, some heuristics have been proposed. For example, knowing that usually a routine is called with a name invoking its function, it is not surprising to find an instance of Functional Decomposition in classes called with prefix as Make or Execute. At the same time, also heuristics based on the structure of a class can support the identification of this anti-pattern. For instance, a functional class can have many dependencies with classes composed by a very few number of methods addressing a single function.

The only approach able to identify this anti-pattern is DECOR [13]. To infer the presence of the anti-pattern, DECOR uses a set of structural

```
RULE_CARD: FunctionalDecomposition {
  RULE: FunctionalDecomposition {ASSOC: associated FROM:
                    mainClass ONE TO: aClass MANY}
  RULE: mainClass {UNION NoInheritPoly FunctionClass}
  RULE: NoInheritPoly {INTER NoInheritance NoPolymorphism}
  RULE: NoInheritance {(METRIC: DIT, SUP_EQ, 1, 0)}
  RULE: NoPolymorphism {(STRUCT: DIFFERENT_PARAMETER)}
  RULE: FunctionClass {(SEMANTIC: CLASSNAME, {Make, Create,
          Creator, Execute, Exec, Compute, Display, Calculate}}
  RULE: aClass {INTER ClassOneMethod FieldPrivate}
  RULE: ClassOneMethod {(STRUCT: ONE_METHOD)}
  RULE: FieldPrivate {(STRUCT: PRIVATE_FIELD, 100)}
};
```

Figure 4.4 Rule card for the Functional Decomposition identification in DECOR [13].

properties together to lexical analysis of the name of a class (see the rule card in Fig. 4.4). Given a class, such class is affected by Functional Decomposition if it is a main class (a class generally characterized by a procedural name, e.g., Display, in which inheritance and polymorphism are poorly used) having many dependencies with small classes (classes with a very few number of methods and many private fields) [13].

2.8.3 Analysis of the Detection Accuracy

The accuracy of the detection algorithm implemented in DECOR has been preliminary validated on Xerces showing that the precision of the approach reaches 52%, while it has a recall of 100%. Then, the study was replicated on other eight systems and the results confirmed those achieved in the preliminary evaluation [13].

2.9. Spaghetti Code

2.9.1 Definition

Classes affected by this anti-pattern are characterized by complex methods, with no parameters, interacting between them using instance variables. As for the Functional Decomposition anti-pattern, this is also a symptom of procedural-style programming [3].

2.9.2 Detection Strategies

The Spaghetti Code anti-pattern describes source code difficult to comprehend by a developer, often without a well-defined structure and with several long methods without any parameter. From a lexical point of view, classes affected by this anti-pattern have usually procedural names.

```
RULE_CARD: SpaghettiCode {
  RULE: SpaghettiCode {INTER: NoInheritanceClassGlobalVariable
                       LongMethodMethodNoParameter}
  RULE: LongMethodMethodNoParameter {INTER LongMethod
                       MethodNoParameter}
  RULE: LongMethod { (METRIC: METHOD_LOC, VERY_HIGH, 0) }
  RULE: MethodNoParameter { (STRUCT: METHOD_NO_PARAM) }
  RULE: NoInheritanceClassGlobalVariable {INTER NoInheritance
                       ClassGlobalVariable}
  RULE: NoInheritance { (METRIC: DIT, INF_EQ, 2, 0) }
  RULE: ClassGlobalVariable {INTER ClassOneMethod FieldPrivate}
  RULE: ClassOneMethod { (STRUCT: GLOBAL_VARIABLE, 1) }
};
```

Figure 4.5 Rule card for the Spaghetti Code identification in DECOR [13].

DECOR [13] is also able to identify Spaghetti Code, once again by using a specific rule card that describes the anti-pattern through structural properties. As you can see in Fig. 4.5, DECOR classifies the anti-pattern using only software metrics able to identify the specific characteristic of classes affected by this anti-pattern. This is possible simply because the Spaghetti Code does not involve any relationships with other classes, but it is a design problem concentrated in a single class having procedural characteristics. Specifically, in DECOR instances of Spaghetti Code are found looking for classes having at least one long method, namely a method composed by a large number of LOC and declaring no parameters. At the same time, the class does not present characteristics of Object-Oriented design. For example, the class does not use the concept of inheritance and should use many global variables.

2.9.3 Analysis of the Detection Accuracy
The empirical evaluation of DECOR indicated that the number of instances correctly detected by DECOR reaches 61%. However, a better detection of this kind of anti-pattern could be possible through the use of some lexical rules. Since a class affected by Spaghetti Code is a class built through procedural thinking, the use of lexical rules can be complementary to the structural rules used by DECOR. For example, the same strategy applied for Functional Decomposition can be applied here: checking the prefix of the class name can aid the identification of this anti-pattern.

2.10. Swiss Army Knife
2.10.1 Definition
A *Swiss Army Knife* is a class that exhibits high complexity and offers a large number of different services. This type of anti-pattern is slightly different

from a Blob, because in order to address the different responsibilities, it exposes high complexity, while a Blob is a class that monopolizes processing and data of the system.

2.10.2 Detection Strategies

A class affected by the Swiss Army Knife is a class that provides answer to a large range of needs. Generally, this anti-pattern arises when a class has many methods with high complexity and the class has a high number of interfaces. For example, a utility class exposing high complexity and addressing many services is a good candidate to be a Swiss Army Knife. The definition of this anti-pattern could seem very similar to the one given for the Blob. However, there is a slight difference between the two anti-patterns: the Blob is a class that monopolizes most of processing and data of the system, having a "selfish behavior" because it works for itself, while a Swiss Army Knife is a class that provides services to other classes.

The characteristics of this anti-pattern suggest that structural information can be useful for its detection. In particular, a mix of software complexity metrics and semantic checks in order to identify the different services provided by the class could be used for the detection. Once again, DECOR is able to detect this anti-pattern through a rule card [13]. In the case of Swiss Army Knife, the rule card characterizes the anti-pattern on the Number of Interfaces metric, which is able to identify the number of services provided by a class. If the metric exceeds a given threshold, a Swiss Army Knife is detected.

2.10.3 Analysis of the Detection Accuracy

The accuracy of DECOR has been empirically validated on 9 open source systems in terms of precision and recall. Results showed that the recall reaches 100%, while the precision obtained was not so high (i.e., 41%) [13]. This result suggests that the use of lexical properties together with the structural ones could produce a more accurate detection tool.

2.11. Type Checking

2.11.1 Definition

A class that shows complicated conditional statements making the code difficult to understand and maintain. One of the most common situation in which a programmer linked to procedural languages can fall down using Object-Oriented programming is the misunderstanding or lack of knowledge on how to use OO mechanisms such as polymorphism. This problem manifests itself especially when a developer uses conditional statements to dynamically dispatch the behavior of the system instead of polymorphism. Such a problem is known as *Type Checking* anti-pattern and, as for all the anti-patterns, in the maintenance phase this problem can grow up, creating problems to the developers.

2.11.2 Detection Strategies

For the identification of symptoms of such anti-pattern, a simple heuristic can be used: when you see long and intricate conditional statements, then you have found a Type Checking candidate. Tsantalis *et al.* [27] proposed a technique to identify and refactor instances of this anti-pattern implemented in the JDeodorant Eclipse plugin. In particular, their detection strategy takes into account two different cases: in the first case, an attribute of a class represents a state and, depending on its value, different branches of the conditional statements are executed. Thus, if in the analyzed class, there is more than one condition involving the attribute, a candidate of Type Checking is found. In the second case, a conditional statement involves *RunTime Type Identification* (RTTI) in order to cast the type of a class in another to invoke methods on the last one. For example, this is the case of two classes involved in a hierarchy where the relationship is not exploited by using polymorphism. In such case, RTTI often arises in the form of an if/else if statement in which there is one conditional expression for each control on the type of a class. However, if the RTTI involves more than one conditional expression, a candidate of Type Checking is found.

2.11.3 Analysis of the Detection Accuracy

The Type Checking detection technique proposed by Tsantalis *et al.* [27] has been evaluated on three teaching examples in the textbooks by Demeyer *et al.* [31] and Fowler [2], and it is able to correctly detect the instances reported by the authors of these books.

3. A NEW FRONTIER OF ANTI-PATTERNS: LINGUISTIC ANTI-PATTERNS

There are several empirical studies in literature showing how linguistic aspects of source code can cause misunderstanding during the development of a software system. Indeed, the lack of comments, ambiguous selected identifiers and poor coding standards increase the risk to have problems during maintenance (see e.g., [32–37]). Based on these observations, Arnaoudova *et al.* [38] defined the linguistic anti-patterns (LAs), a new family of source code design problems that, as for the other anti-patterns in literature, could be described in terms of symptoms and consequences. Whereas "design" anti-patterns represent recurring, poor design choices, LAs represent recurring, poor naming, and commenting choices [38]. The first catalogue of this new family of anti-pattern contains six categories of linguistic design problems. Their detection has been done using linguistic heuristics, which depend on the type of anti-pattern defined. The section reports a brief introduction for each category of this kind of anti-patterns.

3.1. Does More Than it Says

This LA arises when there is a contradiction between the signature of the method and what the method really does. In particular, the method does more with respect to what the signature suggests. One of the examples provided by Arnaoudova *et al.* [38] regards the use of the verb *is* in the name of a method. It suggests that the method performs an action returning a Boolean value. Thus, having an "is" method performing more than returning a Boolean value could be destabilizing for a developers. An example of such anti-pattern is provided in Listing 1.

LISTING 1 An Example of *Does More Than it Says* Linguistic Anti-Pattern [38]

```
public int isValid () {
    final long currentTime = System.currentTimeMillis();
    if ( currentTime <= this.expires ) {
        // The delay has not passed yet
        // assuming source is valid.
            return SourceValidity.VALID;
    }

    // The delay has passed,
    // prepare for the next interval.
    this.expires = currentTime + this.delay;
    return this.delegate.isValid();
}
```

The method *isValid()* of the class *DelayedValidity* from the system *Cocoon* *2.2.0* should return a Boolean value, but it performs more than checking if a component of that class is valid or not. In such cases, the rational behind the choice to design the method in this way should be included in the method summary or in the low-level documentation. In addition, a rename of the method is highly recommended.

The identification of such anti-pattern is based on the identification of all the methods with a signature not conforming to the standard guidelines provided in the catalogue defined by Arnaoudova *et al.* [38].

3.2. Says More Than it Does

This anti-pattern occurs when a method has a signature evoking a liar behavior and the method body does not what the signature says [38]. For example, when a method has a name composed by the verb *get*, a developer might think that this method returns the value of an object instance variable. Listing 2 is provided a case where a "get" method does return nothing. Also in this case, method summary should contain the rationale of this method. However, a renaming should be applied. Also in this case, the identification of methods affected by this kind of anti-pattern could be done exploiting the definition provided in the catalogue.

LISTING 2 An Example of *Says More Than it Does* Linguistic Anti-Pattern [38]

```
protected void getMethodBodies
      (CompilationUnitDeclaration unit, int place) {
      // fill the methods bodies in order
      // for the code to be generated
      if ( unit.ignoreMethodBodies ) {
            unit.ignoreFurtherInvestigation = true;
            return;
            // if initial diet parse did not
            // work, no need to dig into method bodies.
      }

      if ( place < parseThreshold )
            return ; // work already done...

      // real parse of the method...
      parser.scanner.setSourceBuffer(unit.compilationResult
                  .compilationUnit.getContents());
      if (unit.types != null) {
            for (int i = unit.types.length; ‚ài,àii >= 0;)
                  unit.types[i].parseMethod(parser , unit);
      }
}
```

3.3. Does the Opposite

This anti-pattern has been defined as *"the intent of the method suggested by its name is in contradiction with what it returns"* [38]. To understand this kind of anti-pattern, an example is provided in Listing 3. The name and return type of the method *disable()* are inconsistent. The reason is that the method *disable* returns an "enable" state. The problem with anti-pattern like this is that, if the documentation is missing, developers involved in maintenance operations can infer that the return type is a control state that can be enabled or disabled, while the method behavior is different.

LISTING 3 An Example of *Does the Opposite* Linguistic Anti-Pattern [38]

```
/* Saves the current enable/disable state of
 * the given control and its descendents in
 * the returned object;
 * the controls are all disabled.
 * @param w the control
 * @return an object capturing the enable/disable state */

    public static ControlEnableState disable (Control w){
        return new ControlEnableState (w);
    }
```

In order to detect such anti-pattern, a set of heuristics can be applied. For instance, in the case of the example reported above, a contradiction is found looking at the method name and a part of its returned type. Using a thesaurus, it is easy to derive that the two terms (i.e., disable and enable) are antonyms [38].

3.4. Contains More Than it Says

The *Contains more than it says* anti-pattern appears when a variable of a class is declared as a single object, while its type is a collection of elements.

Listing 4 shows an example in which the variable *isReached* is an array of integer values; while a developer expects that its type is a Boolean.

LISTING 4 An Example of *Contains More Than it Says* **Linguistic Anti-Pattern [38]**
```
int[] isReached;
```

A possible consequence is that a developer does not know that changing this variable, he changes multiple objects. Wrong uses in the declaration of variables in a class can be detected using a terms vocabulary, which contains information about the number of a name.

3.5. Says More Than it Contains

This anti-pattern is exactly the opposite of the *Contains more than it says* [38]. In this case, a variable declared as multi-objects, contains only one object (Listing 5). Unlike what happens before, a developer performing maintenance activities on the class affected by this anti-pattern could think to change a collection of objects, while the real meaning of the variable is different. Also for this anti-pattern, wrong uses in the declaration of variables in a class can be detected using a thesaurus.

LISTING 5 An Example of *Says More Than it Contains* **Linguistic Anti-Pattern**
```
private static boolean stats = true;
```

3.6. Contains the Opposite

The goal of this anti-pattern is to find improper use of a variable in a class [38]. In particular, the anti-pattern aims at representing situations where a variable and its type are in contradiction, as shown in Listing 6.

LISTING 6 An Example of *Contains the Opposite* **Linguistic Anti-Pattern [38]**
```
MAssociationEnd start = null;
```

Once again, this anti-pattern can be detected by checking a vocabulary in order to find when the name of a variable is exactly the opposite of one of the terms composing its type.

4. KEY INGREDIENTS FOR BUILDING AN ANTI-PATTERN DETECTION TOOL

This section describes some of the challenges that need to be addressed when building a tool able to detect anti-pattern in software systems. Specifically, there are two critical issues to deal with:

- *Extracting information from source code components in order to identify symptoms of poor design choices.* This is a critical issue because there are different sources of information that can be exploited (e.g., structural or semantic relationship) and in several cases the choice of the type of information to be exploited depends on the kind of anti-pattern to be detected.
- *Define the algorithm to identify candidate anti-patterns.* Each algorithm has strengths and weaknesses. On the basis of the anti-pattern under analysis, an algorithm ensuring a fair compromise of strengths and weaknesses must be chosen.

In the following sections, we present some guidelines on how to deal with these two issues.

4.1. Identifying and Extracting the Characteristics of Anti-Patterns

The first step in the identification of a specific anti-pattern regards the definition of its characteristics. Such characteristics should help in discriminating between components that are affected by the anti-pattern and "clean" components. As said before, there are different sources of information that can be used to extract source code properties that characterize a specific anti-pattern. Most of the techniques existing in the literature exploit structural information extracted by statically analyzing the source code to capture characteristics that could help in the identification of an anti-pattern, such as, the number of calls between two source code entities, variable accesses, or inheritance relations. A second option is dynamic information, which takes into account call relationships between entities occurring during program execution. Finally, historical data (e.g., co-changes) can be exploited to identify anti-patterns that are intrinsically characterized by how source code changes over time. Thus, in the following, we discuss all these sources of information.

4.1.1 Extraction of Structural Properties Using Code Analysis Techniques

In this section, we discuss the sources of information capturing structural properties (e.g., structural coupling) between code components.

4.1.1.1 Method Calls

The most obvious source of information that can be exploited to capture structural relationships between code components is the calls interaction. A measure capturing method call interactions is the Call-based Dependence between Methods (CDM) [39]. CDM has values in [0, 1]; the higher the number of calls between two methods, the higher the CDM value and thus, the coupling between methods. This source of information can be useful for identifying anti-patterns acting at both method (e.g., Feature Envy) and class (e.g., Swiss Army Knife) level. Method calls have been exploited for the detection of many anti-patterns. In particular, different researchers have used them not only to investigate the presence of Blob instances [11,14,29] but also to find instances of Feature Envy [17,18], Refused Bequest [24], Type Checking [27], Divergent Change [25], and Shotgun Surgery [25].

The calls between methods belonging to different classes also represent a particularly useful property for the detection of anti-patterns. Indeed, classes having many call interactions cooperate to implement the same (or strongly related) responsibilities and thus, are highly coupled. This information is particularly important for detecting anti-patterns aimed at causing harms to the modularization of Object-Oriented systems, e.g., Inappropriate Intimacy [2]. There are many metrics available in literature to measure the coupling between classes based on their call interactions. Examples are the Information-Flow-based Coupling (ICP) [40], the Message Passing Coupling (MPC) [41], and the Coupling Between Object Classes (CBO) [41].

4.1.1.2 Shared Instance Variables

The instance variables shared by two methods are an important source of information for detecting anti-pattern (e.g., Blob) inherent to the cohesion of a class. This source of information has been successfully used for the detection of Blob [13,39], Spaghetti Code [13], and Type Checking [27] instances. In fact, they also represent a form of communications between methods (performed through shared data). Thus, methods sharing instance variables are more coupled than methods not sharing any data. A measure to capture this form of coupling between methods is the Structural Similarity between Methods (SSM) [42], used to compute the cohesion metric ClassCoh [42]. SSM has values in [0, 1]; the higher the number of instance variables the two methods share, the higher the SSM value and thus the coupling between methods. Another example of metric measuring the extent to which the methods of a class share instance is the LCOM [28].

4.1.1.3 Inheritance Relationships

Inheritance dependencies among classes is another source of structural information to capture relationships between classes, and thus useful to identify anti-patterns involved in a hierarchy. Generally, the measurement of inheritance relationships between two classes is performed through a simple Boolean value: *true* if two classes have inheritance relationships or *false* otherwise. In the context of anti-pattern detection, inheritance relationships have been exploited to support the detection of Parallel Inheritance [15] and Refused Bequest [24].

4.1.2 Extraction of Lexical Properties Through Natural Language Processing

A source code component contains text, e.g., identifiers, methods' names, and comments. Thus, it can be considered as a textual document. Such a likeness has induced researchers to apply Natural Language Processing (NLP) techniques on source code in order to extract lexical properties. For example, Information Retrieval (IR) [43] techniques have been used to analyze the conceptual cohesion or coupling of classes. For instance, two methods are conceptually related if their (domain) semantics are similar, i.e., they perform conceptually similar actions. In order to compute conceptual cohesion (or coupling), Marcus *et al.* [44,45] proposed the use of Latent Semantic Indexing (LSI) [46], an advanced IR method that can be used to compute the textual similarity between the two methods. The higher the similarity between the methods of a class, the higher the conceptual similarity and thus the conceptual cohesion of the class. On the other hand, the higher the similarity between two classes, the higher the conceptual coupling between them. Empirical studies have indicated that conceptual metrics are orthogonal to structural ones. In other words, using NLP technique, it is possible to identify specific properties of source code that are missed by looking only at structural information.

In the context of anti-pattern detection, lexical properties play a crucial role in the identification of LAs. For instance, a part of speech analysis is required to (i) identify whether a term is a noun, an adjective, an adverb, or other parts-of-speech; (ii) distinguish singular from plural nouns; and (iii) identify dependencies between words, e.g., between subjects and predicates, as well negative form. In addition, thesauruses (e.g., Wordnet [47]) are required to identify synonymous and antonymous relations.

Lexical properties are not only useful for the identification of LA. The analysis of the textual similarity between methods or classes has been used to characterize "design" anti-patterns, such as Feature Envy [17] and Blob [39]. Empirical studies have indicated that using lexical properties it is possible to identify instances of anti-patterns, which are missed by using only structural properties [17].

4.1.3 Extraction of the History Properties Through Mining of Software Repositories

In order to find interesting and/or complementary properties with respect to the structural ones, it would be important to take into account the history of a system. In particular, it is possible to consider the way the code elements changes over time. This is really important when the goal is to detect anti-patterns generally characterized by how code elements evolve during the evolution of the system. For example, in the case of Divergent Change, we have a candidate anti-pattern when a class is commonly changed over time in different ways for different reasons [2]. In the following, we discuss which kinds of historical information could be extracted for the identification of anti-patterns.

4.1.3.1 Co-Changes at File Level

Configuration Management Tools (CMTs) allow to manage different versions of a system. In particular, developers can manage the changes of the artifacts (configuration items) and keep track of changes occurring to configuration items. In addition, by analyzing the log file developers can get information about what was changed, who did the change, when the change was made, and the message left by the developer who made the change. Thus, the log file contains a lot of information that can be mined aiming at finding interesting properties related to the development of a software system. Mining of software repositories is a quite new approach in the sphere of anti-pattern detection, while it has been widely used to support other software engineering tasks, such as [48–56]. In the context of anti-pattern detection, mining log files is worthwhile to detect instances of Parallel Inheritance by simply looking at the way subclasses are added during the evolution of the system.

4.1.3.2 Co-Changes at Method Level

Using the standard APIs of CMTs, it is only possible to mine co-changes at file level. Such a granularity level could not be sufficient to detect some of the anti-patterns defined in the literature. In fact, many of them describe method-level behavior (see, for instance, Feature Envy). This requires the use of an *ad hoc* tool that is able to identify co-changes at method level. A tool supporting such a task has been recently developed in the context of a European project, namely the Markos project.[7] Specifically, the tool is able to identify (i) classes added, removed, moved, or renamed; (ii) class attributes added, removed, moved, or renamed; (iii) methods added, removed, moved, or renamed; (iv) changes applied to all the method signatures (i.e., visibility change, return type change, parameter added, parameter removed, parameter type change, method rename); and (v) changes applied to all the method bodies. This information is particularly useful in the detection of anti-patterns involve methods changing often together during the history of the system, such as Divergent Change.

4.2. Defining the Detection Algorithm

The second step for the definition of an approach for the detection of anti-patterns is related to the choice of the algorithm to use in order to identify candidate instances of the specific anti-pattern. Such a choice depends on two factors:

- The kind of anti-patterns we are interested in detecting.
- The kind of information we want to exploit to characterize the anti-pattern.

Looking at the literature, we can observe that the algorithms proposed so far fall in two categories: (i) heuristic based and (ii) machine learning based.

A lot of anti-patterns can be identified using heuristic-based algorithms. A simple analysis of the dependencies between code components can be sufficient to correctly identify anti-patterns in source code. For example, in order to detect the Feature Envy anti-pattern, two kinds of heuristics can be used:

- A structural heuristic, counting the dependencies (e.g., calls) existing between a method m_i and a class C_j;
- A historical heuristic, counting the number of commits in which a method changes together with methods of the same class (*internal changes*) with respect to the number of commits in which the method change with methods of another class of the system (*external changes*).

The problem with these kinds of algorithms is related to the definition of a set of thresholds to use to identify an anti-pattern. For example, to detect the Feature Envy using a historical heuristic, a threshold is needed to determine the minimum difference between *internal* and *external changes*. In order to

---

[7] http://markosproject.berlios.de.

mitigate this problem, an empirical calibration of the threshold can be performed. However, the value identified empirically could be not sufficient to correctly detect anti-patterns in all the software systems due to the heterogeneity of software systems. Thus, specific tuning should be required on each system to improve the detection accuracy.

Machine learning techniques have also been widely used to detect different kinds of anti-patterns. For instance, rule cards defined by DECOR have been successfully translated into a Bayesian Network using a discretization of the metric values to detect Blobs. In addition, association rule discovery, an unsupervised learning technique, has been used to detect three different anti-patterns (i.e., Divergent Change, Shotgun Surgery, and Parallel Inheritance). Such a technique is able to identify local patterns showing attribute value conditions that occur together in a given dataset [57]. In the context of anti-pattern detection, the dataset is composed of a sequence of change sets, e.g., methods that have been committed (changed) together in a version control repository [58]. An association rule, $M_{\text{left}} \rightarrow M_{\text{right}}$, between two disjoint method sets implies that if a change occurs in each $m_i \in M_{\text{left}}$, then another change should happen in each $m_j \in M_{\text{right}}$ within the same change set. The strength of an association rule is determined by its support and confidence [57], defined as:

$$Support = \frac{\left| M_{\text{left}} \cap M_{\text{right}} \right|}{T}$$

$$Confidence = \frac{\left| M_{\text{left}} \cap M_{\text{right}} \right|}{M_{\text{left}}}$$

where T is the total number of change sets extracted from the repository. In the context of anti-pattern identification, association rule mining has been performed using a well-known algorithm, namely *Apriori* [57]. Note that, minimum *Support* and *Confidence* to consider an association rule as valid can be set in the *Apriori* algorithm. Once again such values can be determined empirically and could be necessary to retune such values when applying the approach on other systems.

4.3. Evaluating the Accuracy of a Detection Tool

The evaluation of an anti-pattern detection tool can consist of different steps and can be done following different strategies. In most of cases, a first evaluation has been done analyzing the accuracy in terms of metrics able to evaluate the goodness of an approach (i.e., *precision* and *recall* [43]). In other cases, the accuracy of the tool can be evaluated directly involving developers who express their opinion regarding the suggestions provided by the tool. In the following, we report a set of evaluation strategies that can be used to evaluate an anti-pattern detection tool.

4.3.1 Evaluation Based on an Automatic Oracle

To evaluate the accuracy of a detection tool, an oracle is required that reports the anti-pattern instances contained in a system. Unfortunately, very few software systems with annotated anti-patterns are available. This means that to have a larger data set for experimenting anti-pattern detection tools a manual identification of anti-pattern instances in the object systems is required to build the oracle. In particular, starting from the definition of the anti-patterns reported in literature, the analysis of each class of a software system should be performed in order to identify instances of those anti-patterns. Once the oracle is defined, the detection tool is executed to extract the set of candidate anti-patterns. Finally, the two sets of anti-patterns (i.e., the manually identified and the candidate sets) can be compared and two widely adopted IR metrics, namely recall and precision [43] can be used to estimate the accuracy of the tool:

$$recall = \frac{|Correct \cap Detected|}{|Correct|}$$

$$precision = \frac{{}^{|}|Correct \cap Detected|}{|Detected|}$$

where Correct and Detected represent the set of true positive anti-patterns (those manually identified) and the set of anti-patterns detected by the approach, respectively. As an aggregate indicator of precision and recall, F-measure, i.e., the harmonic mean of precision and recall can be used:

$$F\text{-measure} = 2\frac{precision \times recall}{precision + recall}$$

4.3.2 Evaluation Based on Developer's Judgment

When an oracle reporting the list of anti-pattern instances present in the system is not available, it is possible to involve developers in order to evaluate the performance of a detection tool. It is worth noting that this is not an optimal solution, because the developers can judge the goodness of a suggestion provided by the tool, while they cannot evaluate the performance of the tool with respect the totality of the anti-pattern instances present in the system (i.e., they can judge the precision of the tool, but they cannot aid in the evaluation of the recall). However, this kind of evaluation is still useful in two cases:

- As complement of the analysis based on the metrics, in order to understand to what extent the tool supports the developer.
- When you have to compare the support provided by two (or more) tools. In this case, a partial oracle can be built as the union of the suggestions provided by the tools. Thus, both the precision and recall can be evaluated.

We distinguish two kinds of studies that could be performed: (i) with the original developers of a system and (ii) with external developers. The evaluations performed with original developers are preferred since external developers do not have a deep knowledge of the design of the subject system under analysis and thus may not be aware of some of the design choices that could appear as suboptimal, but that are the results of a rational choice. However, studies with external developers can complement studies performed with original developers. In fact, even if the original developers have deep knowledge of the system's design, they could be the authors of some bad design choices and consequently could not recognize good suggestions by the tool. This means that the two studies complement each other mitigating the specific threats they have.

5. CONCLUSION AND OPEN ISSUES

Anti-patterns represent symptoms of poor design and implementation choices [2]. Having classes affected by anti-patterns cause time-consuming maintenance operations due to their lower comprehensibility and maintainability. Thus, detecting anti-patterns in the source code is an important activity in order to improve the quality of a software system during its evolution. Some anti-patterns can be detected by using simple heuristics, while others are really complex to identify. This is the reason why in the last decade a lot of effort has been devoted to the definition of approaches able to recommend to developers problematic components that need to be refactored in order to improve their comprehensibility and maintainability.

In this chapter, we have described the state-of-the-art regarding the detection of "design" and "linguistic" anti-pattern. We have also identified and described the challenges that need to be addressed for building a detection tool. Thus, this chapter provides a support to both researchers, who are interested in comprehending the results achieved so far in the identification of anti-patterns, and practitioner, who are interested in adopting a tool to identify anti-patterns in their software systems.

Even if the analysis of the literature reveals that the anti-pattern identification is a quite mature field, there are still some open issues that need to be addressed:

- *Are anti-patterns really harmful?* Despite the existing evidence about the negative effects of anti-patterns (e.g., [4,6,7]) and the effort devoted to the definition of approaches for detecting and removing them, it is still unclear whether developers would actually consider all anti-patterns as actual symptoms of wrong design/implementation choices, or whether some of them are simply a manifestation of the intrinsic complexity of the designed solution. In other words, there seem to be a gap between the theory and the practice. For example, a recent study found that some source code files of the Linux Kernel intrinsically have high cyclomatic complexity. However, this is not considered a design or implementation problem by developers [59]. Also, empirical studies indicated that (i) developers perceived different instances of Blob as not particularly dangerous for the system maintainability, especially because they change these classes sporadically [60] and (ii) some developers, in particular junior programmers, work better on a version of a system having some classes that centralized the control, i.e., Blob [61]. These results suggest that the presence of anti-patterns in source code is sometimes tolerable, and part of developers' design choices.

- *Providing a complete support for the identification of anti-patterns.* Fowler [2] and Brown *et al.* [3] defined more than 30 anti-patterns. In the last years, researchers concentrate their attention only on a small subset of anti-patterns defined in the literature. The world of anti-patterns is still full of interesting points to pick in order to construct more useful and usable tools in a real context. To succeed in this goal, the research community should focus the attention not only on other kinds of anti-patterns but also on novel strategies for improving the accuracy of approaches defined in the literature.

- *On the use of historical and lexical analysis to detect anti-pattern.* A recent study indicates that historical properties of code components are able to complement structural properties in the process of anti-pattern detection [15]. This finding suggests that a better identification of anti-patterns can be achieved with a combined technique using a mix of historical and structural properties. Moreover, together with the structural and historical information, lexical properties could be exploited to better capture the "semantics" of design decisions, in order to have recommendations that are more focused on how developers designed the system under analysis.

• *Analyzing the usability of detection tools.* An important threat to the success of detection tools is related to their usability. Detection tools might require the definition of several parameters. Thus, they might be hard to understand and to work with, making developers more reluctant to use such tools. In addition, it is necessary to define a good strategy for the visualization and the analysis of the candidate anti-patterns. This issue is particular important since the anti-patterns identified by any detection tool need to be validated by the user. Thus, a good graphic metaphor is required to highlight problems to the developer's eye, allowing her to decide which of the code components suggested by the tool really represent design problems.

REFERENCES

[1] M.M. Lehman, On understanding laws, evolution, and conservation in the large-program life cycle, J. Syst. Softw. 1 (1980) 213–221.

[2] M. Fowler, Refactoring: Improving the Design of Existing Code, Addison-Wesley, Boston, MA, USA, 1999.

[3] W.J. Brown, R.C. Malveau, W.H. Brown, H.W. McCormick III, T.J. Mowbray, Anti Patterns: Refactoring Software, Architectures, and Projects in Crisis, first ed., John Wiley and Sons, New York, NY, USA, 1998.

[4] F. Khomh, M. Di Penta, Y.-G. Guéhéneuc, G. Antoniol, An exploratory study of the impact of antipatterns on class change- and fault-proneness, Emp. Softw. Eng. 17 (3) (2012) 243–275.

[5] W. Li, R. Shatnawi, An empirical study of the bad smells and class error probability in the post-release object-oriented system evolution, J. Syst. Softw. (2007) 1120–1128.

[6] M. Abbes, F. Khomh, Y.-G. Guéhéneuc, G. Antoniol, An empirical study of the impact of two antipatterns, blob and spaghetti code, on program comprehension, in: Proceedings of the 15th European Conference on Software Maintenance and Reengineering, IEEE Computer Society, Oldenburg, Germany, 2011, pp. 181–190.

[7] A. Yamashita, L. Moonen, Exploring the impact of inter-smell relations on software maintainability: an empirical study, in: Proceedings of the 35th International Conference on Software Engineering, San Francisco, CA, USA, 2013, pp. 682–691.

[8] R. Arcoverde, A. Garcia, E. Figueiredo, Understanding the longevity of code smells: preliminary results of an explanatory survey, in: Proceedings of the International Workshop on Refactoring Tools, 2011, pp. 33–36.

[9] A. Chatzigeorgiou, A. Manakos, Investigating the evolution of bad smells in object-oriented code, in: Proceedings of the 7th International Conference on the Quality of Information and Communications Technology, Porto, Portugal, 2010.

[10] M.P. Robillard, W. Maalej, R.J. Walker, T. Zimmermann, Recommendation Systems in Software Engineering, Springer, Berlin, Germany, 2014.

[11] F. Khomh, S. Vaucher, Y.G. Guéhéneuc, H. Sahraoui, A Bayesian approach for the detection of code and design smells, in: Proceedings of the 9th International Conference on Quality Software, 2009.

[12] R. Marinescu, Detection strategies: metrics-based rules for detecting design flaws, in: Proceedings of the 20th International Conference on Software Maintenance, IEEE Computer Society, Chicago, IL, USA, 2004, pp. 350–359.

[13] N. Moha, Y.G. Guéhéneuc, L. Duchien, A.F.L. Meur, DECOR: a method for the specification and detection of code and design smells, IEEE Trans. Softw. Eng. 36 (1) (2010) 20–36.

[14] R. Oliveto, F. Khomh, G. Antoniol, Y.-G. Guéhéneuc, Numerical signatures of anti-patterns: an approach based on b-splines, in: Proceedings of the 14th Conference on Software Maintenance and Reengineering, IEEE Computer Society Press, 2010.

[15] F. Palomba, G. Bavota, M. Di Penta, R. Oliveto, A. De Lucia, D. Poshyvanyk, Detecting bad smells in source code using change history information, in: Proceedings of the 11th ACM/IEEE International Conference on Automated Software Engineering (ASE 2013), IEEE, Silicon Valley, CA, USA, 2013.

[16] D.C. Atkinson, T. King, Lightweight detection of program refactorings, in: Proceedings of 12th Asia-Pacific Software Engineering Conference, IEEE CS Press, Taipei, Taiwan, 2005, pp. 663–670.

[17] G. Bavota, R. Oliveto, M. Gethers, D. Poshyvanyk, A. De Lucia, Methodbook: recommending move method refactorings via relational topic models, Trans. Softw. Eng. (2014) (to appear). Available online http://doi.ieeecomputersociety.org/10.1109/TSE.2013.60.

[18] N. Tsantalis, A. Chatzigeorgiou, Identification of move method refactoring opportunities, IEEE Trans. Softw. Eng. 35 (3) (2009) 347–367.

[19] I.D. Baxter, C. Pidgeon, M. Mehlich, Program transformations for practical scalable software evolution, in: Proceedings of the International Conference on Software Engineering, 2004, pp. 625–634.

[20] I.D. Baxter, A. Yahin, L. Moura, M. Sant'Anna, L. Bier, Clone detection using abstract syntax trees, in: Proceedings of the International Conference on Software Maintenance, 1998, pp. 368–377.

[21] L. Jiang, G. Misherghi, Z. Su, S. Glondu, DECKARD: scalable and accurate tree-based detection of code clones, in: Proceedings of the International Conference on Software Engineering, 2010.

[22] T. Kamiya, S. Kusumoto, K. Inoue, CCfinder: a multilinguistic token-based code clone detection system for large scale source code, Trans. Softw. Eng. 28 (7) (2002) 654–670.

[23] V. Wahler, D. Seipel, J.W. von Gudenberg, G. Fischer, Clone detection in source code by frequent itemset techniques, in: Proceedings of the IEEE Working Conference on Source Code Analysis and Manipulation, 2004, pp. 128–135.

[24] E. Ligu, A. Chatzigeorgiou, T. Chaikalis, N. Ygeionomakis, Identification of refused bequest code smells, in: Proceedings of the 29th IEEE International Conference on Software Maintenance, 2013.

[25] A. Rao, K. Reddy, Detecting bad smells in object oriented design using design change propagation probability matrix, in: International Multiconference of Engineers and Computer Scientists, 2008.

[26] A. Rao, D. Ram, Software design versioning using propagation probability matrix, in: Proceedings of Third International Conference on Computer Applications, Yangon, Myanmar, 2005.

[27] N. Tsantalis, T. Chaikalis, A. Chatzigeorgiou, JDeodorant: identification and removal of type-checking bad smell, in: Proceedings of the 23rd IEEE International Conference on Software Maintenance, Paris, France, 2007.

[28] S.R. Chidamber, C.F. Kemerer, A metrics suite for object oriented design, IEEE Trans. Softw. Eng. 20 (6) (1994) 476–493.

[29] M. Fokaefs, N. Tsantalis, E. Stroulia, A. Chatzigeorgiou, Identification and application of extract class refactorings in object oriented systems, J. Syst. Softw. 85 (10) (2012) 2241–2260.

[30] E. Juergens, F. Deissenboeck, B. Hummel, S. Wagner, Do code clones matter? in: Proceedings of the 31st International Conference on Software Engineering, 2009, pp. 485–495.

[31] S. Demeyer, S. Ducasse, O. Nierstrasz, Object-Oriented Reengineering Patterns, Morgan Kaufmann Publishers Inc., Burlington, Massachusetts, USA, 2002.

[32] B. Caprile, P. Tonella, Restructuring program identifier names, in: Proceedings of the International Conference on Software Maintenance, 2000, pp. 97–107.

[33] F. Deissenbock, M. Pizka, Concise and consistent naming, in: Proceedings of the International Workshop on Program Comprehension, 2005.

[34] D. Lawrie, C. Morrell, H. Feild, D. Binkley, Effective identifier names for comprehension and memory, Innov. Syst. Softw. Eng. 3 (4) (2007) 303–318.

[35] D. Lawrie, C. Morrell, H. Feild, D. Binkley, What's in a name? A study of identifiers, in: Proceedings of the International Conference on Program Comprehension, 2006, pp. 3–12.

[36] E. Merlo, I. McAdam, R. De Mori, Feed-forward and re-current neural networks for source code informal information analysis, J. Softw. Maintenance 15 (4) (2003) 205–244.

[37] A. Takang, P.A. Grubb, R.D. Macredie, The effects of comments and identifier names on program comprehensibility: an experiential study, J. Program Lang. 4 (3) (1996) 143–167.

[38] V. Arnaoudova, M.D. Penta, G. Antoniol, Y.-G. Guéhéneuc, A new family of software anti-patterns: linguistic anti-patterns, in: Proceedings of the European Conference on Maintenance and Reengineering, Genova, Italy, 2013, pp. 187–196.

[39] G. Bavota, A. De Lucia, R. Oliveto, Identifying extract class refactoring opportunities using structural and semantic cohesion measures, J. Syst. Softw. 84 (2011) 397–414.

[40] Y. Lee, B. Liang, S. Wu, F. Wang, Measuring the coupling and cohesion of an object-oriented program based on information flow, in: Proceedings of the International Conference on Software Quality, 1995, pp. 81–90.

[41] W. Li, S. Henry, Maintenance metrics for the object oriented paradigm, in: Proceedings of International Symposium on Software Metrics, 1993, pp. 52–60.

[42] G. Gui, P. Scott, Coupling and cohesion measures for evaluation of component reusability, in: Proceedings of the 5th International Workshop on Mining Software Repositories, 2006, pp. 18–21.

[43] R. Baeza-Yates, B. Ribeiro-Neto, Modern Information Retrieval, Addison-Wesley, Boston, MA, USA, 1999.

[44] A. Marcus, D. Poshyvanyk, R. Ferenc, Using the conceptual cohesion of classes for fault prediction in object-oriented systems, IEEE Trans. Softw. Eng. 34 (2) (2008) 287–300.

[45] D. Poshyvanyk, A. Marcus, R. Ferenc, T. Gyimothy, Using information retrieval based coupling measures for impact analysis, Emp. Softw. Eng. 14 (1) (2009) 5–32.

[46] S. Deerwester, S.T. Dumais, G.W. Furnas, T.K. Landauer, R. Harshman, Indexing by latent semantic analysis, J. Am. Soc. Inf. Sci. 41 (6) (1990) 391–407.

[47] G.A. Miller, WordNet: a lexical data base for English, Commun. ACM 38 (11) (1995) 39–41.

[48] S. Bajracharya, C. Lopes, Mining search topics from a code search engine usage log, in: Proceedings of the 6th IEEE International Working Conference on Mining Software Repositories, IEEE Computer Society, Washington, DC, USA, 2009, pp. 111–120.

[49] G. Canfora, L. Cerulo, M. Di Penta, Identifying changed source code lines from version repositories, in: Proceedings of 4th International Workshop on Mining Software Repositories, IEEE CS Press, Minneapolis, MN, USA, 2007, pp. 14–21.

[50] G. Canfora, L. Cerulo, Impact analysis by mining software and change request repositories, in: Proceedings of 11th IEEE International Symposium on Software Metrics, IEEE CS Press, Como, Italy, 2005, pp. 20–29.

[51] T. Chen, S.W. Thomas, M. Nagappan, A.E. Hassan, Explaining software defects using topic models, in: Proceedings of the 9th Working Conference on Mining Software Repositories, 2012.

[52] H. Gall, M. Jazayeri, J. Krajewski, CVS release history data for detecting logical couplings, in: Proceedings of the 6th International Workshop on Principles of Software Evolution, 2003, pp. 13–23.

[53] M. Ohba, K. Gondow, Toward mining concept keywords from identifiers in large software projects, in: Proceedings of International Workshop on Mining Software Repositories, St. Louis, MO, USA, 2005, pp. 1–5.

[54] S.W. Thomas, B. Adams, A.E. Hassan, D. Blostein, Modeling the evolution of topics in source code histories, in: Proceedings of the 8th Working Conference on Mining Software Repositories, 2011, pp. 173–182.

[55] C. Weiss, R. Premraj, T. Zimmermann, A. Zeller, How long will it take to fix this bug? in: Proceedings of the 4th International Workshop on Mining Software Repositories, IEEE CS Press, Minneapolis, MN, USA, 2007, pp. 1–8.

[56] A.T.T. Ying, G.C. Murphy, R. Ng, M.C. Chu-Carroll, Predicting source code changes by mining change history, IEEE Trans. Softw. Eng. 30 (9) (2004) 574–586.

[57] R. Agrawal, T. Imielinski, A.N. Swami, Mining association rules between sets of items in large databases, in: Proceedings of the 1993 ACM SIGMOD International Conference on Management of Data, 1993, pp. 207–216.

[58] T. Zimmermann, P. Weisgerber, S. Diehl, A. Zeller, Mining version histories to guide software changes, in: Proceedings of the 26th International Conference on Software Engineering, 2004, pp. 563–572.

[59] A. Jbara, A. Matan, D.G. Feitelson, High-MCC functions in the linux kernel, in: Proceedings of the IEEE 20th International Conference on Program Comprehension, Passau, Germany, 2012, pp. 83–92.

[60] D. Ratiu, S. Ducasse, T. Gîrba, R. Marinescu, Using history information to improve design flaws detection, in: Proceedings of the 8th European Conference on Software Maintenance and Reengineering, IEEE Computer Society, Tampere, Finland, 2004, pp. 223–232.

[61] S.M. Olbrich, D.S. Cruzes, D.I.K. Sjøberg, Are all code smells harmful? A study of God classes and brain classes in the evolution of three open source systems, in: Proceedings of the International Conference on Software Maintenance, IEEE, 2010, pp. 1–10.

ABOUT THE AUTHORS

Fabio Palomba is a PhD student at the University of Salerno under the supervision of Prof. Andrea De Lucia and Prof. Rocco Oliveto. He received the Master Degree in Computer Science from the University of Salerno (Italy) and the Bachelor Degree in Computer Science from the University of Molise (Italy). His research interests include mining software repositories, refactoring and remodularization, software maintenance and evolution, and empirical software engineering. He is a student member of IEEE.

Andrea De Lucia is a full professor of software engineering at the Department of Management and Information Technology of the University of Salerno, Italy, head of the Software Engineering Lab, and director of the International Summer School on Software Engineering. He received his PhD in Electronic Engineering and Computer Science from the University of Naples "Federico II," Italy, in 1996. His research interests include software maintenance and testing, reverse engineering and reengineering, empirical software engineering, search-based software engineering, collaborative development, workflow and document management, and e-learning. He has published more than 200 papers on these topics in international journals, books, and conference proceedings and has edited books and journal special issues. He also serves on the editorial boards of international journals and on the organizing and program committees of international conferences.

Prof. De Lucia is a senior member of the IEEE and the IEEE Computer Society and was also at-large member of the executive committee of the IEEE Technical Council on Software Engineering (TCSE).

Gabriele Bavota is a research fellow at the Department of Engineering of the University of Sannio (Italy). He received the PhD in Computer Science from the University of Salerno (Italy) in 2013. His research interests include refactoring and remodularization, software maintenance and evolution, and empirical software engineering. He serves and has served on the organizing and program committees of international conferences in the field of software engineering. He is a member of IEEE.

Rocco Oliveto is a assistant professor in the Department of Bioscience and Territory at University of Molise (Italy). He is the director of the Laboratory of Computer Science and Scientific Computation of the University of Molise. He received the PhD in Computer Science from University of Salerno (Italy) in 2008. His research interests include traceability management, information retrieval, software maintenance and evolution, search-based software engineering, and empirical software engineering. He serves and has served as organizing and program committee member of international conferences in the field of software engineering. He is a member of IEEE Computer Society, ACM, and IEEE-CS Awards and Recognition Committee.

CHAPTER FIVE

Classifying Problems into Complexity Classes

William Gasarch

University of Maryland, Maryland, USA

Contents

Advances in Computers, Volume 95
ISSN 0065-2458
http://dx.doi.org/10.1016/B978-0-12-800160-8.00005-X

Abstract

A fundamental problem in computer science is stated informally as: *Given a problem, how hard is it?* We measure hardness by looking at the following question: *Given a set A what is the fastest algorithm to determine if "x ∈ A?"* We measure the speed of an algorithm by how long it takes to run on inputs of length *n*, as a function of *n*. For example, sorting a list of length *n* can be done in roughly *n* log *n* steps.

Obtaining a fast algorithm is only half of the problem. Can you prove that there is no better algorithm? This is notoriously difficult; however, we can classify problems into *complexity classes* where those in the same class are roughly equally hard.

In this chapter, we define many complexity classes and describing natural problems that are in them. Our classes go all the way from regular languages to various shades of undecidable. We then summarize all that is known about these classes.

1. INTRODUCTION

A fundamental problem in computer science is stated informally as:

Given a problem, how hard is it?

For a rather concrete problem, the answer might be *it will take 2 h of computing time on a supercomputer* or *this will take a team of 10 programmers 2 years to write the program.* For a class of problems of the same type (e.g., sort a list), the complexity usually depends on the input size. These are the kinds of problems we will consider. Our concern will usually be how much time or space the problem takes to finish *as a function of the input size.* Our problems will be static, usually set membership: Given a string x is it in set A or not?

Example 5.1 Given a string $x \in \{0, 1\}^n$ we want to know if it is in 0^* (a string of all 0's). An algorithm for this problem is to scan the string and keep track of just one thing: have you seen a 1 or not? As soon as you do, stop and output NO. If you finish the scan and have not seen a 1 then output YES. Note that this take $O(n)$ steps and $O(1)$ space, and scanned the input once. Languages like this are called *regular* or DSPACE($O(1)$) (we will define this later).

Example 5.2 Given a string $x \in \{0, 1\}^n$ we want to know if the number of 0's equals the number of 1's. An algorithm for this problem is to scan the string and keep track of just two things: the number of 0's and the number of 1's. At the end of the scan, see if they are the same. If so, then output YES else output NO. This again takes $O(n)$ steps. How much space does it take? We have to store 2 numbers that are between 0 and n so this takes $O(\log n)$ space. Languages like this are called DSPACE($O(\log n)$) (we will define this later). This particular language is also called *context free*; however, we will not be discussing that class in this chapter.

Most of the sections of this chapter define a complexity class and gives some natural problems in it. In all cases, we are talking about worst case. For example, if we say that a problem requires n^2 steps we mean that for any algorithm there is an input of length n where it takes n^2 steps. As such, some of the problems discussed may not be as complex in real life if the inputs are not the bad ones. We won't discuss this further except to say that a problem might not be quite as bad as it appears here.

We then have additional sections: (1) a look at other complexity measures, (2) a summary of what we've done, (3) a literal discussion *what is a natural problem*,

The natural problems we consider are mainly from graph theory, games, formal language theory, and logic. A good reference for some of the problems in logic (with proofs) is a book by Ferrate and Rackoff [1]. There are many natural problems in other areas (e.g., model checking, artificial intelligence, Economics, Physics); however, to even define these problems would be difficult in a chapter of this nature.

There are many complexity classes that we do not discuss in this chapter. How many complexity classes are there? Literally hundreds. The website *Complexity Zoo* [2] currently lists around 500.

2. TIME AND SPACE CLASSES

The material in this chapter is due to Hartmanis and Stearns [3].

We want to classify problems by how much time or space they take to solve as a function of the length of the input. Say the input is of size n. If the algorithm takes n steps or $n/2$ steps or $10n$ steps, we do not want to care about those differences. While the difference between n and $100n$ matters in the real world, as a first cut at the complexity it does not. We need a way to say we don't care about constants.

Definition 5.3 Let f be a monotone increasing function from $\mathbb{N}$ to $\mathbb{N}$.
1. $O(f)$ is the class of all functions g such that there exists a constants n_0, c such that $(\forall n \geq n_0)[g(n) \leq cf(n)]$.
2. $\Omega(f)$ is the class of all functions g such that there exists a constants n_0, c such that $(\forall n \geq n_0)[g(n) \geq cf(n)]$.

When we define problems we code everything into strings over an alphabet. We are concerned with the complexity of a set of strings.

Notation 5.4 Let A and B be sets.
1. $AB = \{xy \mid x \in A \text{ AND } y \in B\}$.
2. A^i is $A \cdots A$ (i times). If $i = 0$, then A^0 is the empty string.
3. $A^* = A^0 \cup A^1 \cup A^2 \cup \cdots$

Notation 5.5 Let Σ be a finite alphabet (often $\{a, b\}$ or $\{0, 1\}$). A *problem* is a set $A \subseteq \Sigma^*$. The problem is to, given x, determine if x is in A.

Convention 5.6 We will use the term *Program* informally. To formalize it, we would define a Turing Machine.

Definition 5.7 Let T be a monotone increasing function from $\mathbb{N}$ to $\mathbb{N}$. DTIME($T(n)$) is the set of all sets $A \subseteq \Sigma^*$ such that there exists a program M such that
1. If $x \in A$, then $M(x) = YES$.
2. If $x \notin A$, then $M(x) = NO$.
3. For all x, $M(x)$ takes time $\leq O(T(|x|))$.

Definition 5.8 Let S be a monotone increasing function from $\mathbb{N}$ to $\mathbb{N}$. DSPACE($S(n)$) is the set of all sets $A \subseteq \Sigma^*$ such that there exists a program M such that
1. If $x \in A$, then $M(x) = YES$.
2. If $x \notin A$, then $M(x) = NO$.
3. For all x, $M(x)$ uses space $\leq O(S(|x|))$.

Definition 5.9 One can define a function being in DTIME($T(n)$) or DSPACE($S(n)$) similarly.

The program referred to in Definition 7 is deterministic. On input x, there is only one way for a computation to go. We now define non-deterministic programs. We consider them mathematical devices. We do not consider them to be real. However, they will be useful for classifying problems.

Definition 5.10 A *Nondeterministic Program* is a program where, in any state, there is a choice of actions to take. For example, a line might read

$$x := x + 1 \text{ OR } y := y + 4$$

If M is a nondeterminism program, then what does it mean to run $M(x)$? We do not define this. However, we do say what it means for $M(x)$ to accept.

Definition 5.11 Let M be a nondeterministic program. $M(x)$ *accepts* if there is *some* choice of instructions so that it accepts. $M(x)$ *rejects* if there is no choice of instructions that makes it accept.

Definition 5.12 Let T be a monotone increasing function from $\mathbb{N}$ to $\mathbb{N}$. NTIME($T(n)$) is the set of all sets $A \subseteq \Sigma^*$ such that there exists a program M such that

1. If $x \in A$, then $M(x)$ accepts.
2. If $x \notin A$, then $M(x)$ rejects.
3. For all x, any computation path of $M(x)$ takes time $\leq O(T(|x|))$.

Definition 5.13 Let S be a monotone increasing function from $\mathbb{N}$ to $\mathbb{N}$. NSPACE($S(n)$) is the set of all sets $A \subseteq \Sigma^*$ such that there exists a nondeterministic program M such that

1. If $x \in A$, then $M(x) = YES$.
2. If $x \notin A$, then $M(x) = NO$.
3. For all x, any computation path of $M(x)$ uses space $\leq O(S(|x|))$.

Note 5.14 There is no really useful way to define a nondeterministic device computing a function.

Notation 5.15 The class DTIME($n^{O(1)}$) is $\bigcup_{i=1}^{\infty}$ DTIME(n^i). We may use $O(1)$ inside other time or space classes. The meaning will be clear from context.

We will be interested in seeing which time or space class a problem is in. Within a class there may be harder and easier problems. There will be problems that are (informally) the hardest in that class. We do not define *completeness* rigorously; however, we state the following property of it;

Fact 5.16 *Let X and Y be complexity classes such that $X \subset Y$ (proper containment) If a problem is Y-complete, then $Y \not\subseteq X$.*

3. RELATIONS BETWEEN CLASSES

Throughout this section think of $T(n)$ and $S(n)$ as increasing. The following theorem is trivial.

Theorem 5.17 *Let $T(n)$ and $S(n)$ be computable functions.*
1. DTIME($T(n)$) $\subseteq$ NTIME($T(n)$).
2. DSPACE($S(n)$) $\subseteq$ NSPACE($S(n)$).
·3. DTIME($T(n)$) $\subseteq$ DSPACE($T(n)$).
4. NTIME($T(n)$) $\subseteq$ NSPACE($T(n)$).

The following theorem is easy but not trivial.

Theorem 5.18 *Let $T(n)$ and $S(n)$ be computable functions.*
1. NTIME($T(n)$) $\subseteq$ DTIME($2^{O(T(n))}$). *(Just simulate all possible paths.)*
2. NTIME($T(n)$) $\subseteq$ DSPACE($O(T(n))$). *(Just simulate all possible paths— keep a counter for which path you are simulating.)*

The following theorems have somewhat clever proofs.

Theorem 5.19 *Let $S(n)$ be a computable functions.*
1. NSPACE($S(n)$) $\subseteq$ DSPACE($O(S(n)^2)$). *This was proven by Savitch [4] and is in any textbooks on complexity theory.*
2. NSPACE($S(n)$) $\subseteq$ DTIME($O(2^{S(n)})$). *This seems to be folklore.*

The following are by diagonalization. Hence, the sets produced are not natural. Even so, the existence of such sets will allow us to later show natural sets that are in one complexity class and not in a lower one.

Theorem 5.20 *For all $T(n)$, there is a set $A \in$ DTIME($T(n) \log T(n)$)) − DTIME($T(n)$). (The $T(n) \log T(n)$ comes from some overhead in simulating a k-tape Turing Machine with a 2-tape Turing Machine.) This is The Time Hierarchy Theorem and is due to Hartmanis and Stearns [3].*

Theorem 5.21 *Let S_1 and S_2 be computable functions. Assume $\lim_{n \to \infty} \frac{S_1(n)}{S_2(n)} = \infty$. Then there exists a set $A \in$ DSPACE($S_1(n)$) − DSPACE($S_2(n)$). Hence DSPACE($S_2(n)$) $\subset$ DSPACE($S_1(n)$). This is The Space Hierarchy Theorem and seems to be folklore.*

4. DSPACE(1)=REGULAR LANGUAGES

There are many different definitions of regular languages that are all equivalent to each other. We present them in the next definition.

Definition 5.22 A language A is *regular* (henceforth REG) if it satisfies any of the equivalent conditions below.

1. $A \in \text{DSPACE}(1)$.
2. $A \in \text{NSPACE}(1)$.
3. A is in $\text{DSPACE}(1)$) by a program that, on every computation path, only scans the input once. (This is equivalent to being recognized by a deterministic finite automata, abbreviated DFA.)
4. A is in $\text{NSPACE}(1)$ by a program that, on every computation path, only scans the input once. (This is equivalent to being recognized by a nondeterministic finite automata, abbreviated NDFA. When you convert an NDFA to a DFA you may get an exponential blowup in the number of states.)
5. A is generated by a regular expression (we define this later).

The equivalence of $\text{DSPACE}(1)$ and $\text{NSPACE}(1)$ is easy. The equivalence of deterministic and nondeterministic is due to Rabin and Scott [5]. It is in all textbooks on formal language theory. The equivalence of $\text{DSPACE}(1)$ and $\text{DSPACE}(1)$-scan once is folklore but has its origins in the Rabin–Scott paper.

We define regular expressions α and the language they generate $L(\alpha)$.

Definition 5.23 Let Σ be a finite alphabet.

1. $\emptyset$ (the empty set) is a regular expression. $L(\emptyset) = \emptyset$.
2. e (the empty string) is a regular expression. $L(e) = \{e\}$.
3. For all $\sigma \in \Sigma$, σ is a regular expression. $L(\sigma) = \{\sigma\}$.
4. If α and β are regular expressions then:
   a. $(\alpha \cup \beta)$ is a regular expression. $L(\alpha \cup \beta) = L(\alpha) \cup L(\beta)$.
   b. $\alpha\beta$ is a regular expression. $L(\alpha\beta) = L(\alpha)L(\beta)$. (Recall that if A is a set and B is a set then $AB = \{xy \mid x \in A \text{ AND } y \in B\}$.)
   c. α^* is a regular expression. $L(\alpha^*) = L(\alpha)^*$. (Recall that if A is a set then $A^* = A^0 \cup A \cup AA \cup AAA \cdots$.)

We give examples or regular sets after the next bit of notation.

Definition 5.24 Let Σ be a finite set. Let $w \in \Sigma^*$. Let $\sigma \in \Sigma$. Then $\#_\sigma(w)$ is the number of σ's in w.

Definition 5.25 Let $x, y, z \in \mathbb{N}$. Then $x \equiv y \pmod{z}$ means that z divides $x - y$.

Example 5.26 The following sets are regular.

$$\{w \in \{a, b\}^* \mid \#_a(w) \equiv \#_b(w) + 10 \pmod{21}\}$$

You can replace 10 and 21 with any constants.

$$\{w \in \{a, b\}^* \mid abab \text{ is a prefix of } w\}$$

$$\{w \in \{a, b\}^* \mid abab \text{ is a suffix of } w\}$$

$$\{w \in \{a, b\}^* \mid abab \text{ is a substring of } w\}$$

You can replace $abab$ with any finite string.

If A_1, A_2 are regular languages, then so are $A_1 \cap A_2$, $A_1 \cup A_2$ and $\overline{A_1}$. Hence, any Boolean combination of the above is also a regular language. For example,

$$\{w \in \{a, b\}^* \mid abab \text{ is a substring of } w \text{ AND } \#_a(w) \not\equiv \#_b(w) + 10 \pmod{2}1\}.$$

Example 5.27 Throughout this example $w = d_n d_{n-1} \cdots d_0 \in \{0, 1, 2, 3, 4, 5, 6, 7, 8, 9\}^*$ is thought of as a number in base 10.

Is it easy to tell if $w \equiv 0 \pmod 2$? Yes: $w \equiv 0 \pmod 2$ iff $d_0 \equiv 0 \pmod 2$. Hence

$$\{w \mid w \equiv 0 \pmod 2\} \text{ is regular.}$$

Is it easy to tell if $w \equiv 0 \pmod 3$? Yes: $w \equiv 0 \pmod 3$ iff $d_0 + d_1 + \cdots + d_n \equiv 0 \pmod 3$. By keeping a running total mod 3, one can show that

$$\{w \mid w \equiv 0 \pmod 3\} \text{ is regular.}$$

There are also well known divisibility tricks for divisibility by 4,5,6,8,9,10,11. What about 7? There are two questions to ask here

- Is there a trick for divisibility by 7? (This question is not rigorous.)
- Is the set $DIV7 = \{w \mid w \equiv 0 \pmod 7\}$ regular?

One can interpret the second question as a rigorous restatement of the first. When you see the answer you may want to reconsider that interpretation.

We show that $\{w \mid w \equiv 0 \pmod 7\}$ is regular. Note that

$$
\begin{aligned}
10^0 &\equiv 1 \pmod 7 \\
10^1 &\equiv 3 \pmod 7 \\
10^2 &\equiv 2 \pmod 7 \\
10^3 &\equiv 6 \pmod 7 \\
10^4 &\equiv 4 \pmod 7 \\
10^5 &\equiv 5 \pmod 7 \\
10^6 &\equiv 1 \pmod 7
\end{aligned}
$$

Hence $d_n d_{n-1} d_{n-2} \cdots d_0$ is equivalent mod 7 to the following:

$$
\begin{array}{ccccccccccccc}
d_0 & + & 3d_1 & + & 2d_2 & + & 6d_3 & + & 4d_4 & + & 5d_5 & + \\
d_6 & + & 3d_7 & + & 2d_8 & + & 6d_9 & + & 4d_{10} & + & 5d_{11} & + \\
d_{12} & + & 3d_{13} & + & 2d_{14} & + & 6d_{15} & + & 4d_{16} & + & 5d_{17} & + \\
\vdots & + & \vdots & + & \vdots & + & \vdots & + & \vdots & + & \vdots & +
\end{array}
$$

We can use this to show that the set $DIV7$ is regular. To determine if $w \in DIV7$, when scanning w, one only needs to keep track of (1) the weighted sum mod 7, and (2) the index mod 6 of i. This would lead to a 42-state finite automata. Whether you want to consider this a *trick* for divisibility by 7 or not is a matter of taste.

Example 5.28 We want to look at sets like

$$\{(b, c, A) \mid b \in A \text{ AND } c + 1 \notin A\}.$$

Are such sets regular? We first need to have a way to represent such sets. We represent a number x by a string of x 0's and then a 1 and then we do not care what comes next. So for example 000100 represents 3 and so does 000110. we will denote this by saying that $0001 * *$ represents 3 (we may have more $*$'s). We represent finite sets by a bit vector. For example, 11101 represents the set $\{0, 1, 2, 4\}$.

How do we represent a triple? We use the alphabet $\{0, 1\}^3$. We give an example. The triple $(3, 4, \{0, 1, 2, 4, 7\})$ is represented by the following (The top line and the b, c, A are not there. They are Visual Aids.)

	0	1	2	3	4	5	6	7
b	0	0	0	1	0	$*$	$*$	$*$
c	0	0	0	0	1	$*$	$*$	$*$
A	1	1	1	0	1	0	0	1

With this representation the set

$$\{(b, c, A) \mid b \in A \text{ AND } c + 1 \notin A\}$$

is regular.

Much more can be said. We define a class of formulas $\phi(\vec{x}, \vec{X})$, the WS1S formulas, such that the set of $(\vec{a}, \vec{A})$ that make them true is regular. We will use this again in Section 18.

We will only use the following symbols.
1. The logical symbols $\wedge$, $\neg$, $(\exists)$.
2. Variables $x_1, x_2, x_3, \ldots$ that range over $\mathbb{N}$. (We use x, y, z when there are less than 4 variables.)

3. Variables $X_1, X_2, X_3, \ldots$ that range over finite subsets of $\mathbb{N}$. (We use X, Y, Z when there are less than 4 variables.)
4. Symbols: $=$, $<$, $\in$, S (meaning $S(x) = x + 1$).
5. Constants: 0,1,2,3,.....
6. Convention: We write $x + c$ instead of $S(S(\cdots S(x)) \cdots)$. Note that $+$ is not in our lang.

We call this WS1S: Weak Second order Theory of One Successor. Weak Second order means quantify over finite sets. What Does One Successor Mean? Our basic objects are numbers. We could view numbers as strings in unary. In that case $S(x) = x1$. If our basic objects were strings in $\{0, 1\}^*$, then we could have two successors $S_0(x) = x0$ and $S_1(x) = x1$.

Definition 5.29 An *Atomic Formulas* is:
1. For any $c \in \mathbb{N}$, $x = y + c$ is an Atomic Formula.
2. For any $c \in \mathbb{N}$, $x < y + c$ is an Atomic Formula.
3. For any $c, d \in \mathbb{N}$, $x \equiv y + c \pmod{d}$ is an Atomic Formula.
4. For any $c \in \mathbb{N}$, $x + c \in X$ is an Atomic Formula.
5. For any $c \in \mathbb{N}$, $X = Y + c$ is an Atomic Formula.

Definition 5.30 A *WS1S Formula* is:
1. Any atomic formula is a WS1S formula.
2. If ϕ_1, ϕ_2 are WS1S formulas then so are
   a. $\phi_1 \wedge \phi_2$,
   b. $\phi_1 \vee \phi_2$
   c. $\neg \phi_1$
3. If $\phi(x_1, \ldots, x_n, X_1, \ldots, X_m)$ is a WS1S-Formula then so are
   a. $(\exists x_i)[\phi(x_1, \ldots, x_n, X_1, \ldots, X_m)]$
   b. $(\exists X_i)[\phi(x_1, \ldots, x_n, X_1, \ldots, X_m)]$

For any WS1S formula $\phi(\vec{x}, \vec{X})$, the following set is regular:

$$\{(\vec{a}, \vec{A}) \mid \phi(\vec{a}, \vec{A}) \text{ is true }\}.$$

The proof uses the closure of regular languages under union (for $\vee$), intersection (for $\wedge$), complementation (for $\neg$), and projection (for $\exists$). The closure under projection involves taking an NDFA and converting it to a DFA. This results in an exponential blowup in the number of states. Hence, the DFA's one obtains can be quite large.

5. L = DSPACE(log n)

For this section, we let L $=$ DSPACE(log n). It is known that REG $\subset$ L. We give examples of sets in L $-$ REG.

Example 5.31 Intuitively, any set where you need to keep track of the number of a's or any unbounded quantity is not regular. Formally you would prove the following nonregular using the pumping lemma (perhaps together with closure properties). We do not state or use this lemma.

$$\{a^n b^n \mid n \in \mathbb{N}\}$$

$$\{a^n b^m \mid n, m \in \mathbb{N} \text{ AND } n \leq m\}$$

$$\{w \mid \#_a(w) = \#_b(w)\}$$

All of these are in L since you need only keep track of the number of a's and b's which will take $O(\log n)$ space.

Example 5.32 Consider the following problem. The input is an undirected graph together with two nodes.

$$CONN = \{(G, s, t) \mid \text{ there is a path in } G \text{ from } s \text{ to } t \}.$$

$CONN$ is in NSPACE(log n): start with a pointer to s and guess a neighbor x_1 to goto. Then guess a neighbor x_2 of x_1 to goto. Keep doing this. If you ever get to t, then stop and accept. Is $CONN$ in L? Surprisingly yes. Omer Reingold [6] proved this in 2008. What if the graph is directed? This problem is thought to be harder and will be discussed in the next section.

Example 5.33 The following problems are also in L:
1. Given a graph, is it planar? (See [7].)
2. Given two trees are they isomorphic? (See [8].)
3. Given two planar graphs, are they isomorphic? (See [9].)
4. Given n permutations $p_1, \ldots, p_n$, is their product the identity. (See [10].)

6. NL = NSPACE(log n)

For this section, we let NL $=$ NSPACE(log n). Clearly L $\subseteq$ NL. It is not known if this inclusion is proper; however, most theorists think L $\neq$ NL.

Example 5.34 Consider the problem

$$DCONN = \{(G, s, t) \mid \text{there is a path in } G \text{ from } s \text{ to } t\}.$$

(The graph G is directed. This is important.)

This problem may *look* similar to $CONN$; however, it is not. Thought experiment: let $A \in$ NSPACE($\log n$). Let $x \in \Sigma^n$. View the space that the program uses while computing on x to be on a tape of length $O(\log n)$, which we call the *worktape*. Since the worktape is of length $O(\log n)$ there are only a polynomial number of possibilities for it. One can form a directed graph by taking the vertices to be the possible worktapes, and put an edge from u to v if it is possible to go (recall that the machine is nondeterministic), in one step of M, from u to v This directed graph has a path from the start state to an accept state iff $M(x)$ accepts. Hence, we can reduce *any* problem in NSPACE($\log n$) to the problem $DCONN$. Formally $DCONN$ is NL-complete.

If $DCONN \in L$ then $L = NL$. Hence, most theorists think $DCONN \notin L$.

7. P = DTIME($n^{O(1)}$)

Let P $= $ DTIME($n^{O(1)}$), also called *Polynomial Time*. NL $\subseteq$ P by Theorem 19.2. It is not known if this inclusion is proper; however, most theorists think NL $\neq$ P.

P is considered by theorists to be the very definition of *feasible* (though see the next section on randomized polynomial time). Why is polynomial time so revered?

Polynomial time is usually contrasted with brute force search. Lets say you want to, given a Boolean formula $\phi(x_1, \ldots, x_n)$, determine if there is some truth assignment that makes it true. The naive approach is to look at all 2^n possibilities. Lets say you could use symmetries to cut it down to 2^{n-10}. You are still doing brute force search, with a few tricks. But if you got an algorithm in n^{100} steps then you are most definitely **not** doing brute force search. Even though the exponent is large it is likely that the cleverness used to avoid brute force search can be further exploited to obtain a practical algorithm.

We present several natural problems in P. Some are expressed as functions rather than sets as that is more natural for them. They are not believed to be in NL.

Example 5.35 If $G = (V, E)$ is a graph, then $U \subseteq U$ is a *vertex cover* if every edge in E has some vertex of U as an endpoint. Let

$$VC_{17} = \{ G \mid G \text{ has a vertex cover of size 17 } \}.$$

$VC_{17} \in P$ by the following simple algorithm: look at all subsets of 17 vertices and for each one check if it's a vertex cover. This take $O(n^{17})$ time. Can we do better? We'll consider this in Section 9.

Example 5.36 Given a weighted graph $G = (V, E)$ (no negative weights) and a source node s, find, for each node t, the shortest path from s to t. The standard algorithm to put this problem in P Dijkstra's algorithm [11] (it is in many algorithms textbooks) originally took $O(|V|^2)$ time; however, a later implementation using a Fibonacci heap takes $O(|E| + |V| \log(|V|))$.

Example 5.37 Given a weighted graphs $G = (V, E)$ find, for all pairs of vertices $\{s, t\}$ the shortest path between s and t. The Floyd–Warshall algorithm solves this problem in $O(|V|^3)$ time. The algorithm was discovered independently by Floyd [12], Warshall [13], and Roy [14] (it is in many algorithms textbooks).

Example 5.38 Given a weighted graph $G = (V, E)$ find a min weight spanning tree. There are basically two algorithms for this, one due to J. Kruskal [15] and one due to Prim [16] (both are in many algorithms textbooks). Kruskal's algorithm originally took $O(E \log V)$ steps. Prim's algorithm originally took $O(|V|^2)$; however, a later implementation using a Fibonacci heap and adjacency lists takes $O(|E| + |V| \log |V|)$. The best known algorithm for this problem is due to Chazelle [17] and runs in time $O(n\alpha(m, n))$ where $\alpha(m, n)$ is the inverse of the Ackermann function (see Section 19). Note that this is very close to linear. If this was also a lower bound, then the result would be optimal and Ackermann's function would have popped up in a natural place. Alas, Chazelle thinks this is unlikely.

Example 5.39 Linear programming: Given a matrix A and a two vectors b and c find the vector of x that maximizes $c \cdot x$ while satisfying the constraint $Ax \le b$.

Linear programming is particularly interesting. This problem is extremely practical. The Simplex Method, developed by Dantzig in 1947, solves it quickly in most cases but is not polynomial time. It is widely used. In 1979, Khachiyan [18] showed it was in polynomial time using the ellipsoid method. This algorithm was important theoretically in that the problem was now in P; however, it was slow in practice. In 1984, Karmarkar [19] produced a method that is fast in both theory and practice.

8. RANDOMIZED POLYNOMIAL TIME: *R*

Definition 5.40 A problem *A* is in *Randomized Polynomial Time* (henceforth R) if there is a program that flips coins such that the following happens:

1. On all inputs of length n, the program halts in time polynomial in n.
2. If $x \in A$, then the program will ACCEPT with probability $\geq 2/3$.
3. If $x \notin A$, then the program will REJECT.

Note 5.41 The $2/3$ can be replaced by any $\epsilon > 0$ and even by $\frac{1}{2^n}$ where n is the length of the input.

Clearly P $\subseteq$ R. Before 1988, the theory community did not have a strong opinion on if P = R, however, the opinion would have been a tendency towards P $\neq$ R. Michael Sipser [20] was an exception in that he believed P = R. In 1988, Nisan and Wigderson [21] showed that, given certain quite reasonable unproven hypothesis from complexity theory, P = R. Since then the consensus has been that P = R. This remains unproven.

At one time the quintessential natural problem in R that was not known to be in P was primality. Solovay and Strassen [22] and Rabin [23] showed primality was in R. Their algorithms are practical and used. Rabin has pointed out that if the error is (say) $1/2^{100}$ then that is less than the probability that a cosmic ray will hit a computer and flip a bit to make it incorrect. The algorithm by Rabin is sometimes called the Miller–Rabin primality test since Miller had a similar deterministic algorithm that depended on unproven conjectures in Number Theory.

In 2002, Agrawal–Kayal–Saxena [24] proven that primality is in P. Their algorithm is slow and not in use. However, it was very interesting to see that primality really is in P.

There is still one natural problem that is in R that is not yet known to be in P:

Example 5.42 *Given a polynomial* $q(x_1, \ldots, x_n)$ *and a prime* p, *is the polynomial identically 0 over mod* p?

Here is the randomized algorithm: Pick a random $b_1, \ldots, b_n \in$ $\{0, \ldots, p - 1\}$. Evaluate $q(b_1, \ldots, b_n)$ (mod p). If it is not zero, then we KNOW that $q(x_1, \ldots, x_n)$ is not identically zero. If it is zero, then we are not sure. So we plug in another random $b_1, \ldots, b_n$. Do this n times. If you ever get a nonzero value, then you know $q(x_1, \ldots, x_n)$ is not identically zero. If you always get a zero, then you know with high probability that $q(x_1, \ldots, x_n)$ is identically zero.

The following randomized class has also been defined; however, there are no natural problems in it that are not also in R.

Definition 5.43 A problem A is in *Bounded Probabilistic Polynomial Time* (henceforth BPP) if there is a program that flips coins such that the following happens:

1. On all inputs of length n, the program halts in time polynomial in n.
2. If $x \in A$, then the program will ACCEPT with probability $\geq 2/3$.
3. If $x \in A$, then the program will REJECTS with probability $\geq 2/3$.

Note 5.44 The 2/3 can be replaced by any $\epsilon > 0$ and even by $\frac{1}{2^n}$ where n is the length of the input.

Clearly R $\subseteq$ BPP. All that was written above about "P = R?" applies to "P = BPP?". In particular, theorists currently think P = BPP but this remains unproven. We will have a bit more to say about BPP in Section 10.

9. NP = NTIME($n^{O(1)}$)

Let NP = NTIME($n^{O(1)}$), also called *Nondeterministic Polynomial Time*. Clearly P $\subseteq$ R $\subseteq$ NP. It is not known if these inclusions are proper; however, most theorists think P = R $\subset$ NP. We will discuss their thoughts on P versus NP in more depth later.

What about BPP? It is now known if BPP $\subseteq$ NP. Since most theorists think P = BPP and P $\neq$ NP, most theorists think BPP $\subset$ NP. But it's not even known that BPP $\subseteq$ NP. In Section 10, we will state an upper bound for BPP.

NP is the most important class in computer science. It contains natural problems that we want to solve but currently seem hard to solve. Alas, there are reasons to think they will always be hard to solve. But there are ways around that. Maybe.

We give two equivalent definitions of NP.

Definition 5.45 Let A be a set.

1. $A \in NP$ if $A \in NTIME(n^{O(1)})$.

2. $A \in NP$ if there exists a polynomial p and a set $B \in P$ such that

$$A = \{x \mid (\exists y)[|x| = p(|x|) \text{ AND } (x, y) \in B]\}.$$

The intuition here is that y is a short easily verifiable proof that $x \in A$. We often call y *the witness*.

Note that if $A \in NP$ then it is quite possible that $\overline{A} \notin NP$. We know so little about NP that we have no examples; however, most theorists think that NP is *not* closed under complementation. Hence, we need a name for the complement of NP.

Definition 5.46 A set A is in co-NP if $\overline{A}$ is in NP.

Most theorists think $NP \neq co\text{-}NP$.

Example 5.47 A Boolean Formula $\phi(\vec{x})$ is *satisfiable* if there exists $\vec{b}$ such that $\phi(\vec{b}) = TRUE$. Let SAT be the set of all satisfiable formulas. $SAT \in NP$. The intuition is that the satisfying assignment $\vec{b}$ is the witness for $\phi \in SAT$. Formally $p(\phi(x_1, \ldots, x_n)) = n$ and

$$B = \{(\phi, \vec{b}) \mid \phi(\vec{b}) = TRUE\}.$$

Note that while *finding* the assignment $\vec{b}$ such that $\phi(\vec{b}) = TRUE$ may be hard, *verifying* that $\phi(\vec{b}) = TRUE$ is easy. The easy verification *is not* good news for SAT, this *is not* a first step to showing that SAT is easy or in P. But it does indicate why this problem may be hard: finding the right $\vec{b}$ is hard.

You might think that SAT requires a long time to solve since you seem to need to go through all 2^n possible assignments. And this may be true. But we do not know it to be true. What haunts many complexity theorists is that someone will be find a very clever way to avoid the brute force search. What comforts many complexity theorists is that SAT is NP-complete. Hence, it is unlikely to be in P.

Example 5.48 A graph G is *Eulerian* if there is a path that hits every *edge* at exactly once. Let $EULER$ be the set of all Eulerian graphs. $EULER \in NP$. The cycle that hits every edge at least once is the witness that G is Eulerian.

You might think that $EULER$ requires a long time to solve since you seem to need to go through all possible cycles. And this may be true. But we do not know it to be true. What haunts many complexity theorists is that someone will be find a very clever way to avoid the brute force search.

The last paragraph is a joke. *EULER* can be solved quickly! It turns out that a graph is in *EULER* iff every vertex has even degree. Hence, *EULER* ∈ P. Euler, who was quite clever, figured this out in 1736. (though he did not use the terminology of *polynomial time*). This is just the kind of thing I warned about when talking about SAT. There could just some clever idea out there we haven't thought of yet!

Example 5.49 A graph *G* is *Hamiltonian* if there is a path that hits every *vertex* exactly once. Let *HAM* be the set of all Hamiltonian graphs. *HAM* ∈ NP. The cycle that hits every vertex at least once is the witness that *G* is Hamiltonian.

You might think that *HAM* requires a long time to solve since you seem to need to go through all possible cycles. You may also be thinking, given that I fooled you with *EULER*, that you and The Who *don't get fooled again[25]*. However this time, for better or worse, *HAM* does really seem unlikely to be in P. In particular, *HAM* is NP-complete and hence unlikely to be in P.

Example 5.50 If $G = (V, E)$ is a graph, then $U \subseteq U$ is a *vertex cover* if every edge in E has some vertex of U as an endpoint. Let

$$VC = \{(G, k) \mid G \text{ has a vertex cover of size } k \}.$$

$VC \in$ NP. The vertex cover itself is the witness. *VC* is NP-complete and hence unlikely to be in P.

Example 5.51 The *Set Cover Problem)* is as follows: Given $S_1, \ldots, S_m \subseteq \{1, \ldots, n\}$ and a number L, is there a set $I \subseteq \{1, \ldots, m\}$ of size L such that $\bigcup_{i \in I} S_i = \bigcup_{i=1}^{n} S_i$.

The L subsets together is the witness. Set Cover is NP-complete and hence unlikely to be in P.

SAT, HAM, VC, SC are all NP-complete. So are thousands of natural problems from many different fields. Actually this means that *They are all the same problem!* Are these problems not in *P*? Does P $=$ NP? This is still not known.

9.1 Reasons to Think P ≠ NP and some Intelligent Objections

Scott Aaronson [26] gives very good reasons to think that P ≠ NP. William Gasarch [27] gives a simplified version of Scott's reasons. Richard Lipton [28] gives some intelligent objections. We summarize some of their thoughts, and others, below.

(1) For $P \neq NP$

Many of the problems that are NP-complete have been worked on for many years, even before these terms were formally defined. Mathematicians knew that graphs had an Euler cycle iff every vertex had even degree and were looking for a similar characterization for *HAM* graphs. If $P = NP$, then we would have found the algorithm by now.

(2) For $P = NP$

We keep getting better and better algorithms in surprising ways. We give an example. Recall from Section 7:

$$V_{17} = \{G \mid G \text{ has a vertex cover of size 17 }\}.$$

As noted in Section 7 VC_{17}, can be solved in time $O(n^{17})$. It would seem that one cannot do better. AH- but one can! We give two ways to do better to illustrate how surprising algorithms are.

Using the Graph Minor Theorem Robertson and Seymore proved *The Graph Minor Theorem* in a series of 25 papers titled *Graph Minors I, Graph Minors II,* etc. Suffice it to say that this theorem is difficult. We do not state the theorem; however, we state a definition and a corollary.

Definition 5.52 If G is a graph, then H is a *minor* of G if one can obtain H by performing the following operations on G in some order (1) remove a vertex and all the adjacent nodes, (2) remove an edge, (3) contract an edge—that is, remove it but then merge the two endpoints into one vertex.

Definition 5.53 Let $\mathcal{G}$ be a set of graphs. $\mathcal{G}$ is *closed under minors* if, for all $G \in \mathcal{G}$ if H is a minor of G then $H \in \mathcal{G}$. Examples: (1) planar graphs, (2) graphs that can be drawn in the plane with at most 100 crossings, (3) V_{17}.

Definition 5.54 Let $\mathcal{G}$ be a set of graphs. $\mathcal{G}$ has a *finite obstruction set* (FOS) if there exists a finite set of graphs $H_1, H_2, \ldots, H_m$ such that $G \in \mathcal{G}$ iff none of the H_i are a minor of G. Intuitively, if $G \notin \mathcal{G}$ then there must be a solid reason for it. It was known (before the Graph Minor Theorem) that the set of planar graphs has FOS $\{K_5, K_{3,3}\}$.

Fact 5.55 *Fix H. There is an $O(n^3)$ algorithm to tell if H is a minor of G. (This was also proven by Robertson and Seymour).*

We now state the important corollary of the Graph Minor Theorem:

Corollary 5.56 *If $\mathcal{G}$ is a set of graphs that is closed under minors, then it has a finite obstruction set. Using the fact above, any set of graphs closed under minors is in time $O(n^3)$.*

In particular, VC_{17} is in $DTIME(n^3)$. Note that we got a problem into better-time-bound-than-we-thought class using an incredibly hard theorem in math. Could the same happen with SAT?

Before the Graph Minor Theorem, most algorithms were very clever but didn't use that much math and certainly not that much hard math (algorithms in number theory may be an exception). Hence, it was plausible to say *if* P = NP *then we would have found the algorithm by now.* After the Graph Minor Theorem this was a hollow argument. It has been said:

The class P lost its innocence with the Graph Minor Theorem.

We note that the algorithm given above is insane. The constant is ginormous and the algorithm itself is nonconstructive. It can be made constructive but only be making the constant even bigger.

Using Bounded Tree Search There is a clever way to solve VC_{17} in a bound far better than $O(n^{17})$ that does not use hard math. We form a binary tree. At the root put, the graph and the empty set take an edge (a, b) of G. One of $\{a, b\}$ must be in the vertex cover. Make the left subchild of the root the graph without a and the set $\{a\}$. Make the right subchild of the root the graph without b and the set $\{b\}$. Repeat this process. Every node will have a graph and a set. Do this for 17 levels. If any of them lead to the empty graph, then you are done and the set is the vertex cover of size ≤ 17. This takes $O(n)$ but note the constant is roughly 2^{17}.

This algorithm is clever but was not known for a long time. I would like to tell you that the Graph Minor Theorem algorithm came first, and once it was known to be in far less than $O(n^{17})$ people were inspired and thus found the clever algorithm. However, the actually history is murkier than that. Oh well.

The best known algorithm for VC_k is due to Chen, Kanj, and Jia [29] and runs in time $O(1.2738^k + kn)$.

(3) For P $\neq$ NP

Let us step back and ponder how one makes conjectures that are reasonable.

Do Popperian experiments. Karl Popper [30] proposed that scientists should set up experiments that could disprove their theories. That is, experiments that can actually fail. Their failure to fail gives you more evidence in your conjecture. I do not know how one can do this for P versus NP. This would be an interesting approach to P versus NP; however, it is not clear how you would set up such experiments.

Paradigms. Thomas Kuhn [31] proposed that scientists operate within a paradigm and try to fit everything into that paradigm. Great science happens when you have enough evidence for the paradigm to shift. However, most of the time the paradigm is fine. If a theory fits well into a paradigm, that cannot be ignored. (I do realize that if you take this too seriously you may end up with group-think). With regard to P versus NP we *do* know what theorists believe in a more precise way than usual. There have been two polls taken. In 2002, around 60% of all theorists believed P $\neq$ NP [32] and in 2012 around 80% of all theorists believed P $\neq$ NP [33]. Whether or not you see that as evidence is a matter of taste. We will mention this poll later in Section 9.2.

Explanatory power. If a theory explains much data, then perhaps the theory is true. This is how evolution is verified. It would be hard to do experiments; however, given Fossil and DNA evidence, evolution seems to explain it pretty well. (I know that it's not as simple as that.) Are there a set of random facts that P $\neq$ NP would help explain? Yes.

The obvious one: P $\neq$ NP explains why we have not been able to solve all of those NP-complete problems any faster!

More recent results add to this:

1. Chvatal [34] in 1979 showed that there is an algorithm for Set Cover that returns a cover of size $(\ln n) \times OPT$ where OPT is the best one could do.
2. Moshkovitz [35] in 2011 proved that, assuming P $\neq$ NP, this approximation cannot be improved.

Why can't we do better than $\ln n$? Perhaps because P $\neq$ NP. If this was the only example it would not be compelling. But there are many such pairs where assuming P $\neq$ NP would explain why we have approached these limits.

(4) For P = NP:

Fool me once, shame on you, fool me twice, shame on me. There have been surprises in mathematics and computer science before. And there will be more in the future. We mention one: NSPACE$(S(n))$ closed under complementation. While this is not really an argument for P = NP it is an argument for keeping an open mind.

An intriguing Question: Most people in the theory community think (a) P $\neq$ NP, (b) we are very far from being able to prove this. (c) If P $=$ NP, then this might be by an algorithm we can figure out today. I offer the following thought experiment and my answer. You are told that P versus NP has been solved but *you are not told in what direction!* Do you believe:

- Surely P $\neq$ NP has been shown since of course P $\neq$ NP.
- Surely P $=$ NP has been shown since we are nowhere near being able to show anything remotely like P $\neq$ NP. (See Section 9.4 for more on this.)

  Personally I would think P $=$ NP was shown.

9.2 NP Intermediary Problems

Are there any natural problems in NP $-$ P that are not NP-complete? Such sets are called *intermediary*. If we knew such sets existed, then we would have P $\neq$ NP. Are there any candidates for intermediary sets?

Ladner [36] showed in 1975 that if P $\neq$ NP then there is an intermediary set. While this is good to know, the set is not natural.

We now give natural problems that may be intermediary.

Example 5.57 Factoring Consider the set

$$FACT = \{(n, m) \mid (\exists a \leq m)[m \text{ divides } n]\}.$$

1. $FACT$ is clearly in NP. There is no known polynomial time algorithm for $FACT$. There is no proof that $FACT$ is NP-complete. If $FACT$ is in P, then this could probably be used to crack many crypto systems, notably RSA. Hence, the lack of a polytime algorithm is not from lack of trying.
2. Using the unique factorization theorem one can show that $FACT$ is in co-NP. Hence, if $FACT$ is NP-complete then NP $=$ co-NP. Hence, most theorists think $FACT$ is not NP-complete.
3. The best known algorithm for factoring n is the Number Field Sieve due to Pollard (see [37] for the history) and runs in time $O(exp(c(\log n)^{1/3}(\log\log n)^{2/3}))$ where $c = (\frac{32}{9})^{1/3} = 1.922999\ldots$. Note that the length of the input is $\log n$ so this algorithm runs in time roughly $2^{O(L^{1/3})}$ where L is the length of the input. This is still exponential but still better than $2^{O(L)}$.
4. Peter Shor [38] proved that $FACT$ is in Quantum-P. Some people think this is evidence that $FACT$ is easier than we thought, perhaps in P.

Others think that its evidence that quantum computers can do things that are not in P.

5. In the poll [33] about P versus NP, respondents were also asked to comment on other problems. Of the 21 who commented on factoring 8 thought it is in P and 13 thought it is not in P.

6. Gary Miller and others have said: *Number theorists think factoring is in* P, *whereas cryptographers hope factoring is not in* P.

Example 5.58 The Discrete Log Problem Let p be a prime. Let g be such that, calculating mod p,

$$\{g^0, g^1, g^2, \ldots, g^{p-2}\} = \{1, 2, 3, \ldots, p-1\}$$

(This is a set inequality. We are not saying that $g^0 = 1$, $g^1 = 2$, etc.)

Given a number $x \in \{1, \ldots, p-1\}$ we want to know the unique z such that $g^z \equiv x \pmod{p}$. Note that p, g, x are given in binary so their lengths are bounded by $\log_2 p$. Hence, we want to find z in time poly in $\log_2 p$.

Consider the set

$$DL = \{(p, g, x, y) \mid (\exists z \leq y)[g^z \equiv x \pmod{p}]\}.$$

1. DL is in NP. (There is one non-obvious part of this: verifying that g is a generator.) There is no known polynomial time algorithm for DL. There is no proof that DL is NP-complete. If DL is in P, then this could probably be used to crack many crypto systems, notably Diffie–Helman. Hence, the lack of a polytime algorithm is not from lack of trying.

2. DL is in co-NP. Hence, if DL is NP-complete then NP = co-NP which is unlikely. Hence, most theorists think DL is not NP-complete.

3. There are several algorithms for finding the discrete log that take time $O(\sqrt{p})$. See the Wikipedia Entry on Discrete Log for a good overview.

4. Peter Shor [38] proved that DL is in Quantum-P.

5. I have not heard much talk about this problem. In particular, nobody commented on it for the poll.

Note 5.59 (This note is purely speculative. I am invoking the definition of an intellectual: *One who is an expert in one area and pontificates in another.*) Since factoring and discrete log are important for national security I used to say things like *factoring is not known to be in Polynomial time, or maybe that's just what the NSA wants us to think!*. However, one thing I glean from reading about the Snowden leaks is that the NSA seems more interested in bugging your computer *before* you encrypt a message, and convincing you to use keys that aren't long enough to be secure, than it is in hard number theory.

The sociology of research in crypto has changed enormously in the last 50 years. At one time only the NSA worked on it, so they could be way ahead of academia and the private sector. Now many academics, private labs, and businesses work on it. Hence, the NSA cannot be too far ahead. They can read the papers that academics write so they can keep pace. But they cannot talk to people outside of NSA (and perhaps not even to people inside NSA) about what they do, which may be a hindrance.

Hence, I no longer say anything hinting that the NSA may have solved these problems. Nor do I think they have a quantum computer in their basement.

Note again that this is all speculative.

Example 5.60 Graph Isomorphism

$$GI = \{(G_1, G_2) \mid G_1 \text{ and } G_2 \text{ are isomorphic }\}.$$

1. GI is clearly in NP. There is no known polynomial time algorithm for it. There is no proof that it is NP-complete.
2. Even though it has no immediate application there has been much work on it. The following special cases are known to be in P: (1) if there is a bound on the degree, (2) if there is a bound on the genus, (3) if there is a bound on the multiplicity of the eigenvalues for the matrix that represents the graph. There have been connections to group theory as well.
3. The best known algorithm is due to Luks [39] and runs in time $2^{O(\sqrt{n}\log n)}$.
4. If GI is NP-complete, then $\Sigma_3^P = \Pi_3^P$ (see Section 10 for the definition). Hence, most theorists think GI is not NP-complete.
5. In the poll [33] about P versus NP, respondents were also asked to comment on other problems. Of the 21 who commented on Graph Isomorphism (they were not the same 21 who commented on factoring) 14 thought it was in P and 8 thought it was not in P.
6. I give my opinion: Someone will prove P $\neq$ NP between 200 and 400 years from now; however, we will still not know if GI is in P. I pick this opinion not because it's the most likely but because its the most bizarre.

Example 5.61 Group isomorphism You are given representations of elements $g_1, \ldots, g_n$ and $h_1, \ldots, h_n$ you are also given two $n \times n$ tables, one that tells you, for all i, j what $g_i * g_j$ is and one that tells you, for all i, j, what $h_i * h_j$ is. First check if both tables are for groups (there is an identity element, every element has an inverse, and $*$ is associative). This can be done in polynomial time. The real question is then: Are the two groups isomorphic? We call this problem *GPI*.

1. *GPI* is clearly in NP. There is no known polynomial time algorithm for it. There is no proof that it is NP-complete.
2. A long time ago Lipton, Tarjan, and Zalcstein observed that this problem is in time $n^{\log_2 n + O(1)}$ (they never published it but see [40]). Hence, if *GPI* is NP-complete then everything in NP would be in time $n^{O(\log n)}$. This seems unlikely though not as devastating as $P = NP$. Rosenbaum [41] in 2013 obtained a better algorithm for *GPI* that runs in time $n^{0.5 \log_2 n + O(1)}$. This was rather difficult. Lipton is quite impressed with it (see the citation above).

Example 5.62 Grid Coloring Imagine coloring every point in the 5×5 grid (formally all points (i, j) where $1 \leq i, j \leq 5$). A *monochromatic rectangle* (henceforth mono-rect) are four points that form a rectangle (e.g., $(2, 2)$, $(2, 5)$, $(4, 2)$, $(4, 5)$) that are all the same color. The following is known [42]: For all c, there exists n such that for all c-colorings of the $n \times n$ grid there exists a mono-rect. How big does n have to be? We call a grid c-colorable if you can color it with c colors and not get any mono-rects.

Consider the following set

$$GRID = \{(n, c) \mid \text{The } n \times n \text{ grid is } c\text{-colorable }\}.$$

This set seems to be in NP. But it is not. The input (n, c) is of size $\log n + \log c$ since they are written in binary. The witness is a c-coloring of $n \times n$ which is of size roughly cn^2. This witness is of size exponential in the input size.

We get around this problem by writing n, c in unary.

$$GRIDUNARY = \{(1^n, 1^c) \mid \text{The } n \times n \text{ grid is } c\text{-colorable }\}.$$

This problem is in NP. Is it NP-complete? This is unlikely since the set is sparse (see definition below).

Definition 5.63 A set $S \subseteq \Sigma^*$ is *sparse* if there exists a polynomial p such that $(\forall n)[|S \cap \Sigma^n| \leq p(n)]$. Note that this is a good notion of a skinny set since $S \cap \Sigma^n$ could be as large as 2^n.

Mahaney in 1982 [43] proved that if a sparse set was NP-complete then $P = NP$. Hence, it is unlikely that *GRIDUNARY* is NP-complete. Even so, *GRIDUNARY* is believed to be hard.

Consider the following nonsparse variant of the problem: *GRIDEXT* is the set of all $(1^n, 1^c, \rho)$ such that

- ρ is a partial c-coloring of the $n \times n$ grid.
- ρ can be extended to a c-coloring of the entire grid.

GRIDEXT was shown to be NP-complete by Apon, Gasarch, and Lawler [44].

GRIDUNARY and *GRIDEXT* are examples of problems in Ramsey theory. Most of them have this same property: they seem to be hard, the natural version is sparse (hence unlikely to be NP-complete), but the version where you have a partial coloring is NP-complete.

9.3 Have We Made Any Progress on P Versus NP?

No.

9.4 Seriously, Can you give a more enlightening answer to *Have We Made Any Progress on* P *Versus* NP?

1. There have been strong (sometimes matching) lower bounds on very weak models of computation. Yao [45] showed (and later Hastad [46,47] simplified and explained) that PARITY of n bits cannot be computed with an AND–OR–NOT circuit that has a polynomial number of gates and constant depth. Smolensky [48] extended this (with an entirely different proof) to include Mod m gates where m is a power of an odd prime [48].

2. Let ACC be the class of functions that can be computed with a polynomial number of gates and constant depth where we allow AND, OR, NOT and MOD m gates (they return 0 if the sum of the inputs is $\equiv 0 \pmod{m}$ and 1 otherwise). In 2014, Williams [49] showed that ACC does not contain NTIME($2^{n^{O(1)}}$). This was an impressive achievement. This makes one pause to think how much we have to do to get P $\neq$ NP.

3. There have been some weak lower bounds on space-bounded models of computation. Ryan Williams [50,51], proved that (essentially) if your machine has very little space to work with then *SAT* requires $n^{1.8019377...}$ where the exponent approaches $2\cos(2\pi/7)$ as the space goes down. Buss and Williams [52] later proved that the techniques used could not yield a better lower bound.

4. There are proofs that certain techniques will not suffice. These include techniques from computability theory [53], current methods with circuits [54], and a hybrid of the two [55].

5. Ketan Mulmuley has devised a research program called *Geometric Complexity Theory* which, to it credit, recognizes the obstacles to proving P $\neq$ NP and *seems* to have the *potential* to get around them. Ketan himself says the program will take a long time- not within his lifetime. For an overview, see [56] and other papers on his website.

9.5 So You Think You've Settled P versus NP

The following is Lance Fortnow's blog post from January 14, 2009, see blog.computationalcomplexity.org/2009/01/so-you-think-you-settled-p-vs-np.html

which is titled

So You Think You've Settled P versus NP

1. You are wrong. Figure it out. Sometimes you can still salvage something interesting out of your flawed proof.

2. You believe your proof is correct. Your belief is incorrect. Go back to step 1.

3. Are you making any assumptions or shortcuts, even seemingly small and obvious ones? Are you using words like "clearly," "obviously," "easy to see," "should," "must," or "probably"? You are claiming to settle perhaps the more important question in all of mathematics. You don't get to make assumptions. Go back to step 1.

4. Do you really understand the P versus NP problem? To show $P \neq NP$, you need to find a language L in NP such that for every k and every machine M running in time n^k (n = input length), M fails to properly compute L. L is a set of strings. Nothing else. L cannot depend on M or k. M can be *any* program that processes strings of bits. M may act differently than one would expect from the way you defined L. Go back to step 1.

5. You submit your paper to an on-line archive. Maybe some people tell you what is missing or wrong in your paper. This should cause you to step 1. But instead you make a few meaningless changes to your paper and repost.

6. Eventually people ignore your paper. You wonder why you aren't getting fame and fortune.

7. You submit your paper to a journal.

8. The paper is rejected. If you are smart you would go back to step 1. But if you were smart you would never have gotten to step 7.

9. You complain to the editor that either the editor doesn't understand the proof of that it is easily fixed. You are shocked a respectable editor would treat your paper this way.

10. You are convinced "the establishment" is purposely suppressing your paper because our field would get far less interesting if we settle P versus NP so we have to keep it open at all costs.

11. If I tell you otherwise would you believe me?

9.6 Eight Signs a Claimed P $\neq$ NP Proof is Wrong

In 2010, Vinay Deolalikar claimed to have a proof that P $\neq$ NP. After much discussion, some of it in blogs, the proof is now thought to be incorrect and not even close to a real proof. This inspired Scott Aaronson to post a blog on

Eight Signs a Claimed P $\neq$ NP Proof is Wrong

which can be found here: www.scottaaronson.com/blog/?p=458

Below are the eight signs, followed by some comments from me on the signs. Note that they are written in Scott's voice. So if it reads *every attempt I've ever seen* ... it means every attempt Scott has ever seen.

1. The author can't immediately explain why the proof fails for 2SAT, XOR-SAT, or other slight variants of NP-complete problems that are known to be in P. Historically, this has probably been the single most important "sanity check" for claimed proofs that P $\neq$ NP: in fact, I'm pretty sure that every attempt I've ever seen has been refuted by it.

2. The proof doesn't "know bout" all known techniques for polynomial time algorithms, including dynamic programming, linear and semidefinite programming, and holographic algorithms. This is related to sign 1, but is much more stringent. Mulmuley's GCT (Geometric Complexity Theory) program is the only approach to P versus NP I've seen that even has serious aspirations to "know about" lots of nontrivial techniques for solving problems in P (at the least, matching and linear programming). For me, that's probably the single strongest argument in GCT's favor.

3. The paper doesn't prove any weaker results along the way: for example P $\neq$ PSPACE, NEXP $\not\subseteq$ P/*poly*, NP $\not\subseteq$ TC^0, permanent not equivalent to determinant by linear projection, SAT requires superlinear time. ... P versus NP is a staggeringly hard problem, which one should think of as being *dozens of steps beyond anything that we know how to prove today. So then the question arises: forget steps 30 and 40, what about steps 1,2, and 3?*

4. *Related to the previous sign, the proof doesn't encompass the known lower bound results as special cases. For example: where, inside the proof, are the known lower bounds against constant-depth circuits? where's Razborov's lower bound against monotone circuits? Where's Raz's lower bound against multilinear formulas? All these things (at least the uniform version of them) are implied by P $\neq$ NP,*

so any proof of P $\neq$ NP *should imply them as well. Can we see more-or-less explicitly why it does so?*

5. *The paper lacks the traditional lemma–theorem–proof structure. This sign was pointed out (in the context of Deolalikar's paper) by Impagliazzo. Say what you like about the lemma–theorem–proof structures, there are excellent reasons why it's used—amount them that, exactly like modular programming, it enormously speeds up the process of finding buts.*

6. *The paper lacks a coherent overview, clearly explaining how and why it overcomes the barriers that foiled previous attempts. Unlike most* P $\neq$ NP *papers, Deolalikar's does have an informal overview (and he recently released a separate synopsis.* But reading the overview felt like reading Joseph Conrad's *Heart of Darkness*: I've reread the same paragraph over and over because the words would evaporate before they could stick to my brain. Of course, maybe that just means I was too dense to understand the argument, but the fact that I couldn't form a mental image of how the proof was supposed to work wasn't a promising sign.

7. The proof hinges on subtle issues in descriptive complexity. Before you reach for your axes: descriptive complexity is a beautiful part of TCS, full of juicy results and open problems, and I hope that someday it might even prove useful for attacking the great separation questions. Experience has shown, however, that descriptive complexity is also a powerful tool for fooling yourself into thinking you've proven things you haven't. The reason for this seems to be that subtle differences in encoding schemes—for example whether you do or don't have an order relation—can correspond to *huge* differences complexity. As soon as I saw how heavily Deolalikar's proof relied on descriptive complexity, I guessed that he probably made a mistake i applying the results from that field that characterize complexity classes like P in terms of first-order logic. I'm almost embarrassed to relate this guess, given how little actual understanding went into it. Intellectual honesty does, however, compel me to point out that it was correct.

8. Already in the first draft the author waxes philosophically about meaning of his accomplishments, profusely thanks those who made it possible, etc. He says things like "confirmations have already started coming ink." To me, this sort of overconfidence suggests a would-be P $\neq$ NP prover who hasn't grasped the sheer number of mangled skeletons and severed heads that line his path.

I agree with all of Scott's signs. Sign 1 I have used to debunk a paper that claimed to show that P $\neq$ NP. The paper claimed to show that the *HAM* is not in P; however, the techniques would also show that *EULER* is not in P. Since *EULER* actually IS in P, the proof could not be correct. Not that I thought it had any chance of being correct anyway. Lance Fortnow has an easier sign: any proof that claims to resolve P versus NP is just wrong.

Scott uses the male pronoun *He*. This could be because there is no genderless pronoun in English; however, I also note that I have never known a female to claim to have a proof of P $\neq$ NP. Perhaps they know better.

9.7 How to Deal with Proofs that P = NP

Alleged proofs that P $=$ NP are usually code or an algorithm that the author claims works *most of the time*. If its a program for SAT, then the following class of formulas will likely take it a long time and thus disprove the authors claim.

First some preparation. The following seems obvious and indeed is obvious: If you try to put $n + 1$ items into n boxes, then one of the boxes will have 2 items. It is often referred to as the *Pigeon Hole Principle for n*, or PHP_n.

We write the negation of PHP_n as a Boolean formula. The items are $\{1, 2, \ldots, n + 1\}$. The boxes are $\{1, 2, \ldots, n\}$. The Boolean variable x_{ij} is TRUE if we put it item i into box j. Consider the formula that is the AND of the following:

1. For each $1 \leq i \leq n + 1$ $x_{i1} \vee x_{i2} \vee \cdots \vee x_{in}$. This says that each item is in some box.
2. For each $1 \leq i_1 < i_2 \leq n + 1$ and $1 \leq j \leq n$ $\neg(x_{i_1 j} \wedge x_{i_2 j})$. This says that no box has two items.

The Boolean formula $\neg PNP_n$ is not satisfiable. How would one show that? One way is to list out the truth table. This is of course quite long. It is know that in some logical systems this is the best you can do. While these systems are weak, it is likely that the P $=$ NP guy is essentially using one of those systems. So challenge him to run his system on say PHP_{20}. That will shut him up and get him out of your hair.

9.8 A Third Category

I have also gotten papers that claim to resolve P versus NP but from what they write you cannot tell in what direction. Some hint that its the wrong problem or that its model dependent or that its independent of Set Theory; however, even ascribing those aspirations is being generous in that such papers are usually incoherent.

10. PH: THE POLYNOMIAL HIERARCHY

We want to generalize the definition of NP. We first need a better notation.

Definition 5.64 If x is understood, then $(\exists^p y)[B(x, y)]$ means that there exists a polynomial p such that $(\exists y$ AND $B(x, y)$ AND $|y| = p(|x|)$.

With this notation we define NP again.

Definition 5.65 $A \in$ NP if there exists a set $B \in P$ such that

$$A = \{x \mid (\exists^p y)[(x, y) \in B]\}.$$

Why stop with one quantifier?

Definition 5.66

1. $A \in \Sigma_1^p$ if there exists a set $B \in P$ such that

$$A = \{x \mid (\exists^p y)[(x, y) \in B]\}.$$

   This is just NP.
2. $A \in \Pi_1^p$ if $\overline{A} \in \Sigma_1^p$. This is just co-NP.
3. $A \in \Sigma_2^p$ if there exists a set $B \in P$ such that

$$A = \{x \mid (\exists^p y)(\forall^p z)[(x, y, z) \in B]\}.$$

4. $A \in \Pi_2^p$ if $\overline{A} \in \Sigma_2^p$.
5. $A \in \Sigma_3^p$ if there exists a set $B \in P$ such that

$$A = \{x \mid (\exists^p y)(\forall^p z)(\forall^p w)[(x, y, z, w) \in B]\}.$$

6. $A \in \Pi_3^p$ if $\overline{A} \in \Sigma_3^p$.
7. One can define $\Sigma_4^p, \Pi_4^p, \Sigma_5^p, \Pi_5^p, \ldots$.
8. These sets form what is called *the Polynomial Hierarchy*. We define $PH = \bigcup_{i=1}^{\infty} \Sigma_i^p = \bigcup_{i=1}^{\infty} \Pi_i^p$.

   Clearly

$$\Sigma_1^p \subseteq \Sigma_2^p \subseteq \Sigma_3^p \cdots$$

and

$$\Pi_1^p \subseteq \Pi_2^p \subseteq \Pi_3^p \cdots.$$

and

$$(\forall i)[\Pi_i^p \subseteq \Sigma_{i+1}^p \text{ and } \Sigma_i^p \subseteq \Pi_{i+1}^p].$$

These containments are not known to be proper. If there is an i such that $\Sigma_i^p = \Pi_i^p$, then $(\forall j \geq i)[\Sigma_j^p = \Sigma_i^p]$. In this case, we say PH *collapses*. Most theorists think that PH does not collapse.

Clearly NP $\subseteq$ PH and R $\subseteq$ PH. What about BPP? Since most theorists think P $=$ R $=$ BPP, most theorists think BPP $\subseteq$ PH. But is it not even clear that BPP $\subseteq$ PH. However, Sipser [57] obtained BPP $\subseteq \Sigma_2^p \cap \Pi_2^p$ by developing a new theory of time-bounded Kolmogorov complexity, and shortly thereafter, Lautemann [58] proved the same containment with a very clever trick. One might think *Oh, so a problem can be open for a long time and then all of a sudden it's solved. Maybe P versus NP will go that way.* However, I am skeptical of this notion. For clever algorithms and clever collapses of classes that has happened, but never for a separation of classes.

The following are examples of natural problems that are in these various levels of PH.

Example 5.67 This will just be a rewriting of the *SAT* problem. *QBF* stands for *Quantified Boolean Formula.* $\phi(\vec{x})$ will be a Boolean Formula.

$$QBF_1 = \{\phi(\vec{x}) \mid (\exists \vec{b})[\phi(\vec{b}) = TRUE]\}.$$

QBF_1 is Σ_1^p-complete and hence unlikely to be in Π_1^p. This is just a fancy way of saying that *SAT* is NP-complete and hence unlikely to be in co-NP.

Example 5.68 $\phi(\vec{x}, \vec{y})$ means there are two sets of variables that are distinguished.

$$QBF_2 = \{\phi(\vec{x}, \vec{y}) \mid (\exists \vec{b})(\forall \vec{c})[\phi(\vec{b}, \vec{c}) = TRUE]\}.$$

QBF_2 is Σ_2^p-complete and hence unlikely to be in Π_2^p.

Example 5.69 One can define QBF_i. QBF_i is Σ_i^p-complete and hence unlikely to be in Π_i^p.

Example 5.70 Boolean Formula Minimization. Given a Boolean Formula ϕ, is there a shorter equivalent Boolean Formula? Let

$$MIN = \{\phi(\vec{x}) \mid (\forall \psi(\vec{x}), |\psi(x)| < |\phi(x)|)(\exists \vec{b})[\phi(\vec{b}) \neq \psi(\vec{b})]\}.$$

Clearly $MIN \in \Pi_2^p$. It is believed to not be Π_2^p-complete but to also not be in Σ_1^p or Π_1^p. See the paper of Buchfuhrer and Umas [59] for more information.

11. #P

Leslie Valiant defined #P and proved most of the results in this section [60,61].

Definition 5.71 A function f is in #P if there is a nondeterministic program M that runs in polynomial time such that $f(x)$ is the number of accepting paths in the $M(x)$ computation. A set A is in $P^{\#P}$ if membership of $x \in A$ can be determined by a program in poly time that can ask questions to a #P function.

When #P was first defined it was not clear if it was powerful. Clearly $NP \subseteq P^{\#P}$ but it was not clear if $\Sigma_2^p \subseteq P^{\#P}$. However, Toda [62] proved the somewhat surprising result that $PH \subseteq P^{\#P}$. It is not know if this containments is proper. If $PH = P^{\#P}$ then PH collapses, hence most theorists think $PH \subset P^{\#P}$.

We give examples of natural problems in #P.

Example 5.72 Let $f(\phi)$ be the number of satisfying assignments of ϕ. This problem is clearly in #P. Of more importance is that its #P-complete and hence unlikely to be computable in PH.

Example 5.73 For most NP-complete problems, the function that returns the number of solutions (e.g., the number of Hamiltonian cycles) is #P-complete.

Example 5.74 There are some problems in Polynomial time where finding the number of solutions is #P-complete. In particular, (1) finding the number of matchings in a graph and (2) finding the number of Eulerian cycles in a directed graph are #P-complete. Strangely enough, finding the number of Eulerian cycles in an undirected graph can be done in polynomial time.

Example 5.75 The *Permanent* of a matrix is just like the determinant but without the negative signs. Valiant's motivation was as follows: computing the determinant is easy (polynomial time), but computing the permanent seemed hard. Valiant showed that computing the permanent is #P-complete and hence likely quite hard.

12. PSPACE

Definition 5.76 PSPACE is the set of problems that can be solved using space bounded by a polynomial in the length of the input. Formally PSPACE $=$ DSPACE($n^{O(1)}$). By Theorem 19.1 PSPACE $=$ NSPACE($n^{O(1)}$.

Clearly $P^{\#P} \subseteq$ PSPACE. It is not known if this inclusion is proper; however, If $P^{\#P} =$ PSPACE then PH collapses. Hence, most theorists think $P^{\#P} \neq$ PSPACE.

The following problems are PSPACE-complete. Hence, the are in PSPACE and unlikely to be in $P^{\#P}$.

Example 5.77 Given two regular expressions, are they equivalent? Formally

$$REGEXPEQUIV = \{(\alpha, \beta) \mid L(\alpha) = L(\beta)\}.$$

(α and β are regular expressions.)

Example 5.78 HEX is a simple two-player game. Given a position, determining if the player whose move it is wins. Note that we allow any sized board.

Example 5.79 GO is a popular game in Japan and China. There are several versions. Given a position (on an $n \times n$ board) determine if the player whose move it is wins the ko-free version. (The version with ko-rules is EXPTIME complete.)

13. EXPTIME

Definition 5.80 EXPTIME $=$ DTIME($2^{n^{O(1)}}$).

The following problems are in EXPTIME-complete and hence not in P.

Example 5.81 Generalized Chess. Given an $n \times n$ chess board with pieces on it, does the player whose move it is win?

Example 5.82 Generalized Checkers. Given an $n \times n$ checker board with pieces on it, does the player whose move it is win?

Example 5.83 Generalized Go (with Japanese Ko rules). Given an $n \times n$ Go board with pieces on it, does the player whose move it is win, playing Japanese Ko rules?

14. EXPSPACE = NEXPSPACE

Definition 5.84 EXPSPACE $=$ DSPACE($2^{n^{O(1)}}$). By Theorem 19.1 EXPSPACE $=$ NSPACE($2^{n^{O(1)}}$).

Clearly EXPTIME $\subseteq$ EXPSPACE. It is not known if this inclusion is proper; however, most theorists think EXPTIME $\neq$ EXPSPACE. By Theorem 21 PSPACE $\subset$ EXPSPACE.

We present a natural problem that is NEXPSPACE-complete and hence not in PSPACE. The statement is due to Meyer and Stockmeyer [63].

In textbooks, one often sees expressions like $a^5 b^2$. These are not formally regular expressions; however, there meaning is clear and they can be rewritten as such: *aaaaabb*. The difference in representation matters. If we allow exponents, then Regular Expressions can be represented far more compactly. Note that a^n is written in $O(\log n)$ space, where as $aaa \cdots a$ (n times) takes $O(n)$ space.

Definition 5.85 Let Σ be a finite alphabet. A *Textbook Regular Expression* (henceforth t-Reg Exp) is defined as follows.
- For all $\sigma \in \Sigma$, σ is a t–reg exp.
- $\emptyset$ is a t–reg exp
- If α and β are t–reg exps, then so is $\alpha \cup \beta$, $\alpha\beta$ and α^*
- If α is a t–reg exp, and $n \in \mathbb{N}$ then α^n is a t–reg exp.

If α is a t–reg exp, then $L(\alpha)$ is the set of strings that α generates.

Here is the question which we call *t-reg expression equivalence*

$$TRE = \{(\alpha, \beta) \mid \alpha, \beta \text{ are t-reg expressions and } L(\alpha) = L(\beta)\}.$$

Note 5.86 In the original paper, this is called *Regular expression with squaring*. They originally had a formulation like mine but since people thought maybe they were coding things into bits (they weren't) they changed the name. Frankly I think the formulation of t-reg exp is more natural.

Meyer and Stockmeyer showed that *TRE* is NEXPSPACE-complete and hence not in PSPACE. Note that it is also not in P. Is it natural? See the Section 25 for a literal discussion of that issue.

15. DTIME($TOW_i(n)$)

Definition 5.87
1. $TOW_0(n) = n$
2. For $i \geq 1$, let $TOW_i(n) = 2^{TOW_{i-1}(n)}$.

By Theorem 20 we have that, for all i, DTIME($TOW_i(n^{O(1)})$) $\subset$ DTIME($TOW_{i+1}(n^{O(1)})$). For each i, we give an example that is arguably natural.

We give a natural problem that is in DTIME($TOW_3(n)$) and requires at least $2^{2^{cn}}$ time for some constant c. Its exact complexity is known but is somewhat technical.

The problem will be given a set of sentences in a certain restricted mathematical language, determine if it's true. We need to define the language.

We will only use the following symbols.
1. The logical symbols $\wedge$, $\neg$, $(\exists)$.
2. Variables $x, y, z, \ldots$ that range over $\mathbb{N}$.
3. Symbols: $=$, $<$, $+$
4. Constants: 0,1,2,3,.....
We call this *Presburger Arithmetic* in honor of the man who proved it was decidable.

Definition 5.88 A *term* is:
1. If t is a variable or a constant, then t is a term.
2. If t_1 and t_2 are terms, then $t_1 + t_2$ is a term.

Definition 5.89 An *Atomic Formulas* is:
1. If t_1, t_2 are terms, then $t_1 = t_2$ is an Atomic Formula.
2. If t_1, t_2 are terms, then $t_1 < t_2$ is an Atomic Formula.

Definition 5.90 A *Presburger Formula* is defined similar to how a WS1S formula was defined, given that we have defined Atomic formulas.

Is $x < y + z$ true? This is a stupid question since we don't know what x, y, z are. But if we quantify over all of the variables then a truth value exists. For example,

$$(\exists x)(\exists y)(\exists z)[x < y + z] \text{ is true}$$

$$(\exists x)(\exists y)(\forall z)[x < y + z] \text{ is true}$$

$(\exists x)(\forall y)(\exists z)[x < y + z]$ is true

$(\exists x)(\forall y)(\forall z)[x < y + z]$ is false

$(\forall x)(\exists y)(\exists z)[x < y + z]$ is true

$(\forall x)(\exists y)(\forall z)[x < y + z]$ is true

$(\forall x)(\forall y)(\exists z)[x < y + z]$ is true

$(\forall x)(\forall y)(\forall z)[x < y + z]$ is false

A *sentence* is a formula where all of the variables are quantified over. We can now (finally!) define our problem: Given a sentence ϕ in Presburger arithmetic is it true?

- Presburger proved that this problem is decidable. His proof did not yield time bounds.
- Later a proof was found that involved quantifier elimination. Given a sentence we can find an equivalent one with one less quantifier. This algorithm puts this problem in DTIME($TOW_3(n)$).
- Fisher and Rabin showed that there exists a constant c such that this problem requires time at least $2^{2^{cn}}$.

16. DSPACE($TOW_i(n^{O(1)})$)

By Theorem 21 we have that, for all i, DSPACE($TOW_i(n^{O(1)})$) $\subset$ DSPACE($TOW_{i+1}(n^{O(1)})$). For each i, we give an example that is arguably natural. It is a variant of the problem *TRE* from Section 14.

Definition 5.91 Let Σ be a finite alphabet. Let $i \in \mathbb{N}$. An *i-Textbook Regular Expression* (henceforth i-t-Reg Exp) is defined as follows.

- For all $\sigma \in \Sigma$, σ is an i-t-reg exp.
- $\emptyset$ is a i-t-reg exp
- If α and β are i-t-reg exps, then so is $\alpha \cup \beta$, $\alpha\beta$ and α^*
- If α is an i-t-reg exp and $n, k \in \mathbb{N}$, then $\alpha^{TOW_i(n^k)}$ is an i-t-reg exp.

Here is the question which we call *i-t-reg expression equivalence*

$$TRE = \{(\alpha, \beta) \mid \alpha, \beta \text{ are i-t-reg expressions and } L(\alpha) = L(\beta)\}.$$

This problem can be proven to be in DSPACE($TOW_i(n^{O(1)})$) $-$ DSPACE($TOW_{i-1}(n^{O(1)})$) similar to the proof of Meyer and Stockmeyer that *TRE* is not in PSPACE. I believe this is the first time this fact was noted.

17. ELEMENTARY

Definition 5.92 The complexity class EL (for Elementary) is defined by

$$EL = \bigcup_{i=0}^{\infty} DTIME(TOW_i(n)).$$

It is known that, for all i, $DSPACE(TOW_i(n)) \subseteq EL$.

Virtually everything one would ever want to compute is Elementary. In the next section, we give an example of a problem which is computable (in fact, primitive recursive) but not elementary.

18. PRIMITIVE RECURSIVE

We will define the primitive recursive functions in stages.

Definition 5.93 Let PR_0 be the following functions:
1. Let $n, c \in \mathbb{N}$. Then the function $f(x_1, \ldots, x_n) = c$ is in PR_0.
2. Let $n \in \mathbb{N}$ and $1 \le i \le n$. Then the function $f(x_1, \ldots, x_n) = x_i$ is in PR_0.
3. Let $n \in \mathbb{N}$ and $1 \le i \le n$. Then the function $f(x_1, \ldots, x_n) = x_i + 1$ is in PR_0.

Definition 5.94 For $i \ge 1$, the following functions are in PR_i.
1. All $h \in PR_{i-1}$.
2. Let $k, n \in \mathbb{N}$. Let $f \in PR_{i-1}$ where $f : \mathbb{N}^n \to \mathbb{N}$. Let $g_1, \ldots, g_n \in PR_{i-1}$ where $g_i : \mathbb{N}^k \to \mathbb{N}$. Then $h(x_1, \ldots, x_k) = f(g_1(x_1, \ldots, x_k), \ldots, g_n(x_1, \ldots, x_k))$ is in PR_i. (This is just composition.)
3. Let $n \in \mathbb{N}$. Let $f, g \in PR_{i-1}$ where $f : \mathbb{N}^n \to \mathbb{N}$ and $g : \mathbb{N}^{n+2} \to \mathbb{N}$. Let $h : \mathbb{N}^{n+1} \to \mathbb{N}$ be defined by
   a. $h(x_1, \ldots, x_n, 0) = f(x_1, \ldots, x_n)$
   b. $h(x_1, \ldots, x_n, x + 1) = g(x_1, \ldots, x_n), x, h(x_1, x_2, \ldots, x_n, x)$
   (This is just recursion.)

Definition 5.95 A function is *Primitive Recursive* if it is in $\bigcup_{i=0}^{\infty} PR_i$. We denote the set of sets in $DTIME(f)$ where f is primitive recursive by PRIMREC.

One can show that addition is in PR_1, multiplication is in PR_2, Exponentiation is in PR_3, $TOW_n(2)$ is in PR_4. More to the point, virtually any function encountered in normal mathematics is primitive recursive.

Clearly EL $\subseteq$ PRIMREC. In fact EL $\subset$ PRIMREC. We give a example of a natural problem that is in PRIMREC but not EL.

Example 5.96 The problem will be given a sentences in a certain restricted mathematical language, determine if it's true. We need to define the language.

Recall that in Section 4 we defined WS1S formulas.

A *sentence* is a formula where all of the variables are quantified over. As noted in the discussion of Presburger arithmetic, formulas do not have a truth value but sentences do. We can now define our problem: Given a sentence ϕ in WS1S is it true?

- Buchi [64] showed that this problem is decidable using finite automata. This involves using the fact that formulas give rise to regular sets (see Section 4). Using this method, every time there is an alternation of quantifiers you need to do an NDFA to DFA transformation. Hence, this procedure takes roughly $TOW_n(2)$ steps where n is the number of alternations of quantifiers. Therefore the algorithm is primitive recursive; however, since the subscript depends on the input, the function $TOW_n(2)$ is not in EL.
- Meyer [65] showed that the algorithm sketched above is optimal. Hence, the problem is not in EL.
- One can define $S1S$ which allows quantification of infinite sets. Buchi [66] showed that this theory is decidable. The proof uses ω-automata which run on infinite strings. In the algorithm for deciding $WS1S$, DFA's are manipulated and tested but never actually ran. So the fact that an ω-automata takes an infinite string as input is not a problem. The proof that $S1S$ is decidable is rather difficult.
- $WS1S$ and $S1S$ both involve having one successor function. What does it mean to have two successors? Our basic objects are numbers. We could view numbers as strings in unary. In that case $S(x) = x1$. If our basic objects were strings in $\{0, 1\}^*$, then we could have two successors $S_0(x) = x0$ and $S_1(x) = x1$. This yields two theories: $WS2S$ and $S2S$. Rabin [67] proved that both are decidable. The proofs for $S2S$ used transfinite induction and is likely the hardest proof of a theory being decidable. Easier proofs were later found by Gurevich and Harrington [68,69]. Their complexities are primitive recursive but not in EL.

- How expressive is $WS1S$ (and $S1S$, $WS2S$, $S2S$)? Is having them decidable useful? There are two answers to this.
  - $WS1S$ and $WS2S$ have been coded up and used [70]. Even though these theories are not in EL the coding is very clever and the problems they input to it are not that large. The proof that these theories are difficult produce instances that are hard. These instances are somewhat contrived and do not come up. The application has been to search patters, temporal properties or reactive systems, parse tree constraints. It has not been applied to solving open mathematical conjecture. This us unlikely to happen as $WS1S$ seems unable to express anything of interest mathematically.
  - The decidability of $S1S$ and $S2S$ has been use to prove other theories decidable. We do not know of an implementation of either. It is possible to state interesting theorems in $S2S$ (See [67]). Great! So perhaps we can input to an $S2S$ decider an open question in Mathematics and get the answer! There are two problems with this (1) Coding up $S2S$ would be extremely difficult, and getting it to run quickly might be impossible. (2) *Be careful what you wish for— you might just get it:* Lets say we really did have such a decider and its fast. Lets say we input statements of The Goldbach Conjecture, the Riemann Hypothesis, and P versus NP. Lets say it outputs YES, YES, YES. Then we would know that these are all true. Oh. We already sort of know that. It is not the purpose of math to just establish whats true, but also *why* its true. The hope is that the proof of (say) P $\neq$ NP will give great insight into computation. Just the one bit YES would not.
- The last item challenges why we care about a theory being decidable. (1) Hilbert wanted to (in today's terminology) show that mathematics is decidable to give it a rigorous foundation. Even though mathematics is undecidable it is of intellectual interest to see how big a fragment of math is decidable. (2) As the work on $WS1S$ has shown there may be fragments of those fragments that are decidable in good time and can be used elsewhere (though unlikely used for mathematics itself).

We give another example, again a logical theory. We need to define the language.

We will only use the following symbols.

1. The logical symbols $\wedge$, $\neg$, ($\exists$).
2. Variables $x, y, z, \ldots$ that range over $\mathbb{R}$.
3. Symbols: $=$, $<$, $+$

We call this *Theory of the Reals*.

Definition 5.97 A *term* is:
1. If t is a variable, then t is a term.
2. If t_1 and t_2 are terms, then $t_1 + t_2$ and $t_1 t_2$ are terms.

Definition 5.98 An *Atomic Formulas* is:
1. If t_1, t_2 are terms, then $t_1 = t_2$ is an Atomic Formula.
2. If t_1, t_2 are terms, then $t_1 < t_2$ is an Atomic Formula.

Definition 5.99 A *Formula* is:
1. Any atomic formula is a Presburger formula.
2. If ϕ_1, ϕ_2 are Presburger formulas then so are
   a. $\phi_1 \wedge \phi_2$,
   b. $\phi_1 \vee \phi_2$
   c. $\neg \phi_1$
   d. If $\phi(x_1, \ldots, x_n)$ is a formula then so is $(\exists x_i)[\phi(x_1, \ldots, x_n)]$

A *sentence* is a formula where all of the variables are quantified over. We can now (finally!) define our problem: Given a sentence ϕ in the theory of the Reals is it true?

- Tarski [71] showed that this problem is decidable. His proof gave no time bounds.
- There were several different proofs that gave time bounds. Some of the people involved are Seidenberg, Cohen, Collins, Renegar, Heintz, Roy, and Solerno. The papers of Renegar and Heintz–Roy–Solerno both obtain the best known results: time $TOW_2(n)$ where n is the number of quantifier alternations. See [72] for history and details.
- Fisher and Rabin [73] showed that the problem requires time $2^{\Omega(n)}$.

19. ACKERMANN'S FUNCTION

We define a somewhat natural computable function that is not primitive recursive.

Note that any primitive recursive function uses the recursion rule some fixed finite number of times. Ackermann's function (below) intentionally uses recursion a nonconstant number of times. While that is the intuition as to why Ackermann's function is not primitive recursive, the proof is not easy.

Definition 5.100 *Ackermann's function* is defined as follows

$$A(m, n) = \begin{cases} n + 1 & \text{if } m = 0 \\ A(m - 1, 1) & \text{if } m \geq 1 \text{ and } n = 0 \\ A(m - 1, A(m, n - 1)) & \text{if } m \geq 1 \text{ and } n \geq 1 \end{cases} \quad (5.1)$$

Ackermann's function is an example of a function that is computable but not primitive recursive. We have not been able to find a more natural example. This raises the question: How natural is Ackermann's function.

Ackermann's function was originally defined for the sole purpose of obtaining a computable function that was not primitive recursive. Hence, it can be considered unnatural. However, over time they have shown up in natural places. We give one example.

Example 5.101 Data Structures for Union Find

A *Union-Find Data Structure* is a data structure which supports a set of sets. The basic operations are (1) FIND which will, given an item x will determine if it is in the data structure, and if so which set it's in, and (2) UNION given two sets replace them with the union of the two. One could ask how many steps a FIND costs and how many steps a UNION costs. This is not the right question. One anticipates doing many FINDs and UNIONs. So here is the right question: how much time does it take to do n operations? Note that it could be that one of them takes a long time but then many take very little time.

Tarjan and Van Leeuwen [74] showed that this problem (1) can be done in time $O(n\alpha(n))$, and (2) requires time $\Omega(n\alpha(n))$, where $\alpha(n)$ is the inverse of the Ackerman function. This means the problem cannot be done in $O(n)$ time but it can be done in just barely more than that. Of interest to us is that Ackermann's function appears in the analysis of this natural problem!

Definition 5.102 Let ACK = DTIME($A(n)$).

20. THE GOODSTEIN FUNCTION

We do not define a complexity class in this section. We define a somewhat natural computable function that grows much faster than Ackermann's function.

We first define a function that doesn't grow that fast but contains many of the ideas. We do this by example. Say the input is 213. We write this as $(213)_{10}$ to indicate that the number is in base 10. Subtract 1 from the number but put it into base 11 to obtain $(212)_{11}$. Keep doing this go get $(211)_{12}$, $(210)_{13}$. Note that 210 is in base 13 so it's really $2 \times 13^2 + 1 \times 13 + 0 \times 13^0$. Hence, if you subtract 1 then in base 13 you get 20(12). We increase the base to get $(20(12))_{14}$. Keep doing this. Initially the value is going up. But eventually it will come down to 0. $f(213)$ is the number of iterations of this process you need to get down to 0. This function grows pretty fast but is till primitive recursive.

We now define the Goodstein function. First off, we will begin in base 2 (this is not important but lets us give a real example). We'll again take the input 213. First write it in base 2:

$$213 = 2^7 + 2^6 + 2^4 + 2^2 + 2^0.$$

We now write the exponents in base 2:

$$213 = 2^{2^2+2^1+2^0} + 2^{2^2+2^1} + 2^{2^2} + 2^{2^1} + 2^0.$$

We can stop here since all of the exponents are 0,1, or 2. If they were bigger we would again write them in base 2.

We again subtract 1 but then rather than increase the base we increase all of the bases. So in the next iteration we have

$$3^{3^2+3^1+3^0} + 3^{3^2+3^1} + 3^{3^2} + 3^{3^1}.$$

This process will initially increase but eventually decrease to 0. $f(213)$ is the number of iterations before 0 is reached. This function grows much faster than Ackermann's function.

Is the Goodstein function natural? Goodstein used them to investigate various phenomena in logic. Later Paris and Kirby [75] showed that the statement that the Goodstein function always exists (that is, the process always terminates) cannot be proven in Peano Arithmetic. Hence, the Goodstein function is natural *to logicians!* However, since I can explain the function easily, and show it exists easily, and it's fun, I call that natural.

Definition 5.103 Let GOOD be DTIME($G(n)$) where $G(n)$ is the function defined above.

21. DECIDABLE, UNDECIDABLE AND BEYOND

Definition 5.104 A set A is *Decidable* (henceforth DEC) if there exists a program M such that

1. If $x \in A$ then $M(x)$ outputs YES.

2. If $x \notin A$ then $M(x)$ outputs NO.

Note that there are no time or space bounds.

Clearly all the classes defined so far in this chapter are subsets of DEC. Are there any problems that are undecidable? That is, are there any problems that no computer can solve. We give two natural ones.

Example 5.105 The Halting Problem: Given a program M and an input x, does $M(x)$ terminate? We write it as a set:

$$HALT = \{(M, x) \mid (\exists s)[\text{ If you run } M(x) \text{ for } s \text{ steps then it will halt }]\}.$$

One attempt to solve $HALT$ is to run $M(x)$; however, if $M(x)$ does not halt you will never know. This failed attempt *is not* a proof that $HALT \notin$ DEC. However, it is true: $HALT \notin$ DEC. The proof is in most textbooks on Formal Language theory or computability theory. Alternatively, there is a proof in the style of Dr. Seuss [76].

$HALT$ is natural but it refers to programs. Is there a natural problem that is not in DEC that does not refer to programs? Yes!

Example 5.106 Diophantine Polynomials: Given a polynomial $p(x_1, \ldots, x_n)$ with integer coefficients, does there exist $b_1 \ldots, b_n \in \mathbb{N}$ such that $p(b_1, \ldots, b_n) = 0$. This problem turns out to be undecidable.

In 1900, David Hilbert, a very prominent mathematician, proposed 23 problems for mathematicians to work on for the next 100 year. Some of the problems were not quite well defined (e.g., *Problem 6: Make Physics Rigorous*) so it's hard to say how many have been solved; however, experts say that about 90% have been solved. See [77] for more information.

Hilbert's tenth problem was the following: given a polynomial $p(x_1, \ldots, x_n)$ with integer coefficients, determine if there exist $b_1 \ldots, b_n \in \mathbb{N}$ such that $p(b_1, \ldots, b_n) = 0$. To express this as a set,

$$H10 = \{p(x_1, \ldots, x_n) \mid (\exists b_1, \ldots, b_n s)[p(b_1, \ldots, b_n) = 0]\}.$$

Hilbert thought this problem was a solvable problem in Number Theory. He was incorrect. Two papers together, one by Davis, Putnam, and Robinson [78] and one by Matijasevic [79] showed that $H10 \notin$ DEC. They essentially showed that if this could be solved then the Halting problem could be solved.

How do these problems compare to each other? Can there be even harder problems? What does harder mean in this context? For problems of this type, we cannot talk about time or space bounds. But we can talk about how easy it is to express them. We can write the halting problems as membership in the following set:

We rewrite $HALT$. Let

$$B = \{((M, x), s) \mid \text{ If you run } M(x) \text{ for } s \text{ steps then it will halt }\}.$$

Note that B is decidable and

$$HALT = \{(M, x) \mid (\exists s)[((M, x), s) \in B]\}.$$

We can write $HALT$ as a there exists quantifier followed by something decidable. This is analogous to writing SAT as a poly-bounded quantifier followed by something in P. As such, we can define analogies of PH from Section 10. While this is true mathematically this is false historically. The hierarchy we are about to define came first.

Definition 5.107

1. $A \in \Sigma_1$ if there exists a set $B \in$ DEC such that

$$A = \{x \mid (\exists y)[(x, y) \in B]\}.$$

   This class is often called *computably enumerable* (c.e.) or *recursively enumerable (r.e.)*. Both $HALT$ and $H10$ are Σ_1-complete. Hence, they are really the same problem.
2. $A \in \Pi_1$ if $\overline{A} \in \Sigma_1$.
3. $A \in \Sigma_2$ if there exists a set $B \in$ DEC such that

$$A = \{x \mid (\exists y)(\forall^p z)[(x, y, z) \in B]\}.$$

4. $A \in \Pi_2$ if $\overline{A} \in \Sigma_2$.
5. $A \in \Sigma_3$ if there exists a set $B \in$ DEC such that

$$A = \{x \mid (\exists y)(\forall^p z)(\forall w)[(x, y, z, w) \in B]\}.$$

6. $A \in \Pi_3$ if $\overline{A} \in \Sigma_3$.
7. One can define $\Sigma_4, \Pi_4, \Sigma_5, \Pi_5, \ldots$.
8. These sets form what is called *the Arithmetic Hierarchy*. We define $AH = \bigcup_{i=1}^{\infty} \Sigma_i = \bigcup_{i=1}^{\infty} \Pi_i$.

   Clearly

$$\Sigma_1 \subseteq \Sigma_2 \subseteq \Sigma_3 \cdots$$

and

$$\Pi_1 \subseteq \Pi_2 \subseteq \Pi_3 \cdots .$$

and

$$(\forall i)[\Pi_i \subseteq \Sigma_{i+1} \text{ and } \Sigma_i \subseteq \Pi_{i+1}].$$

In contrast to PH, these containments are known to be proper.

The following are examples of problems that are in these classes. Throughout the examples *poly* means *polynomial with integer coefficients*. The quantifiers are over the natural numbers.

Example 5.108 This will just be a rewriting of the $H10$ problem. QP stands for *Quantified Poly*. $\phi(\vec{x})$ will be a poly.

$$QP_1 = \{\phi(\vec{x}) \mid (\exists \vec{b})[\phi(\vec{b}) = 0]\}.$$

QP_1 is Σ_1-complete and hence not in Π_1.

Example 5.109 $\phi(\vec{x}, \vec{y})$ means there are two sets of variables that are distinguished.

$$QP_2 = \{\phi(\vec{x}, \vec{y}) \mid (\exists \vec{b})(\forall \vec{c})[\phi(\vec{b}, \vec{c}) = 0]\}.$$

QP_2 is Σ_1-complete and hence not in Π_1.

Example 5.110 One can define QP_i. QP_i is Σ_i-complete and hence not in Π_i.

For the next few examples, let $M_1, M_2, M_3, \ldots$ be the list of all programs in some reasonable programming language. From the index i, we should be able to recover the code for the program.

Example 5.111 As noted earlier,

$$HALT = \{(M, x) \mid (\exists s)[\text{ If you run } M(x) \text{ for } s \text{ steps then it will halt }]\}$$

is Σ_1-complete and hence not in Π_1.

Example 5.112 Let TOT be the set of program that halt on every input. Formally

$$TOT = \{M \mid (\forall x)(\exists s)[\text{ If you run } M(x) \text{ for } s \text{ steps then it will halt }]\}.$$

TOT is Π_2-complete and hence not in Σ_2. Note that we have not proven this, but it is true.

Example 5.113 Let COF be the set of program that halt on all but a finite set of inputs. Formally

$$COF = \{M \mid (\exists y)(\forall x \geq y)(\exists s)[\text{ If you run } M(x) \text{ for } s \text{ steps then it will halt }]\}.$$

COF is Σ_3-complete and hence not in Π_3. Note that we have not proven this, but it is true.

Are there any natural problems that are not in AH? We give one.

Example 5.114 The problem will be given a set of sentences in a certain restricted mathematical language, determine if it's true. We need to define the language.

We will only use the following symbols.
1. The logical symbols $\wedge$, $\neg$, ($\exists$).
2. Variables $x, y, z, \ldots$ that range over $\mathbb{N}$.
3. Symbols: $+$, $\times$.
4. Constants: $\ldots, -3, -2, -1, 0, 1, 2, 3, \ldots$
We call this *Arithmetic*.

Definition 5.115 A *term* is:
1. If t is a variable or a constant, then t is a term.
2. If t_1 and t_2 are terms, then $t_1 + t_2$ is a term and $t_1 \times t_2$ is a term.

Definition 5.116 An *Atomic Formulas* is: If t_1, t_2 are terms, then $t_1 = t_2$ is an Atomic Formula.

Definition 5.117 A *Formula* is defined the exact same way as for Presburger arithmetic except that the atomic formulas are different.

A *sentence* is a formula where all of the variables are quantified over. We can now define our problem: Given a sentence ϕ in arithmetic is it true?
- This problem is not in AH.
- There are theories even harder that involved quantification over sets.

22. SUMMARY OF RELATIONS BETWEEN CLASSES

Known Inclusions

$$\text{REG} \subseteq \text{L} \subseteq \text{NL} \subseteq \text{P} \subseteq \text{R} \subseteq \text{NP}$$

$$\text{NP} = \Sigma_1^p \subseteq \Sigma_2^p \subseteq \Sigma_3^p \subseteq \cdots \subseteq \text{PH} \subseteq \text{P}^{\#\text{P}} \subseteq \text{PSPACE}$$

$$(\forall i)[\Sigma_i^p \subseteq \Pi_{i+1}^p \wedge \Pi_i^p \subseteq \Sigma_{i+1}^p]$$

$$\text{BPP} \subseteq \Sigma_2^p \cap \Pi_2^p$$

$$\text{PSPACE} \subseteq \text{DTIME}(\text{TOW}_1(n)) \subseteq \text{DTIME}(\text{TOW}_2(n)) \subseteq \cdots \subseteq \text{EL}$$

$$\text{PSPACE} \subseteq \text{DSPACE}(\text{TOW}_1(n)) \subseteq \text{DSPACE}(\text{TOW}_2(n)) \subseteq \cdots \subseteq \text{EL}$$

$$(\forall i)[\text{DTIME}(\mathit{TOW}_i(n)) \subseteq \text{DSPACE}(\mathit{TOW}_i(n)) \subseteq \text{DTIME}(\mathit{TOW}_{i+1}(n))]$$

$$EL \subseteq PRIMREC \subseteq ACK \subseteq GOOD \subseteq DEC$$

$$DEC \subseteq \Sigma_1 \subseteq \Sigma_2 \subseteq \Sigma_3 \subseteq \cdots P^{\#P} \subseteq AH$$

Known Proper Inclusions

$$REG \subset L \subset PSPACE \subset DSPACE(TOW_1(n))$$

$$\subset DSPACE(TOW_2(n)) \subset \cdots \subset EL$$

$$NPDTIME(TOW_2(n)) \subset DTIME(TOW_3(n)) \subset \cdots \subset EL$$

$$(\forall i)[DTIME(TOW_i(n)) \subset DSPACE(TOW_{i+1}(n))$$

$$\subset DTIME(TOW_{i+2}(n))]$$

$$EL \subset PRIMREC \subset ACK \subset GOOD \subset DEC$$

$$DEC \subset \Sigma_1 \subset \Sigma_2 \subset \Sigma_3 \subset \cdots P^{\#P} \subset AH$$

$$(\forall i)[\Sigma_i \neq \Pi_i]$$

What Most Theorists Think

$$L \subset NL \subset P = R = BPP \subset NP \subset \Sigma_2^p \subset \Sigma_3^p \subset \cdots \subset PSPACE$$

$$NP \subset \Pi_2^p \subset \Pi_3^p \subset \cdots \subset PSPACE$$

23. OTHER COMPLEXITY MEASURES

This chapter has focused on worst case analysis where we are interested in time or space. There are other ways to measure complexity which may be more realistic.

1. *Average case analysis*: There has been some work on formalizing average case analysis. Rather than see how an algorithm works in the worst case, one looks at how it works relative to a distribution. But what distribution is realistic? This is very hard to determine.

2. *Approximation Algorithms*: For many NP-complete problems there are approximation algorithms that are fast and give an answer that is close to the optimal (e.g., within twice). There are also lower bounds as well. Some of these algorithms are useable in the real world.

3. *Heuristic algorithms*: There are some rules-of-thumb that seem to work on particular problems. Such approaches tend to work well in the real world but are very hard to analyze.

4. *Fixed Parameter Tractable*: In Section 9, we looked at the Vertex Cover problem. For general k it is NP-complete. For fixed k it is *not* $O(n^k)$ but instead just $O(1.2738^k + kn)$. Many NP-complete problems are *Fixed Parameter Tractable* meaning that if you fix a parameter they can be solved quite fast.

5. *Streaming Algorithms*: The input is a sequence of n numbers where n is quite large. So large that you cannot store n in main memory. We model this by saying we can only pass over the sequence p times and only use $f(n)$ space where $f(n)$ is much less than n. If we want to find the most common element, can we do that with 2 passes and $O(\log n)$ space? Algorithms for these kinds of problems are randomized and approximate. They are called *Streaming Algorithms*

24. SUMMARY

In this chapter, we defined many complexity classes. The classes spanned a rather large swath of complexities from $O(1)$ space to various shades of undecidability. For each class, we gave examples of natural problems that are in them but likely (or surely) not in lower classes. Hence, we have been able to determine how hard many natural problems are.

This classification is a good first cut at getting to the real issue of how hard these problems are. But they are not the entire story since once a problem is discovered to be hard it still needs to be solved. What do you do? W.C. Fields said

If at first you don't succeed, give up.
No use making a damn fool of yourself.

We respectfully disagree. If a problem is hard all that means is that finding a solution that gives the exact answer in quickly in all cases is hard. It could well be that the problem you really want to solve, perhaps a subcase, perhaps an approximation, may still be doable. This is not a pipe dream—many NP-complete problems can be approximated quite well. Section 23 discusses this and other possible ways around hardness results.

We speculate that theory and practice will come closer together as theorists define more realistic classes, and practitioners discover that the size of problems they are working is large enough so that asymptotic results really are useful.

25. WHAT IS NATURAL?

Darling: Bill, since we still don't know that P $\neq$ NP, are there *any* problems that are provably not in P?

Bill: Yes there are such problems! (Thinking of using a diagonalization proof to create one that exists for the sole purpose of not being in P.)

Darling: Great! Unless it's one of those dumb-ass sets that you construct for the sole purpose of not being in P.

Bill: Oh. You nailed it. Okay, so you want a natural problem that's not in P. How about *HALT*.

Darling: Nice try Bill. I want a decidable natural problem that is known to not be in P.

Bill: Do you consider fragments of arithmetic, like Presburger Arithmetic or WS1S, to be natural?

Darling: If it requires a page of definitions then not.

Bill: Oh. OH, I have it! I know a problem that is natural, decidable, easy to describe, and known to not be in P.

Darling: Do tell!

Bill: Add to regular expressions the ability to use exponents like a^{100} instead of writing $a \cdots a$ (100 times). We'll call these t-reg exps. Given two t-reg exp do they generate the same set? This problem is EXPSPACE-complete hence not in PSPACE, hence not in P.

Darling: Why is that problem natural?

Bill: Good question. On the one hand, I didn't construct the problem for the sole purpose of not being in P. So it's not a dumb ass problem. Does it then raise to the level of being natural?

Darling: Perhaps it's intermediary between dumb ass and natural. An intermediary problem. Like graph isomorphism is likely not in P nor NP-complete.

Bill: Okay, I'll take that. Now here is one that might be more natural: Given an $n \times n$ chess board with pieces—interrupted.

Darling: Unless $n = 8$ this isn't really chess.

Bill: I find both t-reg exps and generalized chess natural because people *could have* worked on those problems. The fact that people didn't is not the point. They both use notions people did study.

Darling: You'll call them natural, I'll call them (0.5)natural, and we can agree to disagree.

Bill: Yeah!

ACKNOWLEDGEMENT

I thank Raymond Ng for proofreading. I also thank Scott Aaronson, Lance Fortnow, Richard Lipton, and Ken Regan for many interesting discussions on these points over the years.

REFERENCES

[1] J. Ferrante, C. Rackoff, The Computational Complexity of Logical Theories, Springer, Berlin, 1979.
[2] S. Aaaronsn, G. Kuperberg, C. Granade, Complexity Zoo. https://complexityzoo.uwaterloo.ca/Complexity_Zoo.
[3] J. Hartmanis, R. E. Stearns, On the computational complexity of algorithms, Trans. Am. Math Soc. 117 (1965) 285–306.
[4] W. Savitch, Relationships between nondeterministic and deterministic tape complexities. J. Comput. Syst. Sci. 4 (1970) 177–192.
[5] M. Rabin, D. Scott, Finite automata and their decision problems, IBM J. Res. Dev. 3 (1959) 114–125.
[6] O. Reingold, Undirected connectivity in log-space, J. ACM 55(4) (2008) 17.1–17.26. doi: 10.1145/1391289.1391291.
[7] E. Allender M. Mahajan, The complexity of planarity testing, in: Seventh International Symposium on Theoretical Aspects of Computer Science: Proceedings of STACS 1990, Rouen, France, Lecture Notes in Computer Science, Springer-Verlag, Berlin, 2000. http://ftp.cs.rutgers.edu/pub/allender/stacs0.pdf.
[8] S. Lindell, A log-space algorithm for canonization of planer graphs, in: STOC92, ACM, New York, 1992, pp. 400–404.
[9] S. Datta, N. Limaye, P. Nimbhorkar, T. Thieraf, F. Wagner, A log-space algorithm for canonization of planer graphs, in: Twenty-Fourth Conference on Computational Complexity: Proceedings of CCC '09, IEEE Computer Society Press, New York, 2009, pp. 162–167. http://arxiv.org/abs/0809.2319.
[10] P. M. Stephen, A. Cook. Problems complete for deterministic logarithmic space. J. Algor. 8(3) (1987) 385–394.
[11] E. Dijkstra, A note in two problems in connexion with graphs, Numer. Math. 1 (1959) 269–271.
[12] R. Floyd, Algorithm 97: Shortest path, Commun. ACM 5 (1962) 345. doi:10.1145/367766.368168.

[13] S. Warshall, A theorem on boolean matrices, J. ACM 9 (1962) 11–12. doi:10.1145/321105.321107.

[14] B. Roy, Transitivite et connexite, C.R. Acad. Sci. Paris 249 (1959) 216–218.

[15] J. Kruskal, On the shortest spanning subtree of a graph and the travellings salesman problem. Proc. Am. Math. Soc. 7 (1956) 48–50. doi:10.1090/S0002-9939-1956-0078686-7.

[16] R. Prim, Shortest connection networks and some generalizations. Bell Syst. Techn. J. 36 (1957) 1389–1401.

[17] B. Chazelle, A minimum spanning tree algorithm with inverse-Ackermann type complexity, J. ACM 47 (2000) 1028–1047. Prior version in FOCS 1997.

[18] L. Khachiyan, A polynomial algorithm for linear programming, Dokl. Acad. Nauk, SSSR 244 (1979) 1093–1096. Translation in Soviet Math Doklady, vol. 20, 1979.

[19] N. Karmarkar, A new polynomial time algorithm for linear programming, Combinatorica 4 (1984) 373–395.

[20] M. Sipser, Expanders, randomness, or time versus space, JCSS 36 (1988) 379–383. Earlier version in CCC 1986, then called Structures.

[21] N. Nisan, A. Wigderson, Hardness vs randomness, J. Comput. Syst. Sci. 49 (1994) 149–167. Prior version in FOCS88. Full version at http://www.math.ias.edu/~avi/PUBLICATIONS/.

[22] R. Solovay, V. Strassen. A fast Monte-Carlo test for primality, SIAM J. Comput. 6(1) (1977) 84–85.

[23] M. O. Rabin, A probabilistic algorithm for testing primality, J. Number Theory 12 (1980) 128–138.

[24] M. Agrawal, N. Kayal, N. Saxena. PRIMES in p, Annal. Math. 160 (2004) 781–793.

[25] T. Who, Don't Get Fooled Again, Polydor, 1971. https://www.youtube.com/watch?v=zYMD_W_r3Fg.

[26] S. Aaronson, The scientific case for P$\neq$NP, 2014. http://www.scottaaronson.com/blog/?p=1720.

[27] W. Gasarch. Why Do We Think P$\neq$NP, 2014. blog.computationalcomplexity.org/2014/03/why-do-we-think-p-ne-np-inspired-by.html.

[28] R. Lipton, Could We Have Felt Evidence for SDP$\neq$p?, 2014. http://rjlipton.wordpress.com/2014/03/15/could-we-have-felt-evidence-for-sdp-p/.

[29] J. Chen, L. Kanj, G. Xia, Improved upper bounds for vertex cover, TCS 411 (2010) 3736–3756.

[30] K. Popper, The Logic of Scientific Discovery, Routledge, 1959. The original in German was published in 1934. The English version is online for free.

[31] T. Kuhn, The Structure of Scienfic Revolutions, University of Chicago Press, Chicago, 1962.

[32] W. Gasarch, Computational complexity column 36: the P=NP poll, SIGACT News 33(2) (2002) 34–47.

[33] W. Gasarch, Computational complexity column 74: the P=NP poll, SIGACT News 43 (2012) 53–77.

[34] V. Chvatal, A greedy heuristic for the set-covering problem, Math. Opeart. Res. 4 (1979) 233–235.

[35] D. Moshkovitz, The projection games conjecture and the NP-hardness of ln n-approximating set-cover, Electronic Colloquium on Computational Complexity (ECCC) 18(112) (2011).

[36] R. Ladner, On the structure of polynomial time reducibility. J. ACM 22(1) (1975) 155–171.

[37] C. Pomerance, A tale of two sieves. Notices Am. Math. Soc. 43 (1996) 1473–1485.

[38] P. Shor, Algorithms for quantum computation: discrete logarithms and factoring, in: Proceedings of the 35th Annual IEEE Symposium on Foundations of Computer Science, Santa Fe, NM, 1994, pp. 121–134.

[39] E. Luks, Isomorphism of bounded valence graphs can be tested in polynomial time, in: FOCS80, IEEE, New York, 1980, pp. 42–49.

[40] R. Lipton, Advances on Group Isomorphism, 2013. http://rjlipton.wordpress.com/2013/05/11/advances-on-group-isomorphism.

[41] D. Rosenbaum, Bidirectional Collision Detection and Faster Determinsitic Isomorphism Testing, 2013. http://arxiv.org/abs/1304.3935.

[42] S. Fenner, W. Gasarch, C. Glover, S. Purewal, Rectangle Free Colorings of Grids, 2012. http://arxiv.org/abs/1005.3750.

[43] S. Mahaney, Sparse complete sets for NP: solution to a conjecture of Berman and Hartmanis, J. Comput. Syst. Sci. 25 (1982) 130–143.

[44] D, Apon, W. Gasarch, K. Lawler, An NP-Complete Problem in Grid Coloring, 2012. http://arxiv.org/abs/1205.3813.

[45] A. C. Yao, Separating the polynomial-time hierarchy by oracles, in: Proceedings of the 26th Annual IEEE Symposium on Foundations of Computer Science, Portland, OR, 1985, pp. 1–10.

[46] J. Håstad, Almost optimal lower bounds for small depth circuits, in: S. Micali (Ed.), Randomness and Computation, JAI Press, Greenwich, CT, 1989, pp. 143–170.

[47] J. Håstad, Almost optimal lower bounds for small depth circuits, in: Proceedings of the Eighteenth Annual ACM Symposium on the Theory of Computing, Berkeley, CA, 1986, pp. 6–20.

[48] R. Smolensky, Algebraic methods in the theory of lower bounds for Boolean circuit complexity, in: Proceedings of the Nineteenth Annual ACM Symposium on the Theory of Computing, New York, 1987, pp. 77–82.

[49] R. Williams, Non-uniform ACC lower bounds, J. ACM 61 (2014) 2.1–2.31. Prior version in CCC2011.

[50] R. Williams, Time space tradeoffs for counting np solutions modulo integers, in: Computational Complexity, IEEE, New York, 2008, pp. 179–219.

[51] R. Williams, Alternation-tradings, linear programming, and lower bounds, in: Twenty Seventh International Symposium on Theoretical Aspects of Computer Science: Proceedings of STACS 2010, Nancy, France, 2010.

[52] S. Buss, R. Williams, Limits on alternation-trading proofs for time-space lower bounds, in: Twenty-Seventh Conference on Computational Complexity: Proceedings of CCC '12, IEEE Computer Society, New York, 2012, pp. 181–191.

[53] T. Baker, J. Gill, R. Solovay, Relativizations of the $P =? NP$ question, SIAM J. Comput. 4 (1975) 431–442.

[54] A. A. Razborov, S. Rudich, Natural proofs. J. Comput. Syst. Sci. 55(1) (1997) 24–35. Prior version in ACM Sym on Theory of Computing, 1994 (STOC).

[55] S. Aaronson, A. Wigderson, Algebraization: a new barrier to complexity theory, ACM Trans. Comput. Theory 1 (2009) 2.1–2.54. Prior version in STOC08.

[56] K. Mulmuley, On P versus NP, and geometric complexity theory, J. ACM 58(2) (2011) 26p. Earlier version from 2009 at http://arxiv.org/abs/0903.0544 this version at http://doi.acm.org/10.1145/1667053.1667060.

[57] M. Sipser, A complexity theoretic approach to randomness, Proceedings of the Fifteenth Annual ACM Symposium on the Theory of Computing, Boston, MA, 1983, pp. 330–335.

[58] Lautemann, BPP and the polynomial hierarchy. Inform. Proc. Lett. 17(4) (1983).

[59] D. Buchfuhrer C. Umans, The complexity of boolean formula minimization, J. Comput. Syst. Sci. 77(1) (2011) 142–153. On Umans Homepage, also in ICALP 2008.

[60] L. G. Valiant, The complexity of computing the permanent. Theor. Comput. Sci. 8 (1979) 189–201.
[61] L. G. Valiant, The complexity of enumeration and reliability problems. SIAM J. Comput. 8(3) (1979) 410–421.
[62] S. Toda, PP is as hard as the polynomial-time hierarchy. SIAM J. Comput. 20 (1991) 865–877. Prior version in IEEE Sym on Found. of Comp. Sci. (1989) (FOCS).
[63] A. Meyer, L. Stockmeyer, The equivalence problem for regular expressions with squaring requires exponential space. in: Proc. of the 13th Annual IEEE Sym. on Switching and Automata Theory, 1972, pp. 125–129.
[64] J. R. Büchi, Weak second order arithmetic and finite automata, Zeitschrift Math. Phys. 6 (1960) 66–92.
[65] A. Meyer, Weak monadic second order theory of succesor is not elementary-recursive, in: Logic Colloquium Springer Lecture Notes in Mathematics, vol. 453, 1975, pp. 132–154.
[66] J. R. Büchi, On a decision method in restricted second-order arithmetic, in: Proc. of the International Congress on logic, Math, and Philosophy of Science, 1960, Stanford University Press, Redwood, California, 1962, pp. 1–12.
[67] M. Rabin, Decidabilty of second-order theories of automta on infinite trees, Trans. Am. Math. Soc. 141 (1969) 1–35. www.jstor.org/stable/1995086.
[68] Y. Gurevich, L. Harrington, Trees, automata, and games, in: Proceedings of the Fourteenth Annual ACM Symposium on the Theory of Computing, San Francisco, CA, 1982, pp. 60–65.
[69] E. Borger, E. Gradel, Y. Gurevich, The Classical Decision Problem, Springer Verlag, New York, 2000.
[70] The MONA project, 2002–current. http://www.brics.dk/mona/index.html.
[71] A. Tarski, A Decision Method for Elemenary Algebra and Geometry, 1948. http://www.rand.org/content/dam/rand/pubs/reports/2008/R109.pdf.
[72] V. Weispfenning, Tarski's Decision Procedure FO Theory of Reals, 2012. http://www.cfdvs.iitb.ac.in/meetings/files/tarski.pdf.
[73] M. Fischer, M. Rabin, String matching and other products, in: R. Karp (Ed.), Complexity of Computation, SIAM-AMS Proc., Providence, RI, vol. 7, 1974, pp. 27–41.
[74] R. Tarjan, Worst-caes analysis of set union algorihtms. J. ACM 31(2) (1984) 245–281.
[75] L. Kirby, J. Paris, Accessible independent results for Peano arithmetic, Bull. Lond. Math. Soc. 14 (1982) 285–293. http://blms.oxfordjournals.org/content/by/year.
[76] G. Pullum, Sccoping the Loop Snooper, 2000. http://www.lel.ed.ac.uk/~gpullum/loopsnoop.html.
[77] B. Yandell, The Honor Class: Hilbet's Problems and Their Solvers, A.K. Peters, New York, 2002.
[78] M. Davis, H. Putnam, J. Robinson, The decision problem for exponential diophantine equations, Ann. Math. 74 (1961) 425–436.
[79] Y. Matijasevic, Enumerable sets are diophantine Russian. Dokl. Acad. Nauk, SSSR 191 (1970) 279–282. Translation in Soviet Math Doklady, vol. 11, 1970.

ABOUT THE AUTHOR

Bill Gasarch is a full professor at the University of Maryland, College Park. He received his PhD in Computer Science from Harvard in 1985, with the thesis "Recursion-Theoretic Techniques in Complexity Theory and Combinatorics." Since then he has worked in complexity theory, combinatorics, learning theory, and communication complexity. He has mentored over 30 high school students and over 20 undergraduates on projects. Several of the high school students have won competitions with their research. He is the author or coauthor of more than 50 research papers. He has written a book, with Georgia Martin, on "Bounded Queries in Recursion Theory." He currently co-blogs (with Lance Fortnow) complexityblog which is a well-read blog on complexity theory.

AUTHOR INDEX

Note: Page numbers followed by "*f*" indicate figures, "*t*" indicate tables, "*b*" indicate boxes and "*np*" indicate footnotes.

SUBJECT INDEX

Note: Page numbers followed by "*f*" indicate figures and "*t*" indicate tables, "*b*" indicate boxes.

CONTENTS OF VOLUMES IN THIS SERIES

Volume 71

Volume 72

Volume 73

Volume 94

Printed in the United States
By Bookmasters